Restoration, Reformation and Reform, 1660–1828

Archbishops of Canterbury and their Diocese

JEREMY GREGORY

CLARENDON PRESS · OXFORD

OXFORD

UNIVERSITY PRESS

Great Clarendon Street, Oxford OX2 6DP

Oxford University Press is a department of the University of Oxford
and furthers the University's aim of excellence in research, scholarship,
and education by publishing worldwide in

Oxford New York

Athens Auckland Bangkok Bogotá Buenos Aires Calcutta
Cape Town Chennai Dar es Salaam Delhi Florence Hong Kong Istanbul
Karachi Kuala Lumpur Madrid Melbourne Mexico City Mumbai
Nairobi Paris São Paulo Singapore Taipei Tokyo Toronto Warsaw

with associated companies in Berlin Ibadan

Oxford is a trade mark of Oxford University Press
in the UK and in certain other countries

Published in the United States
by Oxford University Press Inc., New York

British Library Cataloguing in Publication Data

Data available

Library of Congress Cataloging in Publication Data
Gregory, Jeremy. Restoration, reformation, and reform, 1660–1828:
archbishops of Canterbury and diocese / Jeremy Gregory.
(Oxford historical monographs)
Revision of the author's thesis (doctoral)—University of Oxford.
Includes bibliographical references (p.) and index.
1. Church of England. Diocese of Canterbury—History—17th century.
2. Canterbury (England)—Church history—17th century. 3. Church of
England . Diocese of Canterbury—History—18th century. 4. Canterbury
(England)—Church history—18th century. 5. Church of England. Diocese
of Canterbury—History—19th century. 6. Canterbury (England)—Church
history—19th century. I. Title. II. Series.

BX5107.C2 G74 2000   283'.4223—dc21   99–048332

ISBN–0–19–820830–8.

1 3 5 7 9 10 8 6 4 2

Typeset in Ehrhardt MT
by Alliance Phototypesetters, Pondicherry, India
Printed in Great Britain
on acid-free paper by
Biddles Ltd, Guildford and King's Lynn

For
KEITH *and* KATHERINE GREGORY
with love

FOREWORD

It may seem a high presumption, for One, who not many Years since came a Stranger into Kent, to meddle with the Antiquities of the Most Famous City, and Cathedral Church of Canterbury . . . Ever since I came into Kent, I have received continual Favours from the very Reverend the Dean and Canons of this Church. By their leave, and with their consent, I have had free Access to the Archives and Library of this Church; which I do acknowledge with all Gratitude.[1]

Tho' there has been more wrote of this Cathedral than any other whatsoever, yet have none of the Kentish Historians, who have done Honour to their native County, given us any particular Account of the Diocese . . . wherefore as it hath fallen to the Province of a Stranger to attempt it, He humbly hopes that Allowances will be made for any Errors He has committed.[2]

This book is a revised version of a doctoral thesis submitted to the University of Oxford, and in writing it I have been encouraged by a large number of people. It was the late G. V. Bennett who, many more years ago than I care to remember, first suggested that I might like to make a study of the diocese of Canterbury, and Patrick Collinson, Paul Langford, and Anne Whiteman advised me during my researches. John Walsh proved to be much more than a surrogate supervisor, being a source of inspiration and wise counsel. Other friends cheerfully read parts of the book and saved me from some glaring errors. I have benefited a great deal from the suggestions, insights, and comments of Toby Barnard, Jeremy Black, Arthur Burns, Tony Claydon, Mary Elford, Frances Mannsaker, Geoffrey Rowell, Margaret Spufford, Stephen Taylor, and Lucy Wooding. This study could not have been contemplated without the help I have received from the librarians and archivists of Lambeth Palace Library, Canterbury Cathedral Archives and Library, Kent Record Office, the Bodleian Library, the British Library, and Cambridge University Library. In particular, Melanie Barber, the archivist and deputy librarian, Lambeth Palace Library has always been ready to share with me her unrivalled knowledge of the archbishops' papers. I would also like to thank the University of Northumbria for

---

1 Nicholas Battely, *The Antiquities of Canterbury in Two Part. I . . . II Cantuaria Sacra* (1703), (Part II), preface.
2 Browne Willis, *Parochiale Anglicanum* (1733), Av.

granting me a period of teaching relief which enabled me to complete this project, and for providing funding which allowed me to consult documents in the south of England. Above all, I owe more than they will ever know to my friends and colleagues who, in the face of apparent evidence to the contrary, never voiced their doubts to me that one day this work would finally be finished. And as is customary with first books, I dedicate mine to my parents.

J. G.

CONTENTS

LIST OF MAPS

LIST OF TABLES

ABBREVIATIONS

AC	*Archaeologia Cantiana*
Bodl.	Bodleian Library, Oxford
BL	British Library
CCAL	Canterbury Cathedral Archives and Library
Ch. Ch.	Christ Church Library, Oxford
CSPD	*Calendar of State Papers Domestic*
CUL	Cambridge University Library
DNB	*Dictionary of National Biography*
EHR	*English Historical Review*
GM	*The Gentleman's Magazine*
HJ	*Historical Journal*
HMC	*Historical Manuscripts Commission*
JBS	*Journal of British Studies*
JEH	*Journal of Ecclesiastical History*
KAO	Kent Archives Office, Maidstone
LPL	Lambeth Palace Library
PRO	Public Record Office
SCH	*Studies in Church History*
SPCK	Records of the Society for Propagating Christian Knowledge, St Marylebone, London
TRHS	*Transactions of the Royal Historical Society*
VCH	*Victoria County History*

NOTE ON DATES

Before 1752 all dates are given in Old Style, eleven days behind the New Style or Gregorian calendar. The year is taken to begin on 1 January.

Introduction

This book is intended as a contribution to the debates about the nature of the Church of England and its place in society between the Restoration and the reform movements of the 1830s and 40s. Despite the 'minor industry'[1] of studies devoted to individual bishops of the late seventeenth and eighteenth centuries and the growing number of unpublished theses relating to religious life in particular regions, we are still surprisingly ignorant of the teachings and practice of the Anglican Church during these years, especially in comparison with our knowledge of the Church of England in the century following the Reformation and in the Victorian era.[2] Moreover, notwithstanding this burgeoning research, the opinion still received in much of the general literature is of a more or less complacent and pastorally somnolent institution, managed by secular-minded political bishops and staffed either by the stereotypical fox-hunting parson or woefully poor curate.[3] Such views are largely derived from the sweeping generalizations of the Church's varied critics, particularly the Methodists, Evangelicals, Tractarians, and nineteenth-century Church reformers.

[1] The phrase is G. V. Bennett's in *The Tory Crisis in Church and State, 1688-1730. The Career of Francis Atterbury, Bishop of Rochester* (Oxford, 1975), p. vii. Other such studies include, id., *White Kennett, 1660-1728. Bishop of Peterborough* (1957); E. Carpenter, *Thomas Sherlock, 1678-1761* (1936); id., *Thomas Tenison, Archbishop of Canterbury. His Life and Times* (1948); W. M. Marshall, *George Hooper, 1640-1727. Bishop of Bath and Wells* (Milbourne Port, 1976); F. C. Mather, *High Church Prophet. Bishop Samuel Horsley and the Caroline Tradition in the later Georgian Church* (Oxford, 1992); N. Sykes, *Edmund Gibson. Bishop of London, 1669-1748. A Study in Politics and Religion in the Eighteenth Century* (Oxford, 1926); id., *William Wake, Archbishop of Canterbury, 1657-1737*, 2 vols. (Cambridge, 1957); A. Tindal Hart, *The Life and Times of John Sharp, Archbishop of York* (1949); C. E. Whiting, *Nathaniel Lord Crewe. Bishop of Durham (1674-1721) and his Diocese* (1940).

[2] There is a vast historiography concerned with the Church of England in the Reformation era. Of especial importance are P. Collinson, *The Religion of Protestants. The Church in English Society, 1559-1625* (Oxford, 1982); F. Heal, *Of Prelates and Princes. A Study in the Economic and Social Position of the Tudor Episcopate* (Cambridge, 1980); R. O'Day, *The English Clergy: The Emergence and Consolidation of a Profession, 1558-1642* (Leicester, 1979). For the Victorian era, useful studies include: W. O. Chadwick, *The Victorian Church*, 2 vols. (1966-70); A. Haig, *The Victorian Clergy* (Beckenham, 1984); B. Heeney, *A Different Kind of Gentleman. Parish Clergy as Professional Men in Early and Mid-Victorian England* (Conn., 1976); J. Obelkevich, *Religion and Rural Society: South Lindsey, 1825-1875* (1976).

[3] R. Porter, *English Society in the Eighteenth Century* (Harmondsworth, 1982); P. Langford, *A Polite and Commercial People. England, 1727-1783* (Oxford, 1989); and id., *Public Life and the Propertied Englishman, 1689-1798* (Oxford, 1991).

There has indeed been a curious harmony in the way in which High and Low Churchmen have been able to join in condemnation of the Church of the long eighteenth century. The period flanked by the Laudian and Oxford Movements has been castigated by High-Church writers for being a nadir in Church history, whilst evangelically minded historians have bemoaned the supposed lack of zeal within the established Church in the years between the Restoration and the Evangelical Revival.[4] A former historian of the Canterbury diocese and canon of Canterbury Cathedral, writing in 1880 under the influence of nineteenth-century evangelical fervour, and echoing the wider surveys of G. G. Perry, J. H. Overton, and F. C. Relton, consigned this period to a few pages within his diocesan history, dismissing it as a time of 'spiritual deadness and darkness' which made it the 'most lifeless age of all in the history of our Church'.[5] In similar fashion, the early twentieth-century High-Church canons of Canterbury, C. E. Woodruff and W. Danks, who were concerned to highlight the beneficial reforms of the period after 1830, described the life of the cathedral in the years between 1660 and 1828 as 'almost official lethargy bordering on paralysis'.[6]

There have, of course, been attempts to challenge such statements. In the 1870s and 80s, Abbey and Overton offered some evidence which cast the Church of the eighteenth century in a better light,[7] and in 1934 Norman Sykes presented a qualified apologia for the Church, which stressed the structural efficiency of the Church as an institution, but paid little attention to the clergy's relationship with their parishioners, and largely ignored the spiritual role and task of the Church.[8] Rather as Sir Lewis Namier minimized the ideological context of politics, so Sykes was more impressed by the pragmatic and practical elements in Churchmanship. In Sykes's interpretative model the diocese of Canterbury received little attention, save as a backdrop to the wider political and intellectual role of individual archbishops such as William Wake.[9] Significantly too, important sections of the Church's institutional life, which played a dominant role in the

[4] G. G. Perry, *A History of the Church of England*, 3 vols. (1861–4); J. H. Overton and F. C. Relton, *The English Church from the Accession of George I to the End of the Eighteenth Century, 1714–1800* (1906). See also, J. Stoughton, *Religion in England under Queen Anne and the Georges, 1702–1800*, 2 vols. (1878).

[5] R. C. Jenkins, *Diocesan Histories: Canterbury* (1880), 402.

[6] C. Eveleigh Woodruff and William Danks, *Memorials of the Cathedral Priory of Christ in Canterbury* (1912), 376.

[7] C. J. Abbey and J. H. Overton, *The English Church in the Eighteenth Century*, 2 vols. (1878); C. J. Abbey, *The English Church and its Bishops, 1700–1800*, 2 vols. (1887).

[8] N. Sykes, *Church and State in England in the Eighteenth Century* (Cambridge, 1934).

[9] Id., *Wake*, i. 213–43; L. B. Namier's most influential work has been *The Structure of Politics at the Accession of George III* (1929).

diocese—such as the dean and chapter—were for Sykes its most medieval and unacceptable face, and did not feature prominently in his account.[10] The conclusions of the various studies written after Sykes which sought a more positive reassessment of the Church were seldom incorporated into the broader political or social history of the age.

In the past fifteen years a number of powerful interpretations have sought to do just this, but they have, perhaps inevitably, dealt with the world of high politics, not with life in the localities.[11] The work of J. C. D. Clark, in particular his attempt to portray the period as one dominated by the Anglican Church and its vision of the world, has not met with universal acceptance and has reopened controversy concerning the tenor of eighteenth-century society and the position of the Church within it.[12] One reviewer has referred to the rehabilitation of the Church as a campaign 'which is at present going ahead faster than the evidence warrants'; a recent monograph has termed this an 'age of Negligence' in pastoral terms; and a study of the Church in Lancashire has concluded that 'the eighteenth-century Church . . . was unequal to the challenge' facing it.[13] This book would agree with Clark's critics that in several respects he seriously under-estimated the problems faced by the Church in the provinces. In his inter-pretation of events the Church's position was largely unproblematic and untroubled. The Anglican hegemony which he perceived in the ideological sphere was matched by an almost effortless Anglican dominance in the dioceses and parishes of England, an analysis which seems chiefly to gloss traditional notions of eighteenth-century 'stability'. Instead of seeing the

[10] For Sykes' denigration of cathedrals see *Church and State*, 415–16.

[11] J. C. D. Clark, *English Society, 1688–1832: Ideology, Social Structure and Political Practice during the Ancien Regime* (Cambridge, 1985) and S. J. C. Taylor, 'Church and State in England in the Mid-Eighteenth Century: The Newcastle Years, 1742–1762', unpub. Cambridge University Ph.D. thesis, 1987. See also the collection of essays J. Walsh, C. Haydon, and S. Taylor (eds.), *The Church of England, c.1689–c.1833. From Toleration to Tractarianism* (Cambridge, 1993).

[12] The most sustained criticisms of Clark's work can be found in the special edition of *Albion*, 21 (1989), especially the articles by J. Bradley and J. H. Phillips. See also J. E. Bradley, *Religion, Revolution and English Radicalism. Non-conformity in Eighteenth-Century Politics and Society* (Cambridge, 1990), 417–18. Criticisms are also implicit in Langford, *Polite and Commercial People* and id., *Propertied Englishman*. A more pro-Clarkean line is taken by W. A. Gibson, *The Achievement of the Anglican Church, 1689–1800. The Confessional State in Eighteenth-Century England* (Lampeter, 1995).

[13] The review was by W. R. Ward of J. Gascoigne, *Cambridge in the Age of the Enlightenment: Science, Religion and Politics from the Restoration to the French Revolution* (Cambridge, 1989), in *History*, 75 (1990), 497; P. Virgin, *The Church of England in an Age of Negligence. Ecclesiastical Structure and Problems of Church Reform, 1700–1840* (Cambridge, 1989); M. F. Snape, '"Our Happy Reformation": Anglicanism and Society in a Northern Parish, 1689–1789', University of Birmingham Ph.D. thesis, 1994, 458.

period as one which saw the triumph of rationalism and reasonableness over religious fanaticism, we are now asked to see a new kind of stability based on a largely unchallenged faith.[14] Anglicanism, Clark assumes, was virtually unquestioned and its essential tenets seem almost magically to have percolated down the social scale. But, certainly from the clergy's point of view, what was more striking were the tensions and difficulties they experienced in their task. From their perspective the 'confessional state' was something to work for: it had not yet been achieved. Clark's conclusions concerning the Church were largely based on an exploration of political theology gleaned from a study of sermon and printed source material. It was beyond the scope of that work to delve into the local archives or the institutional records of the Church, to see how ideological statements operated within the more earthy context of diocesan administration and parish affairs.

In pursuing the Church into the localities, the book addresses three major historiographical issues: first, the nature of the Restoration ecclesiastical regime; second, the character of the clerical profession and the quality of the clergy's pastoral work; and third, the question of Church reform. These topics have not only provided the book with its title, but they also get to the heart of the controversies surrounding the functioning of the Church in the period. First, historians have debated whether the Restoration Church witnessed a triumph of Laudianism, especially with regard to the treatment of nonconformists, and the high-handed management of ecclesiastical estates, or whether moderation was a more typical ideal.[15] They have differed, too, over the speed of the Restoration process, particularly concerning the resumption of diocesan administration; the filling of livings; and the return of property to the Church.[16] They have also argued about the social and educational status of the parish clergy in these years.[17] By beginning each chapter in 1660, this study examines the Restoration Church from a number of angles (its personnel, its political, social, and economic

---

[14] Clark, *English Society*, 87, 227 and passim. See also id., 'England's Ancien Regime as a Confessional State', *Albion*, XXI (1989), 450–474, and id., 'Eighteenth Century Social History', *HJ*, 30 (1984), 773–88.

[15] For debates concerning the nature of the Church at the Restoration see R. S. Bosher, *The Making of the Restoration Settlement. The Influence of the Laudians, 1649–62* (1951); I. Green *The Re-establishment of the Church of England, 1660–1663* (Oxford, 1978); T. Harris, P. Seaward, and M. Goldie (eds.), *The Politics of Religion in Restoration England* (Oxford, 1990); and J. Spurr, *The Restoration Church of England, 1646–1689* (New Haven, Conn., and London, 1991).

[16] Green, *Re-establishment*; A. Whiteman, 'The Re-establishment of the Church of England, 1660–1663', *TRHS*, 5 (1955), 111–32.

[17] Green, *Re-establishment*.

positions, its relations with dissenters, and its pastoral role) which, taken together, enables an overall assessment of the Restoration regime.

Second, the book considers the quality of the clergy and of their pastoral work in the late Stuart and Hanoverian period. Traditionally, the pastoral shortcomings of the clergy have been highlighted, although recent research has tended to modify such assumptions, and increasingly attention has been paid to how clergy saw their role and to the kinds of pastoral provision they offered.[18] Part of the problem is knowing what yardstick should be used to view the work of the clergy. Negative judgements have often arisen from this being measured against anachronistic late nineteenth-century standards. A rather neglected approach has been to see the clergy's pastoral work in relation to the period more conventionally labelled the Reformation era, for in certain respects the Reformation was seen as unfinished business in the century after 1660.[19] The Reformation endeavour had witnessed the dual desire to improve the standards of the clergy, and their pastoral care, as well as educating the parish, and these aims had not ended in 1640. This book offers a rival interpretation to the usually limited chronological focus (often amounting to less than a century) which has ended consideration of the Reformation in 1559, 1603, or 1640, by emphasizing the long and drawn-out nature of the Reformation in England. Even if the political Reformation had been won by the seventeenth century, there was still much to do in bringing the protestant faith to the hearts and minds of the English people, and this was a process which took centuries rather than years or decades. Furthermore, it is suggested, we will have an improved understanding of what the Reformation implied, and its broad social consequences, if we track its influence and ideology well in to the eighteenth and early nineteenth centuries, for arguably only then were the effects of the Reformation seen in the parishes (such as a professionalized clergy and a religiously educated laity). Chapters on the Church's personnel and on the work of the Church in the parishes directly engage with these themes.

Third, historians have differed over the tone of Church life at the end of the eighteenth and the start of the nineteenth centuries, particularly with regard to the issue of Church reform. Some have argued that reform can be seen only after 1828: their interpretation suggests a 'cataclysmic'

[18] Virgin, *Age of Negligence*; Walsh, *et al.*, *Church of England*.

[19] J. Gregory, 'The Eighteenth-Century Reformation: The Pastoral Task of Anglican Clergy after 1689', in Walsh, *et al.*, *Church of England*, 67–85; id., 'The Making of a Protestant Nation; "Success" and "Failure" in England's Long Reformation', in N. Tyacke (ed.), *England's Long Reformation, 1500–1800* (1998), 307–33; and J. Barry, 'Bristol as a "Reformation City", c.1640–1780', ibid., 261–84.

understanding of reform, which was largely imposed on the Church in the 1830s by outside bodies. Others favour a more 'gradualist approach', arguing that what has been called the third reform movement (after the first reform movement of the sixteenth century, and the second reform movement in the decades immediately after 1688) had its roots in the eighteenth century, and moreover that the impetus for reform came from within the Church.[20] The term 'Church reform' is itself used to cover a number of differing areas such as: institutional revival; the tightening-up of the clerical profession in terms of ordination requirements, residence, and pastoral oversight; and the revival of 'orthodox' or evangelical doctrine, and it is clear that these could have different trajectories. There are also some problems with confining Church reform to a specific period. As indicated above, while most attention has been paid to the ecclesiastical reforms of the 1830s and 40s, historians have also discerned reform movements in the years between 1688 and *c*.1714.[21] But, from the perspective of the diocese, concentrating on these 'reform movements' is rather unsatisfactory. Certainly in the diocese of Canterbury there is a good case to be made for suggesting that the 1660s to the 1680s, the 1720s to the 1740s, and the period from the 1750s to the early nineteenth century deserve as much attention as those years conventionally labelled eras of reform.[22] Chapters relating to the cathedral, to the clergy as a professional force, and to their pastoral oversight indicate that reform was an almost continuous and constant tradition.

In addressing these three issues this book has two overarching methodological premises. The first concerns the way in which Church history should be approached. The major shortcoming of traditional ecclesiastical history has been the habit of treating different facets of Church life in isolation. On the one hand, pioneering diocesan histories have been concerned to investigate the mechanics of Church life, being largely based, in Delumeau's phrase, on the 'dry but necessary study of statistics'.[23] This

---

[20] For the arguments over the nature of the late eighteenth- and early nineteenth-century Church see G. F. A. Best, *Temporal Pillars. Queen Anne's Bounty, the Ecclesiastical Commissioners and the Church of England* (Cambridge, 1964); O. J. Brose, *Church and Parliament: The Reshaping of the Church of England, 1828–1860* (Stanford, Calif., and London, 1960), W. L. Mathieson, *English Church Reform, 1815–40* (1923); K. A. Thompson, *Bureaucracy and Church Reform: The Organizational Response of the Church of England to Social Change, 1800–1965* (Oxford, 1970); and Virgin, *Church in Age of Negligence*, 23–7, 264–7. For criticisms of the cataclysmic approach see R. A. Burns, 'A Hanoverian Legacy? Diocesan Reform in the Church of England, c.1688–c.1833', in Walsh, Haydon and Taylor, *Church*, 265–82.

[21] On the 'second Church reform movement' see N. Sykes, *From Sheldon to Secker. Aspects of English Church History, 1660–1768* (Cambridge, 1959) and Carpenter, *Tenison*.

[22] See below, pp. 68, 84, 141, 172–3, 271, 284–6, 294.

[23] J. Delumeau, *Le Catholicisme entre Luther et Voltaire* (Paris, 1971) [English tr., *Catholicism between Luther and Voltaire* (1978)], 132. The most recent (and most extreme)

genre of ecclesiastical history might be called a materialist approach to the history of the Church, documenting with precision those aspects of the Church which could be tabulated and counted, such as its wealth, the backgrounds and career patterns of its clergy, and the numbers of laity who attended its services. This study has not wished to fight shy of this approach altogether: some kind of quantitative analysis is the necessary context for qualitative assessment. But in the past this has often been done with little reference to religion as theology and belief, and such studies often leave the impression that the Church and the clergy had little to do with religion as conventionally understood.

On the other hand, analyses of eighteenth-century theology have not always been sufficiently rooted in an institutional or parochial context, and have tended to portray religious thought as some kind of free-floating, abstract entity; moreover they have emphasized those aspects of theology which nineteenth-century historians assumed characterized the period, notably the growth of latitudinarianism from the Cambridge Platonists through to Hoadly and Paley.[24] This book aims to redress the balance by amalgamating the history of the Church as an institution with the history of ideas, embracing its social, economic, political, and intellectual dimensions. It is thus rooted in a socio-economic context, but it is also concerned with the attitudes and assumptions expressed by the clergy regarding their own place and role in society, and their understanding of religion.

In part, the reluctance of diocesan historians to deal with matters of attitude and belief has been a consequence of the kinds of documents which they have used. Anglican administrative records are liable to give a rather skewed impression of clerical concerns. It was the exceptional and the problematic which were most likely to have been reported and such sources reveal matters when they were perceived to have gone wrong. It was probably the least conscientious clergy who had to be chivvied, and whose behaviour had to be monitored, and the laity featured largely when they most troubled the Church. The volume of institutional records, seemingly obsessed with patronage and leases, has sometimes focused attention unduly on the secular preoccupations of the eighteenth-century Church

example of this approach is V. Barrie-Curien, *Clergé et pastorale en Angleterre au xviiième siècle: le diocèse de Londres* (Paris, 1992).

[24] Most significantly, L. Stephen, *A History of English Thought in the Eighteenth Century*, 2 vols. (1876). See also I. Rivers, *Reason, Grace, and Sentiment. A Study of the Language of Religion and Ethics in England, 1660–1780*, i. *Whichcote to Wesley* (Cambridge, 1991) and B. Young, "'Orthodoxy Assail'd": An Historical Examination of Some Metaphysical and Theological Debates in England from Locke to Burke', University of Oxford D.Phil thesis, 1990.

and on its apparently archaic bureaucratic structures.[25] Certainly in many respects the administrative framework of the Church in the eighteenth century was medieval. The procedures in the archbishops' registers, the dean and chapter act books, and the court records were little changed from the middle ages.[26] But behind all this a certain energy and modernity of spirit can be seen: in attitudes towards recruitment and the clerical profession; in attitudes to property; and in attitudes towards dissenters and parishioners. If the procedures were old-fashioned, it did not mean that there was no room for manœuvre, and if major changes cannot be found in the legislative structures of the Church, they may nevertheless be found in its local history. Twentieth-century historians have compounded the problem of interpreting the sources by investigating them in the light of modern concerns. Thus institutional records have been analysed from the point of view of social demography, and sermons and pamphlets are often studied more for their literary style than for their doctrinal content.[27]

My desire has rather been to enter into the minds of clergy between the late seventeenth and early nineteenth centuries and to discover how they viewed the world around them and to see the problems of the Church as they saw them. This is an attempt in what has been called 'collective psychology': an effort to map the clerical mind, and to reconstruct not only the activities of the clergy, but also the attitudes and mental framework in which they lived. In doing so I have drawn on a wide range of sources: institutional, archival, and personal correspondence, as well as printed tracts, theological and political pamphlets, and sermons. I have endeavoured to make a virtue out of the fact that the great majority of sources I have consulted are by and large Anglican sources, expressing an Anglican viewpoint. We cannot of course necessarily accept the Anglican emphasis as a description of objective fact. In some ways, the nature of the source material, much of it correspondence with officialdom or visitation returns, might give an over-optimistic view. To some extent incumbents were defending their own practice. Nevertheless, documents such as these can reveal not only what clergy wanted to happen, but how the laity responded to the Church's ministrations.

---

[25] See Porter, *English Society*, 76, 361 and Langford, *Propertied Englishman*, 1; Thompson, *Bureaucracy and Church Reform*.

[26] See I. J. Churchill, *Canterbury Administration: The Administrative Machinery of the Diocese of Canterbury Illustrated from Original Records*, 2 vols. (1933).

[27] For example, J. Downey, *The Eighteenth-Century Pulpit* (Oxford, 1969) and R. P. Lessenich, *Elements of Pulpit Oratory in Eighteenth Century England, 1660–1800* (Cologne and Vienna, 1972).

The second methodological premiss of this book concerns periodization. Too frequently ecclesiastical histories set up artificial boundaries such as 1689, 1714, 1760, 1789, or 1815 which tend to over-compartmentalize periods of Church history, and which have little relevance at the diocesan level.[28] The wide chronological span of this study was chosen deliberately to allow the problems and difficulties often ascribed to the 'eighteenth-century Church' to be viewed as emerging from the seventeenth and continuing well into the nineteenth century. It begins firmly with the re-establishment of the Church in 1660 in the conviction that many of the concerns of the Restoration clergy, especially in the parishes, concerning their wealth, their relationship with their parishioners, and their attitudes towards dissenters, were shared by clergy throughout the eighteenth century. Since many of the previously negative and critical judgements relating to the functioning of the Church have arisen from anachronistic comparisons with the situation in the late nineteenth century, seeing the Church from the perspective of the seventeenth century may allow us better to appreciate its achievements.

One of the benefits of taking this time span is that it allows us to trace continuities and changes over a long period. Just as it has been one of the main thrusts of recent French historiography to emphasize the strong continuities between seventeenth-, eighteenth-, and early nineteenth-century religious behaviour,[29] it is no exaggeration to say that the upheaval of the mid-seventeenth century was the main determinant in shaping the ideologies of clergy in the diocese of Canterbury in the century and a half covered by this book. To a large extent the memory of what happened when the world was turned upside down formed the habits of mind and fashioned the behaviour of Church of England clergy from the late seventeenth and to the early nineteenth centuries. After all, the purpose of the Restoration had been to reconstruct the world which seemed to have been lost.[30] In Canterbury itself the challenge to order and stability posed by religious and political radicals had had tangible expression in the damage inflicted on the interior of the cathedral by parliamentary troops in 1642 and by Richard Culmer and his following in 1643. Religious life in the locality was revolutionized during the 1640s with the stabling of horses and weapons in the cathedral by the 'intruders', the destruction of the archbishop's palace in

---

[28] On the subject of periodization, Spurr, *Restoration Church*, pp. xii–xiv, 104, 376 makes a case for a distinct break after 1689. It is also significant that Clark begins his work in 1688 and not 1660.

[29] For example, Delumeau, *Catholicisme*.

[30] J. Scott, 'Radicalism and Restoration: The Shape of the Stuart Experience', *HJ*, 31 (1988), 458.

the precincts, the abolition of deans and chapters by act of Parliament in 1649, the use of the office of six-preacher to defend the Cromwellian regime,[31] and in the general proscription of Anglican worship in the city and diocese. The memories of the Great Rebellion when the Church had been overthrown, the archbishop of Canterbury executed and Anglican clergy harried in their parishes became extraordinarily deep and fixed within Anglican consciousness and provided a structural coherence to the world of thought and behaviour included here. Because religious pre-occupations were deemed to be central to social, political, and intellectual order, any religious experience which threatened that order needed to be anaesthetized. In this light, the prime object of the Anglican Church in the diocese of Canterbury, as elsewhere, was to be an instrument of religious, and thereby social and political, stability, by preaching orthodox Anglican doctrine and by supporting the forces of order within provincial society. It is often argued that the eighteenth century saw the dawning of the modern age, but this obscures the powerful urge for tradition and continuity with the past which dominated clerical thinking in England. We are witnessing here one of those shifts in the purpose and identity of the Church's position within Kentish society. From being a leader of new ideas under Archbishop Cranmer in the 1540s, and being used by Archbishop Laud as a centre for militant clericalism in the 1630s, its purpose after 1660 had been transposed into a perceptibly different mode: to work for stability within society.[32] Perhaps the purpose of creating and sustaining the sinews of stability resulted in constructing an institution that was itself stable and thus, in the eyes of its critics, liable to the charge of sterility.

The year of Archbishop Manners Sutton's death, 1828, was chosen as the terminal date for this book because developments in the 1830s and 40s (notably the rise of the Oxford Movement and the reforms associated with the Ecclesiastical Commission) provided new challenges for the Church.[33] It should, however, be borne in mind that many of the characteristics of the Church in the eighteenth century continued well into the mid-nineteenth. Indeed Frances Knight has recently remarked that as far as the Church of

[31] M. V. Jones, 'The Divine Durant: A Seventeenth-Century Independent', *AC*, 83 (1968), 193–203.

[32] Clark, *English Provincial Society from the Reformation to the Revolution: Religion, Politics and Society in Kent, 1500–1640* (Hassocks, 1977); K. Fincham, *Prelate as Pastor. The Episcopate of James I* (Oxford, 1990) and N. Tyacke, *Anti-Calvinists. The Rise of English Arminianism, c.1590–1640* (Oxford, 1987).

[33] For Clark, 1828 (with the repeal of the Test and Corporation Acts, to be followed in 1829 by Catholic Emancipation) marked the effective beginning of the end of the *ancien régime* in Church and State: *English Society*, 393–420.

England was concerned the eighteenth century lasted until the 1860s.[34] In the diocese of Canterbury this was literally so, as over 17 per cent of those appointed before 1828 were in post in the 1860s, and at least three of that cohort were still parish incumbents as late as the 1880s.[35] This is not to suggest that there were not profound social, economic, political, and intellectual changes between 1660 and the early nineteenth century, all of which had their part in shaping the Church's position within society, but it is to argue that there were, in the clerical mind at least, underlying continuities and preoccupations, which ought to be considered. It is only by studying a longer chronological perspective than that usually favoured by historians that the deeper trends emerge.

This book focuses on the diocese of Canterbury for three main reasons. First, the records at the diocesan, capitular, and parochial levels are in excellent order. In part the assembling and cataloguing of the sources needed for this study was carried out in the period itself; they were a product of the Church's own desire to record its history, as a succession of administrators and antiquarians associated with Lambeth and Canterbury took it upon themselves to organize documents concerned with the archbishopric, cathedral, and diocese, and individual clergy sorted out the papers of their parishes for their own purposes and for those of future incumbents.

Second, the study of the archbishops' own diocese offers some glimpse into national policy and concerns. While this book concentrates on the archbishops of Canterbury primarily as bishops of a particular diocese and not on their national function, there is inevitably some overlap between the two roles.[36] A complete set of archbishops' registers, act-books, visitation returns, and a largely unstudied series of diocesan correspondence allows an assessment of the aims of the leaders of the Church. It has sometimes been suggested that the Kentish experience was untypical, and is therefore useless as a window into the rest of the nation. But while no diocese can ever

---

[34] F. Knight, *The Nineteenth-Century Church and English Society* (Cambridge, 1995), 3.

[35] Gostwick Prideaux (appointed curate of Upchurch, 1820, promoted to the perpetual curacy of Iwade, 1826–33, and made vicar of Elmstead and rector of Hastingleigh in 1833, posts which he held until 1880); Montagu Oxenden (curate of Chilham in 1823, and rector of Eastwell until his death in 1880); and Charles James Burton (appointed curate of Marden in 1816, made perpetual curate of Ash in 1817, and serving as vicar of Lydd from 1821 until 1887).

[36] The former Lambeth Palace librarian and chaplain to Archbishop Tenison, Edmund Gibson, noted that 'the Records of the See of Canterbury afford more Information upon most Heads, not only than the Records of any other See, but more than the Records of all other Sees put together, as containing the whole exercise of Metropolitical, as well as Ordinary, Jurisdiction through a long series and succession of Archbishops': *Codex Juris Ecclesiastici Anglicani*, 2 vols. (1713), i, p. viii.

claim to be representative, Canterbury offers a useful insight into some of the problems felt and experienced elsewhere in the country. It was in many ways a privileged clerical stronghold, the home of Christianity in England, the archbishop's diocese and the site of a wealthy and prestigious cathedral, yet east Kent also housed a large number of nonconformists. Much of the diocese, like most of England, was predominantly rural, yet parts of the region shared in the population expansion and growth of urbanization found elsewhere in the late eighteenth and early nineteenth centuries. The clergy of the Canterbury diocese had, then, in their efforts to minister to their parishioners, to face problems similar to those in other regions of the country. It may be that the diocese of Canterbury, if not typical, shows up in a more exaggerated form than in most other regions, the strengths and limitations of the Church. In any case, perhaps modern scholars have worried overmuch about the so-called typicality of their chosen area of study. What is increasingly receiving historical attention is the recognition of the importance of region, locality, and environment in creating differences which cannot be reduced to a generalized type. Historians of the sixteenth century have made us aware of the futility of looking for a uniform clerical experience, arguing that we ought to appreciate and understand rather than attempt to iron out the differences between, for example, Kent, as studied by Peter Clark, and Lancashire, as studied by Christopher Haigh.[37]

A third reason for concentrating on Canterbury is that Kent in general, and the diocese of Canterbury in particular, have been well served by historians investigating other periods, whose work has been used as reference points for this study. Those early county historians, Camden and Lambarde, paid especial attention to Kent, providing a structure for that great eighteenth-century county historian, Edward Hasted, whose research has been an invaluable source for this book.[38]

In focusing on a diocese, this book recognizes, however, some of the limitations of the traditional diocesan study. Recent scholarship has indeed

---

[37] Clark, *English Provincial Society* and C. Haigh, *Reformation and Resistance in Tudor Lancashire* (Cambridge, 1976). See also R. Whiting, *The Blind Devotion of the People. Popular Religion and the English Reformation* (Cambridge, 1989).

[38] Edward Hasted, *The History and Topographical Survey of the County of Kent*, 4 vols. (Canterbury, 1778–99); 12 vols. (2nd edn., 1797–1801). Modern studies concerned with the Kentish experience include: Clark, *English Provincial Society*; Collinson, *Religion of Protestants*, which deals extensively with late sixteenth and early seventeenth century Kentish matters; id., 'Cranbrook and the Fletchers: Popular and Unpopular Religion in the Kentish Weald', in P. Newman Brooks (ed.), *Reformation Principle and Practice: Essays in Honour of Arthur Geoffrey Dickens* (1980), 173–202; A. Everitt, *The Community of Kent and the Great Rebellion* (Leicester, 1966); N. Yates, *Kent and the Oxford Movement* (Gloucester, 1983) and id. and R. Hume and P. Hastings, *Religion and Society in Kent, 1640–1914* (Woodbridge, 1994).

revealed the problems associated with studying regional administrative units such as the 'county' or the 'village', demonstrating that they are often either too large or too small to be a sensitive indicator of contemporary experience.[39] The same might be said for the diocese too. How far, for example, did the diocese represent a viable or real focus of loyalty for clergy? Was it merely an institutional construct or could it provide some sense of community? This is a crucial question since it has often been argued that the Church in this period was not only an atomized institution, but that there were insuperable gulfs between the higher and lower clergy which worked against any notion of clerical community and professional identity.[40] This study explores the overlapping and interlocking communities and units represented by the archbishopric, cathedral, diocese, and parish to see how far the Church in Canterbury was able to operate as a unified organization. For example, the cathedral community was a society within a society, with its own rules, officials, customs, lands, and revenues. In this it exemplified the decentralized nature of administration in the Church of England. But it was always more than a closed world, being intimately connected to the wider world of the locality through its ownership of land and its use of patronage. Through the activities and careers of those members who were bound up with the world beyond the precincts, it provided a link between provincial and national society. Likewise parish clergy could have associations outside their parish and diocese, connected to the world beyond east Kent through social, educational, and professional ties. These connections could work towards creating a sense of clerical professional identity and affected the nature of the Church as an institution. As far as the relations between the higher and lower clergy were concerned, John Spurr has argued that, for the Restoration period at least, the Church had a definite top-down management structure, where a 'silent clerical proletariat', lacking self-confidence and initiative, merely responded to the requirements of the authorities.[41] But Spurr's study was essentially based on printed materials. A mass of surviving correspondence reveals that diocesan management was often a question of replying to problems which emerged from the grass-roots experience as the parish clergy bombarded

[39] Amongst others see C. Holmes, 'The County Community in Stuart Historiography', *JBS*, 19 (1980), 54–73; A. Hughes, 'Local History and the Origins of the English Civil War', in R. Cust and A. Hughes (eds.), *Conflict in Early Stuart England. Studies in Religion and Politics, 1603–1642* (1989), 224–52; A. Fletcher, *Reform in the Provinces: The Government of Stuart England* (Princeton, NJ and London, 1986); K. Wrightson and D. Levine, *Poverty and Piety in an English Village: Terling, 1525–1700* (New York, 1979).

[40] Sykes, *Church and State*, 147; Virgin, *Church in Age of Negligence*, 253–5.

[41] Spurr, *Restoration Church*, p. xv.

their seniors with questions which had to be answered. By recognizing the part played by clergy in national, diocesan, and parochial structures, this book hopes to emulate some of those recent county studies which have been aware of the interplay between provincial experience and central concerns.[42] The Church, perhaps *par excellence*, demonstrated this connection between local and national themes.

To help investigate these issues, I have divided the book into three sections. Section I is a study of the personnel of the diocese. Chapter 1 explores those appointed to the hierarchy within the locality—the archbishops and the members of the dean and chapter—looking at their socio-economic backgrounds, their intellectual interests, and their political affiliations. The men who filled these posts have often been castigated for their laziness and irrelevance to the functioning of the Church.[43] Here, the archbishops are shown to have been men of business who had proved their worth in other areas of Church life. Attention is also paid to the management structures of the diocese, especially to the patronage networks which enabled archbishops to have a large amount of control over their clergy, and to the channels of communication which allowed the hierarchy to keep in contact with the clergy in their charge. Moreover, the highly prized prebendaries were not the preserve of the aristocracy and gentry, as has so often been claimed, but were increasingly given to those from clerical backgrounds. Because so much of the cathedral's patronage lay in the hands of the Crown, the community was a stronghold of establishment ideology. Those appointed to the deanery and chapter are demonstrated to have played a central role in defending the Restoration. During the politically sensitive decades following the Revolution of 1688 and in the years after 1714 the cathedral became a centre of support for new regimes. However, the backing given by members of the chapter to Whig governments did not imply any lessening of their commitment to Anglican principles. Many claimed that true Anglican interests demanded attachment to the new order. The educational backgrounds and intellectual interests of the prebendaries reveal the ways in which all branches of knowledge could be utilized for the defence of the Anglican position. In particular, during the second half of the eighteenth century the cathedral became a centre for the dissemination of anti-rationalist and anti-Socinian teachings. The clergy

---

[42] In particular, A. M. Coleby, *Central Government and the Localities: Hampshire, 1649–1689* (Cambridge, 1987) and P. J. Norrey, 'The Restoration Regime in Action: The Relationship between Central and Local Government in Dorset, Somerset and Wiltshire', *HJ*, 31 (1988), 789–812.

[43] John Wade, *The Black Book: or Corruption Unmask'd!* (1820), 258.

associated with the Hutchinsonian circle and later the 'Hackney Phalanx' provided a vigorous defence of the position of the Church at the end of the period, especially in the decades after the French Revolution, indicating the role of the Church's hierarchy in such times of crisis. Attention is also paid to the issue of reform within the cathedral community.

Chapter 2 looks at the parish clergy, examining their backgrounds, training, and political affiliations and focuses on the nature of the clerical profession. Whereas the theme of professionalization has been used in studying clergy in earlier and later centuries,[44] little attention has been paid to the ways in which this period saw an attempt to make the clergy into a homogeneous professional force. This occurred in a number of ways. Socially, in recruitment to the ministry, the period saw a move in favour of those from clerical and other professional backgrounds, which provided some kind of shared experience. Educationally, the great majority of beneficed clergy were graduates, which helped to close the gap between the higher and lower clergy. Institutionally, the hierarchy was able to control the quality of those entering the profession through ordination. Further, valuable work experience could be gained during service as a curate. These factors ensured that the clerical profession was not split into sharply distinct categories as it was in the sixteenth century or as it was in France in the eighteenth century, and it helps explain why movements such as *richerisme* found little outlet in the English situation. Once the clergy were beneficed, their behaviour was monitored by the hierarchy, which was concerned to keep an eye on pastoral standards. Politically too, the period witnessed the creation of a parish clergy whose views were in accord with those of the hierarchy, so that by the 1730s the majority of the clergy in the diocese were Whig supporters. It is suggested that this perhaps contributed to the wider stability of mid-eighteenth century England. Moreover, the creation of a homogenous professional force worked against the development of church parties, which would be a feature of Church life in the decades after 1828, and which arguably hampered the pastoral effectiveness of the Church.

The second section examines the economic role of the Church within the diocese. Chapter 3 is a study of the administration of Church property, which was a sensitive indicator of the Church's relationship with the laity. The way in which a stern management of its estates could sour relations with local society had been seen in the 1630s.[45] Post-Restoration and

---

[44] O'Day, *English Clergy*; Heeney, *Different Kind of Gentleman*; Haig, *Victorian Clergy*.

[45] F. Heal, 'Archbishop Laud Revisited: Leases and Estate Management at Canterbury and Winchester before the Civil War', in R. O'Day and F. Heal (eds.), *Princes and Paupers in the English Church 1500–1800* (Leicester, 1981), 129–51.

eighteenth-century clergy had learned from Archbishop Laud's experience and realized that they had to work within an administrative framework in which they could defend Church rights but did not alienate their supporters. The tension involved in trying to reclaim and protect Church property while also maintaining an amicable relationship with the laity was a central feature of the Restoration in the diocese. Churchmen were anxious to advertise the charitable nature of their treatment of tenants. This policy had the effect of constraining the Church for the next century and is revealed in the difficulties the Church had in increasing its income. In return, lessees were expected to defend and maintain property. In their spending the Church hierarchy repaired buildings, offered charity to the poor and maintained its hospitals. Although a change in policy, promoted by fears of unrest, can be discerned in the last years of the period covered by this book, the greater part of the long eighteenth century saw an attempt at cordial relations with the laity.

Chapter 4 explores the financial position of the parish clergy, looking at the ways in which they obtained and spent their income. In much historical writing, models of conflict have been used to analyse the economic relationship of the clergy with their parishioners and between members of the clerical profession.[46] But to over-emphasize conflict is to obscure the strength of the Church in the parishes and its often uncontested involvement in the economy of the local community. For example, despite the immense difficulties associated with the tithing system, the clergy seem to have been surprisingly successful in obtaining maintenance. The chapter suggests that any account of the economics of the parish should take note of the character of the incumbent in a system where personal relations were often a decisive factor in determining a clergyman's income. Christopher Hill has characterized this relationship as one in which the clergy were economically dependent on the laity, and has relied heavily on evidence produced when the relationship between the incumbent and his parishioners broke down.[47] The more normal situation was the peaceful extraction of tithes. Such disputes as there were decreased during the eighteenth century, rather than building up steadily into the rural outburst of the Swing riots of 1830. In any case, despite the difficulties facing an incumbent in collecting his tithe, the general value of clerical incomes rose during the period. The chapter also looks at the incidence of pluralism, the impact of clerical marriage on incumbents' incomes, and the role of clergy in

---

[46] Virgin, *Church in Age of Negligence*, 8, 11, 124, 242; E. J. Evans, *The Contentious Tithe. The Tithe Problem and English Agriculture, 1750–1850* (1976).

[47] Hill, *Economic Problems of the Church*.

distributing charity. It points to the ability of many incumbents to persuade the laity, both Tory and Whig, to contribute towards the costs of the repair, improvement, and building of parish churches, as indicative of the amicable relations between clerical and lay society in the period between the late seventeenth and the early nineteenth centuries.

The third section concentrates further on the relationship between the clergy and society. Chapter 5 studies the attitude of the clergy towards their nonconformist rivals. The conventional view, propagated by dissenters, Methodists, and Evangelicals, is that the Church of England was a static institution with a limited capacity to absorb new religious impulses.[48] By contrast, this chapter suggests that in their dealings with both Old and New Dissent, clergy often found tolerance more applicable than confrontation. Tolerationist policies emerged in the Restoration period. This is particularly shown in the difficulties that clergy had in defining and in prosecuting dissent, when gentry and incumbents themselves might give tacit support to nonconformists. This charitable treatment extended to groups such as the Huguenots and Walloons which had been persecuted by Archbishop Laud.[49] After 1689, despite party rivalry, the relationship between the Church and dissent was one of competition rather than persecution, as seen in the ways in which the Church devised various strategies to accommodate nonconformists into the Church. In part the increasingly tolerant attitude can be explained by the perceived decline in the dissenting threat. This policy of co-operation, rather than conflict, can be seen even in attitudes towards Catholics in the diocese, which led clergy to support émigré priests after the French Revolution (although they remained suspicious of early nineteenth-century attempts to grant emancipation to Catholics). Attitudes towards Methodism in the diocese show how suspicion of the divisive qualities of dissent could go hand in hand with sympathy. As late as 1786 incumbents happily reported that Methodists still attended the church. The rapid growth of Methodism occurred during the 1790s. Developments in that decade and in the first decades of the nineteenth century hint at a breakdown in the consensus between the Church and nonconformists which had been achieved during the past century. Hitherto, the clergy had been more concerned with the growing section of the populace who did not attend any form of religious worship.

---

[48] G. R. Cragg, *Puritanism in the Period of the Great Persecution, 1660–1688* (Cambridge, 1957); T. Timpson. *Church History of Kent. From the Earliest Period to the Year MDCCCLVIII* (1859).

[49] F. W. Cross, *History of the Walloon and Huguenot Church at Canterbury* (Canterbury, 1898).

How they attempted to deal with absentees from church, and to strengthen the Anglican presence in the parish through pastoral care and parochial education, is the subject of Chapter 6. A large part of the case against the Church in the long eighteenth century has been based on the alleged pastoral failure of its clergy in comparison with previous Puritan and later Evangelical and Tractarian groups.[50] This adverse judgement has been strongly affected by the sources used by historians to evaluate the clergy's pastoral function, most notably the criterion of the number of services supplied, the evidence of which has suggested that clergy were rather under-deployed. However, closer examination, especially of what might be called their back-up pastoral strategies, reveals much in common between the clergy of the Church of England and their so-called rivals. Clerical prescriptive literature stressed the understanding of the faith required for membership of the Church. The principal method of disseminating the faith was held to be through catechizing. But it was often only an elite within the parish which attained the kind of religious commitment demanded by the Church. In their attempts to regularize the religious beliefs and behaviour of their parishioners, Anglican clergy shared ideals which resembled those of the 'godly' of the seventeenth century, and in that they can be seen as participating in the Reformation enterprise.[51] One of the clearest testimonies to the clergy's desire to educate their parishioners lay in their support of parochial education. In this, and especially in the backing given to the Sunday schools in the late eighteenth and early nineteenth centuries, there was little to separate the initiatives of the mainstream clergy from the Evangelicals of the period. The chapter also looks at the religious services offered by the clergy and the difficulties involved in persuading some groups in the diocese to attend. In particular, despite clerical stress on the importance of receiving the sacrament, various sections of the parish were often reluctant to communicate. Behind such parochial pastoral endeavours stood the role of the cathedral as a model for services in the diocese. There, a number of High-Church deans maintained the Anglican liturgy in its full dignity, a practice which suggests that the standards of cathedral worship were by no means as low as later Tractarians claimed. All this pastoral activity was monitored by the archbishops through the visitation system, which became increasingly regularized during the period and was a vital point of contact between the hierarchy and the parish clergy. The process, which relied on returns from clergy rather than churchwardens, is

[50] A. D. Gilbert, *Religion and Society in Industrial England. Church, Chapel and Social Change, 1740–1914* (1976), 27–9.
[51] Collinson, *English Puritanism* (1983).

indicative of the close ties between the various strands of the profession. This chapter further shows that similar pastoral concerns were shared by clergy of varying political persuasions, and indeed by those often deemed to have belonged to different schools of Churchmanship. A common pastoral endeavour was a central feature of the pastoral initiatives of the Church in the Canterbury diocese in the period before 1828.

The book concludes by suggesting that some of the traditional period-izations and characterizations of conventional Church history need modification. Much of the evidence presented here indicates that clergy in the 170 years after the Restoration were preoccupied with difficulties which had concerned their forebears and would concern their successors. In many ways, particularly in areas such as the need to follow through, and in some instances to instigate the pastoral and professional aims of the Reform-ation, and in participating in processes relating to Church reform, clergy in the long eighteenth century continued the work of seventeenth-century clergy, as well as anticipating some of the ideals of the Evangelical and Oxford Movements. Reluctance to recognize this has led historians to ne-glect the strengths of the Church between the Restoration and the 1830s, which, it is argued here, should not be judged primarily for its failure to at-tain the ideals of these other movements, but as an institution possessing its own coherent and positive rationale.

I. Personnel

I

Archbishops and the Dean and Chapter

Of all the ecclesiastical appointments made in the summer of 1660, few were more crucial for the restoration of the Church of England than those to the deanery and chapter of Canterbury. The election of ten new prebendaries to replace those who had died during the Interregnum was even more pressing at Canterbury than elsewhere because of the need for a chapter meeting before the congé d'élire could be issued for the appointment of a new archbishop.[1] Yet we remain largely ignorant of those who filled these posts and their successors during the next 170 years. Part of the reason for this lack of interest has been the barrage of criticism—from Presbyterians and others in the 1640s[2] through to the attacks of radicals in the 1820s[3]—which emphasized not only the laziness and place-seeking of those appointed to these exalted positions within the Church's personnel, but which condemned the whole superstructure of the Church hierarchy as a malevolent influence on the work of the Church.

In this verdict, the archbishops and the dean and chapter of Canterbury were deemed to be far removed from the experience of the parochial clergy, and as such symbolic of the fractured nature of the Church as an institution.[4] However, as defenders of Church hierarchy constantly reiterated, parish clergy could aspire to become prebendaries and prebendaries rise to episcopal office; there existed a ladder of preferment which provided some kind of career structure within the clerical profession.[5] Echoing some of the judgements of Norman Sykes, an analysis of the role and function of cathedrals within French society in this period has similarly condemned them for being 'citadelles du passé', an irrelevance in a world dominated by

---

[1] Bosher, *Restoration Settlement*, 161; Green, *Re-establishment of Church of England*, 66–7.

[2] Richard Culmer, 'Cathedrall Newes from Canterbury' reprinted in G. S[mith], *A Chronological History of Canterbury Cathedral* (Canterbury, 1883), 282–317.

[3] Wade, *The Black Book*, 258.

[4] For the gulf within the Church see the analysis in Virgin, *Church in Age of Negligence*, 253–5.

[5] Defences: Myles Smith: Bodl. MS Tanner 141, fos. 79, 93, 111; William Scott, *The Substance of the Speech . . . delivered in the House of Commons, Wednesday April 7th 1802* (1802), 42–5.

the ideals and values of the Enlightenment.[6] But, as an assessment of those who were appointed to some of the highest posts within the Church of England indicates, they could play a crucial part in defending the restoration of the Church and in providing an intellectual and political defence of the Church's position in society.

ARCHBISHOPS AND MANAGEMENT STRUCTURES

Even the archbishops of Canterbury have been neglected as a group. A general survey of religious life in the long eighteenth century reflects this paucity of information, relying as it does on conventional stereotypes:

another dull appointment [of Herring in 1747] was made to the primacy, to be followed by others over which we need not linger . . . These bishops, as they look out from their portraits, their faces florid under their wigs, often seem as if they have returned from a day's hunting in a vain attempt to shed the effects of the previous evening's drinking.[7]

It is true that six archbishops have been accorded a modern biography, but these, by the very nature of the genre, tend to give a rather oblique approach to diocesan history, by magnifying the role of the particular archbishop concerned and paying little attention to the forces of continuity and the long-term problems which far outlived the archiepiscopate of any one man.[8] And although historians have shown interest in Gilbert Sheldon and

---

[6] B. Plongeron, *La Vie quotidienne du clergé français au xviiie siècle* (Paris, 1974), 113.

[7] D. L. Edwards, *Christian England, ii. From the Reformation to the Eighteenth Century* (1983), 483, 487.

[8] T. A. Mason, *Serving God and Mammon: William Juxon, 1582–1663* (Cranbury, NJ, 1985); V. D. Sutch, *Gilbert Sheldon, Architect of Anglican Survival (1640–1675)* (The Hague, 1973); E. F. Carpenter, *Thomas Tenison, Archbishop of Canterbury. His Life and Times* (1948); Sykes, *Wake*; L. W. Barnard, *John Potter. An Eighteenth-Century Archbishop* (Ilfracombe, 1989); and id., *Thomas Secker. An Eighteenth-Century Primate* (Lewes, 1998). An overview is provided by A. W. Rowden, *The Primates of the Four Georges* (1916). Older studies include: V. Staley, *The Life and Times of Gilbert Sheldon* (1913); G. D'Oyly, *The Life of William Sancroft, Archbishop of Canterbury*, 2 vols. (1821); N. Salmon, *The Lives of the English Bishops From the Restauration to the Revolution*, 2 vols. (1731–8); W. F. Hook, *Lives of the Archbishops of Canterbury*, 11 vols. (1879), which, in typical Tractarian fashion, ends with Juxon; T. Birch, *Life of the Most Reverend Dr John Tillotson* (1752); B. Porteus, 'Life of Archbishop Secker' in *The Works of Thomas Secker, Archbishop of Canterbury*, 8 vols. (1769), i. 1–70. See also J. McKay, 'John Tillotson (1630–1694): A Study of his Life and of his Contribution to the Development of English Prose', unpub. Oxford University D.Phil. thesis, 1952 and R. B. McDowell, 'The Anglican Episcopate, 1780–1945', *Theology*, 50 (1947), 202–9. Of related interest are N. Ravitch, *Sword and Mitre. Government and Episcopate in France and England in the Age of Aristocracy* (The Hague, 1966) and R. A. Soloway, *Prelates and People: Ecclesiastical Social Thought in England 1783–1852* (1969).

William Sancroft as archbishops in the period of fraught Church and State relations between the Restoration and the Glorious Revolution, they have been studied largely as ecclesiastical politicians and their relationship with their diocese has not been adequately assessed.[9] In the late nineteenth century, Canon Jenkins commented of Sancroft, 'nothing of note occurred in relation to the diocese'.[10] The view that archbishops were not much involved with their diocese was largely based on the fact that they did not reside there but at Lambeth. The archbishops were seen as prince-bishops whose main concerns were political and national rather than diocesan and local. Canon Jenkins attributed such lack of involvement to the remoteness of east Kent from the political world of London, suggesting that the pastoral relationship between the archbishops and their diocese only became close during the nineteenth century with the coming of the railways.[11] But, as we shall see, it is not true that archbishops had no contact with their diocese. It is also misleading to imply, as Jenkins did, that archiepiscopal concerns could be sharply separated out into either the 'high political' or the 'pastoral and diocesan', for both could well be part of a coherent programme. It should be recalled that it had never been the custom for archbishops continually to reside in Canterbury. William Laud, so often seen as a model primate by High-Church historians, did not live there.[12] After 1660, with the destruction of great sections of the archbishop's palace during the Civil War, it became not only inconvenient but impossible to do so. William Wake, typically a stickler for form and legal niceties, even had the clause concerning residence removed from his enthronement oath in 1716 since there was no place in which to reside.[13] In any case the diocese, being one day's journey from Lambeth, was easier to administer from London than, say, that of Lincoln. In the century and a half before the railway boom of the 1830s and 40s other strategies were employed to ensure links between archbishops and their see. Volumes of correspondence, registers, and act-books in Lambeth Palace Library are testimony to the strength of the communication between Lambeth, the dean and chapter of Canterbury, and the parish clergy in the diocese, and reveal that several archbishops, even when confined to Lambeth, or Croydon, as they often were at the end of their lives, were very much concerned to know about clergy in their charge.

⁹ Especially Spurr, *Restoration Church*, R. A. Beddard, 'Sheldon and Anglican Recovery', *HJ*, 19 (1976), 1005–17. Also of interest: W. G. Simon, *The Restoration Episcopate* (1965), which is a prosopographical study of bishops appointed between 1660 and 1689.
¹⁰ Jenkins, *Canterbury*, 370.   ¹¹ Ibid., 405.
¹² H. R. Trevor-Roper, *Archbishop Laud* (1940), 148.
¹³ Sykes, *Wake*, i. 205. In 1667 Archbishop Sheldon was granted an exemption from repairs: LPL, Cartae Miscellenae XIII, fo. 2.

Interest in the diocese could serve a wider purpose, as several archbishops, notably Sheldon, Sancroft, Tenison, Wake, Secker, Moore, and Manners Sutton, saw Canterbury, as had Laud, as a model for what might be achieved elsewhere.[14]

A principal function of the archbishops was to superintend and monitor the lives and activities of the clergy under their immediate jurisdiction, and nothing could be done without a satisfactory knowledge of the facts concerning the personnel of the diocese.[15] A series of visitation returns enabled primates to possess detailed knowledge about their clergy. The 'Secker Speculum', essentially a digest of the visitation returns from 1758 to 1766 (but updated by his successors), contains a mass of detail about incumbents and curates.[16] In compiling it Secker had recourse to the archival information deposited by his predecessors. Going through the diocesan material, which Archbishop Wake had left to Christ Church, Oxford, on behalf of the recently elevated Secker in 1759, Edward Bentham, a canon of Christ Church, pronounced himself impressed by Wake's

abilities and application. Neither [*he continued*] is it improper that other people besides the immediate inhabitants of Lambeth Palace should have an authentic proof what a severe tax is constantly paid by the Archiepiscopal dignity in importunicies to be endured as well as real business.[17]

It is significant too that it is precisely in this period that archbishops took care to organize and catalogue records at Lambeth, and if collection of information about the state of the Church and its clergy was a necessary prerequisite for reform, then the knowledge of the clergy and the parishes available to archbishops after 1660 was instrumental in reshaping the Church.[18]

---

[14] Clark, *English Provincial Society*, 361–71. Cf. M. F. Steig, *Laud's Laboratory: The Diocese of Bath and Wells in the Early Seventeenth Century* (Lewisburg, 1982).

[15] Churchill, *Canterbury Administration*, i. 39–42.

[16] LPL, VG 2/5. I have edited the manuscript: *The Speculum of Archbishop Thomas Secker*, ed. J. Gregory, Church of England Record Society, 2 (1995). This compares with the *Speculum Dioeceseos Lincolniensis*, ed. R. E. G. Cole, Lincoln Record Society, 4 (1913) and with *The State of the Bishopric of Worcester, 1782–1808*, ed. M. Ransome, Worcester Historical Society, ns, 6 (1968). Secker's interest in the details of the lives of his clergy was not limited to his time at Canterbury. As bishop of Bristol from 1735 to 1737 he compiled a survey: 'Bishop Secker's Diocese Book', ed. E. Ralph, in P. McGrath (ed.), *A Bristol Miscellany*, Bristol Record Society Publications, 37 (1985), 23–69. See also J. Bettey, 'Bishop Secker's Diocesan Survey', *Dorset Natural History and Archaelogical Society*, 95 (1973–4), 74–5.

[17] LPL MS 1133, fo. 8, Bentham to Secker, 12 June 1759.

[18] See A. Cox-Johnson, 'Lambeth Palace Library, 1610–1664', *Transactions of the Cambridge Bibliographical Society*, 2 (1955), 105–26. H. J. Todd, *Catalogue of the Archiepiscopal Manuscripts in the Library at Lambeth Palace* (1812). Sancroft made notes on his predecessors:

The political considerations involved in the appointment of archbishops are clear. During the Restoration era, Juxon, Sheldon, and Sancroft had impeccable credentials as defenders of the Church and had demonstrated ferocious loyalty to the restored regime. Likewise, Tillotson, Tenison, and Wake were seen as keystones in the construction of the regimes after 1688. In 1737 both Sherlock and Gibson were passed over for political reasons.[19] It was said then of Potter, who was appointed, that 'he is a man after the ministry's own heart, he will not cause trouble; but his learning and thorough knowledge in Divinity does honour to their promotion of him'.[20] The appointment of archbishops also indicates the continuing dominance of the monarchy in Crown appointments throughout the eighteenth century. George II brought Hutton to Canterbury in 1757 and the ecclesiastical cause célèbre of George III's reign was the king's insistence that Manners Sutton (who was dean of Windsor) should succeed Moore in 1805, against the wishes of Pitt who favoured his former tutor Pretyman-Tomline.[21]

Who, then, were the men appointed to this position? A striking fact about the archbishops promoted between 1660 and 1828 is their distinctly un-aristocratic background. Frederick Cornwallis (archbishop, 1768–83) was the first from a noble background since the Reformation, to be followed in 1805 by the nobleman Charles Manners Sutton. The others came from much less elevated families: Tillotson was the son of a grazier, Potter the son of a linen-draper, and Moore was the son of a butcher.[22] It is instructive to compare this with the situation in other countries; in France and Spain all bishops at this time were of strictly aristocratic birth.[23] One of the themes in the historiography of the eighteenth-century Catholic Church is the struggle between the higher dignitaries and the parish clergy: that this

see Bodl. MS Sancroft 45, his commonplace book on 'archbishops'. He is supposed to have intended to leave his books and papers to the library, but decided against this after being ordered to leave Lambeth within 10 days by Queen Mary on 20 May 1691: D'Oyly, *Sancroft*, ii. 467. In the 1770s Cornwallis tried to acquire Sancroft's papers from the Bodleian: John Nichols, *Literary Anecdotes of the Eighteenth Century*, 9 vols. (1812–16), ix. 507. Sheldon, Tenison, and Secker left their entire collections of printed books to LPL: B. Botfield, *Notes on the Cathedral Libraries of England* (1849), 191.

[19] E. Carpenter, *Thomas Sherlock* (1931), 51.

[20] *HMC, Diary of Egmont*, ii. 476. The political nature of the appointment was emphasized in *A Race for Canterbury, or Lambeth Ho! A Poem Describing the Contention for the Metropolitical See* (1747).

[21] Sykes, *Church and State*, 39, 402. On Hutton's elevation see S. Taylor, '"The Fac Totum in Ecclesiastic Affairs"? The Duke of Newcastle and the Crown's Ecclesiastical Patronage', *Albion*, 24 (1992), 422.

[22] Birch, *Tillotson*, 2; Rowden, *Primates*, 115, 248, 348.

[23] Introduction, W. J. Callahan and D. Higgs (eds.), *Church and Society in Catholic Europe of the Eighteenth Century* (Cambridge, 1983), 2.

tension is much less noticeable in the Church of England was perhaps related to the less exclusive social recruitment of those in the highest office.[24] The generally non-aristocratic background of the primates scarcely supports Anthony Russell's contention that the social gap between clergy and bishops became more vast. It fits in well, however, with Geoffrey Holmes' picture of the professions in this period as agents of social mobility.[25] The non-exclusive recruitment of the archbishops is reflected not only in their social origins but perhaps more significantly in their religious backgrounds. Tillotson was of 'Puritan' origins, and Potter and Secker were the sons of nonconformists; Tillotson was educated at Clare during the Interregnum before becoming an Anglican in late 1661, and Secker at the Attercliffe and Tewkesbury dissenting academies before he travelled to Europe in 1721 and enrolled at Leyden University, known for its religious tolerance. When Secker was on the brink of becoming a dissenting minister he was persuaded by Butler and Benson to conform to the Anglican Church.[26]

Olwen Hufton, in an analysis of French bishops, noted that 'the aspirant bishop had never been . . . a parish priest'.[27] This is again very different from the situation in England, since it was through their exertions at the parochial level, and especially in the London parishes, that several future archbishops received the attention of leading patrons. Tenison was promoted for his work in Cambridge during the plague, and then for his pastoral initiatives at St Martin-in-the-Fields.[28] Tillotson was elected to St Mary, Aldermanbury, Wake was rector of St James', Westminster, and Secker built up a reputation in the same parish, where he was rector from 1733 to 1750. The significance of a London living is clear: the availability of an influential audience and proximity to the Court made the capital a recruiting ground for bishops. Others had experience of parish work elsewhere. Sheldon had been vicar of Hackney in 1633, Potter was collated to Great Mongeham in the Canterbury diocese in 1707, and Newington in 1708, and Hutton was presented to Trowbridge in 1726. Secker held the living of Houghton-le-Spring from 1724 to 1727, Cornwallis was presented to the family living of Chelmondiston in 1740, and Manners Sutton was appointed to the rectory of Kelham, Nottinghamshire in 1783. That

---

[24] Ibid.

[25] Russell, *Clerical Profession*, 31; G. Holmes, *Augustan England. Professions, State and Society, 1680–1730* (1982), 15–18.

[26] Birch, *Tillotson*, 2–3; S. Taylor, 'Archbishop Potter and the Dissenters', *Yale University Library Gazette*, 67 (1993), 118–26; LPL, MS 2598, fo. 9.

[27] O. Hufton, 'The French Church', in Callahan and Higgs, *Church and Society*, 16.

[28] *The Diary of John Evelyn*, ed. E. S. de Beer, 6 vols. (Oxford, 1955), iv. 307–8, 21 March 1683.

archbishops had seen something of the reality of ordinary parish life ensured that they appreciated the problems of their clergy, and gave their advice a ring of practicality. Secker, having outlined the role of a parish priest,
urged his audience to remember: 'do not think that I take pleasure in laying
burdens upon you of which I am to take no share myself. I have taken some
care, I hope as much as most of you in the business of my profession ever
since I was in it, and I still do.'[29]

Another kind of work-experience and a valuable source of patronage was
to become chaplain to a nobleman or a bishop. Tillotson had been chaplain
to Sir Edward Prideaux, Hutton to the Duke of Somerset, Secker to the
Talbot family, and Moore was domestic tutor to the son of the Duke of
Marlborough. Sancroft had been chaplain to Bishop Cosin (1660-2) and
Potter was domestic chaplain to Tenison from 1704. It was a huge advantage to have been appointed to a royal chaplaincy, and only Moore and
Manners Sutton failed to be so. Sheldon, Tillotson, and Wake were also
clerks of the closet which cemented their relationship with the Crown.

Besides experience at the parish level, all archbishops had had some kind
of administrative experience, first as members of a dean and chapter and
then usually as bishops of other sees, but the excessive number of trans-
lations of which nineteenth-century critics complained were less in evidence. One to three moves at the most, from their first bishopric to the
primacy, was the typical career pattern. Tillotson and Sancroft became
archbishops without having a previous episcopal appointment, although
they had proved their administrative capabilities elsewhere, serving their
apprenticeship as heads of complex institutions: cathedrals or university
colleges. It was said that Sheldon had been 'born and bred to be Archbishop' on account of his being a successful administrator as warden of All
Souls. Sancroft had been bursar of Emmanuel College, Cambridge, which
may have given him useful training in financial management, before becoming a highly influential master of the college from 1662 to 1664, where
he had been active in moulding the university to the needs of the restored
Church, dean of St Paul's (1664-78), and prolocutor for the lower house
of Convocation (1668-70).[30] Several archbishops had some previous
knowledge of the diocese of Canterbury and county of Kent. Sancroft had
been an active archdeacon of Canterbury (1668-70); Tillotson had been a

[29] LPL MS 1350, fo. 21v. (no date).

[30] C. Grant Robertson, *All Souls: Oxford College Histories* (1899), 108. Sancroft resigned
the mastership on finding that he could not properly attend to its duties: D'Oyly, *Sancroft*, i.
147. For Sancroft's role at Cambridge see Gascoigne, *Cambridge in Age of Enlightenment*, 37-8.

prebendary (stall II, 1670–2), then dean of Canterbury (1672–88), as had Moore (1771–5).

Apart from bureaucratic and administrative training, some of those who were appointed to the archbishopric had made reputations as defenders of Church interests through their writings. All archbishops published something, mostly sermons (of which Tillotson's massive output must claim some kind of pre-eminence). Herring had the reputation of being a fine preacher, but, in accord with his wishes, the majority of his sermons were burnt after his death.[31] Wake and Potter, who was Regius professor of Divinity at Oxford (1707–37), were noted for their works of scholarship on Church history, and Secker's charges and lectures were valued as handbooks on pastoral care well into the nineteenth century.[32] The archbishopric was clearly reserved for men who had proved their worth in the Church. Canterbury was not a wealthy sinecure but a see of 'business', being one of those, along with York, London, and Ely, categorized in the mid-eighteenth century as earmarked for 'men of abilities and learning'.[33] Indeed several archbishops were reluctant to accept the post. It was rumoured that Sancroft did not want to be archbishop in 1678, but was told he could not refuse by Charles II, and although the frequent declarations of unworthiness by archbishops on being appointed may have been no more than conventional platitudes, correspondence does suggest how onerous they found their task. On being offered the post, Herring moaned that

the honour of Canterbury is a thing of glare and splendour, and ye hopes of it a proper incentive to schoolboys to industry; but I have considered all the inward parts and examined all its duties; and if I should quit my present station to take it, will not answer for it that in less than a twelvemonth I did not sink and die with regret and envy at the man who should succeed me here, and quit the place in my possession as I ought to do to one wiser and better than myself.[34]

The impression is not one of bishops greedily grasping after preferment. Nor were they sycophants. Several of those appointed later had been able to show some opposition to the government. In 1745, for example, Herring, often seen as the archetypal Whig primate, acted against the Court party by insisting that the Yorkshire Association formed against the Jacobites

---

[31] Ollard and Walker, *Herring*, iv. 23.

[32] John Tillotson, *Sermons*, 12 vols. (1757); William Wake, *The State of the Church and Clergy of England* (1703); John Potter, *The Theological Works of the Most Reverend Dr John Potter, Late Lord Archbishop of Canterbury*, 3 vols. (Oxford, 1753–4); Thomas Secker, *Eight Charges Delivered to the Clergy of the Dioceses of Oxford and Canterbury* (1769).

[33] Quoted in Sykes, *Church and State*, 157.

[34] D'Oyly, *Sancroft*, i. 151; quoted in Rowden, *Primates*, 194.

should include Tories and Whig dissenters. Secker, too, was well known for his ability to vote against the government in the 1740s.[35]

A problem, however, was that this key post in the Church's hierarchy was consistently given to men of fairly advanced years. It is true that Juxon's appointment in 1660, at the age of 78, when he was virtually senile, was exceptional, and made in order to maintain symbolic continuity with the pre-Civil War regime. The fact that the old man had accompanied Charles I on the scaffold and had said the last prayers for him, was urged in his favour. He was literally a living relic from the past.[36] The average age of those appointed was younger: 60 years. Edmund Gibson, passed over for Canterbury in 1737, refused the see when he was eventually offered it in 1747 on account of his age (he was 78), as did Richard Hurd in 1783, who also pleaded that the political duties of the post would not suit his scholarly character.[37] If any archbishop was to make an impact on the diocese, he needed time. The average duration of the primacy in this period was twelve years. Manners Sutton had the longest period in office (from 1805 to 1828) and at 50 he was the youngest appointed. Tillotson had under four years as archbishop and Hutton only a few months. Because of their age, archbishops, towards the end of their lives, might well lose their grip on administration. Wake's illness from the late 1720s ensured that his son-in-law, Dean Lynch, was responsible for much diocesan business.[38]

One of the fundamental ways in which archbishops of Canterbury were able to make their mark on the Church, and on their diocese in particular, was through the use of the various patronage networks in their control. A valued category of patronage was that to the domestic chaplaincies, of which the archbishop was allowed a total of eight. They could be a useful link between Lambeth and Canterbury, helping archbishops to keep in touch with the cathedral and diocese, acting as patronage brokers, and examining prospective new recruits to the profession.[39] By serving under

[35] R. Browning, *Political and Constitutional Ideas of the Court Whigs* (Baton Rouge, La., 1982), 89–116; Taylor, 'Church and State', 100–1, 157–9. See also M. W. McCahill, *Order and Equipoise; The Peerage and the House of Lords, 1783–1806* (1978), 51–3, 161–2.

[36] See the comments on Juxon's 'superannuation' in Gilbert Burnet, *History of His Own Time*, 6 vols. (1828), i. 320.

[37] Gibson refused the archbishopric in 1747, asserting that 'old age and growing infirmities would not allow him to think of entering upon a new scene of life which was necessarily attended with such a variety of business and required constant application'. Quoted in Sykes, *Gibson*, 385. Similar reasons were given by Richard Hurd in 1783: Nichols, *Literary Anecdotes*, viii. 94. For the controversy over Joseph Butler's supposed refusal of the see: N. Sykes, 'Bishop Butler and the Primacy. Did He Decline the See of Canterbury in 1747?', *Theology*, 33 (1936), 132–7.

[38] Sykes, *Wake*, i. 242.

[39] Thorp acted as a patronage broker in the diocese: Bodl. MS Rawl. lett. 59, fo. 54, Thomas Paramour to Thorp. Gibson played a similar role: LPL MS 954, fo. 85, Stephen

successive archbishops, the chaplains could help to provide continuity in administration. That vociferous defender of the restored Church, Peter du Moulin, was chaplain to Juxon and Sheldon, as well as being a prebendary of Canterbury Cathedral (stall IV, 1660–84). Sancroft's chaplains included George Thorp (stall V, 1680–1719), who sent the archbishop weekly, and sometimes twice-weekly, detailed letters and reports of news from the diocese, John Battely (rector of Adisham and archdeacon of Canterbury, 1688–1708), and Henry Wharton (vicar of Chartham, 1688–91). Tenison promoted two members of his former college, Corpus Christi, Cambridge, Thomas Green and Elias Sydall, to chaplaincies. He collated Green to Minster in 1695, to a prebend (stall VI, 1701–21) and to the archdeaconry of Canterbury in 1708. When the mastership of Corpus became vacant in 1698 (three years after Tenison's appointment as primate), Tenison was actively involved in ensuring Green's election. Sydall was collated by Tenison to Biddenden (1702), Ivychurch (1705), Great Mongeham (1707), and to a Canterbury prebend (stall IV, 1707–28).[40] Wake's chaplains included George Carter, who was born in the diocese and became provost of Oriel (1708–27). Wake collated him to Lydd in 1719. Samuel Lisle became a chaplain in 1722 and Wake made him archdeacon in 1724. Likewise, William Geekie, Balthazar Regis, and David Wilkins were chaplains who all had connections with Canterbury. Wilkins, especially, was a noted scholar and librarian at Lambeth (1715–18). He was made a chaplain in 1719 and was collated to Great Chart and to a prebend (stall XII, 1720–45). His major work, *Concilia Magnae Britanniae et Hiberniae* (1737), based on

Thornton to Gibson, 16 March 1707. Archbishops' chaplains: *Juxon*—W. Brabourne, S. Baker, P. du Moulin, R. Pory, D. Nichol, T. Tomkins, M. Frank; *Sheldon*—G. Hooper, W. Pell, G. Stradling, T. Cooke, T. White; *Sancroft*—G. Thorp, H. Maurice, W. Needham, H. Wharton, L. Turnball, J. Battely, W. Whitear, S. Parker; *Tillotson*—R. Barker, H. Hody, G. Royse, A. Torriano; *Tenison*—T. Green, E. Sydall, E. Gibson, E. Brook, J. Mandeville, J. Potter, B. Ibbot, R. Smallbrook, R. Clavering, R. Ibbetson; *Wake*—D. Trimmell, G. Carter, S. Lisle, W. Geekie, D. Williams, E. Bateman, J. Walker, W. Birch, B. Regis; *Potter*—J. Chapman, W. Ward, J. Tunstall; *Herring*—W. Herring, J. S. Hill, G. Jubb, H. Heaton, N. Foster, H. Hall, J. Holdsworth, J. Piers; *Hutton*—T. Wray, C. Plumptre, C. Hall; *Secker*—B. Porteus, G. Stinton, J. Fowell, T. Wintle; *Cornwallis*—W. Backhouse, W. Vyse, M. Lort, J. Porter, J. Smith; *Moore*—T. Drake, H. Radcliffe, G. Heath, G. Griffiths, G. Moore; *Manners Sutton*—G. Cambridge, G. D'Oyly, C. Lloyd, J. Lonsdale, R. Mant, C. Wordsworth. Some of these served under more than one archbishop. Names are placed under the archbishop of first appointment. Information from A. C. Ducarel, *The History and Antiquities of the Archiepiscopal Palace of Lambeth* (1785), 90, and archiepiscopal registers.

⁴⁰ Richard Masters, *History of the College of Corpus Christi* (1753), 170. John Disney wrote that Tenison was 'not only a very considerable benefactor to that society, but a very generous patron to several of its members': Disney, *Memoirs of the Life and Writings of Arthur Ashley Sykes* (1785), 5.

records belonging to the see and chapter of Canterbury, was a seminal contribution to Church history. Potter's chaplains included James Tunstall
who was rector of Great Chart from 1744 and wrote on classics and theology. Secker made John Fowell his chaplain in 1758: he had been to
Secker's former college, Exeter, and was professor of Moral Philosophy at
Oxford when Secker had been bishop of Oxford. He was collated to
Bishopsbourne in 1764. George Stinton, who had also been a fellow of
Exeter (1750-67), was collated to Wittersham in 1765 and Cornwallis continued to give him preferment. Cornwallis also promoted William Backhouse to a chaplaincy. He became archdeacon of Canterbury in 1769 and
was also rector of Ickham (1771-84) and vicar of Deal (1775-85). Moore's
chaplains included Houston Radcliffe, who was advanced to various livings
in the diocese, to a prebend (stall IV, 1795-1822) and to the archdeaconry
in 1803. Manners Sutton's chaplains who were given preferment in the
diocese were men associated with the High-Church Hackney phalanx:
Christopher Wordsworth, made rector of Woodchurch in 1808; George
D'Oyly, collated to Hernehill in 1815, whose *Life of Sancroft* (1821) is testimony to the pre-Tractarian interest in non-juring history, and who with another of Manners Sutton's chaplains, Richard Mant, published an
annotated edition of the Bible for the SPCK (1814); and John Londsdale,
who was collated to Mersham in 1827.[41]

Chaplains often lived at Lambeth as part of the archbishop's household
and provided information on ecclesiastical matters, helping to create a kind
of clerical enclave at the headquarters of the archbishop's administrative
machine. The medieval tradition of designating the chaplains part of the
archbishops 'family', and the collegiate lifestyle continued throughout the
period. Tenison may have secured Humphrey Hody's appointment as
Regius professor of Greek in Oxford in 1698 because he could stand him no
longer at Lambeth,[42] and Secker's company was usually made up of the domestic chaplains and visiting clergy.[43] The significance of Lambeth as a
hub of national Church affairs should not be underrated. It was here, for
example, that Sheldon entertained influential members of the Anglican

---

[41] See C. Dewey, *The Passing of Barchester. A Real Life Version of Trollope* (Leicester, 1991),
6.

[42] W. R. Ward, *Georgian Oxford. University Politics in the Eighteenth Century* (Oxford,
1958), 29.

[43] *Life of Bishop Beilby Porteus by a Lay Member of Merton College* (1810), 173 and Porteus,
'Life of Secker', 69. D. Gardiner argues that there was a collegiate lifestyle at Lambeth in this
period: *History of Lambeth Palace* (1953), 201. During the 1770s some controversy arose over
the 'routs' held in the Palace by Mrs Cornwallis. But it was claimed that some of these accusations were prompted by dissenting opposition to the archbishop's attempt to revive the fast of
Good Friday in the city: BL Add. MS 5811, fo. 104v.

laity to dinner and helped to cement the alliance between Church and State which was so vital in the Restoration period.[44] It was here too, on the 18 May 1688, that Sancroft held the crucial conference of bishops and prominent clergy, including John Tillotson, the dean of Canterbury, and Thomas Tenison, both future archbishops, as well as Edward Stillingfleet, a Canterbury prebendary (stall XII, 1669–89), which finally led to the refusal of the seven bishops, headed by the archbishop, to comply with James II's order that the Declaration of Indulgence should be read in all parish churches.[45] Sancroft went into seclusion at Lambeth during the winter of 1689–90 before being deprived of his office.[46] Tenison organized an annual dinner at the palace on Easter Tuesday to discuss church policies and problems.[47] Lambeth's role may have been even more necessary to the Church in the eighteenth century, especially since after the Restoration Convocation had a negligible part to play in voicing Church interests (save from 1701 to 1717) and did not effectively meet after the latter date. Recent work on the voting patterns of bishops has demonstrated that there could be a considerable amount of cohesion on the bench when Church interests were felt to be at stake,[48] and archbishops used Lambeth as a venue to discuss Church matters and co-ordinate policy, especially when bishops were in London to attend Parliament. They traditionally held a Boxing Day party at Lambeth for all those bishops present in the capital. In 1743 Potter convened a meeting there to discuss the state of religion in the nation, in 1754 sixteen bishops met at the Palace to discuss the revival of the 1727 royal proclamation for the encouragement of piety, and in 1758 Secker held a meeting of bishops, whose advice he sought when drawing up visitation articles. Again in the 1770s, meetings of the bench were held at Lambeth to discuss opposition to subscription to the Thirty-Nine Articles at the universities.[49] At the diocesan level, Lambeth was also used to entertain

[44] F. Heal. *Hospitality in Early Modern England* (1990), 270; Hasted, *History of Kent*, x. 356; *The London Diaries of William Nicolson, Bishop of Carlisle, 1702–1718*, ed. C. Jones and G. Holmes (Oxford, 1985), 153, 483. Hutton was remembered for his 'easy access' at Lambeth: Nichols, *Literary Anecdotes*, iii. 469. Cornwallis abandoned the distinction between the chaplains' table and high table: *DNB*.

[45] R. Thomas, 'The Seven Bishops and their Petition, 18 May 1688', *JEH*, 12 (1961), 56–70.

[46] D'Oyly, *Sancroft*, I. 449; *HMC, Report on the Finch Manuscripts*, iii. 134, Nottingham to Viscount Sydney, 30 June 1691.

[47] A. Tindal Hart, *The Life and Times of John Sharp, Archbishop of York* (1949), 255.

[48] Taylor, 'Church and State', 166; id., 'Sir Robert Walpole, the Church of England, and the Quakers Tithe Bill of 1736', *HJ*, 28 (1985), 51–77.

[49] For Potter: LPL, Convocation 1/1/22, fo. 21; for Secker: ibid., MS Secker 7, fo. 99; D. A. Winstanley, *The University of Cambridge in the Eighteenth Century* (Cambridge, 1922), 262, 313.

Church tenants, members of the Kentish gentry, and clergy from Canterbury. Wake's diaries, for instance, reveal that he dined with diocesan officials and clergy. The position of Lambeth in national and diocesan ecclesiastical machinery was such that even when Herring chose to reside at Croydon, from 1753, on account of his health, one of his chaplains remained at Lambeth and diocesan officials attended three times a week to receive and dispatch business.[50]

If chaplains could provide some link between the archbishops and their diocese, of added weight was the fact that archbishops also possessed the right of presentation to three prebends in Canterbury Cathedral (stalls I, IV, VI), enabling them to bring men into the cathedral to represent their interests to the dean and chapter and diocese.[51] While living at Lambeth archbishops also relied on the information about the state of their diocese procured by their archdeacons. The role of the archdeacons and other diocesan officials—what might be called the 'middle management' of the Church's administrative organization—in directing Church affairs in the localities, particularly when the archbishop was permanently non-resident, continued the medieval function of being *oculi episcopi*.[52] The status of the archdeacons received some questioning in the late seventeenth century. As part of his plans to rationalize the structure of the Church, Gilbert Burnet, the bishop of Salisbury, had proposed, in a manner which seems uncannily modern to academics living in the 1990s, that such posts could be axed as a wasteful drain on diocesan financial resources.[53] The most vigorous reply came from Thomas Brett, at the time a curate in the diocese and future nonjuror, in his *Account of Church Government and Governors* (1701). Brett outlined the role archdeacons could play in linking the Church hierarchy to the parish clergy and maintained that with all their other commitments, archbishops needed them to help them run their diocese. Some archdeacons were particularly valued as conveyors of information between Lambeth and Canterbury: Thomas Green (archdeacon, 1708–21) acted for both Tenison and Wake, and Secker was heavily reliant on John Head (archdeacon, 1748–69).[54]

[50] Wake's Diary: LPL MS 1770, e.g., fos. 217, 222, 226; ibid., MS Herring 2, fo. 286, William Herring to Hutton.

[51] Some of Thorp's letters are in Bodl., MSS Tanner 33, fos. 156 *et seq.* (27 June 1680–17 Nov. 1689); 123, 125.

[52] Churchill, *Canterbury Administration*, i. 43–53; R. Peters, *Oculus Episcopi: Administration in the Archdeaconry of St Albans (1580–1625)* (Manchester, 1963).

[53] Burnet, *History of Own Time*, vi. 197.

[54] Thomas Brett, *Account of Church Government and Governors* (1701), 121. See a similar defence by John Lewis, quoted in Sykes, *Sheldon to Secker*, 193. Secker's reliance on Head: LPL, MS 2598, fo. 54.

Archbishops might also use the patronage at their disposal to reward or promote members of their own families or dependants, which helped to cement links between Lambeth and the diocese. Sixty per cent of clergy promoted to the 1st, 4th, and 6th stalls were related in some way or other to an archbishop: Sancroft, Tenison, Wake, Potter, Secker, Cornwallis, Moore, and Manners Sutton all advanced relations or former chaplains to Canterbury prebends. John Potter, the son of the archbishop, was presented to a Canterbury stall (XII, 1745–66), later becoming dean (1766–70).[55] Archbishop Moore promoted both his sons, George (stall VI, 1795–1845) and Robert (stall I, 1804–62). It was precisely this kind of nepotistic activity which the critics of the Church saw as the clearest testimony of corruption at the highest level, and early nineteenth-century pamphlets attacked Archbishops Moore and Manners Sutton on these grounds.[56] This use of patronage also received the ire of the first historian of the diocese: 'these were the days of great sinecures and of pluralities worthy of the medieval past'.[57] However, it does not seem that these prebendaries were any less assiduous in their duties than other members of the chapter. Hugh Percy, for example, had received much preferment after marrying one of Archbishop Manners Sutton's daughters, becoming a prebendary in 1816 and dean in 1825. It was under his term of office that the chapter embarked on a vigorous programme of repair.[58] And James Croft, who was collated to a prebend by the archbishop (stall IV, 1822–69) and to the archdeaconry of Canterbury in 1825, and who married another of his daughters, was able to demonstrate in his report to the Ecclesiastical Commissioners in 1834 a high standard of residence and sense of duty among the canons.[59] In any case it made sense for an archbishop to appoint friends and dependants he could trust, so that nepotism may have improved rather than impaired diocesan administration.

The most crucial type of patronage, however, as far as the archbishops' relationship with the diocese was concerned, was patronage to parish livings. The Canterbury diocese was small and compact, split into 11 deaneries, comprising approximately 279 parishes (Map 1).[60] It was untypical in the eighteenth century in that 60 per cent of livings were in the hands of ecclesiastical patrons, belonging to the archbishop, the dean and chapter of

---

[55] See appointments in John Le Neve, *Fasti Ecclesiae Anglicanae, 1541–1857*, iii. *Canterbury, Rochester and Winchester Dioceses*, comp. J. M. Horn (1974), 12–40.

[56] Especially Wade, *Black Book*, 286–98.   [57] Jenkins, *Canterbury*, 414–15.

[58] CCAL, Dean's Book, 1821–1834, 55.   [59] Nockles, 'Canterbury', 257.

[60] This figure has been compiled from visitation returns, and from John Ecton, *Thesaurus Rerum Ecclesiasticum* (1742) rev. edn. The deaneries were Canterbury, Bridge, Charing, Dover, Elham, Lympne, Ospringe, Sandwich, Sittingbourne, Sutton, Westbere.

Canterbury, the bishop of Rochester, the dean and chapter of Rochester, the dean and chapter of St Paul's, and the archdeacon of Canterbury. One hundred and five benefices alone were in the gift of the archbishop.[61] This can be contrasted with the position of the Church in other localities. The bishops of Coventry and Lichfield, for instance, lacked any patronage in the archdeaconry of Coventry and Lichfield.[62] It has often been pointed out that nineteenth-century bishops attempted to increase the standards of professional commitment and competence by greater control over ecclesiastical appointments. Diana McClatchey, for example, has shown that Samuel Wilberforce in the diocese of Oxford in the mid-nineteenth century raised episcopal patronage from 5 to 18 per cent, 'as part of a deliberate policy to gain a more direct influence in the Church'.[63] That archbishops in the eighteenth century had a greater control over ecclesiastical appointments in their diocese than even the most impressive of nineteenth-century 'reformers', had a crucial impact on those appointed to Canterbury livings, the significance of which will be demonstrated in later chapters.

In terms of patronage, the Canterbury diocese was hardly the Church of the landowning classes. The 30.3 per cent of patronage held in private lay hands was not concentrated, as it was in the Oxford diocese, in the hands of a few powerful magnates, like the Duke of Marlborough.[64] Indeed only 3 per cent of patronage belonged to peers, reflecting the social composition

---

[61] The names of patrons from visitation returns, Ecton, *Thesaurus*, and B. Willis, *Parochiale Anglicanum* (1733). The dean and chapter presented to 16 livings in the diocese, the archdeacon to 9 (the 'exempt parishes'), the bishop of Rochester to 2, the dean and chapter of Rochester to 13, the dean and chapter of St Paul's to 2, university colleges to 9 (All Souls': New Romney, Upchurch, Harrietsham, Elmley; St John's, Oxford: Barfreston; St John's, Cambridge: Ospringe, Staplehurst; Merton: Elham; Christ Church: Hawkhurst), the master of Eastbridge Hospital to 1. Secker noted that in total 172 benefices were in the archbishop's gift; of which 105 were to livings in the diocese. LPL, MS Secker 3, fos. 329–31. This contrasts with Warwickshire where only 13.5% of patronage was in ecclesiastical hands: J. L. Salter, 'Warwickshire Clergy, 1660–1714', University of Birmingham Ph.D. thesis, 2 vols., 1975, i. 86. The archbishops also had some patronage in the 'peculiars'. Sheldon proposed their abolition in Bodl., MS Tanner 315, fo. 105 and ibid., Add. MS c. 308, fo. 114. St. Mary's Dover was an elected living: see CCAL, U/3/30/8/3. The Crown presented to 14 livings and 72 had lay patrons.

[62] R. Clark, 'Anglicanism, Recusancy and Dissent in Derbyshire, 1603–1670', unpub. Oxford University D.Phil. thesis, 1979, 1–2. The bishop of Exeter presented to only 17 parishes in the Exeter diocese, while 254 parishes were in the gift of lay patrons: A. Warne, *Church and Society in Eighteenth Century Devon* (Newton Abbot, 1969), 31. The next most powerful episcopal patrons in the country were the bishops of Bangor (61) and Winchester (46). In 1835 only 11.6% of advowsons in the country as a whole were in episcopal hands: Best, *Temporal Pillars*, 345.

[63] D. McClatchey, *Oxfordshire Clergy. 1777–1869. A Study of the Established Church and the Role of its Clergy in Local Society* (Oxford, 1960), 10. See also M. J. D. Roberts, 'Private Patronage and the Church of England, 1800–1900', *JEH*, 32 (1981), 199–223.

[64] McClatchey, *Oxfordshire Clergy*, 5.

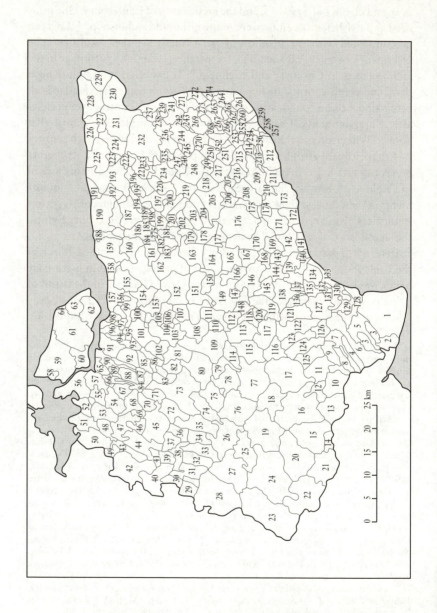

Parishes in the Diocese of Canterbury

227 Acol
175 Acrise
219 Adisham
138 Aldington
209 Alkham
223 All Saints, Thanet
11 Appledore
232 Ash
113 Ashford
106 Badlesmere
89 Bapchild
249 Barfreston
205 Barham
41 Bearsted
200 Bekesbourne
20 Benenden
77 Bethersden
243 Betteshanger
69 Bicknor
19 Biddenden
121 Bilsington
226 Birchington
203 Bishopsbourne
131 Blackmanstone
55 Bobbing
136 Bonnington
54 Borden
111 Boughton Aluph
154 Boughton under Blean
74 Boughton Malherbe
31 Boughton Monchelsea
42 Boxley
146 Brabourne
68 Bredgar
49 Bredhurst
7 Brenzett
202 Bridge
147 Brook
4 Brookland
36 Broomfield
2 Broomhill
254 Buckland near Dover

94 Buckland near Faversham
134 Burmarsh
275 Canterbury, All Saints
275 Canterbury, Holy Cross
275 Canterbury, St. Alphage
275 Canterbury, St. Andrew
160 Canterbury, St. Cosmus & Damien le Blean
275 Canterbury, St. George
275 Canterbury, St. Margaret
275 Canterbury, St. Mary Bredman
275 Canterbury, St. Mary Magdalen
275 Canterbury, St. Mildred
275 Canterbury, St. Peter
184 Canterbury, St. Dunstan
181 Canterbury, St. Mary Bredin
185 Canterbury, St. Mary, Northgate
198 Canterbury, St. Martin
199 Canterbury, St. Paul
211 Capel le Ferne
108 Challock
80 Charing
256 Charlton
115 Great Chart
79 Little Chart
32 Chart Sutton
162 Chartham
172 Cheriton
152 Chilham
246 Chillenden
193 Chislet
251 Coldred
24 Cranbrook
150 Crundale
97 Davington
272 Deal
206 Denton
43 Detling
85 Doddington

258 Dover, St. James
257 Dover, St. Mary
259 Dover, St. Peter
133 Dymchurch
135 Eastbridge
61 Eastchurch
262 East Langdon
244 Eastry
34 East Sutton
102 Eastling
110 Eastwell
12 Ebony
75 Egerton
176 Elham
60 Elmley
165 Elmsted
233 Elmstone
215 Ewell
250 Eythorne
8 Fairfield
99 Faversham
173 Folkestone
189 Fordwich
71 Frinsted
25 Frittenden
151 Godmersham
156 Goodnestone near Faversham
247 Goodnestone near Wingham
23 Goudhurst
157 Graveney
255 Guston
186 Hackington
178 Upper Hardres
179 Lower Hardres
52 Halstow
242 Ham
161 Harbledown
72 Harrietsham
48 Hartlip
62 Harty

166 Hastingleigh
22 Hawkhurst
210 Hawkinge
26 Headcorn
190 Herne
155 Hernehill
18 High Halden
148 Hinxhill
192 Hoath
45 Hollingbourne
129 Hope, All Saints
114 Hothfield
212 Hougham
46 Hucking
137 Hurst
141 Hythe
220 Ickham
56 Iwade
6 Ivychurch
125 Kenardington
112 Kennington
87 Kingsdown
117 Kingsnorth
204 Kingston
245 Knowlton
38 Langley
230 St. Lawrence in Thanet
104 Leaveland
37 Leeds
73 Lenham
63 Leysdown
29 Linton
197 Littlebourne
30 Loose
96 Luddenham
1 Lydd
216 Lydden
170 Lyminge
139 Lympne
92 Lynsted
40 Maidstone
28 Marden

261 St. Margaret's at Cliffe
228 Margate, St. John the Baptist
130 St. Mary's in the Marsh
119 Mersham
3 Midley
183 Milton near Canterbury
57 Milton near Sittingbourne
84 Milsted
59 Minster in Sheppey
231 Minster in Thanet
107 Molash
273 Great Mongeham
268 Little Mongeham
168 Monks Horton
224 Monkton
65 Murston
180 Nackington
127 Newchurch
14 Newenden
80 Newnham
171 Newington by Hythe
53 Newington by Sittingbourne
225 St. Nicholas at Wade
248 Nonington
269 Northbourne
93 Norton
98 Oare
132 Orgarswick
101 Orlestone
86 Ospringe
39 Otham
82 Otterden
263 Oxney
229 St. Peter's in Thanet
174 Paddlesworth
201 Patrixbourne
163 Petham
78 Pluckley
169 Posting
213 Poulton
100 Preston near Faversham
221 Preston near Wingham

58 Quenborough
50 Rainham
191 Reculver
264 Ringwould
265 Ripple
214 River
88 Rodmersham
15 Rolvenden
128 New Romney
5 Old Romney
122 Ruckinge
142 Saltwood
21 Sandhurst
240 Sandwich, St. Clement
239 Sandwich, St. Mary
238 Sandwich, St. Peter
158 Seasalter
144 Sellindge
153 Selling
120 Sevington
116 Shadoxhurst
105 Sheldwich
271 Sholden
217 Sibertswold
66 Sittingbourne
145 Smarden
76 Smeeth
9 Snargate
126 Snave
81 Stalisfield
143 Stanford
235 Staple
27 Staplehurst
177 Stelling
47 Stockbury
195 Stodmarsh
237 Stonar
10 Stone in Oxney
95 Stone near Faversham
167 Stowting
222 Stourmouth
187 Sturry

267 Sutton
33 Sutton Valence
188 Swalecliffe
208 Swingfield
91 Teynham
16 Tenterden
182 Thanington
103 Throwley
44 Thurnham
270 Tilmanstone
90 Tonge
67 Tunstall
35 Ulcombe
51 Upchurch
252 Waldershare
274 Walmer
164 Waltham
64 Warden
124 Warehorne
194 Westbere
260 West Cliffe
140 West Hythe
266 West Langdon
109 Westwell
253 Whitfield
159 Whitstable
196 Wickhambreux
118 Willesborough
234 Wingham
83 Witchling
13 Wittersham
17 Woodchurch
236 Woodnesborough
218 Womenswold
70 Wormshill
241 Worth
207 Wootton
149 Wye

MAP 1. Parishes in the Diocese of Canterbury

of Kent as a county of minor gentry families. In any case, there is no need to see lay patrons as injurious to the Church's best interests: some clergy valued lay patrons as a means of ensuring that the Church was not dominated by the bishops, and Edward Chamberlayne in 1692 called them 'semi-ecclesiastical'.[65] Only a handful of lay patrons in the diocese owned three or more advowsons in the mid-eighteenth century: Sir Philip Boteler, Moyle Breton, William Brockman, and Lord Winchilsea. For the Church as an institution, perhaps the main problem of lay patrons was the abuse of resignation bonds, which required a cleric to resign once a designated dependant of the patron had become suitably qualified. Because of the relatively small amount of private patronage in their diocese, the 'evils' of such bonds were less apparent in Canterbury than elsewhere, but the archbishops had always to think of the interests of the national Church. One of Moore's first acts in 1783 was to give his vote in favour of reversing the judgment in the case of Fytche v. Bishop Lowth, which has been seen as a triumph for the purity of Church administration over real property law.[66]

The ability of any archbishop to effect a thorough change in the complexion of the diocesan personnel was limited, depending as it did on vacancies occurring. These could be rare and it was a constant complaint of archbishops that they did not have enough patronage to satisfy all the legitimate claimants. Archbishop Herring told Samuel Pegge in 1749, after he had written asking to be collated to Harbledown:

I could not help letting you know, that I am not unmoved by your letter, but the mischief and the misery is to me that I can't tell what to say to comfort you. I have many claims upon me, and the opportunities of serving friends in my patronage have as yet been very few. As far as I can, I shall make it a rule to confine my favours to the well deserving clergy of my diocese, and to ease their duty if I can't their situation.[67]

In a similar vein, Secker wrote to Princess Amelia, who had asked him to present Thomas Hebbes to a Canterbury living,

I have now been Archbishop about two years, and in all that time have presented to only one living, and that not worth £100 in Romney Marsh. If my clergy shall continue to be a healthy group (as it is my duty to hope they will), it will be some time before I have it in my power.[68]

---

[65] [E. Chamberlayne], *Angliae Notitia; or, the Present State of England*, 2 vols. (18th edn., 1692), ii. 19. Within the diocese, the patrons of 'donatives' claimed exemption from the visitation of the archbishops: LPL MS Secker 3, fo. 178: the dispute between Brook Brydges and Secker.

[66] Best, *Temporal Pillars*, 53–9; Langford, *Propertied Englishman*, 19–20.

[67] Bodl. MS Eng. lett. d. 43, fo. 223, Herring to Pegge, 14 July 1749.

[68] Quoted in Nichols, *Literary Anecdotes*, v. 407. Hebbes was a lecturer at Kensington. He was presented to Hernehill in 1760 and died in 1766.

He explained to one such petitioner in 1758 that

no one thing hath fallen in my gift hitherto; and though probably in time several may, yt my Relations, Chaplains, Dependants, Friends and acquaintances, the number of wm put together hath risen to a very large one in the many years that I have been a Bp and no Patron, will think, and some of them with very good reason, that they have a title to more preferments from me than I may ever live to bestow.[69]

Richard Bate, the vicar of Chilham, petitioned Archbishop Wake in 1719 for a six-preacher's place in the cathedral. His reasons for doing so provide an interesting insight into the way in which the workings of the patronage system were perceived.

I should not presume to ask this of your Grace before it was vacant, were it not yt I find by long experience nothing of this nature is to be obtained unless sued for before hand, it being certainly true of ye political world which ye French philosopher falsely surmized of as natural, viz. yt there is no vacuum properly speaking, but as soon as any body leave a place, another is ready to step into it.[70]

But if no individual archbishop could dramatically alter diocesan personnel, it did mean that at any one time the majority of the clergy had been primatial appointments. The consequences of this will be seen later.

THE RESTORED CHAPTER

As befitted its status as the metropolitical cathedral, and its proximity to Dover and the coast, Canterbury Cathedral played a major part in the heady celebrations of the summer of 1660. John Reading, who had been vicar of Dover from 1616 until his sequestration in 1647, and who was appointed to a Canterbury stall in 1660 (VIII, 1660–7), was chosen to present Charles II with a Bible on his landing in England on 25 May. His eloquent oration

---

[69] LPL MS Secker 2, fo. 10, Secker to Kennicott, 8 Nov. 1758. Wake made a similar comment: 'I have a pretty many benefices in my gift, but not many desirable, neither the value nor situation of the most part of them being such as to encourage any considerable person to reside upon them. Such as they are, I distribute them as fast as they become vacant to my friends and domestics. For the lesser sort, I have a large list of expectants, whom I endeavour in their order to provide for', quoted in Sykes, *Wake*, i. 239. Horne remembered that Secker had been so harassed with applications for the living of Bethersden that he wished that he had no patronage whatsoever: CUL MS Horne 8134/B/7, fo. 10. The archbishops' ability to influence patronage was not confined to that directly in their gift. Potter and Secker, for instance, were able to influence the disposition of Crown patronage; see D. R. Hirschberg, 'The Government and Church Patronage in England, 1660–1760', *JBS*, 20 (1980–1), 133, 137. For the use of patronage in the diocese in the nineteenth century see Dewey, *Passing of Barchester*.

[70] Ch. Ch. MS Wake 21, fo. 104, Bate to Wake, 10 Feb. 1719.

expressed hopes for the restored regime, and stressed the relationship between political and religious order.[71]

A prime concern was the need for a body of men to defend the restored
regime. It was this task which dominated the activities of the chapter during the 1660s and 70s and which seems to a large extent to have been the
reason for the promotion of particular men to Canterbury stalls. Besides the
dean, Thomas Turner (who had been one of Archbishop Laud's chaplains
and who probably had some knowledge of cathedral business at Canterbury
since he had been appointed to the deanery in 1643), only two prebendaries
had survived to continue the cathedral tradition: Thomas Paske (stall V,
1625–62) and Meric Casaubon (stall IX, 1628–71). Paske had been the
senior resident prebendary in 1642 when parliamentary troops had first
descended on the cathedral.[72] Meric Casaubon was the son of another
Canterbury prebendary, the international scholar Isaac (stall VIII, 1611–
14), and was himself a scholar and Churchman of some repute, publishing
works on a variety of topics. Nothing more dramatically reveals the effect of
the Civil War on Canterbury life than this crisis of personnel; in this respect
at least it seems that the Interregnum was far more calamitous to the life of
the community than the Reformation had been, where there had been a
large measure of a continuity between the monks and newly created prebendaries. Other posts within the community also needed to be filled at the
Restoration. Only a few of the minor canons and lay clerks had survived and
although the six-preachers had been maintained during the Interregnum,
these were all replaced in 1660 in favour of clergy who had not been so
closely involved with the Cromwellian government.[73] Likewise all boys

---

[71] *A Speech made before the King's most Excellent Majesty Charles II, on the shore where he
landed at Dover, by John Reading B.D. who presented his Majesty with a Bible, the Gift of the
Inhabitants there, May 25th 1660.* The New Foundation had been created on 8 April 1541. It
comprised a dean; 12 prebendaries; 6 minor canons; 6 six-preachers; 12 lay clerks; 2 masters of
the King's School, and 50 schoolboys. In 1547 the archbishop was given the right of presentation to the 1st, 4th, and 6th prebends. The statutes were revised by Laud in 1635, as part of his
scheme of reinvigorating his diocese. See Laud's *Works*, ed. W. Scott and J. Bliss, 7 vols.
(1847–60), v. 506–42. They were reissued by Charles II in 1660. At the end of the eighteenth
century Hasted noted that the statutes were still in force: Hasted, *History of Kent*, xii. 547.
Stephen Goffe, who had been presented to stall X in 1644, was still alive in 1660. But he
had converted to Catholicism in 1652 and was deprived of his prebend in May 1660. For a
detailed analysis of the process of restoration at Canterbury and Winchester see Green, *Re-
establishment of Church of England*, esp. chaps. 3 and 5.

[72] He complained to Henry, Earl of Holland, of the treatment received by the cathedral and
members of his family at the hands of Colonel Sandys's regiment. In the absence of the dean,
he had been ordered by the parliamentary commander, Sir Michael Livesey, to give up the
keys. *The Copy of a Letter sent to an Honourable Lord, by Dr. Paske, Subdeane of Canterbury*
(1642).

[73] D. Ingram Hill, *The Six Preachers of Canterbury Cathedral* (Canterbury, 1985).

over fifteen were ejected during late 1660 from the King's School which was governed by the chapter.[74]

The vacant places were filled by August 1660. Six of the new prebendaries had local links and ties, having been born in the diocese or having previously been incumbents of Kentish livings, and were thus familiar with the customs and precedents of the area: Edward Aldey; William Belke; Peter Gunning; Peter Du Moulin; Peter Hardres; and John Reading. The government may well have realized the value of using local men in its attempt to restore its institutions into the interstices of provincial life. Some of the new appointees at Canterbury, together with George Hall, the new archdeacon (1660–8), had conformed to some extent to the Cromwellian regime, which suggests not only a shortage of surviving clergy who were totally unblemished, forcing the restored government to rely on those who had participated in the regimes of the 1640s and 50s, but also perhaps a desire to found the restored order on as broad a base as possible.[75] Not that conformity to the Cromwellian government necessarily meant that these clergy had compromised their Anglican principles. Some of them were noted for their efforts in keeping alive Anglican traditions even in the face of adversity and many clergy had no real option but to stay in England during the Interregnum. While remaining in England, the royalist Du Moulin had written *Regii Sanguinis Clamor ad Caelum* (1652, reprinted 1661), a counter-blast to Milton's defence of Charles I's execution, the title-page appropriately being printed in red. Meric Casaubon had been approached by Cromwell to write a history of the Civil War, which he declined to do. John Reading had been a Calvinist in the diocese and had opposed the introduction of Arminian theology at Canterbury during the 1630s. But he had been imprisoned in the 1640s for his support of Charles I and in 1650 at Folkestone he had attacked the right of unordained people to preach.[76] Peter Gunning, after being deprived from his Cambridge fellowship, spent much of the Interregnum as a private chaplain to royalist families. He lost no opportunity of furthering the Anglican cause by preaching and public disputation, becoming in 1657 chaplain to the Earl of Exeter, in London.

---

[74] CCAL, Register Z, fos. 206–7. Cf. *HMC, 6th Report*, 906: 'Petition by the servants of the Dean and Chapter to the House of Lords'.

[75] Green, *Re-establishment of Church of England*, 70. George Hall (archdeacon of Canterbury, 1660–68), the son of the Jacobean bishop of Exeter, was able to reconcile being one of the legally ordained ministers of the Church of England with a readiness to be moderate: Hall, *God Appearing to the House of Levi* (1655).

[76] John Reading, *The Ranter's Ranting, with the Apprehending Examinations and Confession of John Collins* (1650); id., *Anabaptism Routed: or a Survey of the Controverted Points concerning 1. Infant Baptism 2. Pretended Necessity of Dipping 3. The Dangerous Practise of Rebaptising* (1655).

Here he attracted a large congregation and became the acknowledged leader of Anglican thought and practice, holding monthly communion services and debating with Cromwell. One future Canterbury prebendary who was able to go into exile, John Bargrave (stall V, 1662–80), spent the 1640s and 50s travelling in the Low Countries, France, Germany, and Italy, acquiring a remarkable collection of curiosities which he kept in his house in the precincts.[77]

Those appointed to the cathedral in the 1660s and 70s were men noted and known for their willingness to defend the Restoration in print. John Reading's pamphlet of 1660, *Christmas Revived: or, an Answer to objections made against the Observance of a Day in Memory of our Saviour Christ His Birth* had clear resonance in the Canterbury context. In this task old sermons could be adapted to the new situation. Meric Casaubon reprinted in 1660 a sermon which he had first preached in Canterbury Cathedral in 1643 concerning the need for harmony between the nation and the monarch.[78] Indeed, a distinctive feature of the Canterbury prebendaries in the first two decades after the Restoration was their rigid orthodoxy and their support of Charles II. Their readiness to uphold the position of the government was not the product of servility, but inspired by a desire to exorcize the horrors of the previous two decades. In this vein John Aucher (stall VI, 1660–1701), who had written a damning treatise against the Engagement which required citizens to declare their allegiance to the Cromwellian regime, published *The Arraignment of Rebellion; or the Irresistability of Sovereign Powers Vindicated and Maintained* (1684), which was largely a reworking of his earlier work. Thomas Pierce (stall VII, 1660–91) was known, along with Henry Hammond and Peter Heylyn, as 'the chiefest champion of the old, regular and conformable clergy'.[79] He articulated the widely held belief that the traumas of the mid-century had been a divine judgement on the sins of the nation. He observed that it was 'more than twenty years, since His Rod has been speaking to us in several Dialects of severity'.[80] For this group of clergy the execution of Charles I

---

[77] On Gunning: H. A. Lloyd Jukes, 'Peter Gunning, 1613–84: Scholar, Churchman, Controversialist', *SCH*, 1 (1964), 222–32 and Bosher, *Restoration Settlement*, 37–9. On Bargrave: see N. Ramsay, 'The Cathedral Archives and Library', in P. Collinson, N. Ramsay, and M. Sparks (eds), *A History of Canterbury Cathedral* (Oxford, 1995), 386.

[78] Meric Casaubon, *A King and His Subjects Unhappily Fallen Out and Happily Reconciled. Being the Substance of a Sermon with very little Alteration fitted for the present time. Preached in the Sermon House, Canterbury Cathedral, 15 January 1643* (1660).

[79] Anthony Wood, *Athenae Oxonienses*, ed. P. Bliss, 4 vols. (1813–20), iv. 299.

[80] Thomas Pierce, 'The Embassy of the Rod and the Audience which it Requires', in *A Collection of Sermons upon Several Occasions* (Oxford, 1671), 146.

in 1649 had been the culmination of the nation's sins, and obedience to monarchy was a lesson she had to learn. Samuel Parker (stall II, 1672–85, archdeacon of Canterbury, 1670–88) published a series of works arguing for 'unlimited submission' to monarchy. Originally a Puritan, Parker urged that the later Stuarts should exercise a Hobbesian sovereignty to crush nonconformity and subversion.[81] Another prebendary who shared in the defence of the later Stuarts was James Jeffreys (stall IX, 1682–9) the brother of the notorious judge.

Some of the most significant published work of the Canterbury chapter in the years after the Restoration was devoted to defining the position of the Anglican Church. This rested on an implicit contrast of the Church of England with both the Roman Catholic Church abroad and the emerging nonconformist sects at home. In the aftermath of the Civil War an important consideration was the position of religious institutions vis-à-vis the government and the state. Catholic propaganda had long claimed that Protestantism in all its forms was an act of rebellion, destroying political and social order—a theory to which the Civil War appeared to give some credence. In reply, Anglican apologists claimed that the social and political dislocation manifested in the Great Rebellion was itself the product of Catholic machinations. Peter Du Moulin argued in his *Vindication of the Sincerity of the Protestant Religion* (1664), which reached a fourth edition by 1679, that in its early years the Protestant religion had been warmly embraced by the English ruling elite precisely because it was recognized as a reliable support of the social and political order. He cited the peaceful behaviour of the Huguenots in France, who did not attempt to overthrow governments, but submitted to them, as an indication of the inherently passive

---

[81] Samuel Parker, *A Discourse of Ecclesiastical Politie, wherein the Authority of the Civil Magistrate over the Conscience of Subjects in Matters of Religion is Asserted* (1670); id., *An Account of the Government of the Christian Church for the First Six Hundred Years* (1683); id., *Religion and Loyalty: or, The Power of the Christian Church within itself. The Supremacy of Sovereign Powers over it. The Duty of Passive Obedience, or Non Resistance to all their Commands* (1684). For Parker's association with James's pro-Catholic policies see M. Goldie, 'The Political Thought of the Anglican Revolution', in R. A. Beddard (ed.), *The Revolutions of 1688* (Oxford, 1991), 102–27, and id., 'John Locke and Anglican Royalism', *Political Studies*, 31 (1983), 61–85, which shows how members of the Canterbury chapter such as Gunning, Pierce, and Turner as well as clergy in the diocese such as Lowth resurrected hierocratic principles of Church power against the encroachments of the State. As early as 1674 Parker had compared the chapter of Canterbury to the 'courhon of Rome': Bodl. MS Tanner 123, fo. 181, Parker to Thompson, 8 Oct. 1674. When the bishopric of Chester became vacant in 1686, Sancroft recommended Jeffreys, but James II promoted Thomas Cartwright: D'Oyly, *Sancroft*, i. 235–6. See R. A. Beddard, 'Bishop Cartwright's Death-Bed', *Bodleian Library Record*, 11 (1984), 220–1.

and obedient nature of Protestantism.[82] In contrast, he claimed that it was the infiltration of Catholics within the army and the influence of the Jesuits which had led to the execution of Charles I. In this context, Du Moulin urged that the Church of England still needed a 40th article requiring obedience to the government, the failure to insist on this being, he felt, a prime cause of disorder. This would be one way of countering the political threat of both Catholic and nonconformist adversaries to the restored Church.[83] The position of the Church of England as the only true Church was stressed by Meric Casaubon in his influential tract, *Of the Necessity of the Reformation. In and Before Luther's Time* (1664). This balanced conventional tales of the corruption of late medieval Catholicism with an admission of the often misguided and arrogant zeal of some reformers, including Luther and the Puritans, who had gone too far in their condemnation. In a celebration of the Anglican *via media*, Casaubon described the Church of England as 'the paragon of all Reformed Churches'.[84]

What is also noteworthy about this group of Restoration prebendaries is that some of them held prominent positions in the universities and in other areas of the Church. Peter Gunning was, for example, an influential master of St John's College, Cambridge and Regius professor of Divinity, before relinquishing these offices and his Canterbury stall on his elevation to the bishoprics of Chichester in 1670 and Ely in 1674. He was largely responsible for fashioning St John's into a bastion of loyalty and orthodoxy, whose reputation as a breeding ground for religious traditionalism remained well into the eighteenth century, producing, for example, three times as many non-jurors as any other college.[85] Gunning had resolutely defended the Anglican cause in the Interregnum and was seen as 'the fittest man . . . to settle the university right in their principles, after many corruptions had crept in there by means of the rebellion'.[86] One of his first actions in 1660

---

[82] Peter Du Moulin, *A Vindication of the Sincerity of the Protestant Religion in the point of obedience to Sovereignes, opposed to the doctrine of rebellion, authorised and practised by the Pope and Jesuits* (1664). See also id., *The Great Loyalty of the Papists* (1673) and id., *A Replie to a Person of Honour* (1675), which Dean Turner encouraged him to write.

[83] Bodl. MS Tanner 282, fo. 97, Du Moulin to Sancroft, n.d.[c. 1668]; R. A. Beddard, 'Of the Duty of Subjects: A Proposed Fortieth Article of Religion', *Bodleian Library Record*, 10 (1981), 229.

[84] Meric Casaubon, *Of the Necessity of the Reformation. In and Before Luther's Time* (1664), preface. Amongst other works published by members of the chapter on this theme see John Williams, *The Difference between the Church of England and the Church of Rome* (1687) and George Thorp, *The Fifth Note of the Church Examined* (1688).

[85] J. C. Findon, 'The Nonjurors and the Church of England, 1689–1716', unpub. Oxford University D.Phil. thesis, 1979, 51.

[86] Wood, *Athenae Oxonienses*, iv. 142.

had been to deprive Tillotson of his Clare fellowship on the grounds that this was the same fellowship from which Gunning himself had been ejected.[87] According to the Presbyterian leader Richard Baxter, Gunning was the Church of England's 'forwardest and greatest speaker' at the Savoy Conference in 1661.[88] In 1676 he defended Anglican orthodoxy by writing against Croft's heterodox *Naked Truth* (1675). Thomas Pierce was president of Magdalen College, Oxford and dean of Salisbury. He announced that his royal dispensation for non-residence 'came down from heaven'.[89] Edmund Castell (stall VIII, 1667–86), who had collaborated with Brian Walton on his *Biblia Sacra Polyglotta* (1657) and who could thus be seen as maintaining the traditions of learned scholarship during the Interregnum, was excused the duties of residence as prebendary at Canterbury because he was also professor of Arabic at Cambridge.[90] To some extent this doubling of positions reflects the shortage of men sufficiently learned and well-qualified to fill the leading positions in the restored Church.

APPOINTMENTS TO THE DEAN AND CHAPTER

The dean and chapter formed a clerical elite within the city and diocese. The prebends were highly prized for their prestige and the financial benefit which they conferred upon their holders: in 1698 the ambitious Jonathan Swift attempted to secure a Canterbury stall.[91] Nevertheless, it is somewhat misleading to suggest, as later critics of the eighteenth-century Church have done, that cathedral posts were the pickings for the younger sons of the aristocracy and gentry.[92] Certainly, clerical apologists may have exaggerated the degree to which the eighteenth-century Church remained open to all groups within society, thereby acting as an agent of social cohesion, but it is clear from the social origins of the Canterbury chapter that high birth was not necessary for promotion (see Table 1). If a pattern emerges, it seems that Canterbury prebendaries were increasingly drawn from a clerical background, indicating a growing tradition of family clerical

---

[87] Birch, *Tillotson*, 401–2.   [88] Lloyd Jukes, 'Gunning', 229.

[89] Thomas Pierce obtained a dispensation because he was president of Magdalen and then dean of Salisbury: Bodl. MS Tanner 123, fos. 17, 40. On Pierce see R. A. Beddard, 'The Church of Salisbury and the Accession of James II', *Wiltshire Archaeological Magazine*, 67 (1972), 132–48.

[90] For Castell's dispensation see *DNB*.

[91] For Swift's petition see D. Nokes, *Jonathan Swift: A Hypocrite Reversed* (Oxford, 1985), 34.

[92] Sykes, *Church and State*, 414–16.

Table 1. *Geographical, Social, and Educational Backgrounds of the Dean and Chapter, 1660–1828 (Numbers)*

	1660–90	1690–1720	1720–50	1750–80	1780–1810	1810–28
Geographic origins						
Kent	7	0	5	3	2	0
London	3	5	5	4	2	1
Other	23	15	15	13	21	10
Social origins						
Noble	1	1	1	2	2	4
Gentry	17	6	13	8	9	2
Clergy	9	7	8	9	11	5
Professional[a]			1		1	
Plebeian	4	4	2	1	1	
Educational origins						
Oxford	15	7	12	13	16	5
Cambridge	19	13	13	8	8	6
Elsewhere	1					
Higher Degree	23	17	18	20	22	11
Publication	18	16	12	12	15	10
Further careers						
Archbishop	1	0	0	1	0	0
Bishop	5	3	3	2	6	3
Dean of Canterbury	1	1	1	0	0	0
Prebendary elsewhere	7	3	10	7	6	5
Royal Chaplain	6	7	6	1	2	2
Chaplain to archbishop	5	3	3	2	2	3

[a] Physician or lawyer.

service and the creation of clerical dynasties in the period after 1660. As at Lincoln, the sons of the clergy were more likely to achieve high office within the Church than were the sons of any other social group.[93] Even some of those members of the chapter with aristocratic connections can be placed within this category. William Nelson (stall V, 1803–35), who was the brother of Admiral Nelson and succeeded to the title of Earl Nelson of the Nile, was the son of a Norfolk cleric. Such aristocratic connections were not necessarily as detrimental to the functioning of the Church as later critics have maintained. In 1814 Nelson spoke on behalf of the Church in the

[93] J. H. Pruett, 'Career Patterns among the Clergy of Lincoln Cathedral, 1660–1750', *Church History*, 44 (1975), 208.

Lords during discussions of the Clergy Bill. The majority of successful clergymen came, however, from the less exalted ranks of society. Those who became archbishops and cathedral dignitaries are proof that occupational and vertical social mobility were possible in this period. Men who had talents but few other resources were able to turn their abilities into professional success and obtain a more substantial social position than their fathers.

Patronage was a crucial factor in determining the nature of the cathedral body. The deanery and nine out of twelve prebends were in the gift of the Crown, while the remaining three prebends and the six-preacherships were part of the archbishop's patronage. Thus those making appointments could draw on national patronage and recruitment networks. While the large number of local men appointed during the Restoration period was not maintained, there remained a strong connection between the cathedral, the city, and the county. Julius Deedes (stall IX, 1739–52), for example, the son of a local physician, had been born and educated in Kent. He had begun his clerical career as curate for Dean Sydall in 1717. In 1713 Thomas Brett (unsuccessfully) stressed his Kentish connections as a reason for preferment.

Mr Netterville has encouraged me to acquaint your Lordship with the highest preferment I desire, which is a prebend of Canterbury. Though I cannot plead any desert which will entitle me to such a favour, but a fair plea for it is, that from the foundation of the Dean and Chapter to this day either the Dean or some of the prebendaries have always been natives of Kent. Dr Belk, the last prebendary that died, was also the last Kentish man of the society, and Dr Higden succeeded him; so that there is not at this day one man on that foundation who was born in this county, which never happened before since the Reformation. I acknowledge this cannot give me or any native of Kent a right to a prebend, but if it be allowed that there has been such a custom, and that you are willing to continue it, the gentlemen of the county in general must think themselves obliged by the favour.[94]

Because so much of the cathedral's patronage lay in the hands of the Crown the community was a stronghold of establishment ideology. One of the most likely career patterns before becoming a prebendary was to have been a royal chaplain, thereby gaining monarchical favour. During the politically sensitive years following the Revolution of 1688–9, the cathedral became a centre of support for the new regime: Dean Tillotson was promoted to the archbishopric of Canterbury (stall II, 1670–2; dean of Canterbury, 1672–89; dean of St Paul's, 1689–1, archbishop of Canterbury, 1691–4) and one of the chapter, Edward Stillingfleet (stall XII, 1669–89) became bishop

---

94 *HMC, Manuscripts of the Duke of Portland*, v (1899), 377, Brett to the Earl of Oxford, 31 Dec. 1713. For other solicitations see Bodl. MS Rawl. Lett. 106, fo. 22.

of Worcester. But clearly the wider political tensions can be seen in the differing views held within the chapter. William Beveridge (stall IV, 1684–
1704) was nominated as bishop of Bath and Wells but refused it because the
see had become vacant on the deprivation of the non-juror Thomas Ken.[95]
In this politically charged atmosphere the cathedral pulpit became the
scene for a number of set-piece battles where the various merits and grievances associated with the post-Revolutionary settlement were aired. One
participant was William Cade, the rector of Brook (1682–1722) and a minor
canon, who had married Laud's niece and whose admiration for that archbishop led him to call his son Laud. In 1689 he preached a controversial sermon in the cathedral attacking the legality of the new regime and defending
the behaviour of the non-jurors who had declined to take the oaths of obedience to William and Mary.[96] He later complained of the rough treatment he
received after this sermon. During 1690 government proclamations were
issued in the cathedral, bells were rung in honour of the new king, and a
thanksgiving service was held on William's return from Ireland.[97] Some of
the clergy who had been brought up to believe in obedience and loyalty
were perhaps more readily able to accept the new political situation because
of the stability provided by Queen Mary as a focus of Anglican loyalty. Her
proven devotion to Anglican ceremonies during her time at the Hague
made it possible to believe that Church of England principles were not at
stake. In 1691, during William's absence, Mary promoted George Hooper,
her former chaplain at the Hague, to the deanery (1691–1704). The queen
visited the cathedral in 1694 and presented silver and purple hangings for
the altar, throne, and pulpit, sending to Holland for the material, and
demonstrating her loyalty and commitment to Anglican worship.[98]

Inevitably the 'rage of party' made itself felt in the cathedral after the
Revolution. When Archbishop Tenison visited the diocese in 1702, John
Love, who was described as 'a wild man, against the government', entered
the cathedral as the archbishop was confirming, and insulted him, but was
restrained from acting any further.[99] In the potentially tense years after
1714 the cathedral was a bastion of support for the Hanoverian succession.

[95] G. V. Bennett, 'King William III and the Episcopate', in id. and J. D. Walsh (eds.), *Essays
in Modern Church History* (1963), 121.

[96] BL MS Harleian 3790, fos. 169–72, 'The Case of a Sermon Preach't at Xst Ch. Cant. 9
March 1689'.

[97] CCAL, Treasurer's Book, 1689–90: entries for 6 Mar., 16 Aug., 19 Oct.

[98] G. S[mith], *Chronological History of Canterbury Cathedral*, 330; John Battely, *A Sermon
Preache'd before the Queen, in Christ's Church, Canterbury, May vi 1694* (1694); Marshall,
Hooper, 55. On Mary's role see W. A. Speck, 'William—and Mary', in Lois G. Schwoerer
(ed.), *The Revolution of 1688/9: Changing Perspectives* (Cambridge, 1991), 131–46.

[99] Quoted in *An Examination of the Book lately printed by the Quakers* (1736), 94.

George I was entertained at the deanery in 1717 on his way to the Continent,[100] and members of the chapter were used to keep an eye on politically suspect Tory parochial clergy. Some had received their prebendal preferment for their activity in government service. William Ayerst (stall III, 1724–65), for example, had been secretary and chaplain to the embassy in Holland in 1714 and to France in 1720. John Robinson (stall II, 1697–1710), who became bishop of London in 1714, was for many years chaplain to the embassy at Sweden, securing alliance between England and Sweden in 1692 and negotiating the Treaty of Utrecht in 1713.[101] He was also the last ecclesiastic to be promoted to high political office, being appointed Lord Privy Seal in 1711. One erstwhile non-juror, William Higden, was promoted to Canterbury (stall III, 1713–15), having later conformed to the new regime and written in its support.[102] It is not then surprising to find that members of the chapter were quick to use the pulpit as a means of defending the Hanoverian regime, interpreting the succession as saving the nation from popery and arbitrary government. As explained by preachers in the cathedral, the political changes of 1714 were a necessary defence of true Church principles against the threat of popery. It is sometimes tempting to see such behaviour in terms of political obsequiousness but we should note the urgency with which the chapter defended the Protestant Constitution, and the ways in which they believed that the liberty of the nation was dependent upon its religion. The Jacobite rebellion of 1715 gave cathedral clergy the opportunity to denounce the wickedness of popery. In this context Archbishop Wake's decision to be consecrated in person in the cathedral in 1716 can be seen as a political move, bringing the authority of the new order to Canterbury.[103] Ralph Blomer (stall XI, 1706–32), who was chosen to preach at the ceremony, made it clear that the new archbishop was 'a Prelate of an Hereditary zeal for the Established Church . . . not a zeal instigated by passion . . . but directed by knowledge'. He concluded:

The Protestant succession has so material an Advantage against all Pretenders to the Crown in the Popish line, that men must be strongly tempted before they can

---

[100] Ch. MS Wake 7, fo. 182, Green to Wake, 17 Jan. 1717. See also Elias Sydall, *The Insupportable Yoke of Popery, and the Wickedness of Bringing it again upon these Kingdoms, After So Many Deliverances from it, Consider'd and Apply'd with regard to the Present Rebellion: In a Sermon Preach'd at the Cathedral-Church of Canterbury, on Saturday November 5 1715* (1715).

[101] John Robinson was given dispensation for non-residence in 1712 for his participation in 'a matter so agreeable to his Holy Function as peace': CCAL, Canterbury Letters, no. 184.

[102] William Higden, *A View of the English Constitution, with Respect to the Sovereign Authority of the Prince and the Allegiance of the Subject* (2nd edn., 1709).

[103] N. Sykes, 'The Election and Inthronization of William Wake as Archbishop of Canterbury', *JEH*, 1 (1950), 96–101.

prevail upon themselves to embark in so desperate a Design, as that of introducing a Popish prince, by the Subversion, if it were possible, of a Protestant succession, establish'd upon the most mature deliberations by a most universal consent . . . and after warnings, never to be forgotten, of the utter incompatibility of a Popish Government, with the Religion, Laws and Liberties of this Nation.[104]

This intimate identification of Protestantism and nationalism was a potent image within eighteenth-century discourse. Sermons were thus a way in which Anglican political orthodoxy could be disseminated, and attempts were made to ensure that only orthodox sermons were preached. Of course, not all local clergy accepted these views. Thomas Brett (vicar of Betteshanger, 1703–14), a High Churchman and later a non-juror, attacked the Hanoverian regime while preaching for Dean Stanhope (dean, 1704–28); the dean forbade him to preach in the cathedral again, accusing him of preaching on a 'topical and obnoxious matter'.[105] In 1724 the chapter, encouraged by Wake, required that only those clergy who held an MA degree or higher could preach in the pulpit and it would not allow strangers to do so.[106]

However, the support given by members of the chapter to the Whig government did not imply any lessening of their commitment to Anglican principles. A large number of those who can be considered High Churchmen took the oaths and accommodated themselves to the new situation.[107] Many claimed that true Anglican interests demanded attachment to the new order, an accommodation which would allow clergy to believe they were not guilty of resisting their anointed monarch. The Church of England was safe in Whig hands. In part this may explain the erstwhile Tory Thomas Gooch's decision to side with the Establishment, for which he was rewarded with a Canterbury prebend (stall IX, 1730–8).[108] The history of Canterbury Cathedral shows that the Whig domination of the Church hierarchy did not destroy strong Church principles: rather, they flourished under the guise of High-Church Whiggery. Nevertheless, throughout the period anxieties were expressed that the Church seemed to be in danger, a fear which resulted in some opposition to particular Whig policies. In the 1754 general election, for example, there was quite a furore in Canterbury

[104] Ralph Blomer, *A Sermon Preach'd in the Cathedral and Metropolitical Church of Canterbury, at the Inthronement of His Grace, William Lord Archbishop of the Province, On Friday June 15th, 1716* (1716), 16.

[105] Bodl. MS Eng. Th. c. 25, fos. 192–3, Stanhope to Brett, 3 May 1715.

[106] CCAL, Chapter Act Book, 1711–26, fo. 157.

[107] This point was recognized by C. W. Wordsworth in *Social Life at the English Universities in the Eighteenth Century* (Cambridge, 1874), 80.

[108] C. N. L. Brooke, J. M. Horn, and N. L. Ramsay, 'A Canon's Residence in the Eighteenth Century: The Case of Thomas Gooch', *JEH*, 39 (1988), 546–7. Prebendary Sydall was given a bishopric by Gibson: Sykes, *Gibson*, 140.

in the aftermath of the attempts of the previous year to pass a bill through Parliament naturalizing Jews. This attempt was widely perceived as an attack on the essential Christian underpinnings of the nation, and the Church interest in the city was able to mount a vociferous attack on the MP Matthew Robinson Morris.[109]

Sermons preached by members of the cathedral chapter during the eighteenth century, especially on the fast-days in times of national danger or at thanksgivings for victories, stressed the ways in which political events could be interpreted and analysed in a religious light, as evidence of the workings of God's providence and intervention within the world. The Restoration itself had been explained in this way, and the defeat of the Jacobite rebellions was seen in such terms. Situated near the south coast, Canterbury was always considered liable to foreign invasion and not surprisingly members of the cathedral community were alive to the dangers of their position. For them the wars of the eighteenth century could almost be considered as 'wars of religion'. During the tensions of the Jacobite scare of 1744–5, Samuel Lisle (stall VII and archdeacon of Canterbury, 1728–44) indulged in an overview of past English history from the Elizabethan period, through the Civil War, to the crises of 1688 and 1715 as evidence that God would intervene on the side of the government if the nation repented her sins.[110] The chapter gave £200 to help fight the rebellion 'in defence of our Constitution in Church and State'.[111] The perceived connection between divine providence and politics was a useful way in which clergy could explain England's success or failure and impress the importance of religious behaviour on their congregations. In 1780 James Cornwallis (dean, 1775–81) accounted for the setbacks Britain was facing in the American war in terms of God's providence: divine displeasure was a consequence of the neglect of public devotions.[112] The world-view displayed

[109] T. W. Perry, *Public Opinion, Propaganda and Politics in Eighteenth-Century England. A Study of the Jew Bill of 1753* (Cambridge, Mass., 1962), 169.

[110] Samuel Lisle, *A Sermon Preached before the House of Lords, in the Abbey-Church, Westminster, on Wednesday, April 14, being the Day Appointed by His Majesty's Royal Proclamation for a General Fast, on the Occasion of the Present War* (1744), 19–20. For the invasion scare affecting members of the chapter see *The Letters of Spencer Cowper, Dean of Durham, 1746–74*, ed. E. Hughes, Surtees Soc., 165 (1956), 39.

[111] CCAL, Chapter Act Book, 1727–45, fo. 224, 26 Oct. 1745.

[112] James Cornwallis, *A Sermon Preached in the Cathedral and Metropolitical Church of Christ, Canterbury, On Friday February 4, 1780. Being the Day Appointed to be Observed as a Day of General Fasting and Humiliation* (Canterbury, 1780). A similar message was made by the six-preacher John Duncombe in *The Civil War between the Israelites and the Benjamites. Illustrated and Applied in a Sermon Preached in the Parish-Church of St. Andrew, in the City of Canterbury* (Canterbury, 1778). See P. Langford, 'Old Whigs, Old Tories and the American Revolution', *Journal of Imperial and Commonwealth History*, VII (1980), 106–30.

in such sermons suggests that the logical implications of Newtonian science, that God will not intervene in His creation, could be tempered by religious ideology. Belief in the 'general providence' of God's natural laws did not drive out belief in a particular providence. This providentialism had political uses. By explaining political events in terms of God's intervention, clergy were able to deflect criticism of governmental policies. Such a view also helped to justify the position of the clergy within society. If God intervened within society, it was necessary for society to have clergy who could explain what had gone wrong.[113]

THE CATHEDRAL AND THE WORLD OF LEARNING

The educational and intellectual backgrounds of the members of the chapter reveal them to have been, on the whole, a learned body, closely allied to the universities. Many of the prebendaries in the Restoration period had been educated at Oxford—a choice which reflected the perception of Oxford as the centre of political loyalty and religious orthodoxy. Indeed, it became almost a policy of Restoration Churchmen to turn their attention to the more politically suspect Cambridge, notorious for being a breeding ground of Puritans, in an attempt to win it over towards the restored regime.[114] The activities of clergy such as Peter Gunning at St John's and later the appointment of the Cambridge-educated William Sancroft to the archbishopric of Canterbury in 1678 helped to remove the stigma of dissent at Cambridge, and both universities during the eighteenth century can be seen as operating as clerical seminaries, producing men trained and prepared to defend the Anglican order. In 1781, the year of his promotion to the deanery of Canterbury, George Horne, the president of Magdalen, wrote an open letter to Lord North urging him to reject the schemes for relaxing subscription at Oxford and Cambridge. Horne wanted North to emulate the Earl of Clarendon, uniting Church and State and making the universities into a 'lasting bulwark of the genuine apostolical Church which Popery, Calvinism and Infidelity have hitherto in vain united their efforts to overturn'.[115] Recent research on both universities has modified the

---

[113] P. Langford, 'The English Clergy and the American Revolution', in Eckhart Hellmuth (ed.), *The Transformation of Political Culture. England and Germany in the late Eighteenth Century* (Oxford, 1990), 292–3.

[114] J. Gascoigne, 'Politics, Patronage and Newtonianism: The Cambridge Example', *HJ*, 27 (1984), 3.

[115] George Horne, *A Letter to the Right Hon. the Lord North, Chancellor of the University of Oxford, Concerning Subscription to the XXXIX Articles* (Oxford, 1834), 48.

conventional criticism of them as ineffectual centres of learning.[116] This rehabilitation would have found some favour with some clergy in the eighteenth century. In 1710 Thomas Blomer, a former Canterbury prebendary (stall XI, 1673–1706) and also a fellow of Trinity, Cambridge, took Richard Bentley to task for representing the college as a scandalous place.[117] An intimate connection existed between Corpus Christi College, Cambridge and the cathedral school, through scholarships founded by Archbishop Parker in the sixteenth century. Several members of the Canterbury chapter, such as Leopold Finch (stall XII, 1689–1702), Julius Deedes (stall XI, 1739–52), and John Lynch (stall IV, 1728–34; dean, 1734–60) had themselves attended the school. Corpus came to be known for being 'remarkably attach'd to the Revolution and the succession of the house of Hanover'.[118]

Most of the Canterbury prebendaries held higher degrees, but this is not necessarily a reliable guide to learning. A better indicator of commitment to scholarship is the number of publications produced by clergy in this period. The majority of prebendaries published something, most commonly sermons or religious tracts, but several produced works of a more substantial nature. George Stanhope delivered the prestigious Boyle Lectures in 1701 to an admiring London audience which included John Evelyn, and members of the Canterbury chapter were frequently invited to preach at Court, before Parliament, to the annual meetings of the Society for the Propagation of the Gospel in Foreign Parts (SPG), and before the Corporation of the Sons of the Clergy. An important function of the cathedral in this period was to be a focus for learning, nurturing clergy who would participate in the religious and theological debates of the day. As E. B. Pusey noted in his defence of the cathedrals in 1833, the chapter at Canterbury had in the late seventeenth and eighteenth centuries provided

[116] E. G. W. Bill, *Education at Christ Church, Oxford, 1660–1800* (Oxford, 1988), 87, 99. On the links between the Church and the universities see G. V. Bennett, 'University, Society and Church 1688–1714', in L. S. Sutherland and L. G. Mitchell (eds.), *The History of the University of Oxford*, v. *The Eighteenth Century* (Oxford, 1986), 359–400; Gascoigne, *Cambridge in the Age of Enlightenment*; and id., 'Church and State Allied: The Failure of Parliamentary Reform of the Universities, 1688–1800', in A. L. Beier, D. Cannadine, and J. M. Rosenheim (eds.), *The First Modern Society. Essays in English History in Honour of Lawrence Stone* (Cambridge, 1989), 401–29. On the King's School see the praise showered on it by Eliza Berkeley in her *Poems by the Late George-Monck Berkeley* (1797), pp. xxviii, clxxvi.

[117] Thomas Blomer, *A Full View of Dr Bentley's Letter to the Lord Bishop of Ely. In a Discourse to a Friend* (1710). For a full discussion of the affair see R. J. White, *Dr Bentley: A Study in Academic Scarlet* (1965).

[118] Edmund Pyle, *Memoirs of a Royal Chaplain, 1729–1763. The Correspondence of Edmund Pyle, D.D., Chaplain in Ordinary to George II, with Samuel Kerrich. D.D.*, ed. A. Hartshorne (1905), 53. John Nichols referred to Corpus as a seminary for antiquaries, *Literary Anecdotes*, iii. 525.

a home and a base for a number of influential writers. He picked out Parker, Castell, Stillingfleet, Beveridge, Tenison, and Mill as instances of cathedral clergy who played a part on the national stage.[119] This was part of the cathedral's role in linking local and provincial culture to national concerns. At the Restoration, Meric Casaubon suggested that a series of high-powered lectures should be delivered in the cathedral for the benefit of country clergymen.[120] Indeed, one of the most significant contributions of eighteenth-century prebendaries to the achievement of stability may have been their ability to disseminate ideas and attitudes from the centre to the peripheries. In this, the eighteenth-century cathedral, so fiercely proud of its independence and local ties, might also act as an agent of centralization.

The breadth of learning displayed by the prebendaries in defending the Christian faith is striking. The defence of Anglicanism required a wide range of materials and subjects: history, classics, science, and literature. It has sometimes been suggested that knowledge of such matters is in itself an indication of how far prebendaries in this period had lost sight of the central importance of the Christian faith, and it has been argued that clerical interest in topics such as classical learning and science is a testimony to the growth and dominance of secular forms of thought in the eighteenth century. Clergy are castigated for appearing more interested in secular learning than in defending Christianity. But we ought to appreciate how far these areas of scholarship were seen not as independent of religious and theological considerations, but as part and parcel of a Christian culture; they were defended as legitimate branches of study precisely because they could help shed light on the Christian faith. Judging from the Canterbury evidence, the conventional concentration on the tension between High and Low Churchmen over the acceptance of the new science seems rather misplaced.[121] Within the cathedral chapter three Restoration High Churchmen, Peter du Moulin, Meric Casaubon, and Peter Gunning were all involved in scientific debates. Yet Gunning did not want du Moulin to present a poem to the Royal Society and Casaubon wrote a letter to du Moulin

---

[119] *Diary of John Evelyn*, ed. de Beer, v. 442–3, 6 Jan. 1701; E. B. Pusey, *Remarks on the Prospective and Past Benefits of Cathedral Institutions, in the Promotion of Sound Religious Knowledge, Occasioned by Lord Henley's Plan for their Abolition* (1833), 79–80. See also *The Fruits of Endowment; Being a list of works of Upwards of two Thousand Authors who have, from the Reformation to the Present Time, Enjoyed Prebendal or other Non-Cure Endowments of the Church of England* (1840).

[120] Meric Casaubon, 'On Learning', appendix ii in M. R. G. Spiller, *Concerning Natural Philosophy. Meric Casaubon and the Royal Society* (The Hague, 1980), 201.

[121] For example, B. Shapiro, *Probability and Certainty in Seventeenth Century Thought* (Princeton, NJ, 1985) and M. C. Jacob, *The Newtonians and the English Revolution* (Hassocks, 1976).

arguing about the significance of science. Du Moulin had given Casaubon Glanvill's *Plus Ultra*, which had led Casaubon to take issue with those who were excited by it. What concerned him was not the existence of the new science but the fear that it might come to dominate scholarship.[122]

All aspects of human knowledge could be marshalled for the cause of defending Christianity. There was little disinterested clerical research in this period: the historical, linguistic, and textual studies of the day were part of a sustained endeavour to defend the existing order, and before the mid-nineteenth century Christian scholarship naturally spilled out into these areas. In Canterbury, the first sixty years after the Restoration saw great interest in Anglo-Saxon scholarship as part of the task of demonstrating the historic roots of the Church in England against Catholic arguments: John Battely (stall I, 1688–1708) and John Mill (stall IV, 1704–7) were both noted in this field.[123] From the early eighteenth century even greater interest was shown in classical and philosophical scholarship to meet the threats from science and deism. In such a climate the highest priority was accorded to those disciplines which would help consolidate the Established Church against its perceived enemies: papists and dissenters in the first half of the period, and from the early eighteenth century, increasingly, Deists and Unitarians. Members of the Canterbury chapter seem to have been among the most vociferous in maintaining Christian orthodoxy. John Hancock (stall V, 1719–28), for example, joined in the Whistonian controversy of the early eighteenth century by using evidence from the Church Fathers to show that Arianism was not the form of true primitive Christianity.[124]

The fundamental conception of the relationship between learning and religious faith held by Anglican clerics in this period owed much to the tenets of Renaissance Christian Humanism. The need to understand the Bible contextually drew clergy into other areas of knowledge; their regard

---

[122] Spiller, *Natural Philosophy*, 44, 46, 53.

[123] Cf. S. Taylor, 'Church and Society after the Glorious Revolution', *HJ*, 31 (1988), 978. John Battely, *Antiquitates Rutupinae* (Oxford, 1711); John Mill, Preface to Thomas Bensons's *Vocabularium Anglo-Saxonicum* (Oxford, 1701); Edward Stillingfleet, *Origines Britannicae* (1685); David Wilkins, *Leges Anglo-Saxonicae Ecclesiasticae et Civiles* (1721). For Mill's support of Anglo-Saxon studies cf. D. Fairer, 'Anglo-Saxon Studies', in *History of the University of Oxford*, v. *The Eighteenth Century*, 810–11, 813, 815. Charles Elstob (stall VIII, 1666–1721) was the uncle and guardian to William and Elizabeth Elstob, two of the leading Anglo-Saxon scholars of the early eighteenth century. On the subject more generally see D. C. Douglas, *English Scholars, 1660–1730* (2nd edn., 1951).

[124] John Hancock, *Arianism not the Primitive Christianity; or, the Antenicene Fathers Vindicated from the Imputation of being Favourable to that Heresy, design'd as an Answer (in part) to Mr Whiston's Primitive Christianity Reviv'd* (2nd edn., 1719).

for the Scriptures guided their extra-biblical intellectual pursuits. Thus theological and religious concerns can be seen to permeate all aspects of Canterbury scholarship. William Beveridge, for instance, in his monumental histories of the early Church, stressed the importance of history and tradition in interpreting the Bible against Jean Daillé who in his *Traité de l'employ des saints pères* (1632) had rejected the authority of the Fathers, arguing that scripture alone was sufficient.[125] Samuel Shuckford's (stall X, 1738–54) *The Sacred and Profane History of the World* (1728) was an ambitious attempt to collate biblical and ancient histories. Even Richard Farmer's (stall IX, 1782–8) highly influential *Essay on the Learning of Shakespeare* (1767) can be fitted into this context, arguing as it did for the divine spark which guided the bard's genius. As George Horne observed in his sermon to the King's School in 1784, such scholarship was necessary because the 'days of inspiration have been long since at an end. God has ceased to communicate immediately the treasures of wisdom and knowledge to any man'.[126] Because of this, Anglican clerics were wary of those who claimed to have direct communication with God and thus had no need of an education: this was one of the most dangerous traits of enthusiasm. The Church of England clergy in this period saw their own mastery of such knowledge as distancing them from the perceived superstition of popery and ignorance of the nonconformist ministry.

During the second half of the eighteenth century the cathedral became something of a centre for the dissemination of anti-rationalist and especially anti-Socinian teachings. Dean Horne was the leader of the so-called Hutchinsonian circle which stressed the centrality of the Trinity and the limits of human reason in religious matters. The group took their name from John Hutchinson (1674–1737) whose writings on natural philosophy and theology became the basis of their work. His appeal to such men was obvious: Hutchinson had argued that a proper reading of the Bible demonstrated that both it and the natural world held sure proofs of the Trinity.[127]

[125] William Beveridge, *Synodicon* (Oxford, 1672).

[126] George Horne, *The Character of True Wisdom, and the Means of Attaining it. A Sermon preached in the Cathedral Church of Christ, Canterbury, before the Society of Gentlemen educated in the King's School, on Thursday, August 26 1784* (Oxford, 1784), 4.

[127] For a full analysis of the Hutchinsonian position see A. J. Kuhn, 'Nature Spiritualised: Aspects of Anti-Newtonianism', *English Literary History*, 41 (1974), 400–12; id., 'Glory or Gravity: Hutchinson vs Newton', *Journal of the History of Ideas*, 22 (1961), 303–22; G. N. Cantor, 'Revelation and the Cyclical Cosmos of John Hutchinson', in L. J. Jordanova and R. Porter (eds.), *Images of the Earth* (Chalfont St Giles, 1979), 3–22; C. B. Wilde, 'Hutchinsonianism, Natural Philosophy and Religious Controversy in Eighteenth-Century Britain', *History of Science*, 18 (1980), 1–24; id., 'Matter and Spirit as Natural Symbols in Eighteenth-Century British Natural Philosophy', *British Journal of the History of Science*, 15

Their main targets were the Unitarians and rational dissenters, in particular Joseph Priestley and Richard Price, who were responsible for leading the attack on the Anglican liturgy in this period. The Hutchinsonians were largely Oxford-educated during the 1750s and rose to some prominence within the Church after 1760. George Berkeley, son of the famous theologian and philosopher, had been collated to a Canterbury stall (VI, 1768–95) by Archbishop Secker. He supported the Hutchinsonians, and their views received further backing in the cathedral when Horne was promoted to the deanery in 1781. Horne had been born in Kent, the son of the vicar of Otham, was educated at Maidstone School, and was well connected in the diocese. Whilst at the university he made contact with clergy who would later join him in Kent, and was admired even by those who intellectually had little in common with him as a 'saint in crape'.[128] A constant visitor to the deanery at this time was Horne's great ally, William Jones, who shared his interest in Hutchinsonianism, occasionally preaching in the cathedral and who received preferment within the diocese. In 1776 Horne published his celebrated *Commentary on the Book of Psalms* which maintained that the Old Testament contained a full understanding of Christ's life and purpose, illustrating the crucial connection between the Old and New Testaments. In Hutchinsonian fashion Horne also emphasized the link between the natural world and theology. The Psalms, he argued, used imagery from nature to describe Christ's power and attributes and the blessings of redemption.[129]

The concern of the Hutchinsonians to see a harmony between the Bible and the natural world influenced the popular series of lectures in the early nineteenth century known as the Bridgewater Treatises. Their attitudes also foreshadowed much of the Oxford Movement interest in the relationship between the natural world and theology: John Keble and John Henry Newman cited Horne's writings, and Keble's *The Christian Year* (1827) echoed the Hutchinsonian belief that the Bible and the natural world must be read by analogy. In this as in so much else, the Oxford Movement drew

(1982), 99–131. Because the Hutchinsonians seemed to go against the supposed 'rationalism' of the age, Leslie Stephen called them 'childish': *English Thought in the Eighteenth Century*, i. 392. For more positive appraisals see W. H. Teale, *Lives of English Divines* (1846), esp. pp. 381–9; P. B. Nockles, 'Continuity and Change in Anglican High Churchmanship, 1792–1850' unpub. Oxford University D.Phil. thesis, 1982; R. Sharp, 'New Perspectives on the High Church Tradition: Historical Background, 1730–80', in G. Rowell (ed.), *Tradition Renewed. The Oxford Movement Conference Papers* (1986), 4–23; F. C. Mather, 'Church, Parliament and Penal Law: Some Anglo-Scottish Interactions in the Eighteenth Century', *EHR*, 92 (1977), 540–77; and id., *Horsley*.

[128] W. Derry, *Dr Parr. A Portrait of the Whig Doctor Johnson* (Oxford, 1966), 113.
[129] George Horne, *Commentary on the Book of Psalms*, 2 vols. (Oxford, 1776).

on much of eighteenth-century thought, rather than merely reacting nega-
tively against it.[130] At Canterbury the influence of the Hutchinsonian circle
was strong. Both Archbishops Moore and Manners Sutton were noted for
their support of these High Churchmen, and the minor canon Henry Todd
was a protégé.[131] In 1786, at the primary visitation of Archbishop Moore,
Horne urged the necessity of defending the Trinity. The group also had
links with evangelicals of the period, notably with William Romaine. In
conventional historiography the evangelicals of the eighteenth century are
seen as standing apart from mainstream Anglicanism, but it is clear that
there were areas of overlap. John Wesley, for example, was much impressed
by Horne's *Commentary*, Charles Wesley's *Collection of Hymns on the
Trinity* was written on texts purloined from Jones's *Catholic Doctrine of the
Trinity* (1756), and Horne sent his daughters to be educated at Hannah
More's school near Bristol.[132]

PREBENDARIES AND CAREERS

Many of the Canterbury prebendaries went on to hold more prestigious
posts in the Church. Administrative experience as a member of the chapter,
and especially as dean, could be a valuable preparation for higher office.
Tillotson was the spectacular example of a prebendary who became archbishop. He was an active dean, corresponding with Sheldon and Sancroft,

---

[130] J. H. Newman, *Apologia Pro Vita Sua*, ed. M. J. Svaglic (Oxford, 1967), 18.

[131] See *Memoirs of William Stevens Esquire* (1812), 22; 'a vast number' of Horne's friends
were Hutchinsonians (p. 160). Jones reckoned that he was collated by Archbishop Secker to
Bethersden (1764) and Pluckley (1765) for his defence of Christianity: *Theological,
Philosophical and Miscellaneous Works*, 12 vols. (1801), i. p. x. When Jones went to Holling-
bourne to be inducted he stayed with William Horne (Horne's brother and the rector of
Otham) and was visited by his 'old friend' the Revd Denny Fairfax: ibid., p. xlvii. For
Archbishop Moore's support: BL Add. MS 39312, fo. 122, Horne to Berkeley, 9 Apr. 1791;
A. B. Webster, *Joshua Watson, The Story of a Layman, 1771–1855* (1954), 23–5; George
Horne, *The Duty of Contending for the Faith. A Sermon preached at the Primary Visitation of the
Most Reverend John, Lord Archbishop of Canterbury, in the Cathedral and Metropolitical Church,
on Saturday July 1st, 1786* (Oxford, 1786). The Hutchinsonians were pleased with the eleva-
tion of Moore in 1783: BL Add. MS 39312, fo. 37, Lord Monboddo to Berkeley, 29 Nov. 1784.
Jones dedicated his *Course of Lectures on the Holy Scriptures* (1789) to Moore: Magdalen
College, Oxford MS 471, fo. 24, Moore to Horne, 23 Mar. 1790. Moore, along with many bishops and a great number of clergy, subscribed to Jones's *Works*. For Todd see: BL Add. MS
39312, fo. 154, Todd to Berkeley, 10 Nov. 1794. For Archbishop Manners Sutton's support of
High-Churchmen: *VCH, Norfolk*, ii. 305; and Dewey, *Barchester, passim*.

[132] Horne, *Duty of Contending for the Faith*; CUL Add. MS 8134/A/3, fo. 52. This interplay between Evangelical and High-Church ideals is not surprising. J. D. Walsh has shown
how much the Evangelical Revival owed to High-Church example, and clearly the two strands
kept in tandem: J. D. Walsh, 'The Origins of the Evangelical Revival', in Bennett and Walsh,
Essays in Modern Church History, 132–62.

and after Sancroft had been suspended for refusing to comply with the new regime, it was Tillotson who as dean *sede vacante* played a prominent part in the ecclesiastical settlement after the Revolution.[133] The power to exercise archiepiscopal functions in a vacancy made the dean and chapter of Canterbury unique, and it was at these times that the cathedral attained national significance. From the early years of the Restoration the cathedral chapter were anxious to assert this privilege. Turner had been of importance in the months before Juxon was elected,[134] and in 1663, after Juxon's death, the dean and chapter petitioned the King, 'for a writ vesting in them the accustomed spiritual and ecclesiastical jurisdiction of the see'.[135] In most cases the vacancy was only for a few weeks and the administration was fairly routine, although in 1677 Dean Tillotson exercised the archiepiscopal prerogative of awarding degrees by conferring two MAs and a DMus on the talented John Blow.[136] The most extended period of *sede vacante* came in the long vacancy during Sancroft's suspension when Tillotson and Stillingfleet were given the right to exercise the metropolitical jurisdiction,[137] and with Beveridge had power 'to examine and approve of all clerks as shall be presented to any benefice in the diocese of Canterbury'.[138] Tillotson was involved in advising the new king on ecclesiastical patronage,[139] and as dean had a leading role to play in the commission which met before the Convocation of 1689. In this sense Tillotson can be seen as the obvious successor to Sancroft. Traditional interpretations have made much of the contrast between the two, echoing the contemporary propaganda which exaggerated the differences. In non-juring and High-Church circles Tillotson was seen as an intruder; to the supporters of the Revolution, Sancroft and his 'tribe of Levi' were the last relics of popery.[140] But in administrative terms Tillotson's appointment was less controversial. It was not only deans who were promoted to higher office. Four of those appointed between 1690 and 1720 went on to become bishops, the non-juring secession ensuring that

[133] Sheldon had advised Charles II to give the deanery to Tillotson in 1672: Birch, *Tillotson*, 411.

[134] For example, early fiats were often signed by Turner: CCAL, F/A Induction boxes; LPL, 'unsorted fiats' II/ 1660-9.

[135] Bodl. MS Tanner 128, fo. 47, dean and chapter to Sheldon, 23 Sept. 1663.

[136] N. Sykes, *Canterbury Cathedral Library*, Canterbury Cathedral Papers 9 (1954).

[137] CCAL, Chapter Act Book 1670-1710, fos. 108ᵛ, 113.

[138] *HMC, 9th Report*, 'Appendix', 462.

[139] G. V. Bennett, 'William III and the Episcopate', in Bennett and Walsh, *Essays in Modern Church History*, 117-22.

[140] *The Tribe of Levi: A Poem* (1691); Bodl. MS Rawl Poet 181, fos. 2-3. Sancroft passed his own powers to William LLoyd, bishop of Norwich: Bodl. MS Tanner 26, fo. 11. Sancroft was suspended on 1 Aug. 1689, but was allowed to keep the revenues of the see until his deprivation on 1 Feb. 1690, perhaps to allow him to change his mind: D'Oyly, *Sancroft*, 448-9.

several Canterbury prebendaries would be called upon to fill vacant sees. Some bishops continued to hold their Canterbury prebend *in commendam*, which helped to alleviate the financial hardships of occupants of the poorer bishoprics.

The twelve prebendaries were not required to keep constant residence: the statutes committed them to ninety days' residence a year, with at least twenty-one days' continuous residence, and usually only four or five prebendaries were in Canterbury at a time, except at the general audits in mid-June and mid-November, when leases were renewed and the annual dividend paid out. Measures were taken to deprive those who failed to keep strict residence of some of their financial benefits.[141] Momentous occasions could also attract high attendance. The entry for 5 November 1689 records 'all present', at a time when the dean and chapter had most business, during Sancroft's suspension.[142] At Wake's enthronement on 15 July 1716 nine prebendaries were present.[143] Nevertheless, there was constant pressure for greater attendance. George I informed the chapters of all English cathedrals that full attendance was essential, to fulfil the demands of preaching and of keeping hospitality within their cities.[144] Dean Stanhope was especially concerned to ensure that residence was maintained. He was able to write to Wake in 1724, 'Our Residence is duly observed and generally a very laudable appearance at Prayers, and since my coming not one prebend's course has been preached by a stranger'.[145] Members of the chapter could sometimes get dispensations for non-residence, if they held a university position, were royal chaplains, or were present at Convocation. Yet by their absences they could perform a valuable function by keeping the cathedral in touch with developments elsewhere, notably at Lambeth or Westminster. London was Tillotson's normal place of residence yet he was able to keep in touch with the cathedral throughout the year. Burnet claimed that Tillotson 'did not content himself with such a residence as answered the statute; considering his obligation at Court; but gave as much of his time and his labours to the Cathedral as could agree with his obligations here'.[146] George Thorp suggested to Sancroft in 1684 that a living might be given to Tillotson in the diocese so that he would

---

[141] For example, CCAL., Chapter Act Book, 1727–1745, fo. 208: those who did not reside were deprived of faggots and faggot money.

[142] Ibid., Chapter Act Book, 1672–1710, fo. 183.   [143] Ibid., 1711–1726, fo. 48^v.

[144] Bodl. MS Dep. c. 233, fo. 77, George I to deans and chapters, 9 July 1724.

[145] Ch. Ch., MS Wake 10, fo. 126, Stanhope to Wake, 20 Jan. 1724.

[146] Gilbert Burnet, *A Sermon Preached at the Funeral of the Most Reverend Father in God John . . . Lord Archbishop of Canterbury* (1694), 20.

leave his place at Lincoln's Inn and come and reside here . . . I know your Grace will bear with my only concern to promote residence in our Church, which I fear in a little time we shall want of more and more. I was afraid when your Grace named Dr Beveridge for the prebend the great service he does at London would be a motive for your Grace not to move him thence to a more private station, with which I am confident he would be as well pleased, and we should be much better were we not bound to wish that which may be more for ye public good.[147]

Thorp here articulated the tension concerning the cathedral's function: was it a national or a diocesan body? This 'dualism' was reflected in the activities of its personnel.

Non-residence was one of the disadvantages of having prebendaries who held prominent positions in the outside world instead of residing in their benefices. However, there was a constant group of prebendaries who resided—for instance, the Du Moulin circle in the Restoration period, the Thorp circle in the late seventeenth century, the Berkeley circle in the 1770s and 80s, and the circle around Canon Welfitt in the early nineteenth century, who spent nine months of the year at Canterbury—whilst others were more peripatetic. Another problem was that since there was no concept of clerical retirement, some of the older prebendaries who were sick or dying could not play their part within the life of the community. Minor canons and six-preachers commonly preached on Sundays as substitutes for prebendaries. During the 1760s and 70s in particular, the six-preachers seem to have done much of the preaching, especially George Hearne, John Duncombe, William Bunce, and Osmund Beauvoir. This was partly because in these decades there was a rapid turnover of deans who did not stay long enough to impose their authority on the community. Matters improved in the 1780s and 90s with the longer tenure of Deans Horne and Powys, and by 1800 it was rare for a minor canon to preach on a Sunday. George Berkeley also

set the fashion for prebends assisting the minor canons and city clergy as the late worthy Mrs Gostling, of witty memory, very soon after Dr B. went to reside at Canterbury, on hearing of his frequently not only preaching, but doing the whole of the duty at some city church exclaimed, 'Well, well in a little time, I suppose the minor canons . . . will snuff the moon if they have prebends for curates'.

His example was followed by the 'amicable' Dr Tatton, the 'very worthy' Dr Dering, the 'polite' Dr Benson, and the 'learned' Dr Palmer.[148] Prebendaries were not divorced from the work of the parish clergy, and parochial experience was common before they were preferred to their stall. Those

---

[147] Bodl. MS Tanner 33, fo. 237, Thorp to Sancroft, 30 Oct. 1684.
[148] Quoted in George Berkeley, *Sermons*, ed. Eliza Berkeley (1799), p. xxiv.

who also had livings in the diocese found it possible to perform their parish duties whilst living in Canterbury.[149]

Within the cathedral community, the minor canons and the six-preachers, who were drawn from the ranks of the diocesan clergy, helped to link the cathedral to the diocese. Minor canons were crucial in keeping the life of the community going for if the prebendaries provided a link between the cathedral and the wider world, the minor canons connected it to the life of the city and diocese. It was they who led the daily services, read the lessons, and were responsible for the musical life of the cathedral: the pre-centor and sacrist were chosen from their ranks. In the late seventeenth century the dean and chapter found it difficult to find suitably qualified and talented clergy for these posts. In 1660 two minor canons and seven lay clerks returned to the restored Foundation and they were not necessarily very suitable. Of Henry Nicholls it was said in 1663; 'a pitiful man, of parts scarce sufficient for a minister, once an apothecary, after a pettycanon at the Cathedral. The Church finding him weak gave him £10 to quit his place.'[150] John Langhorne was suspended in 1675 for 'being a reproach to his profession by his vicious and debased manner of life and conversation thereby greatly dishonouring this Church whereof he is a member'.[151] A series of regulations concerning the behaviour of minor canons, lay clerks, and bedesmen during the eighteenth century brought about something of a transformation in the activities of these members of the community so that by the end of the period they had become much more orderly.[152] Nevertheless, they continued to bear the brunt of the dean and chapter's criticism if services were not adequately performed. John Moore (dean, 1771–5), for example, reprimanded one minor canon for not reading early morning prayers because they were not well attended: 'Sir, that shall not be admitted as an excuse; if there are so few, I will pay so much a morning to half a dozen poor aged persons to attend them; for I am fully resolved that they shall never be given up while I am dean of this Church.'[153]

The six-preacherships also went to members of the diocesan clergy and were nominated by the archbishop. From the Restoration the preachers augmented their incomes by renting out their houses in the precincts. Archbishops gave these pieces of preferment to clergy who had often been noted for their pastoral activities. Secker, for example, preferred George

---

[149] In 1668, for example, Peter Hardres (stall X, 1660–78) 'officiates for ye most part' (at Upper Hardres): Bodl. MS Sancroft 99, fo. 89.

[150] LPL MS 1126, fo. 10.   [151] CCAL, Act Book, 1670–1710, fo. 201.

[152] Ibid., 1711–26, fos. 150[v], 54. See R. F. Ford, 'Minor Canons at Canterbury Cathedral: The Gostlings and their Colleagues', unpub. University of California D.Phil. thesis, 1985.

[153] Quoted in Berkeley, *Sermons*, p. xxxix.

Hearne, who was a pioneer in religious education, promoting Sunday schools in the city and the diocese.[154] It is impossible to know how regularly this group performed their duties, although visitation returns suggest that they kept to the statutes. Several six-preachers did, however, leave a substantial number of printed sermons which indicates that they, at least, were fulfilling their function.[155]

REVOLUTION AND REFORM, *c.*1780–1828

During the last two decades of the eighteenth century and in the early nineteenth century the dean and chapter felt itself attacked on many fronts and participated in the renewed movement to defend the position of the Church within the State. Dean Horne and his ally William Jones, for instance, articulated their qualms about the French Revolution from the pulpit of Canterbury Cathedral in September and October of 1789. Horne compared Jones's sermon with the radical Richard Price's famous paean welcoming the Revolution: 'the latter sings his Nunc Dimittis on the sight of Paradise returning upon earth, the former thinks the devil is just broke lose.'[156]

Not only were there dangers from French Jacobins abroad and from radical Unitarians at home: the clergy also felt their position within the State and society threatened by efforts to alter the liturgical formularies of the Church, by the moves to gain emancipation for Catholics and by the attempts to abolish the Test and Corporation Acts which had debarred non-Anglicans from holding office.[157] To the traditionally minded, such schemes were anathema. They seemed to threaten the Anglican hegemony which, since 1660, had been a prime instrument in maintaining social and political stability. Canterbury prebendaries shared in this attitude. In 1773,

[154] For Hearne see the sermon dedicated to him by George Horne: *Sunday Schools Recommended in a Sermon preached at the parish church of St Alphege, Canterbury, on Sunday December the eighteenth, MDCCLXXXV, with an Appendix on the Method of Forming and Conducting them* (Oxford and London, 1786).

[155] For example, John Cooke, *Thirty Nine Sermons on Several Subjects*, 2 vols. (1739); Charles Moore, *Sermons*, 3 vols. (1818). At the 1682 visitation, it was noted that the six-preachers 'preach more sermons in the Cathedral than by Statutes we are required': Bodl. MS Tanner 123, fo. 29.

[156] The quotation is in BL Add. MS 39312, fo. 108, Horne to Berkeley, 5 Dec. 1789. George Horne, 'Submission to Government . . . A Sermon preached in Canterbury Cathedral on 25 October 1789', in *The Works of the Right Reverend George Horne*, 4 vols. (1818), iii. 384–97; and William Jones, 'Popular Commotions to Precede the End of the World. A Sermon preached in Canterbury Cathedral on 26 September 1789', in his *Works*, v. 274–98. Jones attempted to reach a wider audience by writing *A Letter to John Bull Esq., from his Second Cousin Thomas Bull* (1793).

[157] Clark, *English Society 1688–1832*, ch. 6.

when proposals were made to change the liturgy, Richard Farmer warned of the dangers of altering the present state of affairs:

Suppose the Remedy should prove worse than the Disease—it would at least make one Schism more—We shall have the Old Liturgists, and they join'd by the Methodists, would make a formidable figure. Those, who are able to find difficulties in the Old Form are able likewise to explain them: and these bear a very small proportion to the Bulk of Mankind . . . As if Religion was intended for nothing else but to be mended.[158]

Farmer also headed the campaign at Cambridge to block reforms to subscription. William Cole described Farmer as 'such a Whig as those who placed King William on the throne; and of course described a violent Tory by our present Republicans, of whom, to say the truth he could hardly speak with temper'.[159] In a remarkable series of sermons in the 1780s and 90s, members of the cathedral community stressed the urgency of the times and the necessity of maintaining tradition in worship and politics.[160]

This stance is not surprising since governmental patronage had been used to promote orthodox clergy to the Canterbury stalls. Many of the canons in the period after 1780 were intimately linked with William Pitt or Lord Liverpool and with what have been called the forces of 'Tory' reaction. Folliott Cornewall (dean, 1793–7) had been tutor to Lord Liverpool's son, Houston Radcliffe (stall IV, 1795–1822, archdeacon of Canterbury, 1803–22) had been a tutor at Brasenose College, Oxford where his pupils had included Sidmouth, and George Horne had been a friend of Liverpool's since their days at Oxford. Thomas Coombe (stall VII, 1800–22) had defended Britain in America in the 1780s before being banished for his loyalism. The elevation of such men was part of the government's strategy

---

[158] Richard Farmer to Thomas Percy, 18 Feb. 1773, in *The Correspondence of Thomas Percy and Richard Farmer*, ed. Cleanth Brooks (La., 1946), 171. On Farmer's refusal to accept a bishopric, Horne noted that he 'never did live with us much at Canterbury; he used to say it was not a life that suited him; he is still in possession of his beloved Emmanuel': BL Add. MS 311312, fo. 110, Horne to Berkeley, 1 May 1790.

[159] Quoted in Nichols, *Literary History*, ii. 642.

[160] Charles Moore, 'Against Love of Novelty in Religious Matters. Preached in Canterbury Cathedral, 26 May 1794', in his *Sermons*, iii. 340–61. Other sermons on this theme preached in the cathedral include George Berkeley, *The Danger of Violent Innovations in the State Exemplified from the Reigns of the Two First Stuarts, in a Sermon preached at the Cathedral and Metropolitical Church of Christ, Canterbury on Monday, Jan. 31, 1785* (Canterbury, 1785). Writing in 1880, Canon Jenkins observed that 'it is scarcely too much to say that at this period our Church had forgotten her divine origin and was content to be a mere department of state': *Canterbury*, 388. But see Berkeley, *An Inquiry into the Origin of Episcopacy. In a Discourse Preached at the Consecration of George Horne, D.D. late Bishop of Norwich* (1795). Similar sentiments can be found in Houston Radcliffe (stall IV, 1795–1822, archdeacon, 1803–22), *A Sermon Preached in His Majesty's Chapel at the Consecration of William Lord Bishop of Chester, Sunday Jan. 20 1788* (1788), which was a vigorous defence of the divine establishment of the Church.

for strengthening the profile of the Church. In 1791 Dean Horne was promoted by Pitt to the bishopric of Norwich at the same time as Samuel Hallifax and Samuel Horsley were also brought to the bench. Richard Farmer, who was known to be a 'determined enemy of Levellers', was twice offered a bishopric by Pitt because of the Tory principles which he strove to propagate in Cambridge, when master of Emmanuel. It is not surprising that the deanery of Canterbury was noted as being something of a stepping stone for high office in the Church after 1780. Samuel Denne observed in 1797 that

The Deanery of Canterbury has of late been a principal step to a Bishoprick; and I question whether the Ecclesiastical annals of this Country will furnish in any other Cathedral the instance of six Deans in succession being elevated from it within a quarter of a century.[161]

The prebendaries' defence of the Anglican constitution rested on the firm conviction that the world of stability and order would again be turned upside down unless strenuous efforts were made to keep it intact. The dean and chapter asked Archbishop Manners Sutton in 1812 and again in 1827 to petition Parliament against any such legal changes.[162] Their arguments for maintaining the status quo were based on the belief that the lessons of history had shown the necessity of such legislation and moreover that the Anglican Establishment was essentially a tolerant one. The chapter insisted that they were not advocating persecution in petitioning against Catholic emancipation, but rather that they wished to save Great Britain from the nightmare of popish machinations.

Recent occurrences [show] the Romish Church is as zealous as at any former period for the political aggrandizement of Papacy and as hostile to the civil and religious Institutions by law established in this country. Your Petitioners therefore still most earnestly deprecate the dangerous experiment of engrafting the divided allegiance and encroaching spirit of Popery upon our Free Protestant Constitution.[163]

As part of this attempt to buttress the Anglican nature of the constitution, the dean and chapter were supporters of the foundation of King's College, London in 1829, donating £300 to the project.[164] King's was seen as an Anglican counterblast to the recently founded University College, which

---

[161] Quoted in John Nichols, *Illustrations of Literary History*, 8 vols. (1817–58), vi. 687. The deans were Brownlow North, Moore, Cornwallis, Horne, Butler and Cornewall. See 'A Word of Comfort from Bangor to Canterbury, on the Loss of her Dean, 1775' which foresaw Moore's return to Canterbury as a future archbishop: id., *Literary Anecdotes*, viii. 96.

[162] CCAL, Dean's Book, 1793–1822, 199; ibid., Chapter Act Book, 1824–54, 52.

[163] Ibid., Chapter Act Book, 1794–1824, 286: 'A Petition to be presented to both Houses of Parliament respecting the Roman Catholic Claims', 1 Dec. 1812. G. F. A. Best, 'The Protestant Constitution and its Supporters, 1800–1829', *TRHS*, 5th ser., 8 (1958), 107–27.

[164] CCAL, Dean's Book, 1822–54, fo. 61.

admitted dissenters and Unitarians. The foundation of King's and the support it received from the clerical establishment must be seen in the context of the threat to the British constitution and the need to preserve the Church and the State from what were widely perceived to be the destructive influences of liberalism.

It is possible to argue that the volume of criticism of the cathedrals produced in the early nineteenth century was largely a product of theological and political hostility, rather than a reflection of their torpor and sterility. According to hostile accounts the decay and corruption found in early nineteenth-century cathedrals was so pervasive that only parliamentary intervention in the 1830s and 40s could save them. But such an interpretation is misleading in that it seriously underplays not only the vigour with which such institutions participated in the defence of the Church, but also the impulse to reform which can be found within the Church. Testimony to that reforming spirit, and an indication of the activity of the cathedral's personnel, was alluded to in Archbishop Howley's *Visitation Charge* delivered in the cathedral in 1832 where he paid tribute to efforts within the cathedral community since the 1780s to make the Church of England more pastorally effective.[165] The cathedral had given money to the SPG[FP] and in 1824 had contributed to the Society for Building and Enlarging Churches. He pointed to the growth in schools, diffusing spiritual knowledge, which had been founded in the diocese, with support from the chapter. The new archbishop also noted how well the cathedral's functions were performed and the efficiency of its personnel in carrying out their duties.[166] Howley's evidence suggests that long before the changes affecting cathedrals in the 1830s, at Canterbury at least, efforts were being made to make the cathedral a more useful part of the Church's structure. This provides further material to be marshalled on behalf of the 'gradualist' case concerning Church reform, supporting the argument that the 'eighteenth-century Church' was not only reformed by outside pressures acting on it in the 1830s, but had itself been participating in reform.[167] How this desire for reform and efficiency was displayed in other areas of the cathedral's operation will be considered in later chapters.

---

[165] Wiliam Howley, *A Charge Delivered at his Primary Visitation in August and September, 1832* (1832), 15, 19, 49. In this, the chapter of Canterbury was perhaps participating in the 'intellectual repulse of revolution' noted by I. R. Christie, *Stress and Stability in late Eighteenth Century Britain: Reflections on the British Avoidance of Revolution* (Oxford, 1984), 155–78.

[166] Howley, *Charge*, 49.

[167] See Virgin, *Church in Age of Negligence*, 26–7, 264, 266–7; W. R. Maynard, 'The Response of the Church of England to Economic and Demographic Change: The Archdeaconry of Durham, 1800–1851', *JEH*, 42 (1991), 457.

2
The Parish Clergy

In administering the diocese, a major concern of the Church authorities was the parish clergy, for without them efforts to maintain and strengthen the presence of the Church in the local community would be fruitless. Given the extent of Anglican influence in eighteenth- and early nineteenth-century society it is surprising that historians have paid relatively little attention to the parish clergy as a body.[1] Most estimates, relying on gener-alizations heavily based on quotations from Fielding, Goldsmith, Jane Austen, and Trollope, have suggested that the clergy did not operate as a group in any positive sense—any common identity there may have been was largely limited to negative traits.[2] Analysis has tended to concentrate on social, educational, and political divisions, not only between the bulk of the parish clergy and the Church dignitaries, but also between the affluent parish clergy and the underpaid clerical proletariat, which worked against any professional cohesion.[3] Little effort has been made to explore how far the clergy could be seen as a professional community. This chapter investi-gates the forces which helped to provide the clergy with some kind of shared interests. A problem in such an analysis, however, is to decide what is meant by 'professional identity'. Attention here will be paid to what might be called socio-cultural group formation and also to those elements within the Church, such as institutional collegiality and professional ties, which encouraged clergy to think of themselves as sharing a common role and experience.[4] This is not to suggest that clerics identified themselves solely as members of a professional body: other sorts of loyalties—familial, regional, and economic—competed for the allegiance of the parish clergy.

Though ecclesiastical historians have studied the professionalization of the parish clergy from the Reformation to the Civil War, the theme has not been taken up again until discussions of the Evangelical and Oxford

[1] B. R. Wilson, *Religion in Secular Society* (1966), 76.

[2] Though W. A. Speck, *Society and Literature in England, 1700–1760* (Dublin, 1983), 55, 72–5, 159–61 does place some of these authors in perspective.

[3] Virgin, *Church in Age of Negligence*, 216–51; Russell, *Clerical Profession*, 31–3.

[4] For a pioneering assessment of the 'clerical tribalism' of the early seventeenth-century clergy see Collinson, *Religion of Protestants*, 115–40.

Movements, which have traditionally been portrayed as reacting against 'the eighteenth-century Church'.[5] 'Reformers' blamed the parish clergy for becoming so worldly that by the end of the period there was often nothing to distinguish them from fox-hunting country gentlemen. The eighteenth-century cleric has often been placed in the category of 'un-reformed' or 'pre-professional'.[6] In particular, much has been made of the transfer from 'status' to 'occupational' professionalism in accounting for the changes in the nineteenth century.[7] In the studies of Russell, Haig, and Heeney, the 1830s are taken as the effective starting point for a profession-alization which represented a vigorous reaction against the 'gentlemen-status' of the eighteenth-century parson.[8] But this perception rests on a failure to recognize that Church authorities in the long eighteenth century, together with many of the parish clergy themselves, were anxious to define a professional clerical role. The idea of 'reaction' can be a dangerous con-cept, if simplistically used. In matters of the professionalization of person-nel, as in others, there was as much continuity as reaction between these two movements and the Established Church. Focusing on the personnel of the parish clergy, their backgrounds, training, and politics, can help in our understanding of the clerical profession in the period before 1830.

For the purpose of analysis only those clergy beneficed to livings in the diocese proper have been considered, but there was always some movement between the diocese and the peculiars, especially the nearby deanery of Shoreham. Names have been taken from diocesan material, archbishops' registers, and act books, and information recorded concerning ordination and university education has been used to trace socio-geographic origins.[9] The period has been divided into thirty-year blocks, allocating each incum-bent to a grouping depending on his initial presentation to a benefice in the

[5] R. O'Day, *The English Clergy: The Emergence and Consolidation of a Profession, 1558–1642* (Leicester, 1979); id., 'The Anatomy of a Profession: The Clergy of the Church of England', in W. Prest (ed.), *The Professions in Early Modern England* (1987), 25–63.

[6] Russell, *Clerical Profession*, 6; Heeney, *Different Kind of Gentleman*; Haig, *Victorian Clergy*. These works are influenced by the sociologist P. Elliot and his *The Sociology of the Professions* (1972), esp. ch. 2.

[7] Heeney, *Different Kind of Gentleman*, 4; Russell, *Clerical Profession*, 28–49.

[8] Recent literature on the concept of 'professions' includes Prest, *Professions in Early Modern England*; Holmes, *Augustan Professions*; W. J. Reader, *Professional Men: The Rise of the Professional Classes in Victorian England* (1966).

[9] LPL, Archbishops registers, Juxon to Manners Sutton; ibid., VB 1/1–15: act books, 1663–1828. Other sources include CCAL Add. MS 19, 'Notitia Diocesis Cantuar', compiled by Archdeacon Green in 1716 and continued by his successors. Biographical information has been found in J. Venn and J. A. Venn, *Alumni Cantabrigienses*, 10 vols. (Cambridge, 1922–7; 1940–54); J. Foster, *Alumni Oxonienses*, 8 vols. (Oxford, 1888; 1891–2); G. D. Butchaell and T. U. Sadleir, *Alumni Dublinienses, 1505–1905*, 2 vols. (1924); Hasted, *History of Kent, passim*.

diocese. What follows is a prosopographical study of clerical recruitment which will help assess changes over time in the composition of the parish clergy, and in the nature of the clerical profession.

The experience of the 1640s and 50s had consequences for the way in which the clerical profession was viewed. Amongst other things that had to be restored in the 1660s was the perception that the role of the clergy was to bring stability to parishes. The ejection of ministers had a marked effect upon the religious and communal life in a number of parishes in the diocese. Before the 1640s many incumbents had served in their parishes for decades. Barnaby Knell, for example, had been vicar of Reculver for forty years before being ejected in 1646,[10] but during the Civil War there was a constantly changing succession of ministers. After Richard Bands had been ejected from Boughton Malherbe in 1643, a total of five incumbents succeeded him before 1660.[11] The stability of parish life must have been disturbed, and the esteem in which clergy were held undermined by the ease with which they were ejected. However, because of the shortage of episcopally ordained men in 1660, there was, of necessity, a large amount of continuity between those who served in the Cromwellian and in the Restoration Church. As many as 183 (60 per cent) parishes in the diocese in 1663 were filled by incumbents who had served cures or been to university during the 1650s.[12] Such continuity was common partly because there were in 1660 no theological or doctrinal tests.

GEOGRAPHIC, SOCIAL, AND EDUCATIONAL BACKGROUNDS OF THE PARISH CLERGY

The social status and educational experience of the parish clergy in the century and a half after the Restoration has been a subject of historical debate. In its crudest form, the received opinion is that the parish clergy were on the whole of low social status and poor education until later in the eighteenth century, when the sons of the gentry were attracted into the Church

[10] G. L. Ignjatijevic, 'The Parish Clergy in the Diocese of Canterbury and Archdeaconry of Bedford in the Reign of Charles I and under the Commonwealth', unpub. University of Sheffield Ph.D. thesis, 1986, 226.

[11] Everitt, *Kent*, 300.

[12] Information from LPL MS 1126. John Spurr suggests that perhaps 70% of all parish ministers had remained in possession of their benefices till their death or the Restoration: *Restoration Church of England*, 6. Of the 194 Warwickshire clergy in possession after 1662, 29 had served from the 1630s, 15 from the 1640s, and 46 from the 1650s: Salter, 'Warwickshire Clergy', ii.

because livings had become more profitable, thanks to agricultural improvement or enclosure. This fits in with the view of the period as one of growing gentry domination of the Church.[13] The Canterbury evidence, as we shall see, modifies such an interpretation.

Although there was a group of local families who provided personnel for the parishes, even in the period between 1660 and 1690 less than 40 per cent of the incumbents whose geographical origins are known were natives of Kent (see Table 2).[14] Nearly 15 per cent came from the London area, reflecting the close connections between the capital and the diocese.[15] Several of those born in London were in fact sent to the King's School in Canterbury. A high percentage (46 per cent) came from further afield, showing the national mobility towards the south-east, and the high proportion of ecclesiastical patronage in the diocese, which exercised a greater pull than in other regions. The geographical mobility of the archbishops and the cathedral clergy was largely responsible for promoting clergy from without the area, and illustrates the ways in which the Church in the Canterbury diocese drew on a national patronage network. In 1682 Jonathan Maude, from Halifax, was presented by the dean and chapter to Tenterden; a note in the chapter act-book reveals that he was a 'kinsman of Mr. Dean'.[16] Archbishop Herring brought John Langhorne to Folkestone from the diocese of York in 1753. He had caught the archbishop's eye by preaching vigorously against the 1745 Jacobite rebellion,[17] and Secker was congratulated in 1759 for 'transplanting into your diocese so valuable a stock' as Thomas Forster from the diocese of Oxford.[18] So too, Manners Sutton promoted Christopher Wordsworth to Woodchurch in 1816, whom he had ordained when bishop of Norwich in 1797. In the Restoration era a few of the clergy came from as far off as Scotland, Wales, and France. In 1661 it was noted of John Lodowick that he was 'a Fleming lately put in'.[19] The continental connection

---

[13] Virgin, *Church in Age of Negligence*, 110–14.

[14] These included the families of Bate, Boys, Harvey, Waterhouse, Dering, Honeywood, Papillon, and Marsh. Likewise, in the diocese of Chichester in the early eighteenth century, just over 30% of clergy were born in the diocese: Chamberlain, 'Sussex', 61.

[15] P. Laslett, 'The Gentry of Kent in 1640', *Cambridge Historical Journal*, 9 (1948), 152. See also C. W. Chalklin, *Seventeenth Century Kent: A Social and Economic History* (2nd edn., Rochester, 1975), 218.

[16] CCAL Act Book, 1672–1710, fo. 57.

[17] Quoted in G. M. Ditchfield and B. Keith-Lucas (eds.), *A Kentish Parson. Selections from the Private Papers of the Revd Joseph Price of Brabourne, 1767–1786* (Stroud, 1991), 137.

[18] LPL MS 1133, fo. 8, Bentham to Secker, 12 June 1759.

[19] Ibid., MS 1126, fo. 17. Lodowick is an example of a cleric who was beneficed in the early years of the Restoration perhaps because of a shortage of totally qualified candidates. But by the 1680s he attracted the attention of diocesan officials for his shoddy credentials: Bodl. MS Tanner 33, fos. 176–8. He was later dismissed: CCAL, U3/30/8/2, fos. 2–4. At Godmersham,

TABLE 2. *Geographical, Social, and Educational Backgrounds of the Parish Clergy, 1660–1828*

	1660–90	1690–1720	1720–50	1750–80	1780–1810	1810–28
Geographic origins percentage (of those known)						
Kent	39.5	40.0	39.0	38.4	38.2	22.2
London	14.5	18.2	16.0	11.0	12.3	18.8
Other	46.0	41.8	45.0	50.6	49.4	58.9
Unknown	36.0	31.0	35.0	34.0	35.0	13.0
Social origins percentage (of those known)						
Noble	0.0	0.0	1.5	1.0	1.6	3.4
Gentry	28.0	29.4	39.0	32.0	35.0	65.0
Clergy	23.0	32.0	34.5	38.0	37.7	20.0
Professional[a]	1.0	1.0	1.0	1.5	4.2	6.9
Plebeian	48.0	37.6	24.0	27.5	14.2	8.6
Unknown	34.0	38.0	37.0	34.0	32.0	20.0
Educational origins percentage (of those known)						
Oxford	30.4	35.0	43.9	51.0	53.0	57.0
Cambridge	65.7	62.5	53.8	48.0	37.5	38.8
CCCC[b]	10.0	18.0	5.5	7.7	8.8	3.1
Elsewhere	3.9	2.5				
Unknown	29.0	27.0	26.0	28.0	20.0	15.0
Publication	8.0	10.0	8.0	8.0	12.0	11.0
Further careers (numbers)						
Chaplain	20	38	26	23	17	14
Prebendary	21	10	17	14	18	12
Minor Canon	13	8	11	8	16	4
Six Preacher	17	10	4	8	12	3
Total beneficed	445	237	217	285	263	130

[a] Physician or lawyer.
[b] Those attending Corpus Christi College, Cambridge.

These figures do not include assistant curates. Clergy are recorded on their first appointment to a Canterbury living. The higher number appointed in the Restoration period reflects the greater turnover because of the ejections of 1660–2 and the fact that many restored in 1660 were significantly older than most clergy on their initial presentation.

remained strong throughout the eighteenth century because of the Huguenot and Walloon communities who settled in Canterbury, Sandwich, and elsewhere in the diocese after persecution in Europe. At least twenty-three Anglican clergy in the eighteenth century in the diocese had Walloon backgrounds. Some, like Gerald de Gols, were educated at Leyden. He was the

because of old age and unsuitability, four vicars were presented between 1660 and 1664: T. Tatton-Brown, 'The Parish Church of St. Laurence, Godmersham: A History', *AC*, 106 (1989), 62.

incumbent of St Peter's, Sandwich (1706–37), as well as being the minister of the Dutch congregation there. Several were presented by Wake, reflecting his ecumenical interests.[20]

The social origins of the parish clergy can only be estimated roughly since the sources are often vague or incomplete. In this analysis, university registers have been heavily relied on, but there are many 'unknowns' and thus the picture is tentative. The Oxford registers used social categories such as 'nobility', 'gentleman', 'clergyman', and 'plebeian', whilst the Cambridge registers recorded institutional categories (fellow-commoner, pensioner, sizar), although the father's occupation was often noted as well. Such categorization is notoriously imprecise, leading Peter Virgin to omit Oxford-educated clergy from his recent study of the profession. The term 'plebeian' in the Oxford registers, for example, was used to cover a broad social spectrum, ranging from the genuinely poor to prosperous merchants, and some described their fathers in this way in order to avoid higher fees payable at matriculation. Nevertheless, Macaulay's picture of the Restoration clergy, which can also be found in modern studies, is substantially incorrect for the diocese of Canterbury. He portrayed the clergy as split into two sharply contrasted groups, the well educated and well born, 'found without scarcely a single exception, at the universities, at the great Cathedrals, or in the Capital', and the rural clergy who were 'ignorant plebeians'.[21] There certainly was a wide variety in social origins, but the parish clergy cannot be described as 'low born and ignorant'. Ian Green has shown how successful the Church had been in the decades before 1640 in attracting ordinands from the middling and upper ranks of society, and this continued to be the case after 1660.[22]

Over a quarter of those beneficed in the diocese between 1660 and 1690 whose origins can be traced were the sons of gentry. In practice the percentage was rather less, since 'unknowns' were more likely to be the sons of plebeians. Ecclesiastical historians have tended to criticize heavy gentry recruitment to the clergy, seeing it as a threat to clerical identity, but as early as 1692 Edward Chamberlayne believed that it was beneficial if the Church attracted the gentry, since this showed that the profession possessed

---

[20] Sykes, *Wake*, ii. 1–89. In 1721, for example, he collated John Henry Ott, the son of the Archdeacon of Zurich, to Blackmanstone. Ott acted as Wake's representative in negotiations in France and Switzerland.

[21] Virgin, *Church in Age of Negligence*, 281; T. B. Macaulay, *The History of England from the Accession of James II*, 4 vols. (1906 edn.), i. 246.

[22] I. M. Green, 'Career Prospects and Clerical Conformity in Early Stuart England', *Past and Present*, 90 (1981), 73–6.

standing within society.[23] And in relations with the landowning classes it may have been a positive advantage that the Church was represented by people who could deal with them more or less as equals. This contrasts with the situation in France where there was a marked fall in the social backgrounds of the parish clergy, and a corresponding decline in the way in which the profession was perceived.[24] However, there was never the wholesale domination by the gentry which was supposed to have made the second half of the eighteenth century the age of the 'fox-hunting parson'. Very few sons of the nobility held a parochial benefice (the few who did revealing the attractiveness of the Church as a profession to this social group after 1740, and in particular after 1810), and at the other end of the scale, the sons of plebeians did not disappear. Over a quarter (27.5 per cent) of those appointed between 1750 and 1780 were of plebeian origins. Such findings mirror evidence from elsewhere in Europe. Over 20 per cent of ordinands in the diocese of Lyons in the mid-eighteenth century were from the lower orders.[25] The typical European parish priest of the ancien régime was less of a cultural alien within the parish than the simple popular/elite sociological model might suggest.[26]

None the less, from the 1720s those of low social origin were becoming an increasing minority within the diocesan clergy, and this contrasts with the still largely plebeian clergy of the pre Civil War era.[27] A prime reason for this was the decline in the number of undergraduates from poorer backgrounds after 1700, since the general costs of a university degree had increased by the early eighteenth century, and the sizar system was in decay.[28] The gradual shift from this social group in clerical recruitment had less to do with any Church policy than with the composition of the universities which provided the Church with its personnel. However, the decrease in the number of clergy with plebeian origins was a consequence of a move in

---

[23] [E. Chamberlayne], *Angliae Notitia; or, the Present State of England* 2 vols. (18th edn. 1692), ii. 207–8.

[24] T. Tackett, 'The Social History of the Diocesan Clergy in Eighteenth Century France', in R. M. Golden (ed.), *Church, State and Society under the Bourbon Kings of France* (Kansas, 1982), 333. See also A. J. La Volpa, *Grace, Talent and Merit: Poor Students, Clerical Careers and the Clerical Profession in Eighteenth Century Germany* (Cambridge, 1988).

[25] P. T. Hoffman, *Church and Community in the Diocese of Lyon, 1500–1789* (New Haven, Conn., 1984), 158.

[26] P. Burke, *Popular Culture in Early Modern Europe* (1978), 207–81.

[27] D. M. Barratt, 'The Condition of the Parish Clergy between the Reformation and 1660', unpub. Oxford University D.Phil. thesis, 1949, 4–6.

[28] In the mid-eighteenth century there were only 20 servitors in the whole of the University of Oxford: L. Sutherland, *Politics and Finance in the Eighteenth Century*, ed. A. Newman (1984), 560, 840.

favour not only of those from gentry backgrounds, but also of those from clerical and professional families. The substantial number whose fathers had also been incumbents was instrumental in advancing a sense of 'professionalism' and group identity within the Church. In some ways, despite the anti-clericalism and hostility to clerical separatism which had been a driving force behind the acceptance of the Reformation in Kent and remained the classic way of demonstrating the useful social role of Anglican clergy vis-à-vis their popish rivals, it can be suggested that the late seventeenth- and eighteenth-century Church fostered a new kind of clericalism, based upon family service and clerical connections. Evidence for this can be found in the growth of clerical dynasties. These do not appear to have been very common among the later Stuart clergy, if the evidence of Leicestershire is typical: in Canterbury, however, they can be seen increasing as the eighteenth century progressed.[29]

The Bagnall family was one such dynasty. William, a native of the diocese, was rector of Badlesmere from 1662 until his death in 1713. His sons were beneficed in the diocese. Henry, after being curate to John Johnson at Appledore in 1698, was presented to Hawkhurst (1704-26), Lympne (1723-48), and Frittenden (1726-37). Thomas was presented to Chillenden in 1710. Henry's son, also Henry, was the rector of Shadoxhurst (1734-61), and succeeded his father at Frittenden (1737-61). Clerical dynasties might affect the nature of the profession in several ways. They could provide a sense of continuity between the parishioners and the clergy, and to some degree they allowed prospective clergy to gain an insight into the demands of the profession before ordination, ensuring that many recruits already had direct experience of clerical life as the son of a parish minister. This trend is visible in other professions; it is in the late seventeenth and early eighteenth centuries that Geoffrey Holmes has established the really dramatic development of family professional groupings.[30]

Those from clerical backgrounds were, however, never a majority, and although their percentage increased for most of the period under review, the years after 1810 saw a decline in this group (although the evidence may well

---

[29] Pruett, *Leicestershire Clergy*, 36. In the diocese of Exeter in the early eighteenth century the largest group of clergy came from clerical backgrounds: Smith, 'Exeter', 287. Similar evidence has been found for the diocese of Durham: J. C. Shuler, 'The Pastoral and Ecclesiastical Administration of the Diocese of Durham, 1721-71: With Particular Reference to the Archdeaconry of Northumberland', unpub. University of Durham Ph.D. thesis, 1975, 24. The evidence for Canterbury also accords with Paul Langford's findings that in the archdeaconries of Chichester, Dorset, and Gloucester 40% of clergy between 1750 and 1775 had clerical fathers: Langford, 'English Clergy and the American Revolution', 304.

[30] Holmes, *Augustan Professions*, 107-8, 208. See also A. Everitt, 'Dynasty and Community since the Seventeenth Century', in id., *Landscape and Community in England* (1985), 327.

be misleading since matriculation registers were now more likely to record wealthy clergy as 'gentlemen' rather than as 'clergymen').[31] Other groups which provided sons who entered the Church included the medical profession. Not only were clergy drawn from medical backgrounds, but in some parishes they continued to perform a semi-medical function. During the Restoration era several became ordained having previously studied for other careers, especially medicine, because of the disruption caused to the clerical profession during the Interregnum.[32] In looking for more preferment in 1683 Robert Coombe, who had been curate of Appledore for fifteen years, stressed that he had 'some skill in physick'.[33] This talent was encouraged by writers on the clerical profession. It was held that the clergyman should be physician to the body as well as the soul, and clergy in the diocese saw it as a legitimate part of their function to publish on medical matters.[34] It might be thought that subsidiary occupations such as this reduced pastoral effectiveness by robbing clergy of valuable time. However, such occupations may have enhanced contacts with their parishioners.[35] Law was another profession which provided recruits for the ministry, and several clergy had law degrees.[36] In shaping the complexion and attitudes of the eighteenth-century clergy, connections with professional groups may have been as decisive as the traditional concentration on links with the landed gentry.

The educational background of the parish clergy was a matter of concern to the diocesan officials. Ever since the Reformation the ideal of a graduate ministry at the parochial level had been something for which the hierarchy had striven, and this had strengthened the ties between the Church and the universities. In 1570 200 of the lower clergy in the diocese

---

[31] See Virgin, *Church in Age of Negligence*, 281.

[32] Holmes, *Augustan Professions*, 109. Tenison, Hooper, and Secker all had some medical training.

[33] Bodl. MS Tanner 33, fo. 246, Thorp to Sancroft, 6 Mar. 1683. See also MS Tanner 125, fo. 22, where complaints were made at the 1682 visitation about John Bate, the incumbent of All Saints, Hope, who had 'abandoned his function for his practice of Physic'.

[34] Gilbert Burnet, *A Discourse of the Pastoral Care* (1692), 183. For examples of clergy writing on medical matters: Theodore Delafaye, *A Vindication of a Sermon entitled Inoculation an Indefensible Practice in which Dr Kirkpatrick's Arguments in Favour of the Operation are Consider'd and Repli'd To* (1754); Edmund Marshall, *A Candid and Impartial State of the Evidence of a Very Great Probability, that there is Discovered . . . a Specific for the Gout* (Canterbury, 1770).

[35] Smith, *Oldham*, 80.

[36] In the late eighteenth century 5.5% of those admitted to Lincoln's Inn were later ordained: P. Lucas, 'A Collective Biography of the Students and Barristers of Lincoln's Inn', *Journal of Modern History*, 46 (1974), 238. Frances Hender Foote (incumbent of Boughton Malherbe, 1751–73) is an example of a barrister who took orders: Hasted, *History of Kent*, v. 3.

were classified as *non gradus*, representing a clear educational gap between the higher and lower clergy.[37] By 1637 90 per cent of Canterbury incumbents had attended universities, and 87 per cent had degrees, confirming D. M. Barratt's assertion that by 1642 only a tiny percentage of the parish clergy were non graduate.[38] Thereafter, the dislocation within the profession caused by the Civil War led to a dramatic fall in the numbers of university men amongst the clergy. By 1662 only 69 per cent of beneficed clergy in the diocese had been to university and only 66 per cent had degrees.[39] In the years immediately following the Restoration the shortage of suitably qualified clergy meant that the Church had to rely on those whom the hierarchy deemed to be under-educated. Not surprisingly they caused problems. Thomas Phillips of Headcorn, for example, was considered in 1663 to be 'a poor and mean qualified man', and five years later he was prosecuted for scandal and suspended.[40] By the end of the seventeenth century, however, it was an exception to be a non graduate in the Canterbury diocese; the result of the efforts of Restoration archbishops to form a well-educated parochial force. Sancroft's articles of 1685 decreed that no one should be ordained without being a graduate.[41] The interest shown by the hierarchy in educational qualifications was part of its attempt to differentiate its clergy from the supposedly badly educated dissenting ministers, and its need for a cadre of interpreters who could impose orthodoxy on the parishes.

The gap between the higher and lower clergy in matters of education was closing by the late seventeenth century. Whilst there were enormous divisions in the wealth of clergy, in Canterbury their educational experience was increasingly homogeneous, and those clergy who were not graduates had little chance of promotion to a benefice. In 1681 Samuel Pratt hoped that 'my not being a graduate may not rank me in exemption for holy orders with ye most profligate villaine'.[42] In other dioceses the move of the clerical body to an overwhelmingly graduate status can also be found, though it was not always so marked. In the late seventeenth century only 32 per cent of clergy in the poorer diocese of St David's were graduates.[43] It may be that better

[37] Bodl. MS Eng. Lett c. 43, fos. 86–7.   [38] Barratt, 'Parish Clergy', 86–7.

[39] Ignjatijevic, 'Canterbury', 33.   [40] LPL MS 1126, fo. 37.

[41] David Wilkins, *Concilia Magnae Britanniae et Hiberniae*, 4 vols. (1737), iv. 612–14.

[42] Bodl. MS Tanner 36*, fo. 114, Samuel Pratt to Thorp, 11 Sept. 1681.

[43] G. H. Jenkins, *Literature, Religion and Society in Wales, 1660–1730* (Cardiff, 1978), 213. Between 1660 and 1672 12.5% of Warwickshire clergy did not have a degree: Salter, 'Warwickshire Clergy', i. 51. As late as the 1740s the clergy of the diocese of York were often not graduates: *Archbishop Herring's Visitation Returns, 1743*, ed. S. L. Ollard and P. C. Walker, The Yorkshire Archaeological Society, Record Series, 71, 72, 75, 77 (1928–32), introduction, p. xx. This is indicative of the regionalism which has to be borne in mind in discussing the clerical

qualified men were more attracted to the centre of the province of Canterbury. Nevertheless, Secker admitted as late as 1763, 'What you say of ordaining persons without academical distinctions is very just, and not confined to the distant counties. I have found such ordinations necessary in Kent'.[44]

Attendance at a university meant that future parish clergy would meet others there who would follow a similar career, which helped to provide a basis for a sense of shared identity. Contacts made at universities could prove important both for careers and for the consolidation of the clerical profession as a whole. The overall numbers of those matriculating at Oxford and Cambridge declined in the period after 1660, ensuring that they became more like clerical seminaries than they had been in the previous century.[45] For reasons of proximity Cambridge was the 'natural' university for Kentish incumbents. In the Restoration period nearly two-thirds of the clergy who attended a university were Cambridge graduates. Scholarships from the King's School reinforced this bias, as scholars were encouraged to go to Corpus Christi College and Emmanuel. The original Canterbury scholarships, founded by Archbishop Parker in 1569, were augmented in 1728 by Dean Stanhope, who gave £250 for an exhibition.[46] Prebendary George Thorp left lands and buildings in Ash, in 1719, for the endowment of five exhibitions to enable BAs to reside until they had taken their MAs, with preference to 'the sons of orthodox ministers of the Church of England from the diocese of Canterbury, and educated at the King's School'.[47] In 1775 the dean and chapter purchased £50 worth of stock in New South Sea Annuities to augment these exhibitions.[48] Most of those who were awarded these scholarships returned to the diocese after ordination, such as Thomas Paramour, later rector of East Langdon; John Bunce, vicar of Brenzett; William Halford, vicar of Egerton.[49]

The King's School scholarships were not the only ones available to prospective clergy. In 1658 John Smith of Wickhambreux gave £15 p.a. for

profession: Fincham, *Prelate as Pastor*, 182. Nevertheless, it was still quite common to go to university but not to take a degree: this was the case of George Hearne, who matriculated at Trinity Hall in 1743, and was collated to St Alphege's, Canterbury in 1761.

44 Quoted in Nichols, *Literary Anecdotes*, v. 487, Secker to Archdeacon Robinson, 5 Dec. 1759.

45 J. A. Venn, 'Matriculations at Oxford and Cambridge, 1544–1906', *Oxford and Cambridge Review* (1908), 48–66; L. Stone, 'The Size and Composition of the Oxford Student Body', in id. (ed.), *The University in Society*, 2 vols. (1974), i. 3–110.

46 Masters, *Corpus Christi*, 34.   47 Hasted, *History of Kent*, x. 513.

48 CCAL, Chapter Act Book, 1761–1775, fo. 360.

49 LPL MS 1125, fo. 303. James Ford, son of a minor canon at Canterbury founded the Ford Lectureships in 1788 to tighten links between Canterbury and the universities: D. L. Edwards, *History of the King's School, Canterbury* (1957), 116.

the maintenance of a student at Lincoln College, Oxford for eight years, enabling the holder to stay on after taking a BA for theological work.[50] A striking 9 per cent of all incumbents in the diocese appointed between 1660 and 1828 whose educational experience can be traced were Corpus Christi men. This concentration has parallels in other dioceses. In the late seventeenth century 24.3 per cent of the Oxford-educated parish clergy in the Hereford diocese had been to Brasenose, and a large number of clergy in the Exeter diocese had attended Exeter College, Oxford.[51] But the Cambridge monopoly declined and after 1750 was reversed, possibly because Potter, Secker, and Moore had close connections with Oxford and brought Oxford-educated clergy into the diocese.

A further indication that Macaulay's assessment of the low academic credentials of the parish clergy was too crude is provided by the proportion of those who managed to get their work into print. Of the incumbents appointed between 1660 and 1690, 8 per cent published some item, as far as can be traced, and this proportion reached 12 per cent in the last quarter of the eighteenth century. Parish clergy in the diocese were not the 'silent clerical proletariat' envisaged by John Spurr; rather, through publication, and through reading the publications of their fellow clergy, they were able to participate in some of the issues of the day, which helped further a sense of common endeavour and concern.[52] In many areas of clerical debate it was the parish clergy who led the field.

The clergy's critics did not deny that most had had a university education; rather they complained that prospective ordinands received the wrong type of training there. John Eachard's criticisms in the 1670s were taken up by nineteenth-century reformers who bemoaned the lack of specifically pastoral or theological instruction,[53] which seemed symptomatic of a Church dominated by secular concerns. However, research into university life in this period suggests that not all future incumbents followed a completely secular course. In any case, after the Restoration the MA (where theological studies were pursued) became the most common degree, and those with only BAs were more likely to remain unbeneficed. Reading lists

---

[50] Hasted, *History of Kent*, x. 45.

[51] W. M. Marshall, 'The Administration of the Dioceses of Hereford and Oxford, 1660–1760', University of Bristol Ph.D. thesis, 1978, 102; Smith, 'Exeter', 287.

[52] Information taken from D. Wing, *Short Title Catalogue, 1641–1700*, 3 vols. (1945–51) and F. J. G. Robinson, *et al.*, *Eighteenth Century British Books: An Author Union Catalogue*, 5 vols. (Folkestone and Newcastle upon Tyne, 1981); Spurr, *Restoration Church*, p. xv.

[53] John Eachard, *The Grounds and Occasions of the Contempt of the Clergy* (1670). Many of these criticisms were not ignored by the Church hierarchy. Wake, indeed, agreed with them: Bodl. MS Ballard 3, fo. 64, Wake to Charlett, 27 June 1716.

which survive indicate how thorough and wide-ranging theological reading was supposed to be. Dean Stanhope, in a letter 'to a young relation' (*c*.1710), advised the student to obtain an interleaved Bible into which he could add remarks from his reading of the Fathers; he should also read Stillingfleet and Tillotson, to understand the pastoral role of a clergyman.[54] Thomas Curteis, vicar of Wrotham, published in 1725 an *Advice to a Son at the University, designed for Holy Orders*, which is a revealing indication of what one clergyman connected to the diocese saw as necessary training and preparation for the aspirant pastor. His ordinand son was instructed to read St Chrysostom on the sacred function of the clergy, and urged to be 'conversant in the ecclesiastical writings of the past ages, the collection of those genuine epistles published by Wake; the works of St. Julian Martyr, of St. Irenaeus, St. Clement Alexandrius, St. Cyprian, St. Gregory, St. Ambrose and St. Jerome.' Curteis also recommended modern authors: 'Bishops Bull, Pearson, Stillingfleet; Chillingworth, Archbishop Tillotson, Hooker, Potter's *Of Church Government* . . .'.[55] The list is interesting not least since it urges the study of patristics. Later High-Churchmen lamented that the Fathers were little read during the Hanoverian period,[56] yet they are here prescribed undergraduate reading. Curteis concluded his advice by warning his son not to spend too much time on the classics,[57] a corrective to the impression that eighteenth-century clergy, and universities in general, were under the spell of the classical authors. Clergy were generally well aware of the potential dangers of the Enlightenment's admiration for the pagans of the ancient world. William Jones of Pluckley exhorted ordinands in 1769 to read the Fathers, for he believed that the destruction of Christianity would be brought about 'by this growing

---

[54] Quoted in Weeden Butler, *Some Account of the Life and Writings of the Reverend Dr George Stanhope* (1797), 73.

[55] Thomas Curteis, *Advice to a Son at the University, designed for Holy Orders* (1725), 74–6. The 'advice' seems to have worked—his son became a Canterbury prebendary (stall XI, 1755–75). For Curteis senior see L. P. Curtis, *Chichester Towers* (New Haven, Conn., and London, 1965), 90–101; Sykes, *Church and State*, 175–6; and Jeffrey S. Chamberlain, 'The Limits of Moderation in a Latitudinarian Parson: or, High-Church Zeal in a Low Churchman Discover'd', in Roger D. Lund (ed.), *The Margins of Orthodoxy. Heterodox Writing and Orthodox Response* (Cambridge, 1995), 195–215. Secker informed one candidate whom he had failed that 'my reason for it was that a minister of a parish is to teach his people, not mathematics or natural philosophy, but the word of God and [you] appeared to me surprisingly ignorant of the content of the Bible': LPL MS Secker 3, fo. 147, Secker to Matthew Kenrick, 26 Apr. 1762.

[56] G. V. Bennett, 'Patristic Tradition in Anglican Thought, 1660–1900', *Oecumenia* (Gutersloh, 1972), 63–76; Sykes, *Sheldon to Secker*, 142.

[57] Curteis, *Advice*, 76.

affection to heathenism'.[58] The prominence of Archbishop Tillotson in these reading lists is significant. It has been suggested of Tillotson that he broke with the theology of his predecessors as archbishops of Canterbury by believing that natural religion and revealed were very nearly the same, and he has often been castigated for ushering in Deism into the Anglican Church.[59] The jibes against the 'paganism' of archbishops such as Tillotson were, however, a propagandist charge, owing less to his actual beliefs than to his taking of the oaths to William and Mary.[60]

At the universities, dominated by clerical fellows, the aspiring clergyman could gain an understanding of his future career. In 1773 Beilby Porteus (an intimate of Secker's and rector of Ruckinge from 1764 to 67) proposed the introduction of lectures on pastoral care at Oxford, and he reported that in many colleges fellows ably expounded the 'fundamentals of revelation'.[61] By the end of the century bishops were requiring candidates to attend the divinity lectures at Oxford—first instituted by Edward Bentham in 1764— and the Norrisian Lectures at Cambridge. It has been argued that the intention behind the founding of theological seminaries by Tractarians and Evangelicals after the 1830s was to provide graduates with a grounding in the knowledge of the Christian tradition, supervision in developing professional skills such as preaching and pastoral care, and guidance in the acquisition of an appropriate life-style. Yet these ends were also being pursued by the hierarchy in the previous century. Indeed it might be suggested that many nineteenth-century 'reformers' destroyed some of their forebears' methods of clerical education when they sold the parochial libraries built up by their eighteenth-century predecessors for the promotion of clerical, and to some extent lay, learning.[62]

---

[58] Quoted in W. H. Teale, *Lives of English Divines* (1846), 363. See also William Jones, 'A Letter to a Young Gentleman at Oxford, intended for Holy Orders' (1769), in his *Works*, i. 243–300. This was originally a visitation sermon preached before Secker at Ashford in 1766. Jones's fear of the Enlightenment can also be seen in his 'Letter from a Tutor to his Pupils', ibid., xi. 201–43, which was written whilst he was the rector of Pluckley (1765–77).

[59] H. R. McAdoo, *The Spirit of Anglicanism. A Survey of Anglican Theological Method in the Seventeenth Century* (1965), 175.

[60] G. R. Reedy, *The Bible and Reason. Anglicans and Scripture in Late Seventeenth-Century England* (Philadelphia, 1975), 81. See J. Marshall, 'The Ecclesiology of the Latitude Men, 1660–1689: Stillingfleet, Tillotson and "Hobbism"', *JEH*, 36 (1985), 407–27. Also John Williams, A *Vindication of the Sermons of Archbishop Tillotson Concerning the Divinity and Incarnation of our Blessed Saviour* (1695).

[61] R. Hodgson, *Life of Beilby Porteus* (1810), 18. D. A. Winstanley, *The University of Cambridge in the Eighteenth Century* (Cambridge, 1922), 176.

[62] N. Yates, 'The Parochial Library of All Saints, Maidstone, and other Kentish Parochial Libraries', *AC*, 99 (1983), 163.

Archbishop Secker published the most comprehensive work on pastoral care in this period, in the series of charges which he delivered to his clergy, first as bishop of Oxford, and then as archbishop.[63] They were issued free to the clergy of his dioceses and elsewhere. Secker's Charges went some way to make up for the lack of pastoral training, covering a wide range of topics from how to deliver a sermon to the ways in which clergy should deal with refractory parishioners. The charges articulated the tension in the clergy's role, the need to win the support of society, yet without sacrificing clerical ideals.[64]

ORDINATION AND WORK EXPERIENCE

One way in which archbishops were able to influence the complexion of the diocesan clergy was by their control of ordination. Orders were issued to suffragan bishops in an attempt to regulate the standards of those entering the profession.[65] This was especially necessary in the years after the Restoration; not only was episcopal ordination used as a touchstone of conformity, but there is some indication that the temporary shortage of available clergy meant that bishops were forced to ordain those who in Sheldon's eyes were 'unworthy persons that ... have crept into the ministry'. Through stricter regulations concerning ordination archbishops hoped to improve the quality of their profession. As Edward Hughes has shown, the financial cost of entering the ministry was significantly lower than for other professions and standards had to be maintained by a careful regard to ordination.[66] For most of the period under review, archbishops held ordinations at Lambeth for those to be created deacon or priest for the Canterbury

---

[63] Thomas Secker, *Eight Charges Delivered to the Clergy of the Dioceses of Oxford and Canterbury* (1769).

[64] Ibid., 206, 166.

[65] Sheldon's 'Orders and Instructions concerning Ordination', 7 July 1665 was reprinted in Wilkins, *Concilia*, iv. 582; Sancroft's 'Directions from the Archbishop of Canterbury to his Suffragans' of 1678, ibid., 600; Sancroft's Articles, ibid., 612–14. See also the *Instructions given by the King's Majesty for the Better Regulation of Ordination and Institutions to the Archbishops of this Realm* (1695); Bodl. MS Tanner 25, fo. 13: Tillotson's circular letter demanding strict care about ordinations and testimonials. See also Wake's letter of 5 June 1716 in Wilkins, *Concilia*, iv. 670–1; [John Potter], *The Archbishop of Canterbury's Letter to the Right Reverend Lord Bishops of his Province* (Stamford, 1737); [Thomas Secker], 'The Archbishop's Directions to the Bishops of his Province, Concerning Orders and Curates, 1759', in John Bacon, *Liber Regis* (1785), appendix; and C. Hodgson, *Instructions for the Use of Candidates for Holy Orders* (1817).

[66] Wilkins, *Concilia*, iv. 582; E. Hughes, 'The Professions in the Eighteenth Century', *Durham University Journal*, 44 (1952), 55.

diocese, although visitations provided an opportunity to ordain in the diocese itself (as Wake did in Canterbury Cathedral in 1720).[67] Manners Sutton established a trend for ordaining much more regularly at Canterbury from 1808 onwards, thereby helping to strengthen the links between the archbishop and his diocese in the early nineteenth century; this was a trend which would be followed by archbishops after 1828.[68] Information from the registers also shows that some archbishops ordained more frequently than others; Secker, for example, ordained regularly, but others issued more letters dimissory. Sheldon, because of his commitments at Court in the late 1660s and early 1670s, seems to have relied on other bishops to ordain Canterbury clergy.[69]

The canons of 1604 remained the basic guide to ordination requirements. In the diocese these were followed, although they were not always observed in full: prospective clergy were sometimes ordained deacon and priest in one day. In attempting to ensure the quality of their appointments, archbishops urged the need for detailed and realistic testimonials from other clerics. In 1731 Dean Lynch informed Samuel Pegge, who wanted promotion:

It is necessary for you to have testimonials for the three last years, and as they have been divided between college, Sundridge and Bishopsbourne, you must bring one from each of those places for such time as you have resided in them, that you may not err in forms pray transcribe out of Ecton's *Liber Valorum*, for we are very exact here in these things.[70]

There is some evidence to suggest that the Church hierarchy used these clerical connections as a kind of quality control for the profession. In 1759 Secker pointed out the usefulness of testimonials in the selection of ministers, for 'when a clergyman is shunned by most of his Brethren, it may very well set him to examine himself strictly whether he hath given them no occasion for it, or temptation to it'.[71] Archbishops stressed that candidates needed to show a sufficient knowledge of theology, and they and their chaplains were able to test this in their examinations. Secker wrote 'Instructions given to candidates for orders after their subscribing to the articles', which advised the ordinand how to prepare himself for office:

spend a due share of the Remainder of this Day in what, I trust, hath employed not a little of your Time already; weighing diligently the Nature and Importance of the

---

[67] LPL, VB 1/6, 311.   [68] LPL, VB 1/13, 336.

[69] This explains the number of letters dimissory for Canterbury clergy; see LPL, VB 1/1–15.

[70] Bodl. MS Eng. d. 43, fo. 315, Lynch to Pegge, 3 June 1731.

[71] LPL MS Secker 3, fo. 206, Secker to George Burnett, 6 July 1759.

undertaking, which you are about to engage . . . and earnestly begging that Grace of God, which alone can make you able ministers of the New Testament.[72]

After ordination, valuable professional experience could be gained whilst serving as a curate. Curates were employed for a variety of reasons. They might serve the cure whilst the incumbent was absent through pluralism, or incapacitated through illness or old age. In his 'Speculum' Secker was careful to record the names of curates, with their qualifications. He had complained in his charge of 1758 that many curates in the diocese had not obtained a licence, and although he admitted that these could be expensive, he insisted:

you cannot think it right that I should be left in Ignorance, who serves a Church under my Care, till I learn it by Accident, or private inquiry . . . through which Omission Men of Bad character . . . might intrude . . . I am far from looking on the past failures of giving notice, as designed Negligence of your flocks . . . but I shall have cause both to think of them and treat them as such, if continued after the Warning which I now give that no one is to officiate, or employ another to officiate . . . unless he first obtain my consent . . .[73]

It was often difficult for the diocesan hierarchy to know exactly who curates were, since their turnover could be rapid. Appledore, for instance, had forty-three curates between 1660 and 1828.[74] This was because curacies were often a step on the ladder to acquiring a benefice, not an office for life. The percentage of those clergy beneficed who had previously been curates, either in the living they held, or in another, which they sometimes continued to serve with their own benefice, was fairly high: 14 per cent of those beneficed in the Restoration period, rising to 35.5 per cent between 1810 and 1828. This suggests that the idea that curates were a permanent clerical lumpen proletariat who suffered from an insufficient salary and insecure tenure needs modification.[75] Curates were more likely to be the younger clergy, who were in the process of gaining pastoral experience. It has been argued that the period after 1830 saw a shift in the role of the curate, from the stipendiary curate to the assistant curate,[76] but this is to pose too abrupt a transition. The concept of a curacy as a kind of preparation for parochial responsibility as an incumbent was also held in the eighteenth century. The growth in the number of curates might also have been an institutional response to what has been seen as the overcrowding of the clerical profession

---

[72] Thomas Secker, 'Instructions Given to Candidates for Orders', in Charges, 327–8.

[73] LPL, VG 2/5; Secker, *Charges*, 221. See also LPL MS Secker Diocesan 3, fo. 272, Secker to Pearsall, 26 Mar. 1767, demanding his right to know who was supplying the cure.

[74] Sir John Winnifrith, 'Land Ownership in Appledore, 1500–1900', *AC*, 97 (1981), 1–6.

[75] Sykes, *Church and State*, 206; Virgin, *Church in Age of Negligence*, 218–22.

[76] Haig, *Victorian Clergy*, 216–19.

by the late eighteenth century, providing at least some kind of employment for the new recruits.[77] In 1713 George Thorp wrote to Tenison on behalf of his curate John Brownrigg, supporting his application to become vicar of Herne. Thorp noted that Brownrigg

has lived in my family for four years, and hath done me very good service in the supply of my cure here, to my own and my parishioners very good satisfaction and hath behaved himself always very soberly and modestly, both by diligence in his study as well as the execution of his office.[78]

The position of the curate within the professional structure helped to ensure that the Church in Canterbury in the eighteenth century was not broken into a hierarchy of distinct career patterns. To some extent this helped to make the clergy an integrated body. Proving oneself as a humble curate might be the way to gain the attention of a patron who could provide a benefice, although this might take time. Benjamin Burridge was curate at High Halden for nearly thirty years before being finally made rector by Archbishop Secker in 1759.[79] Nevertheless this career structure is significantly different from the situation in the diocese in the sixteenth century, when, as Michael Zell has shown, the clerical profession was highly stratified, and when it was unlikely for curates ever to become beneficed.[80] It is in contrast also to the Catholic Church in Europe where friction between the upper and lower clergy grew in the eighteenth century, to produce the dissident movement of French *richerisme* among the poorer curés, with its economic and class-conscious reform programme.[81] In England, however, the Church's hierarchy attempted to alleviate the financial position of curates by trying to safeguard a minimum wage through Acts of Parliament in 1713 and 1796.[82]

MONITORING THE CLERGY

One way in which archbishops attempted to create a sense of professional identity was by exhorting the clergy to a specific type of behaviour, and

[77] Virgin, *Church in Age of Negligence*, 136–7. Henry Wharton and George Stanhope claimed that one of the advantages of pluralism was that it allowed young clergy to train as curates: *Defence of Pluralities, or Holding Two Benefices with Cure of Souls, As Now Practised in the Church of England* (1692), 191.

[78] LPL MS 953, fo. 101, Thorp to Tenison, 5 Aug. 1713.   [79] *Speculum*, 59.

[80] M. Zell, 'The Personnel of the Clergy in Kent in the Reformation Period', *EHR*, 89 (1974), 523–33.

[81] R. F. Necheles, 'The Curés in the Estates General of 1789', *Journal of Modern History*, 46 (1974), 89–114; J. McManners, *French Ecclesiastical Society under the Ancien Regime* (Manchester, 1960), 167–90.

[82] Virgin, *Church in Age of Negligence*, 222–5.

disciplining them when they fell short. In the 1680s one of Sancroft's pastoral initiatives was to revive in the diocese the office of rural dean as a kind of self-regulating mechanism by which designated clergy reported back to the archbishop on the behaviour of their fellows.[83] The office was not continued after Sancroft's deprivation and this has sometimes been instanced as another sign that the managerial energy displayed in the Restoration period soon gave way to inertia. However, in a small diocese such as Canterbury there may not have been the need for this extra tier in the diocesan administrative structure. In any case, archbishops and archdeacons often chose to exercise discipline over their diocesan clergy in a less formal and more private manner—not surprisingly when one considers the potential effect of the open censure of an incumbent on his professional relationship with parishioners. Such private regulation, usually through correspondence, was another channel by which reasonably effective communication and contact were maintained between the authorities and the parish clergy.[84]

The professional ideal of a pure and moral life was reiterated in visitation articles and sermons. It was accepted that only by living a blameless life could the clergy convince their parishioners of the truths they preached. By upholding high moral standards, Secker realized, clergy might find themselves at odds with the world around them: 'Too possibly a great part of our People may like the Lukewarm amongst us the better for Resembling themselves, and giving them no uneasiness or Comparison, but seeming to authorize their indifference. But then such of Us can do Them no good.'[85] While the clergy were encouraged to strive to uphold the dignity and purity of the clerical character, Secker also urged them not to be aloof from the life of their parishioners, warning that

clergymen, who are Serious in their whole Behaviour . . . are often too inactive amongst their People; apt to think, that if they perform regularly the Offices of the Church, exhort from the pulpit . . . and answer the Common occasional calls of Parochial duty, they have done as much as they need . . .[86]

Parishioners themselves expected their clergy to live up to these ideals of clerical behaviour. Professional identity was not merely defined from

[83] For the appointment of George Thorp to Canterbury, Giles Hinton to Charing, John Castillion to Westbere, Henry Ullock to Sandwich, William Wickens to Ospringe, and James Wilson to Sutton: Bodl. MS Tanner 124, fo. 75 (1683); MS Rawl lett. 59, fo. 100, Wilson to Sancroft, 14 Oct. 1684, complaining that Mr Green was marrying clandestinely; ibid., fo. 481, Wilson to Sancroft, 15 Nov. 1683, concerning Mr Stoughton, who neglected his cure.

[84] For some of Secker's attitudes towards disciplining his clergy see Nichols, *Literary Anecdotes*, iii. 751.

[85] Secker, *Charges*, 250.   [86] Ibid., 267–8.

within the profession: it was at times imposed upon it by the demands of the laity, who were not slow to assess the character of their pastors. In 1715, in defence of John Benson, the curate of Deal, parishioners informed Tenison of 'his sober good life, a certain demonstration to us of his being himself convinced of the sacred and tremendous truths he teaches us'. And in 1785 the inhabitants of Eastchurch, who wanted to dismiss their curate, accused of adultery, told Archbishop Moore that 'we feel that the life of a minister is the best comment upon his doctrine'.[87]

Very few clergy were, however, dismissed on account of misconduct. Samuel Bickley, the vicar of Bapchild, was deprived by Secker in 1764 on a charge of attempting to commit sodomy.[88] Since it was difficult to remove clergy from their benefices, the majority stayed within the diocese once they had been presented to a living. There was some movement in the early stages of a clergyman's career as he worked up from a curacy to a benefice, but most spent the rest of their life in the same parish or parishes. Thus some parishes in the period between 1660 and 1828 saw a remarkably low turnover of incumbents. There were, for example, only six vicars of Appledore, despite the high turnover of curates. In visitation returns clergy prided themselves on the length of time they had served in a parish, contrasting this 'stability' with the 'instability' of nonconformist preachers. In 1724 the vicar of Linton boasted to Wake that 'I have resided for 40 years and more than 38 in the same house. Have not been absent from my parish 5 months, putting all together during ye said 40 years'.[89] Such length of tenure must have had an effect on the relationship between the clergy and parishioners, though the nature of that influence depended on the character of the incumbent. In some cases this long-standing association explains much of the strength of the Church of England in this period. Historians have told us much about the unpopularity of the Church, but what has not been accounted for satisfactorily is the affection shown by parishioners for their minister during the century: an affection often based on long service and social familiarity.

It is clear that the ideal at which clerics aimed was not that of a landed gentleman. As John Firebrace wrote in 1733, 'the dignity of a clergyman and that of a modern gentleman are different things. We must be the losers by confounding them; since there will be so many to outshine us in that way,

[87] LPL MS 941, fo. 54, Churchwardens and parishioners of Deal to Tenison, 8 Nov. 1715; MS Moore 2, fo. 42, Petition of vicar, Churchwardens, and principal inhabitants of Eastchurch, 19 Aug. 1785. See also ibid., fo. 243, complaints of parishioners of Kingsdown, 27 Jan. 1785.

[88] Ibid., MS 2598, fos. 60–1.

[89] Ch. Ch. MS Wake Visitation Returns C, fo. 447.

shine we ever so brilliantly'.[90] The 'gentrification' of the clergy was not encouraged with the relish that has been assumed. Of far more concern was
the fear that the clerical ideal might be lost. One of the ways in which historians have felt that the clerical function was compromised was through participation on the magistrates' bench. The combination of clergyman and
civil magistrate, the 'squarson', has been taken as symbolic of the supposed
erosion of clerical by gentlemanly ideals in the second half of the eighteenth
century. Research, however, has indicated that this was rather more of an
early nineteenth century phenomenon (as indeed so many so called 'abuses'
of the eighteenth-century Church turn out to be), and in the Canterbury
diocese it occurred fairly infrequently. There was a convention that clerics
would not be appointed to the magistrates' bench in Kent, and proximity to
London ensured that there would usually be enough gentry in the area to
fulfil this function.[91] In any case it is not clear that participation in the
magistracy represented an intrusion on the clerical profession. As early as
1692 Edward Chamberlayne had maintained that clerics were well suited to
being magistrates:

for who so proper to make and keep peace as they whose constant duty it is to preach
peace?, who so fit as they whose main business and study is to reconcile those that
are at variance . . . since the Restoration as well as before divers grave, discrete
divines have been J.P.s . . . many differences have been composed without law suit,
in a more Christian and less expensive way.[92]

The few Canterbury clergy who were appointed magistrates meant that in
1831 the Kent Bench had only two clerical members as opposed to 145 laymen.[93] And those clergy who served as magistrates generally lived in areas
of the diocese in which there was a dearth of leading gentry.[94] Richard
Harvey, vicar of St Lawrence, Thanet (1766–93), was a member of an old

[90] John Firebrace, *The Clerical Character Considered with Respect to the Times of Improvement* (1767), 18. But see the comments in [Anon.], *A Letter Written by a Country Clergyman to
Archbishop Herring, in the Year MDCCLIV* (1771), 27–8.

[91] R. Quinault, 'The Warwickshire Magistracy and Public Order, c. 1830–1870', in
R. Quinault and J. Stevenson (eds.), *Popular Protest and Public Order* (1974), 187–9. The most
forthright defence of clerical magistrates came not from an orthodox Anglican, but from the
Unitarian, John Disney. See Disney, *Considerations on the Propriety and Expediency of the
Clergy, acting in the Commission of the Peace* (1781).

[92] Chamberlayne, *Present State of England*, 91. For the view that clerical magistracy was
harmful to the clerical profession see Langford, *Propertied Englishman*, 367.

[93] Virgin, *Church in Age of Negligence*, 285.

[94] This was also true of Derbyshire and Sussex: S. Webb and B. Webb, *English Local
Government from the Revolution to the Municipal Corporations Act*, 9 vols. (1906–29), i. 384. See
also B. Keith-Lucas, *Parish Affairs. The Government of Kent under George III* (Maidstone,
1986), p. 16.

east Kent family. He was a magistrate in the Isle of Thanet, and was the only clergyman named as a commissioner for the redemption of the Land Tax in Kent. Another clerical magistrate, John Duncombe, vicar of St Andrew's, Canterbury, maintained that the principal inducement for him in accepting office was to see justice done to the poor.[95] Henry Hall tried to influence the Duke of Dorset in 1763 to have his name placed on the commission, 'that I might be able to protect myself, and several of my parishioners, from the malicious designs of a certain person in the neighbourhood. It might likewise probably have prevented a suit which I find it necessary to commence against him'.[96] Other research has revealed that clerical JPs were more likely to settle disputes without recourse to other legal tribunals than their pre-Restoration predecessors.[97]

In the 1790s it looked as though the clerical ideal might be compromised as some clergy joined the army not as chaplains but for normal military duties. A few of the Canterbury clergy were appointed to be recruiting officers, but in general this was frowned upon in the diocese. Archbishop Moore and other bishops met at Lambeth to counter Bishop Horsley's exhortation to the Rochester clergy to sign up. Moore urged the Canterbury clergy not to abandon 'the proper business of your profession in order to take up the soldier's execution'.[98] The bishops resolved 'that it was not conducive in any considerable degree to the defence and safety of the kingdom, if the clergy were to accept commissions in the army, be installed in any military corps, or be trained to the use of arms'.[99]

PARTY AND POLITICS

One of the factors which has been seen as working against a common clerical identity was the involvement of the clergy in politics. In particular, much has been made of the existence of Church parties in the late seventeenth and early eighteenth centuries, which divided clergy into Tory and Whig. However, G. V. Bennett has reminded us of the need to penetrate the

[95] Quoted in Nichols, *Literary Anecdotes*, viii. 274.

[96] LPL MS 1163, fo. 156, Henry Hall to Ducarel, 26 Apr. 1763.

[97] N. Landau, *The Justices of the Peace, 1679–1760* (Berkeley, Calif. and Los Angeles, Calif., 1984), 191. In any case, some matters, such as licensing dissenting meeting houses seriously affected the position of the Church.

[98] 'To the Revd. the Clergy of the Diocese and Peculiars of the See of Canterbury, 29 April, 1798', *GM* (1798), 385.

[99] 'Resolution of 28 April 1798', *GM* (1798), 386. Thus, instead of taking up arms, clergy preached sermons. See Nehemiah Nisbett, *Ezekiel's Warning Applied to the Threatened Invasion of Great Britain. A Sermon Delivered at Ash 8 March 1797* (Canterbury, 1797).

party slogans of High and Low Church,[100] and the careers of the leading clerical politicians in the Canterbury diocese show that such divisions were far less clear-cut than they might seem. They also complicate the rather crude correlation which has often been made between High Church and Tory on the one hand and Low Church and Whig on the other. What is striking were the areas of common concern. John Johnson, Thomas Brett (leaders of the High-Church party), and John Lewis, a champion of the Whig interest, had all been united in their concern for pastoral improvement and their interest in historical researches; Johnson and Lewis were firm friends until the Convocation controversy tore them apart.[101] All these three had received preferment from Archbishop Tenison. Lewis was collated to St John's Margate and Eastbridge in 1706 and to Minster in 1708–46; Brett was appointed to Betteshanger in 1703 and to Ruckinge in 1705; Johnson was presented to Appledore in 1697 and to Cranbrook in 1707. The Convocation controversy created a 'parting of friends' in the diocese; Lewis remained a fervent Whig, Brett became a non-juror, and Johnson stayed in the Church but clung on to High-Church, and often non-juring, views. Brett's career is of significance since in his attempts to mobilize the High-Churchmen in the diocese he came into contact with Francis Atterbury and other leaders of the High-Church camp. It also illustrates ways in which national and local themes might coincide. In 1710 Brett and Johnson stood for election as one of the proctors for the diocese in the new Convocation.[102] Convocation is usually seen as part of the organization of the national Church, bringing together Church leaders, but it was also a unique expression of diocesan opinion. Election campaigns for a seat to represent the diocese were just as intense as those for a seat in Parliament. These occasions were an opportunity for the clergy to meet and discuss matters of common concern, and it was at such times that they saw themselves as possessing a self-consciously diocesan identity. Brett failed to be

---

[100] Bennett, *Crisis*, p. vii.

[101] Brett had been brought up as a Whig, but at school had been taught by a Mr Pratt, the curate of Gervase Needham, brother of Sancroft's chaplain, and had come across Tory views: BL Add. MS 34106, fos. 97–9. Johnson styled Lewis a 'middle region man', i.e. neither High nor Low: Add. MS 28651, fo. 15v. At *Vindication* (1714), 4 Lewis himself called Johnson a 'moderate'. Lewis was also on friendly terms with the non-juror Thomas Hearne until disputes over Whitgift: Bodl. MS Rawl. lett. fos. 162–7. See J. Shirley, 'John Lewis of Margate', *AC*, 64 (1951), 39–56.

[102] For the 1710 Convocation see G. V. Bennett, 'The Convocation of 1710: An Anglican Attempt at Counter-Revolution', *SCH*, 7 (1971), 311–19; id., *Crisis*, 125–30; Bodl., MS Eng. Th.c. 24, fo. 604: 'Papers relating to ye Proceedings at ye elections of Convocation men, 26 Oct. 1710'. For the importance of Lambeth Palace Library in the Convocation controversy see Sykes, *Gibson*, 31. Tenison gave Convocation Books to the Library: LPL MS 1163, fo. 32.

elected and, in true party style, blamed his failure on the machinations of the archdeacon. He complained that not all the clergy had been notified. Whilst all the Low-Church supporters had been cited, he claimed that many, who had promised to vote for him, had not been. Brett maintained that 'if we have no redress, ye right of election, which ye diocesan clergy have in the relation to their proctors in Convocation is worth nothing'.[103] He congratulated Atterbury on his election as Prolocutor of the Lower House: 'it being a testimony that ye clergymen of ye province are not to be influenced like too many of ye Canterbury diocese'.[104] Brett wanted Atterbury to take up his case in Convocation, and order another election, but Atterbury warned that it would be unadvisable to create any breach within Convocation at such a time.[105] Johnson was elected in 1710, and stood again in 1713. Brett feared that their friendship would be ruined by their rivalry, even though they supported the same party.[106] Again Brett failed in his attempt.

Brett's dissatisfaction with the Whigs and the Low-Church party became more intense after being reprimanded by Tenison in 1711 for delivering a sermon in the cathedral which was described as 'popish'.[107] In 1715, he wrote to the archbishop resigning his living. Tenison was reluctant to lose a man who clearly could do much for the Church, and tried to persuade Brett to retract his resignation. Other clergy in the diocese were less lenient and in 1716 there appeared a *Letter of Advice*, which reprimanded both Brett and Johnson for their attitude towards Tenison, since they had 'spoken and written such works as no way becomes a priest towards his Bishop, nay his Archbishop and Primate, a Metropolitan, and his own diocesan'.[108] Brett took pains to show that neither he nor his doctrines was papist.[109]

[103] Bodl. MS Eng. Th. c. 24, fo. 662, John Eve to Brett, 3 Jan. 1711.

[104] Ibid., fo. 642, Brett to Atterbury, 28 Nov. 1710.

[105] For the difficulty in Atterbury's position, Bennett, *Crisis*, 156.

[106] Bodl. MS Eng. Th. c. 24. fo. 648, Johnson to Brett, 9 May 1713; ibid., fo. 650, Brett to Johnson, 14 May 1713.

[107] Bodl. MS Eng. Th. c. 53. fo. 151, Tenison to Brett, 7 Dec. 1711. The sermon had 'urged the necessity of the Absolution of the Priesthood much further than is consistent with the Doctrine of the Church of England': LPL MS Gibson 941, fo. 28, William Quarles to Tenison, 5 Dec. 1711.

[108] Bodl. MS Eng. Th. c. 38, fo. 185, Brett to Tenison, 4 Apr. 1715; MS Eng. Th. c. 25, fo. 173, Tenison to Brett, 12 Apr. 1715; [Anon.], *A Letter of Advice to Thomas Brett, LLD, and with it a Rebuke for Late Offences Given by Him to God and the King* (1716), 123.

[109] Thomas Brett, *Dr Brett's Vindication of Himself* (1715), 31. Even when he resigned, Brett thanked Tenison: Bodl. MS Eng. Th. c. 38, fo. 197, Brett to Tenison, 1 Oct. 1715. Johnson too praised Tenison in his *The Unbloody Sacrifice and Altar Unvail'd and Supported*, 2 vols. (1714–24), i. p. xxxiv.

The party strife and political changes of the late seventeenth and early eighteenth centuries had some effect on the diocesan personnel. Fifteen incumbents were deprived between 1689 and 1716 as non-jurors and most of these were connected with Brett and Johnson. They were all Cambridge men, except for the Aberdeen University educated Alexander Innes. This shows that the stereotype of Oxford as the centre of so-called reactionary and Tory ideals in this period needs modification. The ever vigilant John Lewis informed Wake in 1726 that the pretender's health was drunk at St John's, Cambridge.[110] In the Canterbury diocese most of the non-jurors came from livings presented by clerical patrons, and some of them came from clerical families. The 'vicars of Bray' were probably more likely to have been men presented by local lay patrons, the representatives of parochial erastianism.[111] However, it took time for some of those who became non-jurors to decide to do so. Whilst it was not so difficult for those like Brett, who came from a wealthy Kentish family and had private means, to become a non-juror, the poverty which secession might entail must have persuaded many to compromise and stay within the Church. It seems too that some became non-jurors partly out of disappointment when their career hopes were thwarted. Simon Lowth, who had held livings in Canterbury, had long been concerned with the question of Church authority and in 1685 charged the Low-Church party, especially Gilbert Burnet, with erastianism. Lowth came from a staunchly royalist family and was nominated by James II to the deanery of Rochester in 1688. His installation was postponed when it was discovered that he had no higher divinity degree. William III presented Henry Ullock in his place. It appears from a note in the register at St Cosmus Blean that Lowth had publicly prayed for the new regime until the deanery had been given to Ullock.[112] In 1699 Lowth published his *Historical Collections Concerning Church Affairs*, demonstrating the typical non-juring interest in historical studies as a means of displaying fidelity to tradition—especially the tradition that the deprivation of bishops should not have been carried out by the lay power. Other non-jurors later recanted and conformed, perhaps through necessity. Thus Michael Bookey, a non-juror in 1692, became vicar of St Lawrence, Thanet

[110] Ch. Ch. MS Wake 7, fo. 148, Lewis to Wake, 30 Aug. 1716.

[111] Findon, 'Nonjurors and the Church', 100.

[112] Simon Lowth, *Of the Subject of Church Power* (1685); id., *Historical Collections Concerning Church Affairs . . . A Reply to Dr Hody* (1696). Burnet responded in his *Letter to Dr Lowth* (1685). See also *DNB* and Le Neve, *Fasti Ecclesiae Anglicanae*, 56. Cf. M. Goldie, 'The Political Thought of the Anglican Revolution', in R. Beddard (ed.), *The Revolutions of 1688* (Oxford, 1991), 125.

from 1700 to 1740. William Symes who had been deprived in 1691 from Chislet, was later an incumbent in Lincolnshire after 1691.[113]

Non-jurors in other dioceses sometimes conformed and were presented to Canterbury benefices. Shadrach Cooke who had been deprived from his London lectureship and who was known as 'absolution Cooke' for absolving the men who had attempted to assassinate William III in 1696, later took the oaths and was presented to Faversham in 1715. Cooke offered a theoretical defence of his position at the archdeacon's visitation of 1718, pouring scorn on the non-jurors' commitment to the principles of indefeasible hereditary right. He claimed that 'when I was among them, as I was for many years, and suffer'd much with them, perhaps none of the Clergy more, nor with more loyalty of Heart, I bless God for it, I own I was not of that opinion'. He also condemned the 'Oliverian regicides', presenting his own more pragmatic position as an alternative to theirs.[114] Other clergy, though not officially non-jurors, were suspected of being clandestinely so, and worried the diocesan hierarchy.[115] In this situation the Church was fortunate to have clergy like John Ramsay, the incumbent of Herne (1713–24), noted for being

a profound Divine, an Engaging Preacher, a solid Reasoner, of human and generous principles, and extensive views, an avowed enemy to unlimited power and superstition, an acute detector of the sophistry of their maintainers, a Preservative against the delusions of the age, a perpetual assertor of the Glorious Revolution and an unwearied Propagator of loyalty and obedience to the present happy establishment, by which he became a bright ornament of this Church.[116]

As the career of Thomas Brett has shown, High-Church views received some support in the diocese. Yet he was unable to get himself elected to represent the diocesan clergy in Convocation, despite several attempts. High-Church voting in the diocese resulted in the election of the more moderate John Johnson and although the parish clergy could sympathize with Tory sentiment in the years after the Revolution, they did not associate themselves with the high-flying Toryism of Atterbury or Brett. Johnson himself could declare that he was above party, having friends in both camps.[117]

---

[113] Venn, *Alumni Cantabrigienses*.

[114] Shadrach Cooke, *Legal Obedience the Duty of a Subject: considered in a Sermon* (1718), 10.

[115] In 1716 John Lamb, the late curate of Minster, was noted as being 'a very ill man: disaffected to the Government, Drunkard': LPL, VG/2/a, fo. 36. John Johnson, in particular, caused concern: Ch. Ch. MS Wake, 9, fos. 234, 277, 293, 297. For a list of clergy supposedly influenced by Johnson see Bodl. MS Eng. Th. c. 53, fo. 153.

[116] LPL MS 1024, fo. 203.

[117] Bodl. MS Ballard 15, fo. 99, Johnson to Charlett, 17 Jan. 1711.

Indeed, a measure of the increasing homogeneity of the clergy can be seen in the healing of political divisions in the diocese by the 1730s. No doubt this was more apparent in Canterbury than elsewhere since so many of the incumbents were ecclesiastical nominees and a large proportion of them were educated at the staunchly Whig Corpus Christi College. It has been estimated that 80 per cent of the parish clergy throughout England were committed Tories in Anne's reign.[118] In 1705 Defoe complained that of the 318 parsons in Kent over 250 were Tory 'plumpers', 'in conjunction with the Papists, Nonjurors and Tackers'.[119] Propaganda insisted that the Whigs were violently anti-clerical. In the 1710 election the Tories in Kent persuaded even the moderate clergy that if the Whigs were returned 'all the pulpits in England [would be] put under padlock'.[120] Johnson believed that 'the proceedings against Dr Sacheverell have convinced a great number of men that no good was intended to the Church'.[121] The Tory commitments of the Canterbury clergy were revealed again in 1713, when Johnson rejoiced that 'this time three years [ago] there were 10 Whigs elected in this county, and but 8 Churchmen: now we have 13 Churchmen and but 5 Whigs'.[122] It has been suggested by Peter Humphries that the Toryism shown by the clergy in Canterbury in these elections was due to respect for Tory gentry patrons.[123] But a more likely explanation is that most of these incumbents were the appointees of Sheldon or Sancroft, and as such were imbued with principles of passive obedience and non-resistance.[124] Tory sympathies remained after 1715. In the Kent election that year the dramatic change in the county as a whole from Tory to Whig was not shared by a similar change in the clerical vote.[125] In the 1722 election Charles Bean, the rector of Bishopsbourne, writing to Wake about the Tory affiliations of the diocesan clergy, which did not seem to him to have changed since the Revolution, complained that 'the sentiments of the clergy are not so much

---

[118] G. Holmes, 'Religion and Party in Late Stuart England', repr. id., *Politics, Religion and Society in England, 1679–1742* (London and Ronceverte, 1986), 211.

[119] D. Defoe, *Review*, 29 May 1705, quoted in W. A. Speck, *Tory and Whig. The Struggle in the Constituencies, 1701–1715* (1970), 24.

[120] Bodl. MS Ballard 15, fo. 96, Johnson to Charlett, 19 Jan. 1710.

[121] Ibid., fo. 99, Johnson to Charlett, 15 Sept. 1710.

[122] Ibid., fo. 107, Johnson to Charlett, 5 Sept. 1713.

[123] P. L. Humphries, 'Kentish Politics and Public Opinion, 1768–1832', unpub. Oxford University D.Phil. thesis, 1981, 14. That indefatigable Whig John Lewis claimed that 'a great majority of the clergy . . . are possessed that King William had no affection for the Church': BL Add. MS 28651, fo. 31.

[124] Spurr, *Restoration Church of England*, 82.

[125] The Tory John Johnson complained in 1715 that 'the Whigs govern us with an absolute sway and the honest Church-men, tho' in equal commission with them dare not show their faces': Bodl. MS Ballard 15, fo. 118, Johnson to Charlett, 22 Aug. 1715.

amended as might have been expected in near 34 years'.[126] But gradually a shift can be perceived. In 1723 Wake investigated the political leanings of his clergy after they had been accused of Jacobitism, concluding that 'this diocese is in as good temper and as well affected towards His Majesty as ever it has been at any other time and as any diocese in the kingdom'. He considered that accusations of an increase in Jacobitism in the diocese were 'groundless'.[127] In the election of 1734 Thomas Curteis wrote to the Duke of Dorset, the most influential Whig magnate in the region, that 'if the clergy were only to decide the election we should carry the point'.[128] Despite the fact that the Tory candidate, Dering, was elected, it does not seem that he owed his victory to clerical sentiment. The majority of clergy whose votes can be traced in the poll book voted Whig.[129] This represents a remarkable change in the political attitudes of the parish clergy. Their commitment to the Whig regime can also be seen behind the votes for Convocation given by the Canterbury clergy. The candidates chosen by the lower clergy in 1734 were both Whig, a result paralleled only in the dioceses of London, Lincoln, and Chichester.[130] This is worth noting since it has been suggested that in general there was still a fundamental split between the Whig dignitaries and the overwhelmingly Tory sympathies of the parish clergy.[131] That the Canterbury experience differed is partly explained by the patronage system in the diocese. In the nearby diocese of Rochester, where there was less clerical patronage, there were more problems in securing a Whig majority.[132] By the 1754 election the Whig allegiance of the Canterbury clergy was even more pronounced. Of the 209 Kent clergy whose names can be found, 145 (70 per cent) supported the Whig candidates.[133] William Byrch, the minister at Dover, wrote to Lord George Sackville that he would 'now obey him in voting for Fairfax and Watson' (the Court candidates). He had hesitated because Archdeacon Head was his patron, but now Head 'out of regard to his relationship to Sir

---

[126] Ch. Ch. MS Wake 9, fo. 203, Bean to Wake, 11 May 1722.

[127] PRO., S.P. 1729 36/16, fo. 37.

[128] KAO MS C148, fo. 48, Curteis to Dorset, 29 Dec. 1733.

[129] A. N. Newman, 'Elections in Kent and its Parliamentary Representation, 1715-1754', unpub. Oxford University D.Phil. thesis, 1957, 172.

[130] P. Langford, 'Convocation and the Tory Clergy, 1717-61', in E. Cruickshanks and J. Black (eds.), *The Jacobite Challenge* (Edinburgh, 1988), 114.

[131] L. Colley, *In Defiance of Oligarchy: The Tory Party 1714-1760* (Cambridge, 1982), 104-7.

[132] Langford, 'Convocation', 114.

[133] Newman, 'Elections in Kent', 173. Norman Sykes argued that Gibson's efforts had been 'to bind the clergy by ties of material interest to the cause of the Hanoverian dynasty and to create a Church–Whig alliance to replace the tradition of loyalty to the Stuarts', but he also talks of the 'breakdown of that alliance': *Gibson*, pp. xv–xvii.

Edward [Dering] as his parishioner . . . votes for him himself yet . . . he does not desire to influence his friends'.[134] The Tory clergy could, of course, still exercise some kind of influence. At Waldershare, for example, the tenants of Lady Guildford gave the two Whig candidates 163 and 161 votes, the Tories 10. Careful investigation revealed why some of these votes were lost: two men were noted as being 'seduced by Revd. Mr Turney'.[135]

Linda Colley has argued that the survival of the Tory party in the eighteenth century owed much to the dissatisfaction displayed by the parish clergy to the Whig regime. In her account 'the parson was the backbone of the Tory party', stiffening much of the party's ideology.[136] This is certainly not true of the Canterbury diocese where, although there was strong Tory sentiment, it owed little to clerical feelings. The flaw in Colley's argument is that she assumes that the Whig government was seen as inimical to true Anglican interests and that Anglican attitudes found their natural outlet in Tory politics. She tells us much about Tory Anglicanism, but perhaps the most interesting development of the period after 1714 is not so much this traditional alliance as the creation of Whig Anglicanism. Geoffrey Holmes has also noted the change in the political affiliations of the parish clergy from Tory to Whig, but he accounts for this in terms of erastianism, inertia, and ideological torpor, implying that such a transference was the work of secular considerations.[137] But in fact there were more positively religious reasons for voting Whig and it was perfectly possible to be a firm supporter of Church interests and to be a Whig ally. Certainly in Anne's reign, and after, clergy might feel that the Whigs and the Hanoverians would attack the Church, but despite the propaganda of 'Church in danger', by the 1730s the Tories could no longer realistically claim, as they had done in Anne's reign, that they were the only Church party. The Anglican clergy were decreasingly of use as a base of support for the Tories. The Church was actually safe in Whig hands. Archbishops such as Wake, Potter, and Secker, who can be described as High-Church Whigs, did much to reconcile the Tory clergy to the Whig regime; and Herring too has been termed a 'High Churchman'.[138] In their efforts to strengthen the pastoral force of

---

[134] Quoted in Newman, 'Elections in Kent', 135.

[135] KAO MS Guildford, U/31091, 'Countess of Guildford's estate voters, 1754'.

[136] Colley, *Defiance of Oligarchy*, 107, 131–2, 153–4.

[137] Holmes, 'Religion and Party', 211–21; also E. J. Evans, 'The Anglican Clergy of Northern England', in Clyve Jones (ed.), *Britain in the First Age of Party, 1680–1750. Essays Presented to Geoffrey Holmes* (London and Ronceverte, 1987), 221–40.

[138] Ollard and Walker, *Herring*, iv. 24. The rapprochement between the Whigs and High-Churchmanship can also be seen in the Sussex clergy: Chamberlain, *Accommodating High Churchmen*.

the Church in the parishes, to defend Church property, and to maintain Anglican doctrine, they were clearly acting in the interests of the Church. Even John Johnson could say of Wake, 'I have always said that he was the best clergyman in England that was not a Tory'.[139] Wake summed up his own position, 'all I would desire is that they with hearty zeal for the Church are by no means inconsistent with a most firm and steady adherence to the King'. Rather disingenuously Wake described himself: 'I do not know that I am of any party in the Church of England more than another'.[140] Such a policy was not a new development; Tillotson and Tenison desired the reconciliation of the post-Revolution regime with the Church of England.[141] They did not see themselves acting against but for the interests of the Church. The change in the political affiliations of the clergy was instrumental in the move to consensus which has been seen as a hallmark of the mid-eighteenth century. It may be that the Church which had been so prominent in creating party divisions in the late seventeenth century later helped to heal them. Colley maintains that the period saw a continued gulf between the Whig dignitaries and the Tory lower clergy,[142] but in Canterbury the voting patterns suggest a developing homogeneity; an increasingly similar outlook. The divisions that disfigured the Church in the early eighteenth century do not appear to have continued throughout the period.[143] Thomas Curteis tried to argue in 1725 that the late distinctions between High and Low were groundless. He urged his fellow clergy to

live peaceably with all men . . . and you will find the more Reason to do so, if you consider (what I make no doubt of) that very many, notwithstanding their different ways of thinking, sincerely aim at the same end, viz., the Public Good, or the common safety of our excellent constitution in Church and State and it being once granted that men may go under the distinguishing characters of High or Low, Tory

---

[139] Bodl. MS Ballard 15, fo. 140, Johnson to Charlett, 6 Mar. 1718.

[140] MS Ballard 3, fo. 164, Wake to Charlett, 27 June 1716.

[141] Bennett, 'William III and the Episcopate', Bennett and Walsh, *Essays in Modern English Church History*, 104–31. Gascoigne, *Cambridge*, 238–9, makes too clear a distinction between the methods of Sheldon and Sancroft and those of Tillotson and Tenison. In 1701 Tenison brought a bill into the Lords 'for the security of the Doctrine, Liturgy and Rights of the Church of England': *Nicolson Diaries*, 158.

[142] Colley, *Defiance of Oligarchy*, 105, 153.

[143] The rapprochement can be found in other areas of the country: J. F. Quinn, 'Yorkshiremen Go to the Polls: County Contests in the Eighteenth Century', *Northern History*, 21 (1985), 137–74. Similar events happened in Norfolk: W. M. Jacob, 'Clergy and Society in Norfolk, 1707–1806', unpub. University of Exeter Ph.D. thesis, 1982, 93–4. However, contrasting evidence of a continued division between Tory and Whig clergy has been found in Cheshire: S. W. Baskerville, 'The Political Behaviour of the Cheshire Clergy, 1705–1752', *Northern History*, 23 (1987), 74–97.

and Whig, and yet be good Christians, True Lovers of our Church, Good Subjects and Good neighbours.[144]

This is in itself a propagandist position, but it is clear that political divisions between clergy were dying down. In part, as we have seen, this can be attributed to the large amount of patronage that lay in ecclesiastical hands. Changes in the voting patterns of the clergy can be explained by the replacement of those clergy presented by Sheldon and Sancroft by the appointees of Whig archbishops. There is no doubt that Wake expected the clergy to whom he had given preferment to vote for the Hanoverian Court candidates. Dean Lynch of Canterbury, Wake's son-in-law, informed the Duke of Newcastle in 1734 that the archbishop would do all he could to win the votes of his clergy for the Whig candidates:

if yre be any whom the Archbishop has obliged of wch your Grace is doubtful, if your Grace be pleased to let me be inform'd of them, I am sure my Lord Archbishop will cause his Secretary to write to them in the most pressing terms to desire yr vote and Interest for these Gentlemen.[145]

The archbishops of Canterbury, through their example and their patronage, ensured that the majority of their clergy would vote Whig by the mid-eighteenth century, and did much to ensure that the parochial clergy were a united professional force. For a short while in the late 1770s and early 1780s, when a more radical whiggery emerged in Kent in support of Wyvill and Lord Mahon's reform critique of the government, at least six of the diocesan clergy were associated with the movement, and it has been suggested that in their parishes 'the pulpit was effectively employed in spreading the radical gospel'.[146] But this movement, at least amongst the clergy in Kent was shortlived, and after 1790 clergy in the diocese once again wholeheartedly supported the establishment.[147]

CONCLUSION

This survey of the parish clergy between 1660 and 1828 is intended to shed some light on the development of the clerical profession. An analysis of

---

[144] Curteis, *Advice*, 83.

[145] Quoted in B. Williams, 'The Duke of Newcastle and the Election of 1734', *EHR*, 12 (1897), 469.

[146] Humphries, 'Kentish Politics', 87–9. These included Edmund Marshall, the vicar of Charing, 1766–97; Ralph Drake-Brockman, vicar of Newington, 1770–81; and Frederick Dodsworth, perpetual curate of Bredhurst, 1763–82, and later chaplain to the earl of Shelburne.

[147] Ibid., 115, 224–8.

Catholicism in France has suggested that the theme of strife must permeate any discussion of ecclesiastical history; strife between the clergy and between the clergy and the laity.[148] The Anglican experience differs from this French model in a number of significant ways. The common social and educational backgrounds of the various strands in the clerical profession in England worked against such divisions between higher and lower clergy as were found in pre-Revolutionary France. The degree of internal strife which plagued the French Church, particularly that between Jansenists and Jesuits, is absent from Anglicanism, especially after 1714. This is not to suggest that the Church did not display a variety of opinions and different styles of Churchmanship. But these differences were not so strong as to preclude cooperation and mutual respect between clergy of contrary views.[149]

We should be wary of accepting the idea that there was a weak conception of clerical identity in this period: this assumption shows a lack of understanding of the efforts of pre-Victorian Churchmen to improve the standards of the clerical body, both in the quality of those ordained, and in the behaviour and attitudes of the parish clergy. In some respects they anticipated the later reformers, though steering clear of the insistence on the 'apartness' of the clergy which characterized the Oxford Movement and in this way they held the support of a laity suspicious of sacerdotalism. The eighteenth-century Church is often seen as an aberration between the ideals of the sixteenth- and nineteenth-century reformers: it is time that it should be seen in a different light, as a period of some importance for the development of the clerical profession. The concern to tighten up the clerical vocation is as visible in the Established Church in this period as in those groups which are supposed to have reacted against it. John Wesley, usually seen as a stern critic of the eighteenth-century Anglican clergy, recognized this:

It must be allowed that ever since the Reformation, and particularly in the present century, the behaviour of the clergy in general is greatly altered for the better . . . Most of the Protestant clergy are different from what they were. They have not only more learning of the most valuable kind, but abundantly more religion. In so much

[148] R. M. Golden, 'Introduction', in id. (ed.), *Church, State and Society under the Bourbon Kings of France* (Kansas, 1982), 1. For a more recent corrective see N. Aston, *The End of an Elite: The French Bishops and the Coming of the Revolution, 1786–1790* (Oxford, 1992).

[149] In this respect, at least, the Church of the eighteenth century continued the ideological consensus found in the Restoration period as described in Spurr, *Restoration Church of England, passim*. See also, Nockles, *Oxford Movement*, who finds that serious divisions between Evangelicals and High Churchmanship occurred only after 1828.

that the English and Irish clergy are generally allowed to be not inferior to any in Europe, for piety as well as knowledge.[150]

How this attempt to create a professional force affected the pastoral work of the clergy, how it was translated in the parishes, and how it altered the clergy's dealings with nonconformists will be explored in later chapters.

[150] John Wesley, *Works*, 14 vols. (1872), vii, *Sermons*, ii. 179.

II. The Church and the Economy

3

The Administration of Church Property

The hostile picture of the eighteenth-century Church projected by much historiography has centred on its economic activities. Nineteenth-century reformers portrayed the Church of the previous century as a money-grabbing organization which typified the evils of 'Old Corruption'. Whig bishops and cathedral dignitaries were seen as too concerned with lining their own pockets to be effective diocesans or Churchmen.[1] The diocese of Canterbury has often been cited to support this argument: the wealth of both the archbishopric and the cathedral received adverse attention from 'Blue Dick' Culmer's attack in 1644 through to the criticisms of the Unitarian and political radical, John Wade, who in his *Black Book: or Corruption Unmasked!* (1820) singled out Canterbury as a special object for his venom.[2] This chapter argues that the concern shown by the archbishops of Canterbury and members of the dean and chapter in the administration of their property is not to be dismissed as an indication of the Church's pre-occupation with merely secular matters. On the contrary, an involvement in the realm of property and finance was seen as a way of holding back the secularizing forces within society by maintaining the Church in full vigour.

At the Restoration, ecclesiastics in the diocese were restored to some of the most lucrative properties in the Church. Canterbury was one of the richest sees and the dean and chapter ranked amongst the most highly paid dignitaries. Lands belonging to the archbishop were concentrated in a triangle between Canterbury, Sandwich, and Folkestone. The archbishop also owned property in the diocese of Rochester, in London and in Lancashire. The dean and chapter's estates were not so compact; outside the diocese the

---

[1] Abbey and Overton, *English Church in the Eighteenth Century*, i. 12; Langford, *Propertied Englishman*, 1, 15; W. D. Rubinstein, 'The End of "Old Corruption" in Britain, 1780–1860', *Past and Present*, 101 (1982), 55–86.

[2] R. Culmer, Cathedrall Newes from Canterbury, repr. in G[eorge] S[mith], *Chronological History*, 282–317; Wade, *Black Book*, 286, 298. But despite the criticisms which highlighted the wealth of Canterbury it is clear that other cathedrals were even more lucrative. Sykes, *Church and State*, 149, shows that in the mid-century prebends at Windsor, Oxford, and St Paul's were worth more than at Canterbury. A sympathetic treatment of Church finance is C. Clay, '"The Greed of Whig Bishops"?: Church Landlords and their Lessees, 1660–1760', *Past and Present*, 87 (1980), 128–57.

cathedral held lands in Norfolk, Suffolk, Sussex, Essex, Surrey, London, and Devon. Nevertheless 87 per cent of its property lay in Kent. In all, the dean and chapter with its 33 manors, 34 rectories and urban properties (including 240 buildings in Canterbury itself) owned 16,100 acres.[3]

Such a concentration of ecclesiastical wealth in the diocese meant that property was bound to be a sensitive issue in the Church's relationship with the laity. Church income came from leasing out property and collecting substantial entrance and renewal fines. Setting fines was the result of negotiation between ecclesiastics, their estate officials, and the prospective tenant. The reserved rent on Church estates was usually minimal and variation from year to year in income was explained by the fact that properties were renewed at different times, depending on when the original lease was taken out. The majority of the Church's properties were leased for a period of twenty-one years and fines were paid at least every seven and on some estates every four years. In theory this ensured that there was a regular and steady income. However, there was always the temptation for Churchmen to accrue heavy entry fines from long leases for a period of lives; thereby generating a large income for themselves but possibly creating problems for their successors. Because of this, Archbishop Whitgift had converted some of the three-life leases on the Canterbury estates back into twenty-one-year grants.[4] Part of the difficulty in changing the length of the leases was that a lease for three lives was advantageous to the tenant family. None the less, Archbishop Laud continued to alter the length of leases and the Commonwealth surveys indicate that only four leases for lives remained on the archbishop's estates.[5]

However, the way in which a stern administration of property could sour relations with local society had also been seen during the 1630s. The consequences of the economic dimension of Laud's aggressive clericalism in the diocese had been disastrous, alienating a powerful section of the laity.[6]

[3] For the archbishop's estates see F. R. H. Du Boulay, *The Lordship of Canterbury* (1966) and N. Brooks, *The Early History of the Church of Canterbury* (Leicester, 1984), 311–13. For the cathedral: D. A. Heaton, 'A Study of the Structure of Corporate Estate Management of the Lands of the Dean and Chapter of Canterbury, 1640–1760', unpub. University of Kent at Canterbury M.A. thesis, 1971, 27–8. Likewise in York, the estates of the archbishop were concentrated around the city: I. Gentles and W. J. Sheils, *Confiscation and Restoration: The Archbishopric Estates and the Civil War*, Borthwick Papers, 59 (1981), 2. For the kind of involvement which the estates necessitated within local society see R. L. Smith, *Canterbury Cathedral Priory. A Study in Monastic Administration* (1943) and M. Mate 'Property Investment by Canterbury Cathedral Priory, 1250–1400', *JBS*, 23 (1983–4), 1–21.

[4] Bodl. MS Tanner 127, fos. 1–47, copies of letters; Heal, *Of Prelates and Princes*, 100–24.

[5] Heaton, 'Dean and Chapter', 28.

[6] Clark, *English Provincial Society*, 367; F. Heal, 'Archbishop Laud Revisited: Leases and Estate Management at Canterbury and Winchester before the Civil War', in R. O'Day and

Post-Restoration and eighteenth-century clergy had learned the lesson from his experience: they realized that they had to work within an administrative framework in which they could defend Church rights, but did not alienate their supporters. In a county like Kent, where leading members of the laity had long been sensitive to the question of lay and clerical relations, the Church was not free to act without considering the implications for its position within lay society. Support for Anglicanism did not mean support for clericalism: support for the economic and political power of the Church was qualified by the need to take careful consideration of the gentry's wealth, freedom, and position.[7] Clergy had to understand the limitations within which they worked. The management of Church lands required careful handling and the administration of its property involved the Church hierarchy in Kent in a series of complex and sensitive relationships with lay society. Churchmen needed to maintain their estates and the rights inherent in their property, yet most clerics had little experience in estate management and their other commitments meant that they could not become directly involved in the day-to-day running of their estates.

THE RESTORATION OF CHURCH PROPERTY

In 1660, a major obstacle to the resumption of the Anglican order might well have been the question of its properties for, as Ian Green has suggested, the 'land question' at the Restoration was a potentially explosive one.[8] The parliamentary regime had funded itself and its armies partly by selling off ecclesiastical lands. Between 1647 and 1659 a total of £73,031 14s. 9d. was raised by the sale of lands that had belonged to the archbishopric. The original Church tenants were given the right to purchase the land within thirty days.[9] Some of the Canterbury lessees availed themselves of this opportunity. Sir John Roberts, who had rented 60 acres of marshland at Chislet,

---

F. Heal (eds.), *Princes and Paupers in the English Church 1500–1800* (Leicester, 1981), 129–51; Heaton, 'Dean and Chapter', 28; P. Heylyn, *Cyprianus Anglicanus* (1668), 244–1; *Proceedings in Kent*, ed. L. B. Larking, Camden Society Publications (1862), 60–4; 160–75; 196–8.

[7] P. Seaward, 'Court and Parliament: The Making of Government Policy, 1661–1665', Oxford University D.Phil. thesis, 1986, 24. One might note the fear that James II's pro-Catholic policies would lead to former monastic lands, now in the hands of lay landowners, being taken back by the Church: J. R. Western, *Monarchy and Revolution: The English State in the Sixteen Eighties* (Blandford, 1972), 202.

[8] Green, *Re-establishment of Church of England*, 99.

[9] Everitt, *Community of Kent*, 161 argues that perhaps one-eleventh of the revenues raised in this manner came from the diocese of Canterbury; G. B. Tatham 'The Sale of Episcopal Lands during the Civil Wars and the Commonwealth', *EHR*, 22 (1908), 104.

bought 156 acres of marsh and 758 acres of woodland for £5,394 5s. 11d., and Sir Robert Honeywood purchased the lands belonging to St Gregory's Priory and Lecton manor, where he had been the major tenant, for £1,411 15s. 0d.[10] Most of the immediate tenant purchasers were not the lessees of the larger estates. They may well have found it difficult to raise the necessary purchase price within thirty days, and it is possible that some refrained from doing so out of a disapproval for the selling off of Church property. The majority of the tenant purchasers in the first instance were the lessees of the small tenements and properties in Canterbury and Deal: 'obscure people who bought for trivial amounts.'[11] Some of the former Church tenants of the larger estates may have purchased the lands later, buying them from the initial purchasers.

The tension involved in trying to reclaim Church property while also maintaining an amicable relationship with the laity was a central feature of the Anglican restoration in the diocese. On the one hand there could be no question that lands would not be restored to the Church; on the other this had to be tempered by the necessity of justifying that wealth to the wider world. Historians, following Bishops Burnet and White Kennett, are apt to complain of the lost opportunity in 1660 for a fundamental reorganization of the Church's economic position.[12] Yet this is to misjudge the mood of both clerics and lay Anglicans and their desire to found the regime on past precedent. To help them do this Churchmen relied on the register books and act books which contained information about the location of ecclesiastical lands and the leasing policies which governed them. The Church in Canterbury was fortunate that William Somner, a prominent antiquarian, had survived the Interregnum and was appointed auditor to the restored dean and chapter.[13] He possessed the intimate local knowledge required to restore to the Church its properties and estates. There is some indication that the Church hierarchy also found the surveys, made of the archiepiscopal and cathedral property prior to the sale of Church lands, of use.[14] However, it took time to recover all the Church's property. In 1682 Dr Parker complained that a large part of the glebe land belonging to

---

[10] I. Gentles, 'The Sale of the Bishops' Lands in the English Revolution, 1646–1660', *EHR*, 95 (1980), 580–1.

[11] Ibid., 580.

[12] Burnet, *History of Own Time*, i. 338; White Kennett, *The Case of Impropriations and of the Augmentations of Vicarages and Other Insufficient Cures* (1704), 249–51.

[13] For Somner, see White Kennett, *Life of Mr William Somner* (1693).

[14] The survey of the dean and chapter of Canterbury was made in 1650: LPL, TR, 34, fo. 150. See C. E. Woodruff, 'The Parliamentary Survey of the Precincts of Canterbury Cathedral in the Time of the Commonwealth', *AC*, 49 (1938), 195–222.

Faversham had been sold to 'one Knowler in the late times and is not yet returned to ye Church'.[15]

In the Restoration period Churchmen were anxious to advertise their generosity in taking low fines, and in treating tenants charitably. The Church was commonly believed to have done very well out of the Restoration, and the wealth of its hierarchy was sometimes compared unfavourably to Cavalier poverty.[16] In his account of the attitudes of the Church in the early years of the Restoration, Clarendon made allowance for the understandable bitterness of diocesans and cathedral dignitaries, but he claimed that 'they made haste to enter upon their own' and, in the treatment of their tenants, showed 'more passion than justice'.[17] In the Canterbury diocese this was too harsh a verdict: it is clear that the Church was willing to take into account the 'suffering' of their tenants when setting fines.

It is difficult to explain the zeal shown by the Kentish gentry for the resumption of the Anglican order without recognizing that many landowners saw this as a chance to reclaim their former possessions, which included their right to be tenants. It is puzzling that there is not more evidence of friction between Civil War purchasers and the restored Church; those instances which survive, such as the lawsuit between the archbishop and William Rand in November 1664 regarding the ownership of twelve houses in Deal in which the archbishop's rights as owner were being contested, relate to houses, rather than large tracts of land.[18] It has been suggested that many purchasers retired gracefully because they knew that they had already made a fair profit from their acquisitions. In any case, many of the largest purchasers of lands throughout England, like Arthur Haselrig, were specifically exempted from the Act of Pardon of 1660.[19]

The Crown's directives to the Church in 1660 stressed the need to avoid any unnecessary confrontation.[20] The first leases were given out on 17 July 1660.[21] Church landlords were prohibited from forcing an entry until

[15] CCAL, Dr Parker's Memorandum Book, 1681, 84.

[16] Seaward, 'Court and Parliament', 23.

[17] *The Life of Edward, Earl of Clarendon Containing I. An Account of the Chancellor's life . . . to the Restoration in 1660 II. Continuation of the History of England, Written by himself* (Oxford, 1759), 98-9.

[18] KAO, U 3/13/T3. The disputes seem to have lasted for some time. In 1678 the archbishop's steward was still advising tenants about the case: LPL, TS 2, fo. 8.

[19] J. Thirsk, 'The Sales of Royalist Land during the Interregnum', *Economic History Review*, 2nd ser., 5 (1952/3), 188-207. See also H. J. Habbakuk, 'Landowners and the English Civil War', ibid., 2nd ser. 18 (1965), 130-51; and P. G. Holiday, 'Land Sales and Repurchases in Yorkshire after the Civil Wars, 1650-1670', *Northern History*, 5 (1970), 67-92.

[20] LPL MS 952, fo. 781.   [21] CCAL, Register Z, 1660-1, fo. 26.

Parliament had made more specific recommendations and on 13 October 1660 the king declared that Church landlords should give regard to pre-Civil War tenants as well as giving satisfaction to purchasers.[22] During the first year of the Restoration Archbishop Juxon and the dean and chapter received petitions from former tenants. Some made excuses for their purchase of the freehold land, claiming that they had bought in order to preserve the lands, and gave back to the chapter their deeds of purchase.[23] The Earl of Winchilsea, writing on behalf of Richard Nevet, a former tenant of chapter property, explained that Nevet's purchase was 'rather from necessity than choice and yet is the only he hath for himself, his wife and diverse small children'.[24] In 1662 Christopher Darrell confessed that he had made a purchase 'under the State as they so termed themselves'. Another former tenant claimed that he had been 'forced to kiss the Rod' to preserve himself and his family.[25]

Those tenants who had been ousted from their properties were able to regain their position. Sir John Boys complained that 'William Molins did lately purchase of certain persons in a pretended Act of Parliament for sale, of manors and lands belonging to the archbishopric'.[26] Boys was a descendant of the steward to the Elizabethan archbishops and a member of a staunchly Anglican family.[27] For such families history did repeat itself, and the Boyses once more became tenants to the Church. Others were not so fortunate. Thomas Monins petitioned Juxon, pleading that his father and grandfather had been 'time out of mind tenants unto his Grace's predecessors, of the manor and rectory of Lydden and farms in Barton in East Kent'.[28] But Captain Monins had been a parliamentary supporter in Kent, being appointed treasurer general of the sequestered cathedral estates, although he claimed at the Restoration to have been a crypto-royalist.[29] By 1673 Lydden was leased to Thomas Heath, one of Sheldon's officials, and Barton Farms were leased to Richard Swain, from Sussex.[30]

The charitable treatment given to lessees included letting some tenants off their fines altogether. This was especially common on the smaller properties. Sometimes this was because the tenant had 'suffered' for the Anglican and royalist cause. On other occasions the bestowing of Church lands were viewed as a legitimate way of rewarding the friends, families, and dependants of the Church hierarchy. No fine, for example, was demanded

[22] *CSPD*, 1660–1, 60; Wilkins, *Concilia*, iv. 557–60.

[23] CCAL, Register X, 14, 2. nos. 90–9.   [24] CCAL, Canterbury Letters, i, no. 87.

[25] Ibid., no. 90.   [26] LPL, TR 19, fo. 10.

[27] Collinson, *Religion of Protestants*, 63–4.   [28] LPL, TR 19, fo. 8.

[29] CCAL Add. MS 80 and Bodl. MS Gough Kent 19, fos. 148–84.

[30] Bodl. MS Sancoft 119, fos. 56, 150.

for Barton Manor since the tenant was Juxon's nephew.[31] Similarly Juxon's sister leased Bekesbourne Manor in 1662 for no fine, and no fine was taken for Crophill on the grounds that the tenant was 'an old servant'.[32] Others were able to lease on reduced terms. The rich manor of Hull and Shoulden, valued in 1663 by the auditor to the archbishop at a clear annual value of £188, was leased to one of the archbishop's officials for a fine of £50.[33] The abatements to the Canterbury tenantry in the form of low fines were so extensive that Churchmen cited them as an indication of Anglican charity. Such examples were useful to meet criticism of the Church's tenure of property. In 1670 Sheldon asked Dean Turner for an account of 'what you have abated to your tenants (having been loyal and suffered for His Majesty's Cause)'.[34] It was estimated that the cathedral had given at least £12,000 to tenants in this way and Archbishop Juxon was supposed to have donated at least £16,000 in this form of charity.[35]

The method of raising income through fines, while annual rents were kept at a minimal level, contrasts with the rack-renting found on lay estates and was viewed as another instance of the way in which the Church could be considered as a charitable landlord. The policy of beneficial leasing was kinder to tenants and certainly easier to administer than the more active policy of rack-renting, which necessitated constant supervision. Churchmen were well aware that their policy was a lenient one, and at times when the Church was attacked for its temporal possessions they were quick to point this out. During the early years of the Restoration, when both the archbishop and the dean and chapter had received high incomes through the more than usually lush crop of fines, Myles Smith, secretary to Archbishop Sheldon, noted this difference between Church and lay landlords:

The tenants to the Churches, when they shall live upon ye Rack, will not be able to serve the King and Country as they do now, their fines being very reasonable, for now a lease being out for 21 years, and 7 years thereof run out, they take the known profit for 1 year . . . which upon a strict account is worth hard upon 2 years profit.[36]

THE MANAGEMENT OF ESTATES, 1660–c.1780

After the Restoration, both archbishops and cathedral dignitaries took pains to acquaint themselves with the history of their estates in earlier eras,

[31] LPL, TC 9, 'View of Estates, 1805', fo. 16.
[32] Ibid., fos. 17, 79.   [33] Ibid., fo. 151.
[34] Bodl. MS Tanner 128, fo. 57, Sheldon to Turner, 29 July 1670.
[35] Bodl. MS Tanner 123, fo. 68, Turner to Sheldon, 22 Nov. 1670.
[36] Bodl. MS Tanner 141, fo. 87ᵛ.

when the rights and privileges belonging to the see and cathedral had been established. In a period when clergy found it necessary to defend such privileges, a knowledge of their title was essential. Archbishops like Sheldon, Sancroft, Wake, Secker, Moore, and Manners Sutton, deans, and those most concerned with the administration of the cathedral's property, the receiver and treasurer, took the trouble to familiarize themselves with the extent of their lands, with the names of tenants, and with the intricacies of individual leases.[37] This was no purely antiquarian interest. A knowledge of the historical formation of their estates was, to a legally minded age, necessary for an understanding of the present position and responsibilities of the Church in the local economy.

Clergy were anxious to preserve in good order the records relating to their property. At the Restoration Dean Turner admitted that 'our Audit Bookes . . . were not soe exactly kept as they ought' and the problem was exacerbated by the destruction of many records in a fire which burned down the Audit House in 1670.[38] Likewise in 1684 Prebendary Thorp complained to Sancroft that 'the long time of Rebellion made a great devastation in our records'.[39] The two most substantial collections of documents relating to the customs, privileges, and rights of the Anglican Church produced in the period, Edmund Gibson's *Codex Juris Ecclesiastici Anglicani* (1713) and David Wilkins's *Concilia Magnae Britanniae et Hiberniae* (1737) made extensive use of the medieval and post-Reformation records at Lambeth which referred to the rights of the archbishops and the cathedral at Canterbury. In both cases the records of the see and the cathedral were used to reveal the rights of the national Church.

However concerned the Church authorities were to safeguard their rights, their freedom for manœuvre was severely constrained by custom and local demands, and in some cases by self-interest and inertia. Charles II, in the tradition of his father and Archbishop Laud, forbade the cathedral in 1660 to convert leases for years into leases for lives, in an attempt to keep a tighter check on Church property.[40] But in 1660–1, fourteen of the cathedral's estates were newly leased for a period of three lives, and despite constant pressure from the dean and chapter out of 173 leases in 1800 six were held for three lives.[41] A three-life lease was considered a better bargain than one for twenty-one years and most changes from lives to years happened

---

[37] For example: LPL MSS 1126, 1134, 1138, VG 2/5, TC 9; Bodl. MSS Tanner 122, 127, 128; CCAL Add. MS 19.

[38] Bodl. MS Tanner 123, fo. 68, Turner to Sheldon, 22 Nov. 1670.

[39] Ibid., fo. 21, Thorp to Sancroft, 11 Dec. 1684.

[40] Bodl. MS Tanner 128, fo. 41, Charles II to dean and chapter, 22 June 1662.

[41] Heaton, 'Dean and Chapter', 86.

where a lease changed hands or where the contents of the demise were altered, as at Monkton Manor in 1731.[42] The dean and chapter were pleased to have changed the lease of Leysdown in 1749 to years.[43]

The revenue of both the archbishop and the cathedral remained fairly static for nearly a century after 1660, despite the fact that between the Restoration and the mid-eighteenth century, increased costs, inflation, and rising taxes put pressures on both to increase their income. In 1677 Archbishop Sheldon received a total income of £5,841 13s. 0d., in 1682 Sancroft obtained £6,075 7s. 10d. and in 1761 Secker's income was £7,000.[44] In the late seventeenth century the deanery was worth about £540 and prebendaries about £220, and similar figures were obtained in the 1740s.[45] The strength of Restoration anti-clericalism had left its mark on clerical landed incomes which fell significantly behind those of lay contemporaries in the century after 1660: this was partly the result of the refusal of lay tenants to permit clerical landowners to extract the same rents and fines as they did themselves.[46] The Restoration policy of treating tenants charitably had the effect of constraining the Church for the next century: having once leased at easy rents, it proved difficult to change. In 1718 Archdeacon Thomas Bowers reckoned that:

Tis probable that the low value of money, the dearness of all things belonging to house-keeping and the more expensive way of living among all ranks and degrees of men, may awaken Churchmen to look more carefully into their estates, and to go a little out of the old track which their predecessors for a long time have gone in, without due thought or consideration, regarding only what had formerly been taken and not considering the present state of the world, or the low value of money . . .[47]

During the 1720s the dean and chapter did try to alter the basis of their fines from 1¼ years value for a renewal of seven years, to 1½ years value.[48] In

---

[42] Ibid.   [43] CCAL, Chapter Act Book, 1741–60, fo. 20.

[44] Bodl. MS Tanner 127, fos. 69–70, 112. Secker's income is recorded in LPL MS TF 18, fo. 8. In 1715 it was claimed that the annual income was 'usually' £6,000: Edward Tenison, *The True Copies of Some Letters, Occasion'd by the Demand for Dilapidations in the Archiepiscopal See of Canterbury* (1716), 5.

[45] Bodl. MS Tanner 123, fo. 32; CCAL, 'Dr Potter's Book'. However, by 1759 the deanery was worth £900, the prebends £350: E. N. Williams, *The Eighteenth-Century Constitution, 1688–1815* (2nd edn., Cambridge, 1970), 348. In 1767 Dr Benson received £315 11s. 9d.: CCAL, 'Dr Benson's Book', fo. 23.   [46] Best, *Temporal Pillars*, 101.

[47] Thomas Bowers, *The Value of Church and College Leases Considered and the Advantages of the Lessees made very Apparent* (2nd edn., 1722), 12. He wrote to Wake in 1718 concerning the need to raise fines: Ch. Ch. MS Wake 10, fo. 16, Bowers to Wake, 19 July 1718. The 'beneficial' system can also be seen in that quit rents, reliefs, and heriots were no longer claimed on Church lands: B. M. Short, 'The South East, Kent and Sussex', in J. Thirsk (ed.), *The Agrarian History of England and Wales*, v. i. (1985), 296.

[48] Westminster Abbey Muniments, 25096 A/B, fo. 79.

1720 Dean Stanhope explained to Archbishop Wake that they had attempted this with the largest lease and had informed the dean and chapter of Rochester 'so we do not stand alone'.[49] It was necessary to do this, he argued, because of the different ways in which clerical and lay landlords dealt with their tenants:

> Upon debate here concerning the present condition of affairs with regards to the sinking interest, the rise of the value of land and the very different proportions by which our tenants and those of the lay landlords are dealt with in renewals, we think it necessary to change our measures in this respect.[50]

The attempt, however, met with a great deal of hostility and the tenants' complaints forced the cathedral to revert to its former policy in 1727.[51] The chapter had to move warily. In 1722 Sir Hewart Aucher protested against the new policy and in 1723 John Penton wrote a hectoring letter to the chapter about the 'exorbitant fine'.[52] In some ways such protests fit into the concept of a 'moral economy', in which tenants used arguments based on tradition and past practice to justify their opposition.[53] In the face of such attacks the dean and chapter defended their action on the grounds that the fines they asked were still less than the real value of the land, that they were also less than the amounts taken by lay landlords and that 'some men would always have the Church tied down by old fines'. They concluded:

> it is said that the Church by Raising their Fines, Grow Harder Landlords than they were Formerly: And that it is by no means a Proper Time for Churchmen to do this, when they have so much need of doing Evr'y thing to Oblige the Laity to stand by them from their Enemys.[54]

The 1720s and 1730s were a time of virulent anti-clericalism, when there was a loud outcry against excessive ecclesiastical power. The Church went through a period of crisis, a main object of attack being its wealth and property. Norman Sykes likened the intensity of this hostility to that experienced by the Church in the 1530s, and it also presents close similarities to the situation in the 1830s when radical politicians once again denounced the affluence of the Church.[55] In each of these periods the cathedrals were viewed as the most overt symbols of the Church's privileges, and became

---

[49] Ch. Ch. MS Wake 8, fo. 20, Stanhope to Wake, 25 June 1720.
[50] Ibid.   [51] CCAL, Dean's Book, 1718–42, 75.
[52] Ibid., 75. In 1723 the dean and chapter of York informed the cathedral of their fining practices: ibid., letter interleaved between pp. 98 and 99.
[53] E. P. Thompson, 'The Moral Economy of the English Crowd in the Eighteenth Century', *Past and Present*, 50 (1971), 76–136.
[54] CCAL, Dean's Book, 1718–42, p. 2 of 3 pp. inserted between 100 and 101.
[55] Sykes, *Gibson*, 149.

the prime targets of attack. In 1723 the chapter advised 'any prebendaries in London to resist any attempt to bring a Bill for ascertaining fines or rents of Ecclesiastical estates',[56] and in 1736 the dean and several prebendaries met together for a similar purpose.[57] During the previous parliamentary session a bill to let Quakers off paying their tithes had been debated and the bishops and cathedral dignitaries rallied against it, in support of the rights of the Church.[58] Concern for ecclesiastical interests here overrode the sense of the duty to comply with the wishes of the government. In such times of crisis, the decentralized Church could unite. Likewise in 1769 the chapter noted with concern that a 'dangerous Association [has been] formed among the Farmers in Essex and Suffolk to destroy the rights of collecting and gathering Tithes in the usual and legal way in defence of which we think ourselves and all persons concerned'.[59]

Some idea of the constraints under which the dean and chapter operated as landlords can be seen in the hostile reaction to those who tried to defend and strengthen Church interests. The laity were quick to react when they felt that changes were afoot. In 1748 a vicious satire on Dean Lynch included criticism of his handling of Church lands.[60] The pamphlet is revealing not as an accurate portrayal of the dean's behaviour, but as an indication of how the laity expected clerical landlords to act. It was alleged that the dean had disregarded the traditional policy of 'being prudent and easy with tenants'. Instead he treated 'yeoman and farmers . . . as his dogs'.[61]

In part, the generally static nature of the Church's revenues between the Restoration and the mid-eighteenth century can be explained by the economic state of the region as a whole. In this respect the difficulties of Church landlords mirrored those of the laity. The archbishop's revenues suffered during the agricultural depression of the 1680s and 1690s. Reports to Sancroft from his estate officials indicate that the Church had problems with tenants who could not pay their rents. The matter was so grave that a new column appeared in the records of the receiver, Ralph Snow, in which arrears were split into two categories, 'sperate' (those which offered some

---

[56] CCAL, Chapter Act Book, 1711–26, fo. 135ᵛ.   [57] Ibid., 1727–45, fo. 112ᵛ.

[58] Taylor, 'Walpole, the Church and the Quakers', 51–77.

[59] CCAL, Dean's Book, 1761–76, fo. 135.

[60] *The Life of Dean L—ch by a Yeoman of Kent. No Canterbury Tale. And shall they escape for such Wickedness?* (1748). Pyle called Lynch a 'vast carcass', quoted in *Memoirs of a Royal Chaplain*, 288. For some defences of Lynch from within the cathedral community, which stress his charity, see *Poems by the late George-Monck Berkeley*, p. ccxl; William Jones, *Memoirs of the Life, Studies, and Writings of the Most Reverend George Horne* (1795), 339.

[61] *Life of L—ch*, 29.

hope of being recovered) and 'desperate', which did not.[62] Between 1720 and 1750 Church landlords in east Kent shared with the laity the problems of another period of depression and there was little change in the level of incomes.[63]

However, a major factor in explaining the inability of clergy to secure a realistic return from their lands was their estate management techniques, especially their reliance for the greater part of the century on their own members to survey and value their lands, and their acceptance of the values given by tenants when negotiating a fine. During the early years of the Restoration, and at periodic intervals thereafter, prebendaries valued the cathedral's estates. John Bargrave's notes of his tours of the estates during the 1670s, when he was receiver, survive, as do Ralph Snow's, made for Archbishop Sancroft.[64] The dean and chapter were concerned to have accurate surveys made of their properties since the Restoration and from 1681 members of the Hill family, Canterbury map-makers, had been employed to survey particular estates from time to time.[65] This seems to have been a rather haphazard policy and it was not until 1762 that the dean and chapter agreed that 'for the future all such of our estates as are not mapped, shall be surveyed and mapped'.[66] In 1772 the chapter agreed to purchase a theodolite to help in their assessments.[67]

Gradually this casual process changed. This was largely the result of the increasing sophistication of estate management techniques, as first the dean and chapter and then the archbishop employed professional agents to survey and value their lands.[68] Reliance on members of the chapter, untrained in such matters, had always posed problems, since some of the prebendaries were more competent than others in this task. Prebendary de L'Angle made such a mess of the accounts during his turn as treasurer that Henry Foche, the vicar of Monkton, was asked to come in to help out.[69] Hasted observed that Lynford Caryl was a 'person to whom the body is much indebted for his indefatigable care and industry in the regulation and improvement of their estates'.[70] During Caryl's tenure of office in 1769

---

[62] Bodl. MS Tanner 127, fo. 131.

[63] G. E. Mingay, 'The Agricultural Depression, 1730–1750', *EHR*, 8 (1956), 323–38.

[64] Bodl. MS Tanner 123, fo. 68; CCAL, Surveys 12–21; C. E. Woodruff, 'A Seventeenth-Century Survey of the Estates of the Dean and Chapter of Canterbury in East Kent', *AC*, 38 (1926), 29–44; id., 'A Survey of the Sussex Estates of the Dean and Chapter of Canterbury, Taken in 1671', *Sussex Archaeological Collections*, 53 (1910), 192–7.

[65] See A. Oakley, 'The Hill Family of Canterbury, St Paul, Mapmakers', in Margaret Sparks (ed.), *The Parish of St Martin and St Paul, Canterbury* (Canterbury, 1980), 68–70.

[66] CCAL, Chapter Act Book, 1761–75, fo. 28.　　　[67] Ibid., fo. 297.

[68] Ibid., Dean's Book, 1718–42, fo. 11.　　　[69] Ibid., Treasurer's Book, 1679–80.

[70] Hasted, *History of Kent*, xi. 528.

entries were made in books and not on parchment, which made cross reference easier, and in 1772 the chapter agreed that a week before each chapter meeting the mason and carpenter would inspect cathedral property in the precincts, as a way of ensuring that improvements were kept up.[71]

But it was not only the lack of expertise which inhibited the Church from raising more money from their lands; it was also a matter of policy. The Church wished to present itself as a paternalistic landlord. In 1718 Archdeacon Bowers acknowledged that lay landlords took 'more than double of what most Churches take'.[72] He urged Churchmen and fellows of colleges to 'be better landlords than laymen are', citing 'prudence' as one reason which should encourage them to be so. Being charitable to tenants and agreeing on moderate fines was part of a conscious tactic of building up lay support within local society. The chapter act books are full of references to the needs of tenants being taken into consideration. This form of charity was also prompted by the Church's desire to maintain its own position with the locality; through its network of tenants in the diocese the Church could establish and maintain what one official termed in 1663 'friends to the Church'.[73] Such friends were viewed as the backbone of lay Anglicanism: giving support in the localities against dissenters; providing funds for the repair and maintenance of parish churches; and ensuring that a significant proportion of the leading members of the Kentish gentry had a vested interest in the Church's economic prosperity.

Critics of the Church's landed wealth stressed the precarious nature of the tenants' position. In the 1730s Archbishop Wake received demands for an act to give tenants clearer rights. The petitioner claimed that

It is the power and pleasure of Bishops, Deans and Chapters, whether they will permit the present tenants to renew their leases or not, or else suffer the lease to run out and turn the tenant to his utter ruin, and give a lease of the said lands to a relation or friend or to any stranger who will give a great rent or fine.[74]

This allegedly arbitrary power was said to have greatly discouraged the improvement of property. But the records of both the archbishops and the dean and chapter indicate that tenants were often sure of their tenure. Lease-books show the same family names running from the Restoration until the early nineteenth century. This was especially the case on larger properties where the tenants included the leading families in Kent county

[71] CCAL, Chapter Act Book, 1761–75, fos. 212, 284.

[72] Bowers, *Value of Church Leases Considered*, 7. It seems that French canons were also more interested in maintaining revenues, rather than enhancing profits. See O. Hufton, *Bayeux in the Late Eighteenth Century. A Social Study* (Oxford, 1967), 28.

[73] For example, LPL MS 1126, fo. 6 (s.v. 'St John's, Thanet').

[74] Ibid., MS 950, fo. 23.

society, such as Hales, Honeywood, Knatchbull, Oxinden and Brook-Brydges, the continuity of the names from the Restoration to the early nineteenth century being in itself a consequence of the stability which the restored Church brought to the provinces. It was this level of Kentish society which Jane Austen came to know well in the early nineteenth century: for much of the period her relations at Godmersham were tenants of the cathedral and in her correspondence she noted the importance of audit day, when civilities were exchanged between the prebendaries and local gentry.[75] The continuity in the lessees, especially on the larger estates, was in any case beneficial, encouraging tenants to spend money on improvements. The Church needed tenants with enough local prestige to ensure that the Church was well protected, and rich enough to pay their fines.

Such lessees seem to have met with the same benefits as that 'charmed circle' of Church tenants noted by David Marcombe in the diocese of Durham.[76] The placement of manors in the hands of such local notables made the administration of vast properties much more straightforward. The Church favoured letting its estates to substantial men, even for less than the market value. In return, ecclesiastical landlords expected their tenants to take on the more routine burdens and expenses themselves. In this way the archbishops and the members of the dean and chapter preserved their source of income as well as ensuring that the administrative weight was lightened. This smooth-running relationship between the archbishops and the dean and chapter and their tenants was only impeded when tenants refused to comply with the Church's requirements; more often than not this concerned the tenant's failure to repair chancels or an undue exploitation of the woodlands on the estate.

This charitable attitude, formed at the Restoration, continued during the eighteenth century. Fines were frequently lessened to tenants who had served the Church in some way. A 'moderate fine' was taken at Cranbrook, for instance, 'not adhering to the rigid rules of calculation'.[77] In 1773 Lord Sondes wanted to renew for Sheldwich, and the dean and chapter appointed

---

[75] Among the larger estates which remained in the hands of the same gentry family throughout this period were Adisham (Oxinden family); Tenterden (Hales); East Peckham (Twysden); and Eastry (Bargrave). For this see CCAL, C. R. Bunce's Schedule (1805); *Jane Austen's Letters to her Sister Cassandra and Others*, ed. R. W. Chapman (2nd edn., 1952), 215, 20 June 1808. The Austens had leased from the cathedral since 1669: T. Tatton-Brown, 'The Parish Church of St. Laurence, Godmersham: A History', *AC*, 106 (1989), 62. The use of estates to build up a body of support in the area had long been a feature of leasing policy. See Clark, *English Provincial Society*, 43.

[76] D. Marcombe, 'Church Leaseholders: the Decline and Fall of a Rural Elite', in O'Day and Heal, *Princes and Paupers*, 255–76.

[77] CCAL, Dean's Book, 1777–93, fo. 89.

Mr Harvey of Barfreston to survey the lands, telling him to be moderate.[78] In 1801 the lessee of Appledore did not have to pay the full price.[79] Such a policy could be a substantial indirect investment, since allowances and abatements encouraged tenants to maintain and improve the lands and buildings they leased. It goes some way to explain why the Church did not attempt to obtain a true economic return from its estates.

A prominent group of Church tenants was MPs. Ian Green has estimated that nine or ten of the tenants of the Church in the Canterbury and Rochester dioceses were Kentish MPs in the early years of the Restoration.[80] This was an ideal way to cement relations between clerical and lay society. MPs representing the city of Canterbury had an intimate connection with the Church, and some were active supporters of the Anglican interest in Parliament. During the Anglican reaction during Anne's reign the leading Canterbury MP was John Hardres (MP, 1705-22). Hardres was related to several clergy in the diocese and was a member of the extreme Tory October Club, his name being sent to the Pretender in 1721 as a probable supporter of a Jacobite rising.[81] Another member of the family, Sir William Hardres, represented the city from 1727 to 1735.[82] An indication of the economic function of Church lands can be seen in the career of George Gipps who, from a humble background as a poorly paid apothecary in Canterbury, became successful by investment in the hop business. He purchased the lease of St Gregory's Priory from Archbishop Cornwallis in 1773, on the death of the Earl of Chesterfield.[83] The social influence and prestige gained through leasing so much land no doubt helped him in his political career and in 1780 he was elected MP for Canterbury.

The gentry tenants in the diocese, as well as those who found that the holding of Church lands could help them on the road to acceptance within polite society, leased rural manors and estates. They were frequently non-resident and below them was a whole network of under-tenants for whom they were directly responsible. Some of the under-tenant families themselves were as much entrenched in the system as the tenants proper. The Hulse family, for example, were under-tenants at Appledore Court Lodge for over two hundred years.[84] If Church landlords were reluctant to extract the full economic worth of their estates, their tenants showed no such

---

[78] Ibid., 1770-6, fo. 150.   [79] Ibid., Chapter Act Book, 1794-1824, fo. 43.
[80] Green, *Re-establishment of Church of England*, 198.
[81] R. Sedgewick (ed.), *The History of Parliament: The House of Commons, 1715-1754*, 2 vols. (1970), ii. 109.   [82] Ibid.
[83] L. Namier and J. Brook (eds.), *The History of Parliament; The House of Commons, 1754-1790*, 3 vols. (1964), ii. 503.
[84] Sir J. Winnifrith, 'Land Ownership in Appledore, 1500-1900', *AC*, 97 (1981), 1-6.

reticence. The majority of occupiers paid large annual rents to the Church tenant who had sub-let them. The Church lessee made his profit from rack-renting the land at the real value. Estate officials were aware that their tenants not infrequently did their best to hide the real sums they made out of their under-tenants.

Tenants of the rectories belonging to ecclesiastical patrons were a significant group since their existence denied the incumbents the great tithes of about sixty-seven parishes in the diocese. White Kennett complained that at the Restoration, 'we hear of no offer made for the restitution of tithes . . . though it might have been done with great ease . . .'.[85] In fact, as Christopher Hill has noted, the situation was more complex than this remark suggested.[86] The availability of such leases had helped to root the Church within the locality and the possibility of taking them back was not considered. Nevertheless, the Restoration Church did attempt to remedy the situation by augmenting the income of many of the poorer incumbents in the diocese from profits made on the lease of the great tithes. This was in accordance with the king's letter of 1660 which directed Church authorities to covenant with their tenants to pay augmentations so that each incumbent had an income of at least £80 or £100.[87] Archbishop Juxon himself made a total of £1,210 6s. 8d. over in augmentations; special concern being shown to the poor incumbents of the parishes belonging to St Gregory's Priory.[88] Tenants would only agree to the payment of such augmentations when leases were taken out or renewed. Sir George Sandys delayed renewing his lease, 'lest he should be forced to make an augmentation' and in 1663 a memorandum noted that at Whitstable the Church was to 'move for augmentation to curate when renewed'.[89] In 1679 the inhabitants of St John the Baptist, Thanet petitioned Sancroft to make an augmentation to the incumbent upon the renewal of the lease of Salmanstone Grange.[90] The difficulty for the Church authorities was to make sure that their tenants did in fact pay the augmentations. Archdeacon Battely noted that this was not always the case.[91]

Church officials did their best to crack down on tenants who neglected to pay the augmentations. Sir Thomas Culpepper informed them that he had failed to pay the required £20 to the incumbent of Hollingbourne because of family debts.[92] The archbishops and the dean and chapter were also

[85] Kennett, *Case of Impropriations*, 251.   [86] Hill, *Economic Problems*, 138–9.
[87] Wilkins, *Concilia*, iv. 556.   [88] Bodl. MS Tanner 141, fo. 101.
[89] LPL MS 1126, fos. 16, 7.   [90] Bodl. MS Tanner 124, fo. 165, 22 Dec. 1679.
[91] Bodl. MS Tanner 333, fo. 82.
[92] Bodl. MS Tanner 124, fo. 226, Culpepper to Sancroft (1684).

concerned to make sure that their tenants kept the chancels of the parish churches in good repair and were prepared to take tenants to court who evaded this duty. This is an indication that tenants had non-secular responsibilities. In most cases being threatened with a presentation to the ecclesiastical courts seems to have had the desired effect. Ralph Snow used the threat of not renewing Mr Warren's lease at St Margaret's at Cliffe if he failed to repair the chancel.[93] In 1721 William Brockman was presented to the archdeacon's court for failing to repair his chancel at Saltwood. In the following year he showed a certificate signed by the incumbent to testify that the work had been completed.[94] Secker urged his tenants to repair the fabric of their parish churches, arguing that the obligation to maintain and adorn them fell strongly on lessees, 'because they have a more beneficial interest in the estate than the lessors. Being possessed of the greater share of what was orginally given for the support of the service and fabric, they are bound at least in conscience to take care of both'.[95]

The lease of the rectories belonging to St Gregory's Priory was a constant worry for the archbishops' administration. It included the great tithes of twelve parishes in the diocese, leaving the tenant with the responsibility of paying augmentations to the incumbents and repairing the chancels. For much of the period the undertenant for the Church tenants was the Roberts family. In 1678 Snow observed that the chancels of Bekesbourne and Bethersden were out of repair.[96] It was noted that Captain Roberts had repaired Bekesbourne handsomely by 1684 but in 1706 Archdeacon Green complained to Tenison that the then Mrs Roberts was ill-treating the parish of Nackington:

ye [church] Roof of which Mrs Roberts has in several places mended with ordinary painted paper such as in alehouses and looks scandalously . . . they complain heavily of her, for being very hard to them and particularly for very lately taking fourteen acres from ye parish under pretence of its being glebe, though they have enjoyed it for many years without disturbance . . . The minister complains too, as indeed everybody does that has to with her.[97]

Moreover, Mrs Roberts refused to pay the annual augmentation, claiming that the Church tenant, the Earl of Chesterfield, had given her orders not to pay.[98] One incumbent complained to the archbishop that 'the lease of St. Gregory's does not oblige the curates to go to unknown parts to receive

---

[93] LPL, TS 2, fo. 77.   [94] CCAL, X. 79, fo. 189.   [95] Secker, *Charges*, 178.
[96] LPL, TS 5, fo. 37.   [97] Ibid., fo. 82; ibid., TR 12, fo. 15, Green to Tenison, 1706.
[98] Ibid., fo. 16, Simon Hughes to Tenison, 1706. See other complaints from Bethersden, Bekesbourne, Westgate: ibid., fos. 20–36.

their stipends'.[99] More problems arose in the mid-century. Benjamin Dawney informed Secker in 1759, 'after all, this pension is originally due from your Grace, for it is payable out of this rectory'.[100] Secker examined all the evidence brought before him and was anxious to find out how much the Robertses were making out of the lands, for on a large lease like the Priory there were usually several layers of tenants. He discovered that the Robertses had concealed the true value of the lands and cut timber without permission. His dilemma was that he could not afford to upset the Church tenant, the Earl, since it was difficult to find a lessee like Chesterfield who was willing to pay the substantial fine and rents and take on the administrative responsibility for a large collection of manors and parsonages. Secker had to bear this in mind, especially at a time when other landlords were being forced to make considerable rent reductions to their tenants. But Secker would not tolerate the Robertses' attempt to deduct the land tax from the augmentations. In treating with Chesterfield for the renewal of the lease, he agreed to accept the Earl's valuation of the estate, providing that, 'if your lordship can legally exempt the pensions of the incumbents from the payment of the land-tax, I would purchase that exemption of you with part of the fine'.[101] Chesterfield refused to have this written into the lease since this would bind his successors to an obligation that might devalue the land. Secker, 'fearful of the bad consequences from making any alteration in the lease', told the incumbents that he would pay the land-tax himself, 'since nothing more is in my power'.[102]

It has been worth looking at this case in some detail, for it shows both the considerations and the problems facing Church landlords. The archbishops' concern was with the upkeep of the parish churches and the stipends of their clergy and they expected their tenants not to let them down. There is no evidence to suggest that such a prolonged problem was typical of the attitudes of most tenants. Such cases, and the presentation of tenants to the courts, only tell of a breakdown in the scheme: they do not tell of those tenants who regularly repaired chancels and paid the requisite stipends.

When tenants could be seen to act on behalf of the Church, they might be rewarded at the next renewal. The dean and chapter asked Sancroft's advice in 1680 since they wanted to reward one of their tenants who had defended their lands. They thought that the archbishop might know of

---

[99] Ibid., fo. 46, Thomas Randolph to Secker, 4 Oct. 1758.
[100] Ibid., fo. 94, Dawney to Secker, 1 Aug. 1759.
[101] Ibid., fo. 93, Secker to Lord Chesterfield, 18 July 1759.
[102] Ibid., fo. 95, Secker to incumbents, 13 Aug. 1759.

a precedent and told him that 'we do not want to expose ourselves to censure'.[103] In 1709 the lessee of Maidstone had to pay only £80 out of a £126 fine, 'in consideration of a troublesome suit'.[104] In return for the co-operation which tenants gave to the Church, their leases, as the arch-bishop's receiver, Christopher Hodgson, informed Parliament in 1837, were very open.[105] Apart from clauses safeguarding timber, buildings, and fences, there was not the same interest in shaping in detail the form of leases whereby agricultural innovators like Coke of Norfolk achieved far-reaching changes.[106] Fines were lowered to encourage the repair of build-ings and tenants covenanted to use the buildings on Church lands which they might be tempted to neglect in favour of their own. The tenant of Northbourne in 1671 had to 'store in the barn all ye corn and hay growing and tithes, and to fold ye sheep on ye premises'.[107] The lessee of Coldred Manor in 1675 agreed to 'lay upon ye premises all ye compost arising from Hay or Corn after ye first three years'.[108] Some tenants were charged with giving food rents. In the sixteenth century nearly half of the archbishop's kitchen requirements was provided by the tenantry but after the Restor-ation such charges were unusual and were commuted, although several lessees still covenanted to entertain the archbishop's officials when they were in Kent on business.[109] When lessees failed to keep up buildings, petitions to the Church officials showed how vital Church properties could be in the local economy. The parishioners of Godmersham complained to Tenison that the mill belonging to the dean and chapter was unusable after the last tenant failed to renew: 'the poor have to go to a lot of trouble to have their grain ground . . . which is a very great burden'.[110]

There were other types of property besides the manors and rectories that could be leased. The urban tenements were let to members of other social orders: shopkeepers, innkeepers and tradesmen. This meant that the Church's links were far broader than merely with the gentry classes. The urban properties, some of which were let to fairly poor families, changed hands at a much greater rate than the large rural estates. The 300 tenements in Deal belonging to the archbishop were clearly something of an adminis-trative problem for his estate officials. In the early years of the Restoration it was complained that they were 'in a very poor and deplorable condition

---

[103] LPL, TC 9, fo. 144.   [104] CCAL, Chapter Act Book, 1670–1710, fo. 236.
[105] Parliamentary Papers 1837, ix, *Select Committee Report on Church Leases*, 25.
[106] R. A. C. Parker, *Coke of Norfolk: A Financial and Agricultural Study, 1707–1842* (Oxford, 1975), 50, 54–5, 67–8, 137–47.
[107] Bodl. MS Sancroft 119, fo. 8.   [108] Ibid., fo. 16.
[109] Heal, *Of Prelates and Princes*, 294; e.g. Bodl. MS Sancroft 119, fo. 141.
[110] LPL MS 952, fo. 46: Petition of parishioners of Godmersham, 20 May 1695.

made for by the last plague, of which died in that little town (most of ye houses being his Grace's) 1200–1400 . . .'.[111] Officials often had to sort out disputes over tenure since there were more people who could afford to rent these properties than was the case for the larger blocks of land. The Deal properties were usually leased for thirty years at a time, and the wide variation in the dates of the initial lease meant that there was a considerable difference in the income received from these from year to year. In 1676 fifty Deal leases were renewed at a total fine of £114, but in 1677 only eleven leases were up for renewal, £20 being taken in fines.[112]

Much of the responsibility for maintaining a satisfactory relationship between the Church landlords and their tenants rested on the estate officials. The archbishops and the dean and chapter employed a host of receivers, agents, and wood-reeves to administer their estates. These could be a vital bridge between the interests of the Church and lay society. Their intimate knowledge of the economic position of the Church within the diocese was often crucial in helping successive archbishops and prebendaries to obtain information about their lands. As far as the cathedral administration was concerned, the most vital post was that of auditor. Some indication of the interpenetration of ecclesiastical and secular considerations connected with the auditor's position was revealed in a memorandum: it 'deserves a person more experienced in ecclesiastical affairs than secular; the making of a lease or auditing of accounts being as I conceive ye easiest part of ye business'.[113]

The relationship between the Church hierarchy and their tenants benefited from the continuity of administration offered by those officials who served for a long time. The archbishopric was fortunate in having Ralph Snow as an estate official from the Restoration until 1707. As treasurer and registrar he proved to be an invaluable advisor to a number of archbishops, corresponding about all aspects of estate business, and making his annual 'Journeys into Kent' to talk with tenants and check up on repairs of buildings and the upkeep of chancels, fences and woods.[114] Most of the time Snow, along with the other officials, lived at Lambeth where he was something of a character, fond of drinking and horse-play. In 1706 Gibson wrote to Arthur Charlett, 'My Lord Archbishop is now in Kent upon his

---

[111] LPL., TC 4, fo. 100 'The Town of Deal (1667)'.   [112] Ibid., TS 5, fos. 11, 51.

[113] BL MS Harleian 7377, fo. 34ᵛ, Sheldon to Tillotson, 1672. For the problems in finding a successor to the omniscient William Somner: Bodl. MS Rawlinson 93, fo. 47; MS Tanner 123, fo. 8, dean and chapter to Sheldon, 28 Aug. 1672.

[114] LPL., TC 4. There was, however, no such journey in the politically charged summer of 1688: TC 5 2, fo. 87.

visitation, has left the care of his family to me in sacris; and to Mr Snow in secularibus. The old gentleman is still hearty'.[115]

Estate officials could help iron out tenants' grievances, especially during the delicate time when fines were being assessed. They were so important in maintaining the relationship between the Church and local society that it was essential to employ men who had the confidence of the tenantry. Edward Lawrence, the well-known writer on estate-management, advised that stewards and estate officials must be reasonable with tenants, not employing 'the blustering manner of agents sent down from London'.[116] Once such rapport had been gained, the Church authorities might be able to learn more about their property. John Middleton, who was an agent for the archbishop's properties in Deal, wrote to Secker on behalf of some of the tenants in 1760, reporting that they 'think their rents were set too high in that list, and indeed so did I, considering the case in all its circumstances. The Fountain is not an Inn in the sense you mean it, but a common ale-house, used only by common sailors and the meanest company'.[117] He also pointed out that one of the properties was leased by two sisters, 'who are very ancient and have but little means of support'.

There was much competition among local families for posts in the management of estates. A report to Sancroft in 1681 acknowledged that 'wood-reeves places in Kent are to my knowledge coveted by ye best gentlemen in Canterbury'.[118] The position of gamekeeper was sought after, and these were often given to rich men and thus amounted to no more than gaming licences. In 1673 Sir James Oxinden, the lessee of Adisham was granted the patent of gamekeeper, and in 1732 the same patent was given to Sir Robert Hales.[119] In 1728 Thomas Munter, a gamekeeper of Ickham Manor, and Robert Stead, the keeper of Chartham Manor covenanted with the chapter to provide pheasants, woodcock, and hares.[120] Local men did not have a monopoly on such posts, however. Every archbishop had relatives and clients who had to be rewarded and maintained, and such posts were regarded as legitimate fodder for this purpose. What was critical was to ensure that there were always enough positions in the estate administration for local men. Archbishops' relatives could prove to be a liability in such

[115] Bodl. MS Ballard, 6, fo. 113, Gibson to Charlett, 20 June 1706. Snow's abilities seem to have been wide-ranging. He helped decode intercepted letters from suspected Jacobites: LPL MS 1029, fos. 79, 104, 197.

[116] Edward Laurence, *The Duty and Office of a Land Steward* (Dublin, 1731), 11.

[117] LPL, TR 20, fos. 26, 38.   [118] Bodl. MS Rawl. Lett. 106, fo. 181.

[119] CCAL, Chapter Act Book, 1670–1710, fo. 20ᵛ; ibid, 1727–41, fo. 68. There were also negotiations over who could catch fish, for example: LPL, TR 12, fo. 133, Cuming to Moore.

[120] CCAL, Chapter Act Book, 1727–45, fo. 40.

posts. Sir George Juxon, a nephew of the archbishop, was given the position of wood-reeve at the Restoration. Ralph Snow had to reprimand him in 1664 for felling trees without permission and thus defrauding the diocese of some of its assets.[121] The danger of relying too heavily on officials was that they could always make the system work to their own advantage. Wood-reeves appear to have been especially prone to taking more than their dues. In 1716 the dean and chapter had to investigate the activities of their reeve Jacob Janway.[122] Secker had to take an equally firm line with John Herring and his deputy Edward Denne in 1763. Herring's patent limited his perquisites to only certain woods but he had extended it by taking more than was necessary for repairs and was dismissed.[123] The existence of a network of officers in the diocese ensured that the Church was firmly entrenched in provincial society. The deep roots which the Church had in Kent can partly be explained by the fact that it could provide posts and prestige for local men.

PROPERTY IN CANTERBURY

A distinctive type of urban property owned by the cathedral were the houses in the precincts at Canterbury. Part of Archbishop Laud's policy in the diocese had included an attempt to remove lay tenants from the precincts as a concomitant of the clericalist revival which aimed to clear away secular interferences in Church life.[124] At the Restoration some effort seems to have been made to revive this aspect of Laudian policy. But Laud's vision of the collegiality of the clerical community, set apart from lay society, had little relevance after 1660 now that clergy's wives were such a feature of the precincts. In the early seventeenth century, only four of the prebendaries were married, but after 1660 clerical marriage became the norm.[125]

During the 1660s some difficulty was experienced in getting all the property in the precincts back from the parliamentary occupiers. Captain Owen, for instance, was still in possession of the deanery in 1661. It was reported that he had 'pull'd down the Dean of Canterburies Chappel and part of his house', but that he 'yet forcibly lived in the [rest] of it'.[126] The chapter complained that 'some of the inhabitants are very disorderly persons, such as

---

[121] LPL, TC 4, fo. 29. [122] CCAL, Canterbury Letters, 1661–1760, no. 185.

[123] LPL, TR 18, fo. 23. [124] Clark, *English Provincial Society*, 393.

[125] A great deal of information relating to life in the precincts in the late eighteenth century can be gleaned from the gossipy preface to *Poems by the late George-Monck Berkeley*, ed. Eliza Berkeley (1797); D. Gardiner, 'The Berkeleys of Canterbury', *AC*, 69 (1956), 117–24.

[126] *Mercurius Publicus* (1661) 2, 10–17 Jan. 31.

despise the Prayers of the Church and hold conventicles and some keep ale-houses. In the mean time many members of the Church are destitute of houses, and [we] are forc'd to provide houses for them, or pay their rent'.[127]

A particular problem in the years immediately after 1660 were the widows and relatives of former prebendaries, who frequently pleaded with the archbishops and the dean and chapter for charity, stressing the loyalty of their husbands to the royalist cause. Charles II wrote to the dean on their behalf, and royal dispensations were issued to permit Eliza Turner, Damien Kingsley, and Eliza Bargrave to stay in their houses, even though this was against the statutes.[128] He insisted that they should continue to renew the leases to such fit objects of charity. Backed by royal support the widows became 'cocksure' and the chapter objected to their occupation, citing Laud's warning that such practices could lead to an alienation of Church property.[129] Charles tried to get Archbishop Sheldon to persuade the dean and chapter to renew their leases. In 1666 the king wrote to the chapter:

Upon reading the humble petition of Damian Kingsley, of Canterbury, widow, setting forth that the sufferings of her late husband, for his loyalty to us and in our service hath reduced her to so low a condition, that the greatest part of her subsistence is a term of years and tenant right in a house built within the precincts of the Cathedral . . . for some reason the lease has not been renewed . . . renew it at a moderate rent.[130]

The king threatened to use his power of dispensation but the chapter retorted that as the house in question was not built on the churchyard, there was no statute forbidding the renewal. They did point out, however, that many of the houses within the precincts were inhabited by disorderly strangers, some of whom attended nonconformist conventicles. Such activity was anathema to the restored clergy who informed Charles that they felt bound not to renew:

the tenants speak high and threaten us with the law . . . and complain to those who shall over-rule us. But we fear them not. If it shall happen that we be hindered from doing this Right to ye Church . . . it shall content us that we have done our best endeavour.[131]

In a minor way, the problem mirrored the wider concern which the Church faced in this period of trying to balance the claim of loyalty and obedience

---

[127] CCAL, 'unmarked box' 1/4; Bodl. MS Tanner 123, fos. 92–3; Bodl. MS Add.c. 308, fo. 36, Sheldon to Turner, 13 Feb. 1666. A similar problem occurred at York where members of the chapter had to rent houses in the city. Dorothy M. Owen, 'From the Restoration until 1822', in G. E. Aylmer and R. Cant (eds.), *A History of York Minster* (Oxford, 1977), 234.

[128] Bodl. MS Tanner 123, fo. 89, draft, 26 July 1665.

[129] Ibid., fo. 92, Turner to Sheldon, 1 Feb. 1666.

[130] Ibid., fo. 91, Charles II to dean and chapter, 31 Mar. 1666.   [131] Ibid., fo. 92.

to the Crown with the need to maintain its independence, and fore-shadowed the need to establish the limits to passive obedience which was to be demonstrated against James II.[132]

The chapter was also wary about leasing out property in the precincts to members of the city. In 1687 when John Younger (stall II, 1685–92) leased his house to Colonel Henry Lee, the mayor of Canterbury, an agreement was drawn up which necessitated the mayor leaving his mace, the symbol of his authority, outside the precincts.[133] The houses in the precincts belonging to the six-preachers were rarely used as their places of residence and were also leased out. But relations between the lay and clerical residents in the precincts were not without their tensions. George Stanhope was anxious to safeguard his prestige as dean of the metropolitical cathedral and reacted strongly whenever he felt that his status was being undermined. After a particularly exuberant soirée at the house of Sir Richard Head, the dean claimed to have been woken up and insulted by members of the party.[134] Yet by the 1780s Hasted could refer to the 'genteel families who form a very respectable neighbourhood within these Precincts which are kept remarkably clean and neat, and being gravelled and well planted with rows of trees, make a most pleasant and desirable residence'.[135]

Another source of potential grievance was the tendency for shopkeepers and house-owners in Canterbury to extend their own properties in ways that might be detrimental to the cathedral's property. Orders were issued to prevent people depositing rubbish in the precincts.[136] The cathedral authorities were trying to preserve the peace and separate character of the precincts. They demanded the removal of cattle, horses, and geese from grazing within the cloisters and in 1722 ordered the keeper of their gaol to drive out all beggars 'and not to suffer such Nastiness about the church or Precincts as is so intolerably otherwise at present'.[137] In the early nineteenth century the dean and chapter were concerned about the havoc caused by the annual fair, because it was disorderly. In 1810 by their resolution 'All Puppet Shews, Gin Stalls, Roundabouts, Wild Beasts, Swings etc. were refused admission, and no stalls allowed but on the Broad

---

[132] For the problem of resistance to James II see Goldie, 'Political Thought of the Anglican Revolution'.

[133] CCAL, Treasurer's Book, 1663–4, copy of a letter from Lord Treasurer Southampton to Sir Thomas Peyton and Sir Anthony Aucher, 22 Oct. 1664; ibid., Register 29, fo. 291, Col. Lee's Agreement, 28 Oct. 1687; Bodl. MS Add. c. 307, fo. 174. For the wider issue of maintaining corporate independence see R. A. Beddard, 'The Privileges of Christchurch, Canterbury: Archbishop Sheldon's Enquiries of 1671', *AC*, 87 (1973), 81–100.

[134] CCAL, Chapter Act Book, 1711–26, fos. 71ᵛ, 75; ibid., Dean's Book, 1718–42, fo. 197.

[135] Hasted, *History of Kent*, xi. 542.   [136] CCAL, Dean's Book, 1776–93, fo. 63.

[137] Ibid., Chapter Act Book, 1711–26, fo. 51.

Pavement and one under the Gateway for Gingerbread, Toys and Merchandise'. In 1814 it was agreed to remove the fair from the precincts altogether and move it to the Cattle Market in the city.[138]

The presence of lay tenants within the precincts was symptomatic of the Church's relations with the city at large. The dean and chapter were a dominating force within city life: they owned many of the inns, shops, and properties within Canterbury; they provided employment for many of its inhabitants; they contributed to the upkeep of the roads; and they played a large part in shaping the economic fortunes of the city. Most of the houses in the parishes of St Andrew, St Mary Magdalen, and St Alphege, the major trading area of the city, were held under lease from the chapter and the number of people employed on a regular and part-time basis made the cathedral the largest employer within the city and its environs.[139] The range of employment is also striking—from the holders of important offices such as the auditor to the rat-catcher (paid 6*d.* a rat) and the old people who were given small jobs such as sweeping the library and making brooms, mending carpets, and washing surplices.[140] In 1676 the chapter paid for people to go to London to be touched for the King's Evil and in the next year it gave money to a dying man and a woman to watch over him.[141] All this was part of the cathedral's paternalist role within the city: providing help and giving alms to the poor, who were paid after sacrament; paying for the education of tradesmen's sons and finding apprenticeships for choristers; looking after the relations of former employees and administering the charity to look after clergy widows; and maintaining a prison.[142] A testimony to the relationship between the cathedral, the city, and the county was the foundation of the Kent and Canterbury Hospital in 1791. The dean and chapter helped contribute towards its building and paid for the maintenance of the hospital chaplain.[143] Canterbury Cathedral, alongside other such institutions of the *ancien régime* was a considerable employer within the local economy.

The chapter also contributed to the spate of improvements in the city at the end of the eighteenth century, participating in Canterbury's 'urban renaissance'. These helped transform it from being Defoe's 'general ruin a

---

[138] Ibid., Dean's Book, 1793–1822, 158, 169, 210.

[139] Hasted, *History of Kent*, xi. 100.

[140] CCAL, Treasurer's Book, 1670–1.   [141] Ibid., 1676–7.

[142] CCAL, Records of Sykes' Charity; ibid., Charity; ibid., Chapter Act Book, 1761–75, fo. 105.

[143] F. M. Hall, R. S. Stevens, and J. Whyman, *The Kent and Canterbury Hospital, 1790–1987* (Ramsgate, 1987).

little recovered'.[144] The cathedral gave generously to the programme of lighting and paving, subscribing £50 to the new corn-market and in 1827 installing gas lighting in the precincts.[145] Hasted noted that the new paving had been in imitation of London styles

> and the improvements would have been carried still further, had not the short tenure by which most of the Houses in it were still held under Church lease (which is in every place the bane of all industry) deterred the lessees from hazarding more on such uncertain property.

Hasted claimed that save for this the city 'would in all likelihood have been second to few others in the kingdom'.[146]

THE MANAGEMENT OF WOODLAND

The Church authorities spent a great deal of effort in ensuring that their woodlands were well maintained. They had proved invaluable to the parliamentary forces who felled large quantities for fuel, being unable to obtain coal from Newcastle.[147] At the Restoration the dean and chapter estimated that £8,000 worth of timber had been taken from Sturt Wood between 1647 and 1660.[148] However, Snow's accounts show that post-Restoration archbishops still owned 3,324 acres of woodlands.[149] His annual inspections involved advising wood-reeves which trees to fell and what prices to ask. There was a ready market for timber at the shipyards at Chatham, for fuel and for building purposes.[150]

Snow not only checked up on the activities of wood-reeves; he found that tenants were liable to take more wood than they were allowed. Tenants were meant to preserve woodlands on their estates, although they were allowed to use wood towards the repair and upkeep of buildings and fences. Snow was careful to show that this was given at pleasure and was not a tenant right. As a result of numerous disputes with tenants, the dean and chapter attempted to tighten up the wording of clauses concerning timber on their estates. In 1720 an attorney submitted his proposals 'to make clear what

---

[144] P. Borsay, 'The English Urban Renaissance: The Development of Provincial Urban Culture, c.1680–c.1760', *Social History*, 5 (1977), 581–603; Daniel Defoe, *A Tour Thro' the Whole Island of Great Britain*, ed. G. D. H. Cole, 2 vols. (1968) i. 118.

[145] CCAL, Chapter Act Book, 1775–94, fo. 323.

[146] Hasted, *History of Kent*, xi. 99.

[147] C. Firth and R. Raith (eds.), *Acts and Ordinances of the Interregnum, 1642–1660*, 2 vols. (1911), i. 170.

[148] Heaton, 'Dean and Chapter', 9.   [149] LPL, TC 4, fo. 12.

[150] Chalklin, *Seventeenth-Century Kent*, 23–4, 105–6.

proportion of types (of timber) must not be touched', showing that the dean and chapter had liberty of access to 'come in, cut, mark, grub up, cart and carry away'.[151]

Critics of the Church's leasehold system maintained that the position of tenants was so insecure that they were given no incentive to protect young trees so that Church leasehold estates were noticeably bare of timber.[152] Yet the concern of the Church officials in the diocese to regulate and supervise the timber sales and planting on their estates suggests that clergy were well aware of the importance of timber to their income and it was partly their careful husbanding of such resources during the eighteenth century and the profitable sales during the Napoleonic Wars which account for the dramatic increase in Church revenues in this period.[153]

Disputes concerning woodland might occur when, as was often the case, the tenant was a landowner in his own right and had lands which bordered those he rented from the Church. The failure to identify Church lands where the tenant had adjacent freehold was part of the problem of inadequate land surveys. This may have been aggravated by the uncertainty of the situation at the Restoration; George Lynch informed Secker in 1758 of the 'shaving' and 'paving away a little from each parcel when returned to the Archbishop'.[154] In trying to identify the archbishop's lands at the Restoration, Snow had to rely on old surveys and information from local inhabitants. He even used the parliamentary surveys, finding that the wood at Ashley Grange had been completely cut down by the 'rebels'.[155] It was also observed that Longbeach Wood had been 'wasted and destroyed when it was in the hands of Queen Elizabeth'.[156] In 1759 Secker ordered a complete survey of archbishop's woods, and this indicated on whose lands the Church woods bordered.[157]

A report from the sixty-six-acre wood at Herne was indicative of a wider problem. The agent told Secker that the woods had been totally neglected by estate officials and had been appropriated by a Mr Mills, the lessee of the great tithes:

If my Lord, from particular facts I may be allowed to judge of general grievances, I apprehend the Church of Canterbury can meet with no difficulty in accounting for the loss of her patrimony, for 'tis evident that either the inactivity of some, or the

---

[151] LPL, TC 4, fos. 13, 1667.
[152] CCAL, Chapter Act Book, 1711–26, interleaved between fos. 96 and 97.
[153] By 1804 the archbishop was making £2,458 5s. 11d. from woods: LPL, TS 140, fo. 99, Pettman to Young, 18 Feb. 1804.
[154] Ibid., TR 20, fo. 90.   [155] Ibid., TC 5, fo. 56.
[156] Bodl., MS Sancroft 119, fo. 12.   [157] LPL, TS, 5.

negligence of others may have furnished an agreeable opportunity of effecting such an alienation . . . Recent instances there are in the parish, too notoriously known, where the Church formerly possessed large tracts of land which now she can only show on a map.[158]

The Church authorities attempted to ensure that their tenants provided a terrier of the lands before leases were renewed. Dean Tillotson informed George Thorp that, concerning Mr Hales' lease, 'I shall never consent to ye renewing it, till a perfect terrier be made and our lands set out by him'.[159] In 1678 Sancroft demanded a terrier from Oxenden before renewing, and noted that Sir Edward Monins had a 'pretended title to [Southwood Lands] by virtue of Queen Elizabeth and other mean conveyances'.[160] Some leases included covenants which directed the tenants to mark out leasehold land with stones.[161] But the complaint that Churchmen did not have adequate knowledge of their lands was a frequent one. In 1742 Samuel Shuckford noted that the 'Church has suffered in Appledore, what I fear we shall never recover, by making a new lease too hastily'.[162] Other methods of protecting timber included forbidding unmuzzled horses to work in the woods, and inserting clauses in leases demanding that trees be planted.[163]

If tenants had to be prevented from despoiling the Church's woods, there were also threats from other sections of society. In parts of the Weald of Kent labourers had customarily appropriated an almost continual supply of fallen wood, which helped to eke out their income.[164] As Cobbett found out in his rides round Kent in the early nineteenth century, a wooded landscape was apt to offer relative prosperity to the poor.[165] The Church authorities attempted to clamp down on such behaviour. Snow complained of forest inhabitants who damaged woodland by letting cattle trample through them and gathered wood for fuel. In 1684 he noted that Bevis Wood, six miles from Canterbury, 'near a Beggarly place called Upstreet . . . is much prejudiced by those poor people who will in winter never want fuel so long as there is underwood there'.[166] He ordered that the fences around the wood should be strengthened. There had been attempts to discipline wood-gatherers from at least the thirteenth century, but this

---

[158] LPL, TR 25, fo. 232.
[159] CCAL, Canterbury Letters, 1661–1760, no. 165, Tillotson to Thorp, 5 July 1682.
[160] Bodl. MS Sancroft 119, fo. 17.   [161] Ibid., and LPL, TC, 'View of Estates'.
[162] CCAL, Canterbury Letters, no. 218, Shuckford to Lynch, 17 Nov. 1742.
[163] Ibid., Chapter Act Book, 1761–75, fo. 195.
[164] A. Everitt, 'Farm Labourers', in J. Thirsk (ed.), *The Agrarian History of England and Wales*, iv. (1967), 404.
[165] William Cobbett, *Rural Rides*, ed. G. Woodcock (1967), 206.
[166] LPL, TS 52, fo. 74.

appears to have taken on a new dimension during the seventeenth and eighteenth centuries. All over England the eighteenth century witnessed concern shown to the woodland regions of the kingdom.[167] The Church landlords in east Kent were no exception. Perhaps this was partly because these regions were centres of nonconformity in the diocese and as such were considered to be areas of alternative political, social, and religious activity.[168] Attacks on wood-gathering can also be seen as another indication of the breakdown of the 'moral economy' within society.[169]

EXPENDITURE

So far this chapter has been concerned with the ways in which the Church landlords received their income. What also has to be considered are the various types of expenditure which contributed to the economic function of the Church. As Felicity Heal has shown, there had always been a tension in the objects of archiepiscopal and capitular spending: that between caring for the poor on the one hand, and winning the support of influential members of the laity and preserving the clergy's status in society on the other.[170] One of the most pressing problems for the Church dignitaries in the years after 1660, on which they spent a large proportion of their income, was the physical maintenance of Church buildings. Myles Smith reckoned that the damage inflicted on English cathedrals and Church buildings during the Interregnum amounted to more than £½ million.[171] The prebendaries of Canterbury Cathedral were quick to point out the destruction which their cathedral had suffered at the hands of 'Blue Dick' Culmer and the parliamentary troops in 1642–3.[172] In 1660 William Cooke petitioned the recently reconstituted chapter for a reward for his help in resisting Culmer when

[167] B. Bushaway, *By Rite. Custom, Ceremony and Community in England, 1700–1800* (1982), 207–33.

[168] A. Everitt, *The Pattern of Rural Dissent: The Nineteenth Century*, University of Leicester, Department of Local History Occasional Papers, 4 (1972).

[169] Thompson, 'Moral Economy of the English Crowd'; id., 'Patrician Society, Plebeian Culture', *Journal of Social History*, 8 (1974), 382–405. But there were powerful countervailing forces, such as the distribution of charity at the parish level, which are discussed below, pp. 165–7.

[170] F. Heal, 'The Archbishops of Canterbury and the Practice of Hospitality', *JEH*, 33 (1982), 544–63. Hirschberg, 'Episcopal Incomes', 221 shows that hospitality and household accounts might take up half of the income.

[171] Bodl., MS Tanner 141, fo. 90.

[172] For the destruction: A. L. Rowse, *Reflections on the Puritan Revolution* (1986), 26; W. H. Hunt, *The Puritan Moment: The Coming of Revolution in an English County* (Cambridge, Mass., 1983), 299, 300, 308; D. Underdown, *Revel, Riot and Rebellion: Popular Politics and Culture in England, 1603–1660* (Oxford, 1985), 139, 177–8.

smashing the stained glass.[173] The scale of the destruction inflicted upon
the cathedral fabric is revealed in an account of 1662:

we shall here recount and represent the sad, forlorne, and languishing condition of
our Church at our returne; which (in short) was such as made it look more like a
ruined Monastery than a Church; so little had the fury of the late Reformers left
remaining to it besides the bare walles and roof, and these, partly through neglect,
and partly by the daily assaults and batteries of the disaffected so shaken, ruinated
and defaced, as it was not more unserviceable in the way of a cathedral, then justly
scandalous to all who delight to serve God in the beauty of holiness. The windows
(famous both for strength and beauty) so generally battered and broken down, as it
lay exposed to the injury of all weathers: the whole roof, with that of the steeples, the
Chapter house and cloister extremely impaired and ruined both in timber work and
lead; the water tables, pipes and much other lead in almost all places, cut off . . .; the
choir stripped and robbed of rich godly hangings; the organ and organ loft, communion table and the best and chiefest part of the furniture with the rail before it
and the screen of the tabernacle . . . and many monuments shamefully abused.[174]

The inventory is revealing not only of the damage, but also of a frame of
mind determined to recreate 'the beauty of holiness'. The physical repair
of cathedrals and their refurbishment was a necessary, if expensive, duty of
the Restoration Church. Gradually, relics of the past were restored to place.
Some items were returned, like the magnificent font which had been presented by John Warner in the 1630s, damaged during the soldiers' occupation of the cathedral and had been lovingly hidden away by William
Somner, the auditor to the new chapter.[175] The font was fully repaired and
set in position by 1663, attracting appreciative comments from visitors to
the cathedral. The chapter informed Warner that they wished to preserve
it 'from the rude, unhallowed and sacriligious hands and approaches of a
sordid and malignant generation in these licentious times, whose meat and
drink it is to invade, abuse and violate all that ever may adorn either the
house or service of God'.[176] They were clearly aware of the ideological
significance of their activities, recognizing that their recreation of decency
and order would not be effected without some opposition.

[173] CCAL, Petition 32.
[174] Quoted in J. C. Robertson, 'The Condition of Canterbury Cathedral at the Restoration
in A.D. 1660', *AC*, 10 (1876), 95–6.
[175] Bodl. MS Tanner 123, fo. 57, 13 Dec. 1662.
[176] Quoted in C. E. Woodruff, 'Some Seventeenth Century Letters and Petitions from the
Muniments of the Dean and Chapter of Canterbury', *AC*, 42 (1930), 123, dean and chapter to
Bishop Warner of Rochester, 5 Oct. 1663. The first person to be baptized in the restored font
was Sophia, the daughter of Prebendary John Aucher, on 8 Oct. 1663. See *The Register Booke
of Christninges, Marriages, and Burialls within the Precinct of the Cathedrall and Metropoliticall
Church of Christe of Canterburie*, ed. R. Hovenden (London, 1878), 12.

In the early 1660s the precincts must have been a scene of almost frenetic activity as builders, glaziers, plumbers, carpenters, ironsmiths, cleaners, and workmen were employed in the task.[177] This involved not only structural repair but also the refurbishment of the choir. Money was also laid out on the purchase of rich hangings for the choir, communion plate, a lectern, linen, candles, and candlesticks.[178] Central to this activity was the dean, Thomas Turner, who lavished time and attention on the matter. Turner brought down prayer books from London and also arranged for cushions for the choir to be delivered. He presented to the cathedral a magnificent folio Bible, covered in silver.[179] Spurred on by Turner, the chapter spent £5,248 on the fabric by 1662.[180] Archbishop Juxon gave money towards the repair of the precinct gates.[181] So much had been achieved by 1665 that John Evelyn noted that the cathedral was 'exceedingly well repaired since His Majesties returne'.[182] Such expense was used as a justification by cathedral clergy for the high fines they received. Peter du Moulin, replying to lay criticism that the clergy had obtained an inordinate sum of money from their tenants, maintained that without this the cathedral would have been a 'heap of ruines'. He was quick to point out the relationship between the physical manifestation of the Church as an institution within society and its spiritual role:

And it is that ruin, and another following upon it of a better Church than the material, which such men as the libeller aim at, when they cry out against fines and would have them converted to other uses. God keep the Church from such stewards; and enrich us with a better patrimony of the Church, than this temporal wealth, which brings little plenty and much envy.[183]

Du Moulin was particularly sensitive to nonconformist criticisms of the wealth of the restored Church. His brother Lewis had been a supporter of

---

[177] CCAL, Treasurer's Books, 1660-1, 1661-2, 1662-3, 1663-4, 1669-70.

[178] Bodl. MS Tanner 123, fo. 59, 13 Dec. 1662.

[179] For some of Turner's gifts to the cathedral see Peter du Moulin, *A Sermon Preached in the Metropolitical Church of Canterbury, October 17 1672, at the Funeral of the Very Revd. Thomas Turner, D.D.* (London, 1672), 23.

[180] Bodl. MS Tanner 128, fo. 57, 13 Dec. 1662.

[181] *Diary of John Evelyn*, ed. de Beer, iii. 395, 6 Jan. 1665. For evidence of a similar restoration at Salisbury see R. A. Beddard, 'Cathedral Furnishings of the Restoration Period: A Salisbury Inventory of 1685', *Wiltshire Archaeological Magazine*, 66 (1971), 147-55.

[182] *Mercuricus Publicus*, no. 23 (5-12 June, 1662), 358-60.

[183] [Peter Du Moulin], *A Letter to a Person of Quality, Concerning the Fines Received by the Church at its Restoration. By a Prebendary of the Church of Canterbury* (1668), 5; and Bodl. MS Tanner 45, fos. 159-60, Du Moulin to Sheldon, 1668. It may be that over £17,000 had been received in fines by November 1661. But this was clearly an anomaly. By 1663-4, fines were only £1,121: see Green, *Re-establishment of Church of England*, 105.

the Cromwellian regime and had been appointed to the chair of History at Oxford and had attacked the revenues of the Church.[184] The first two decades of the Restoration saw much inter-familial squabbling and Peter persuaded his fellow prebendary John De L'Angle to intervene. This was unsuccessful, although on his deathbed Lewis appears to have recanted his attacks.[185]

In 1670 Archbishop Sheldon asked the dean for a breakdown of the chapter's spending, urging: 'you cannot be ignorant with what an evil eye have men looked upon ye possessions of ye Church'.[186] By this time £9,178 had been spent on repairs.[187] The act-books of the chapter reveal a continued concern with the physical maintenance of the cathedral. The repair of the fabric was a continuing problem. The running costs for repairs were high, largely caused by the detrimental effects of weather and erosion on a medieval building. The great storm of 1703, which proved so disastrous to cathedral buildings all over England, and which killed Bishop Kidder of Bath and Wells, took its toll at Canterbury by damaging the Arundel Tower.[188] Although some repairs were made to the tower it remained a constant source of worry and was eventually replaced in 1832.[189] Traditionally, the costs for such repairs came from the 'timber money', but this proved insufficient. Early in the eighteenth century it was agreed that the money customarily given by new prebendaries on their installation as well as that given by archbishops at visitations should now be used for repairs and decoration.[190] From time to time some of the money from fines was used for this purpose too. In 1704, for example, the architect Nicholas Hawksmoor was consulted on the best way to spend £400, part of Colonel Lee's fine, on beautifying the cathedral, and in 1751, after a specially lush crop of fines, money was set aside for ornamenting the building.[191] But a survey in 1721 showed that at least £14,000 would be needed to put the fabric in decent repair, and in 1722 the dean and chapter added up their expenses on the fabric since the Restoration and asked Archbishop Wake about the possibility of some kind of public provision for the cathedral, 'which being the metropolitan and first in dignity of all England, we hope it will find a

---

[184] *DNB.*

[185] Lewis Du Moulin, *A Short and True Account of the Several Advances the Church of England Hath Made Towards Rome* (1680).

[186] Bodl. MS Tanner 128, fo. 57, Sheldon to Turner, 29 July 1670.

[187] Ibid., fo. 123, Turner to Sheldon, 22 Nov. 1670.

[188] William Gostling, *A Walk In and About the City of Canterbury* (6th edn., Canterbury, 1825), 148.

[189] CCAL, Dean's Book, 1822–54, 113.

[190] For example, CCAL, Chapter Act Book, 1727–45, fo. 48[v].

[191] Ibid., 1670–1710, fo. 191[v]; ibid., 1746–60, fo. 68.

prominent place in his Majesty's and the parliament's care and regard'.[192] The attempt was unsuccessful. But clergy and members of the local laity also made gifts to the cathedral, indicating the affection in which it was held. In 1706 Archbishop Tenison gave a throne elaborately carved by Grinling Gibbons. Some prebendaries left money in their wills to be spent on the fabric: Samuel Shuckford and John Grandorge, for instance, bequeathed money for a new altarpiece, which was designed by Sir James Burroughs, and candlesticks.[193] Despite all the problems with the fabric, a report of 1768 by the architect Robert Mylne stated that few Gothic churches were in as good repair.[194] From 1773 the dean and chapter collected money to repave the nave, a scheme finally carried out in 1787. This received much criticism in the nineteenth century, especially from the Gothic Revivalists, but at the time Hasted noted that it was 'much admired for its simplicity and neatness'.[195] Other indications of concern for the fabric were the purchase of a lightning conductor in 1775 after a series of English churches had been damaged by lightning and the taking out of an insurance policy in 1796.[196]

In the early nineteenth century Dean Percy took great pains to improve the state of the fabric, importing Caen stone, as had been used in the medieval building. He was something of an amateur architect and he saw his work at Canterbury as part of his policy of making the building and services more orderly. In gratitude for this work, the Chapter agreed to place his armorial bearings in the Cathedral.[197] There is no doubt that his term of office saw a great deal of activity on this front, which was not always appreciated by fellow members of the community. Canon Welfitt commented on Percy's 'rank activity and alertness on the scaffold of promotion'.[198] By the 1820s, however, the Dean and Chapter were overwhelmed by the financial problem of maintaining a large medieval building, and a crisis began to loom as expenditure on fabric greatly exceeded the sum reserved for the

---

[192] Ibid., Dean's Book, 1718–42, fo. 62.

[193] Gostling, *Walk*, 289; For a more detailed account of Grandorge's charities see Ralph Blomer, *A Discourse Concerning Conscience. With an Appendix Occasioned by the Death of the Reverend Dr Grandorge, late Prebendary of Canterbury, and Chaplain to the Right Honourable the late Earl of Thanet. A Sermon Preach'd in the Cathedral-Church of Canterbury, February 1 1729/30* (1730), 40.

[194] CCAL, Fabric V, 22, Mylne's Survey and Report, 1768.

[195] Hasted, *History of Kent*, xi. 353. For Horace Walpole's criticisms see *The Correspondence of Horace Walpole*, ed. W. S. Lewis, 48 vols. (New Haven, Conn., 1937–83), xii. 109.

[196] CCAL, Chapter Act Book, 1775–94, fo. 105; ibid., Dean's Book, 1793–1822, fo. 42.

[197] Ibid., Dean's Book, 1822–54, 53, 55.

[198] Ibid., Add. MS 298, Canon Welfitt's Diary, fo. 33.

purpose. In 1817 it was agreed that 10 per cent of fines should be used to augment this sum, and in 1830 matters had become so bad that the Chapter petitioned parliament to be allowed to borrow on the security of their woods.[199] George Pellew (stall VI, 1822-8) was later to argue that instead of taking money from expressed canonries to augment stipends of parochial clergy, the Ecclesiastical Commission ought to encourage more expenditure on cathedral fabrics.[200]

The archbishops were similarly concerned with the upkeep of their buildings. During the Civil War their palaces at Foord and in Canterbury were much damaged, and havoc was wrought on the palace at Lambeth which had been demolished in 1648 by Colonel Thomas Scott, the regicide and army leader. The hall at Lambeth had been the centre for the hospitality given by pre-Civil War archbishops and as part of the attempt to recreate the position of the Church in society at the Restoration Archbishop Juxon insisted that the architect design it exactly like the previous building.[201] Money was also spent on Croydon, but the ruined palaces in the diocese were were let out to tenants. These could sometimes cause trouble for the archbishops. Wake was particularly incensed at the tenant of the palace at Canterbury, Mrs Juxon, for allowing strolling players to perform there; 'it is an unspeakable grief to me to hear that my tenant . . . has so little regard to the honour and dignity of that venerable palace'.[202] Maintaining the palaces of Lambeth and Croydon consumed a fair proportion of the archbishops' revenue. With the large costs of entertaining and providing hospitality, it is not surprising that new archbishops were ready to sue the estate of their predecessor for dilapidations. Tillotson found the deprived Sancroft unwilling to leave the premises and had to issue a subpoena upon his predecessor to answer the charge of appropriating the revenues of the see.[203] The most notorious case of this kind was between Wake and the nephew of Tenison.[204] The expenses of coming into a new see were such that it was reckoned that the first four years of the archbishop's income went on necessary costs and repairs. Some impression of these costs can be gained from the account books of various archbishops. During his ten-year archiepiscopate, Sancroft paid the clerk of the kitchen a staggering £18,124 17s. 3d.[205] The expenses of the household took up well over half of

[199] Ibid., Dean's Book, 1793-1822, 262; ibid., 1822-54, 99.

[200] Pellew, *Letter to Peel*.

[201] P. Hembry, 'Episcopal Palaces, 1533-1660', in E. W. Ives, R. J. Knecht, and J. J. Scarisbrick (eds.), *Wealth and Power in Tudor England. Essays Presented to S. T. Bindoff* (1978), 165.

[202] Ch. Ch. MS Wake 22, fo. 197, Wake to Sydall, 12 Mar. 1722.

[203] Bodl. MS Tanner 26, fo. 54.   [204] Tenison, *Demand for Dilapidations*.

[205] Bodl. MS Tanner 127, fo. 87.

Archbishop Secker's revenue, the costs for 1767 reaching £4,692 6s. 2d.[206] He entertained clergy and bishops at Lambeth, buying 4,266 stones and 7lb of meat in 1767.[207]

Charity and gifts of money took up part of the Church's income. For instance, the dean and chapter were asked to contribute liberally to collections for the plague relief fund in 1665 and to the collection of 1667 for the war against the Dutch.[208] In 1662 Dean Turner noted that the chapter had given a 'royal present of £1,000'.[209] The subscription for the rescue of the captives at Algiers in 1662 was of special concern to the Canterbury hierarchy since one of the prebendaries, John Bargrave, was given the task of going to Algiers where he claimed he 'bought' 162 Englishmen, one by one, like horses in Smithfield.[210]

Charity to the poor was another area of the Church's concern. In 1660 Sheldon declared that the Church should show its gratitude to God for the Restoration by relieving the wants of the poor.[211] The archbishops were keen to set the standard, and a liberal feeding of the poor at the gates of Lambeth was practised. They were besieged by petitions for charity and alms. The dean and chapter fulfilled a similar function within Canterbury. During the series of disastrous harvests in the early 1660s the cathedral gave 'considerable sum of money by way of stock' so that corn could be 'bought in and provided for at reasonable rates, for the supply of the necessity of the poor'.[212] In 1733 they agreed that the list of the poor usually relieved by 6d. a month should be increased to 80, each now to receive a shilling.[213] It is impossible to measure the amount that individual archbishops and dignitaries donated in personal charity, but there is no doubt that they wanted to appear charitable. It was said of Sancroft that he was 'greatly loved in the neighbourhood for his charities were unbounded, and the door of his palace at Lambeth were never closed against poverty and

---

[206] LPL, TG 36, fo. 56.   [207] Ibid., fo. 158.

[208] Bodl. Add. MS c. 308, fo. 7, Sheldon to E. Pierce, W. Somner, and M. Hirst, 31 July 1665; ibid., fo. 33. It was agreed that the money raised in Maidstone should be used to relieve the plague there: ibid., fo. 40, Sheldon to Mr Davis, 16 Aug. 1665 (draft).

[209] Bodl. MS Tanner 48, fo. 15, Turner to Barwick, 27 June 1662.

[210] Bodl. MS Tanner 124, fo. 159.

[211] Gilbert Sheldon, *David's Day of Deliverance and Thanksgiving. A Sermon Preached before the King at Whitehall, 28 June 1660, being the Day of Solemn Thanksgiving for the Happy Return of His Majesty* (1660).

[212] *Mercuricus Publicus*, no. 23 (5–12 June 1662), 358–60; no. 13 (27 Mar.–3 Apr.), 207–8. Such charity was especially necessary in the early Restoration period. W. G. Hoskins shows that the harvests of 1660 and 1661 were bad, 'Harvest Fluctuations and English Economic History, 1620–1759', *Agricultural History Review*, 16 (1968), 16.

[213] CCAL, Dean's Book, 1718–1742, fo. 261.

distress'.[214] Tillotson was supposed to have spent one-fifth of his income in charity, and Secker's account book reveals a desire to help the poor and needy.[215]

In the diocese the archbishops had a special concern for the administration and oversight of three hospitals for the poor: St Nicholas, Harbledown, and St John's, Northgate, founded by Archbishop Lanfranc in the eleventh century, and St Thomas, Eastbridge.[216] Archbishops had a duty to oversee their administration, the management of their funds, the choice of inmates, and the selection of masters. The hospitals were seen as a part of the public image of the Church in the diocese, highlighting a historic tradition going back to the Middle Ages, and emphasizing a concern for the poor. In 1665 Sheldon issued a questionnaire to the bishops asking for information concerning the state of the hospitals.[217] Those in his own diocese had fallen into disrepair during the Interregnum. He contributed towards their upkeep and in 1678 Archdeacon Parker informed Sancroft, the new archbishop, that they had largely been rebuilt with Sheldon's help; 'he, as he was always, my best cashier'.[218]

But it was not only the upkeep of the fabric which was of concern. Enquiries among the inmates of the hospitals revealed that, in some cases, they had become a refuge not only for the poor and needy, but also for nonconformists. The hospital of St Bartholomew in Sandwich, maintained by the corporation, was described as a nest of dissent, harbouring regicides and fanatics.[219] Thus special care had to be taken to ensure that only 'deserving' inmates were chosen. Archdeacon Parker, who was also the master of Eastbridge, complained that this could be very time-consuming: 'I must endure the complaints and importunity of so many miserable people, and it is now come to that pass that there never fails that I am wearied out of from morning to night with the solicitations of at least 10 or 12 poor widows.' He added that 'they trouble me more than all my other affairs. I can learn a good deal from them, because I do not a little delight to do kind offices to the poor, but I would not be besieged with their complaints'.[220]

The financial affairs of the hospitals were another concern of the archbishops. Secker instigated a survey into the value of the lands owned by the

[214] D'Oyly, *Sancroft*, ii. 467, 498.
[215] For Tillotson: J. Meadows Cowper, *Lives of the Deans of Canterbury* (Canterbury, 1900), 110; LPL, MS 1483, *passim*.
[216] M. Gibson, *Lanfranc of Bec* (Oxford, 1978), 185–6.
[217] Wilkins, *Concilia*, iv. 581.
[218] Bodl. MS Tanner 123, fo. 179, Parker to Sancroft, 19 Dec. 1678.
[219] Bodl. MS Tanner 126*, fo. 115, 1 May 1684.
[220] Ibid., fo. 181, Parker to Thompson, 8 Oct. 1674.

hospitals, being keen to ensure that a realistic fine was paid by the lessees, 'for the sake of the poor people'.[221] He thought that the year's income demanded from tenants of the lands attached to the hospitals as a fine was too low and was pleased when his efforts to increase them to 'a very moderate' 1¼ year's income was effected.[222] Secker left £500 in his will to each of the hospitals in the diocese.[223] Attention was also paid to the inhabitants of the hospitals. Secker's enquiries showed that most of them were local people, recommended by parish clergy and overseers of the poor. However, he was concerned to ensure that they were truly deserving, although Archdeacon Head made it clear that the proper objects of charity at the almshouses were people who were able to do something towards their own support.[224]

Archbishop Cornwallis continued his predecessor's concern, taking care to ensure that lessees did not enroach on hospital property. The same necessity of having their lands properly mapped, found on the larger archiepiscopal properties, was echoed here. The attention paid by successive archbishops of Canterbury to the state of the hospitals in the diocese (they were also responsible for hospitals in Lambeth and Croydon), modifies the image of the Church-managed almshouses in this period. Such institutions received a large amount of criticism from Church reformers in the nineteenth century, who saw them as presenting, in miniature, all the evils and neglect of 'Old Corruption'.[225] Those in the Canterbury diocese, however, were repaired and maintained during this period and provided a form of subsistence for the poor and infirm.

THE CHURCH AND PROPERTY, *c.*1780–1828

There are indications of an alteration in the Church's attitude towards its property and its tenants in the late eighteenth century. This change of attitude can be explained, in part, by the fear engendered by reports of the fate of the Church and Monarchy in France during the Revolution. The old anxieties of social anarchy were renewed and the Church intensified its attempts to maintain its full rights and privileges.[226] As a contribution to the war effort the dean and chapter gave money to the Canterbury Volunteers and in 1815 subscribed 100 guineas to the casualties in the British army at

---

[221] LPL., MS Secker 3, fo. 51, Secker to Heaton, 3 Dec. 1762.   [222] Ibid.
[223] Ibid., MS Secker 7, fo. 363.   [224] Ibid., fo. 136, Head to Secker, 17 Mar. 1767.
[225] Ibid., MS Cornwallis 3, fos. 30–43; G. F. A. Best, 'The Road to Hiram's Hospital', *Victorian Studies*, 5 (1961–2), 135–50.
[226] CCAL Add. MS 298, Canon Welfitt's Diary, fo. 21, 10 Jan. 1801.

Waterloo.[227] The Kentish coast was always vulnerable to invasion and in 1814 the dean and chapter were pleased to note that their lessee at Leysdown had erected a semaphore system at Sheerness.[228] Such defence of Church revenues might necessitate the abandonment of the previous policy of leniency towards tenants. A pamphlet of 1802 regarded 1½ years' income as usual for the renewal of leases and noted that the chapter of Canterbury had recently increased its fines to that level.[229] In 1804 the dean and chapter agreed to follow the precedent of other cathedral and collegiate bodies and demand 1½ years' income for a seven-year lease.[230] Estates were now more regularly surveyed and more interest was shown in getting an economic return from them. From the 1790s complaints from tenants about the prebendaries began to appear in the act books and relations became more strained. In 1799 Isaac Bargrave refused to pay a fine demanded for Eastry. By November Bargrave 'yielded' and paid the fine. In 1803 the fine asked by the chapter for Milton Rectory was refused.[231] In 1837 Christopher Hodgson informed Parliament that there had been a distinct change in policy since the end of the eighteenth century.[232]

Evidence of this new attitude can be found in the voluminous archive left by Archbishop Manners Sutton (1805–28). In 1815 he received a petition from the tenants of the Deal properties which illustrated the change. They asserted that from 'time immemorial' the fines had been a ½ year's rent on buildings and 1¼ year's rent on land.[233] This had been kept to by Archbishop Moore and the result had been that because of the 'constant and uniform adherence' to the archbishop's policy, there had been a 'progressive development' at Deal in building and repairs.[234] By 1815 the rents had been doubled and the fines increased. The petitioners concluded:

When your Grace considers the situation of your Grace's property in Deal, that a large part of it lies contiguous to a bold and open shore . . . considerable improvements were made on the estate from a general confidence that has prevailed in the tenure beyond most other lease holders by reason of the immemorial terms adhered to on the renewals.

[227] CCAL, Chapter Act Book, 1794–1824, 9.
[228] CCAL, Dean's Book, 1793–1822, fo. 232.   [229] Ibid., f. 220.
[230] CCAL, Dean's Book, 1793–1822, fo. 232: 'Ordered & agreed that as since the incumbency of the present Dean, the principal Estates belonging to the Dean & Chapter have been survey'd and estimated by Messrs. Kent, Pierce & Kent, & other smaller estates by competent surveyors; The Dean & Chapter do adopt the principle already establish'd in almost all Ecclesiastical & Collegiate Bodies in the Kingdom of not taking a fine of less than a year and a half for a septennial renewal of Estates on 21-year leases.'
[231] CCAL, Dean's Book, 1793–1821, fo. 104.
[232] Parliamentary Papers, 1837, ix, *Select Committee Report on Church Leases*, 23.
[233] LPL, TR 34, fo. 104.   [234] Ibid.

Church revenues changed dramatically as higher prices for agricultural products enabled the Church to demand larger returns on its lands. In 1797 the income of the Canterbury prebendaries had risen to £600 p.a., and that of the dean to £1,200 p.a. By 1805 total income from the archbishop's estates had soared to £16,791 4s. 8d.[235] Such increases were, however, by no means as impressive as those enjoyed by some lay landlords.[236] Nor were they as great as those taken by the dignitaries of some other dioceses. Properties in the diocese of Oxford, for example, grew even more quickly because of the enclosure in the Midland counties.[237] The increase at Canterbury does not accord with the general increases seen after 1805, whereby archiepiscopal income rose to £28,434 6s. 9d. by 1828, while the prebendaries were worth £1,044 and the dean drew £2,111.[238] Despite this augmentation of incomes the radical critics of the early nineteenth century exaggerated the riches which leading ecclesiastics exacted from their profession. It was commonly believed that Archbishop Moore died a millionaire in 1805, the implication being that he made this out of the profits of the lands belonging to the diocese. In fact the bulk of Moore's wealth came from his marriage to the daughter of the wealthy Chief-Justice of South Carolina, Robert Wright.[239]

One of the consequences of the war with France was that in response to the Act for the Redemption of the Land tax (1797) the dean and chapter agreed to sell off all their tenements in the city, except those in the precincts, and all those estates which were held for lives out of Kent. The Act was one of Pitt's measures for financing the war and it enabled ecclesiastical bodies to sell their estates to lessees at terms advantageous to the tenants. In 1800 the dean and chapter sold parcels of land to Jane Austen's relative at Godmersham.[240] The effect of such sales was to concentrate the cathedral's estates even more compactly in the diocese. Indeed, the argument that the cathedral had an intimate and inalienable right to its Kentish lands was strongly made in the 1830s when the dean and chapter urged that money from lands in Kent should not be taken to support the Church in other areas of the country.[241]

---

[235] LPL, E.D., 1916, fo. 69.   [236] Parker, *Coke of Norfolk*, 76–7, 95–6.

[237] Virgin, *Church in Age of Negligence*, 62.

[238] For the archbishop: LPL, E.D., 1916, fo. 69; for the prebends: Parliamentary Papers, 1835, 22, *Report of the Commissioners appointed by His Majesty to inquire into the Ecclesiastical Revenues of England and Wales*, 30–111.

[239] Rubinstein, 'Old Corruption', 56; R. Soloway, *Prelates and People: Ecclesiastical Social Thought in England, 1783–1852* (1969), 72; *DNB*.

[240] CCAL, Dean's Book, 1793–1822, fo. 104.

[241] Parliamentary Papers, 1837, 41, *Return of all the Remonstrances made to the Church Commissioners respecting the union of the Sees of St. Asaph and Bangor and Further . . . Memorials . . . Relating to Cathedrals*, 4.

The surge in the incomes of the Church landlords at the end of the eighteenth century produced some concern amongst Churchmen themselves. Bishop Watson of Llandaff reminded the archbishop in 1783 of the fine line which lay between having sufficient money to fulfil the demands incumbent on the episcopal office, and having too much:

I do not take upon me to fix the precise sum which would enable a Bishop not to pollute Gospel Humility with the Pomp of Prelacy, not to emulate the noble and opulent in such luxuries and expensive levities as become neither Churchmen nor Christians; but to maintain such a decent establishment in the world as would give weight to his example, and authority to his admonitions . . . and to recommend his religion, by works of charity, to the serious unbelievers of every denomination.[242]

Here was a defence of Church wealth, but it also pointed to the objections which were increasingly to be raised in the early nineteenth century when the wealth of Church landlords reached new levels.

The image of the eighteenth-century Church as an insensitive institution making the most out of its tenants was largely a myth fuelled by radical demonology. It was only at the end of the period that the Church was able to adopt a realistic attitude to the maximization of income from its estates. Tenants found that their supposed 'right of renewal' no longer seemed to hold. William Heseltine, tenant to the dean and chapter, complained in 1839 of the 'despotic power' of surveyors which had developed from the early nineteenth century. He warned that

Their boldness may well be reserved for some better occasion than when their temporalities only are concerned. The land which has shaken off the lazy slumbers of a cloistered priesthood will not easily submit to ecclesiastical oppression by their Protestant successors.[243]

These sentiments found their most trenchant expression in the radical historiography of critics of the Church like John Wade and William Cobbett.[244] They compared the use of wealth by the Anglican Church with that of the medieval monasteries, claiming that the pre-Reformation Church had a much better record, and that the Church of England now had a power and wealth in society which exceeded that of the medieval period. In maintaining that the Reformation had been economically detrimental to

---

[242] Richard Watson, 'Letter to the Archbishop of Canterbury, 1783', printed in *English Historical Documents*, 10, *1714–1783*, ed. D. B. Horn and M. Ransome (1957), 362–3.

[243] William Heseltine, *A Tenant's Statement of the Conduct Recently Pursued towards him by the Dean and Chapter of Canterbury, on the Occasion of his Renewing his Lease* (2nd edn., 1839), 21. It was, however, maintained by the archbishop's officials that tenant right was 'certain': *Select Committee on Church Leases*, 25.

[244] Wade, *Black Book*, 281; William Cobbett, *History of the Protestant Reformation* (1824).

society these nineteenth-century critics disagreed with three centuries of Anglican rhetoric which had stressed the economic benefits of the Anglican regime. The outcry in the 1830s was not so much a damning indictment of the position of the eighteenth-century Church as such, but was rather a critical reaction to a different, and essentially early nineteenth-century situation. Through the administration of its property, the Established Church was involved in many aspects of life in the diocese during the eighteenth century. The Church's concern for the management of its lands went beyond the merely financial need to secure a revenue. By eschewing the aggressive policies of the Laudian Church, the post-Restoration and eighteenth-century Churchmen in the diocese echoed the policies of 'tactful affability' demonstrated by those Jacobean clergy who had been similarly aware of the need to work with the grain of local opinion if the Church's position was to be maintained.[245] In understanding this, the Church was able to present its relations with the laity as a beneficial consequence of the entrenchment of Anglicanism within provincial society.

[245] Collinson, *Religion of Protestants*, 79; Fincham, *Prelate as Pastor*, 82.

4

The Economy of the Parish

One of the most pressing institutional problems for the Church was the funding of the parish clergy. From the failure to provide a reasonable income for all incumbents stemmed the grievances which have preoccupied both ecclesiastical and social historians: much of the pluralism and non-residence, which impaired the pastoral work of the clergy, and the dependence on tithes which was a source of contention between parishioners and their ministers,[1] becoming in the diocese of Canterbury an allegedly major cause of the anti-clericalism behind the Swing riots of 1830.[2] Differences in the values of livings have also been used as evidence for what has seemed to be an insuperable gulf between affluent dignitaries and pluralists and poor curates: testimony to the divisions within the clerical body.[3]

Historians have frequently analysed the economy of the parish clergy in terms of conflict: conflict between clergy and parishioners and conflict within the clerical profession itself.[4] This model accords with that of French ecclesiastical historians who have concentrated on the strains between the French Church and society over its economic position and have studied the development of *richerisme*, the battle between the lower and higher orders of the Church, which was to have such telling consequences in the years prior to the French Revolution.[5] Certainly the economics of the parish clergy provide us with a sensitive indicator of the relationship between clerical and lay society, but it can be suggested that the model of conflict is not the only possible way of analysing the situation in the Canterbury diocese. To overemphasize conflict between clergy and parishioners is to obscure the strength of the Church in the parishes and its often uncontested involvement in the economy of the local community.

[1] Virgin, *Church in Age of Negligence*, 8, 11, 124, 242; E. J. Evans, 'Some Reasons for the Growth of English Rural Anti-Clericalism, c.1750–c.1830', *Past and Present*, 66 (1975), 84–109; W. R. Ward, 'The Tithe Question in England in the Early Nineteenth Century', *JEH*, 16 (1965), 67–81.

[2] E. J. E. Hobsbawm and G. F. E. Rudé, *Captain Swing* (1969), 76–7.

[3] Abbey and Overton, *Eighteenth-Century Church*, ii. 16; Sykes, *Church and State*, 76–7.

[4] Most systematically in E. J. Evans, *The Contentious Tithe. The Tithe Problem and English Agriculture, 1750–1850* (1976).

[5] T. Tackett, *Priest and Parish in Eighteenth-Century France* (Princeton, NJ, 1977), 225–41.

TITHES

What is at first sight striking is not the reluctance, but rather the willingness, of lay society to pay for the parish clergy. Kent had had a long tradition of economic anti-clericalism, surfacing, for example, during the 1450s, with cries of 'kill the pluralists'.[6] The problem of achieving adequate funding for the parish clergy in the diocese had been debated in the sixteenth and early seventeenth centuries, and radicals in Kent had then sought alternatives to the tithe system, which provided the bulk of the clergy's income.[7] Yet the Puritan clergy of the Interregnum, however much they had railed against the economic situation of the Church of England, found it difficult to replace the tithe system with an effective alternative method of funding. William Belcher, for instance, had made tithes an issue in Ulcomb during the 1650s,

by which strategem he work'd the Doctor [Horsemonden] out, and himself into the affections of the parish, after which he lived some time on contributions; but these at length failing, he sued them for tithes, even from the first moment of his coming there among them.[8]

The experience of the 1640s and 50s had provided a lesson for Restoration clergy, demonstrating the need to get on with the laity, especially the leading men of the parish, if they were to be adequately maintained. Clerical incomes had suffered during the Civil War and the 1650s and any realistic prospect of recovery suggested the need for an amicable relationship between clergy and parishioners.[9]

In 1660 there was no overwhelming hostility to paying for a national Church again, although in areas of the diocese where nonconformists were strong, it was noted that this 'must trouble the parson, [since they are] an ill paymaster of their tithes'.[10] The early years of the Restoration were marked by a series of bills in Parliament for the more effectual collection of

---

[6] R. L. Storey, *The End of the House of Lancaster* (1966), 9.

[7] Richard Culmer, *The Ministers Hue and Cry* (1651); Charles Nicholls, *The Hue and Cry after Priests* (1651); M. R. James, 'The Political Importance of the Tithes Controversy in the English Revolution, 1646–1660', *History*, 26 (1941), 13.

[8] A. G. Matthews, *Walker Revised* (Oxford, 1948), 211. On the problem more generally, R. O'Day and A. Laurence, 'Augmentation and Amalgamation: Was There a Systematic Approach to the Reform of Parochial Finance, 1640–60?', in O'Day and F. Heal (eds.), *Princes and Paupers in the English Church, 1500–1800* (Leicester, 1981), 167–94.

[9] Ignjatijevic, 'Canterbury', 225. Of the schemes to relieve distressed clergy the most famous was that by the former Canterbury prebendary and bishop of Rochester, John Warner. It is discussed in E. Lee-Warner, *The Life of John Warner* (1901), 56, 58–9.

[10] LPL MS 1126, fo. 32.

tithes. In this campaign Canterbury clergy received some support from Sir Edward Dering, who attempted to bring bills to Parliament in 1668, 1669, 1670, and 1673 to help them recover tithes, but these did not succeed.[11] The preoccupation of the period immediately following the Restoration was, as in other areas of Church life, the reconstruction of a system which had all but petered out during the previous years, but whilst the resumption of the Church estates by the hierarchy was achieved fairly easily, the return to normal of the system for funding the parish clergy created more difficulty. In part this was because the system itself had perhaps never worked completely satisfactorily, grounded as it was in a medieval framework.

The value of a benefice was wholly dependent on a number of variables: the accidents of historical endowment, topography, geography, the economy of the parish, and the size of its population. Parishes in Kent had been formed by the thirteenth century, many with churches going back to 1100 or beyond, and apart from an abortive attempt to divide the unwieldy parish of Wrotham in the Civil War, no further parishes were created until the nineteenth century.[12] Hasted stressed the socio-economic differences between the regions of the county which made Kent 'an epitome of the whole kingdom'.[13] Economically, the parishes in the diocese were separated into three broad regions: the east, the Weald, and the marsh to the south. Towards the east, around Canterbury, were the smallest and most compact parishes, some under 3,000 acres, and here could be found some of the richest livings. Parishes in the north-east were situated in rich corn-growing areas: here the livings were fairly wealthy, but here too were also some of the poorest livings in the diocese—the urban parishes of Canterbury and Dover. Christopher Hill demonstrated the failure of the pre-Civil War Church to collect tithes in urban centres, and his findings appear to be borne out by the livings within the city of Canterbury. These received their income from a nominal rate of 2s. 6d. on houses.[14] In some cases the incomes may have been augmented by parishioners, but without voluntary contributions it is not clear how some city parishes continued a regular church life. One pragmatic answer which had developed before the mid-seventeenth century had been to present minor canons of the cathedral to

---

[11] *The Diaries and Papers of Sir Edward Dering, 2nd Bt., 1644–1684,* House of Lords Record Office, Occasional Publications, 1 (1976), 169.

[12] A. Everitt, *Continuity and Colonisation: The Evolution of Kentish Settlement* (Leicester, 1986), 184.

[13] Hasted, *History of Kent,* i. 266.

[14] Hill, *Economic Problems of the Church,* 107. This custom was established in the 1570s: Hasted, *History of Kent,* x. 213.

these livings, thereby harnessing diocesan and cathedral resources. The northern coastal parishes could be unpalatable. James Wilson wrote to Sancroft, complaining from Preston of

the corroding quality of the sea air which has already damaged marble in the monuments of the Church, and I fear it will find an easy passage through the breaches of my crazy body. If your Grace permit me to reside in Canterbury, where I shall meet with more frequent opportunities to attend ye publick worship of God, have ye advantage of ye library in my great penury of books, ye comfort of good society, ye most desired convenience of education for my children, especially my son at ye King's School, and ye benefit of riding to officiate on Sundays.[15]

The Wealden parishes towards west Kent, bordering on the diocese of Rochester, were much larger and spread out. Cranbrook, for example, was over 15,000 acres. Their churches were not sited in established communities but as ecclesiastical centres of a nexus of scattered farms and dispersed hamlets.[16] The most unpopular region, as far as clergy were concerned, was the marshland, and archbishops received petitions from clergy requesting dispensation from residence on account of its unhealthy situation and the prevalence of 'marsh fever'. In the early eighteenth century John Deffray, the incumbent of New Romney, informed Archbishop Wake that he 'would always consider curates who have took some pains in the marsh, and are in a manner naturalized in it, by some continuance in this air, which proves fatal to a great many living'.[17] Edward Hasted's comments on the topography of the parishes and their healthiness in the 1780s provide a useful insight into the mentality of the educated, university classes, from which most of the clergy were drawn, including his son (rector of Hollingbourne, 1790–1855).[18]

These regional differences within the diocese were also complicated by the disparities between rectories, vicarages, and perpetual curacies, which resulted in the inequality of the values of the benefices. At the bottom end, 59 per cent of livings in 1663 were worth less than £50 p.a., such as Wingham, worth less than £20 at this time.[19] This roughly accords with the situation in Warwickshire where 70 per cent of livings in this period were

---

[15] Bodl. MS Rawl. lett. 59, fo. 361, James Wilson to Sancroft, 28 Dec. 1683. For evidence that the unhealthiness of the Isle of Sheppey discouraged people from accepting benefices there: LPL MS Moore 2, fo. 71, Thomas Hey to Moore, 20 Jan. 1786. Even that model cleric, Edmund Gibson, declined the offer of a living on the Isle of Thanet because of its unhealthy situation: Sykes, *Gibson*, 23.

[16] Everitt, *Continuity and Colonisation*, 183.

[17] Ch. Ch. MS Wake 7, fo. 100, Deffray to Wake, 29 Jan. 1716.

[18] *History of Kent, passim.*   [19] Figures taken from LPL MS 1126.

valued at £60 or under.[20] At the other extreme, rich rectories like Adisham and Ickham were worth well over £250. What complicated matters further was the fact that several of the most populous and demanding parishes— such as that of Maidstone—were rated as perpetual curacies. Broadly speaking, the rectories were paid the whole of the tithes, the vicarages the small tithes, and the perpetual curacies a fixed monetary payment, which fell in real value as prices increased. The great tithes consisted of corn, hay, wood, and other products that grew directly out of the ground, while the small tithes consisted chiefly of animal produce and fruit. In parishes endowed with vicarages, the great tithes had usually been taken over by monasteries for their own use and had normally passed into lay hands at the Reformation, leaving vicars only the small tithes. But this general pattern could easily be blurred by local variations. The vicar of Eastchurch, for example, received all the tithes. There was also the problem of knowing whether certain produce rated as great or small tithes. In 1793 Archbishop Moore received a query from Thomas Squire, the son of the chief parishioner of Hernehill, wondering whether 'potatoes when put in fields or in hop grounds' were his mother's tithes or the vicar's.[21] Various districts were exempt from tithe. Treatises by farmers in the Weald claimed that the area was tithe free. In the parish of West Langdon only 81 of the 606 acres were tithable.[22] In the early eighteenth century the Tory cleric John Johnson of Cranbrook related such claims to broader party political matters, portraying those who refused to pay tithes as anti-Church Whigs.[23]

A related issue was the problem of deciding how 'new' crops should be assessed. In particular, discussion centred on the issue of whether hops, which in Kentish legend had come to England at the same time as the Reformation, along with other 'new' and market gardening crops, were in fact tithable. Jonathan Maude complained in 1682 that at Tenterden there was no tithe on hops, flax, hemp, or fruit.[24] If allowed, this clearly could have damaged the financial position of many Canterbury clergy, especially as the period after 1660 saw a greater diversification amongst Kentish farmers into fruits, market gardening, and new crops.[25] The period was

---

[20] Salter, 'Warwickshire', i. 24.

[21] LPL, TR 20, fo. 101, Thomas Squire to Moore, 30 August 1793.

[22] R. J. P. Kain, 'The Tithe Commutation Surveys', *AC*, 89 (1974), 113.

[23] Bodl. MS Ballard 15, fo. 105, Johnson to Charlett, 15 Sept. 1711. See also his *The Clergyman's Vade Mecum; or, an Account of the Ancient and Present Church of England; the Duties and Rights of the Clergy, and of their Privileges and Hardships* (1706), 186. In 1786 the earl of Guildford maintained that the parish of Langdon was tithe free: LPL, TR 20, fo. 9. Gibson recorded that 20 parishes in the Weald claimed exemption: *Codex*, 716.

[24] Bodl. MS Tanner 126, fo. 159.   [25] Chalklin, *Seventeenth-Century Kent*, 92–5.

punctuated by a series of bills in Parliament which attempted to forbid the tithing of hops. Kentish incumbents expressed concern over the proposed bills and some petitioned Archbishop Wake to represent them in Parliament. Richard Bate, the vicar of Chilham, claimed in 1719 to be 'in a nest of hornets' where he had been living for 'many years in a state of downright persecution from implacable enemies in these parts, for no other reason that I know of, but asserting the rights of ye Church according to your Grace's direction'.[26] He pointed out how damaging the bill would be to the interests of the Church, calculating that if it came into force the Church would lose £99,356 6s. 5d.; if passed, it would take away the tithe easiest to collect and further impoverish poor vicarages.[27] The rector of Boughton Blean, Edward Plees, told Wake that his living had been so improved by hops that he had rebuilt the house.[28] In 1749 an attempt was made by hop planters around the city of Canterbury to petition against a recent attempt to exact the payment of tithes in kind.[29] Other new crops were tithed without too much trouble. In 1792 John Price noted that the annual revenue of Herne had risen to £158 'as canary seed has lately been much cultivated here'.[30]

Archbishops were concerned to get as detailed a picture as possible of the livings in their charge. Sheldon, Sancroft, Herring, Secker, and Moore all instigated surveys of the parochial benefices which are useful in charting the movement of clerical wealth.[31] Interpreting these figures is, however, problematic. Clergy may have exaggerated their plight and certainly the figures they submitted were only rough estimates based on the experience of the past few years, which can hardly be used with precision. The need for accurate information was as much a problem for the Church in the period as it is for the modern historian, for an income which depended so heavily on agricultural produce changed annually according to the harvest. And, especially in the towns, variables such as surplice dues (fees for marriages, burials, and other special services) often complicated matters even further. Also, it was not usual for any extra income to be allocated to a clergyman in lieu of a parsonage house, yet few other professional men were likely to have free accommodation. Of course the problem of maintaining a house might

---

[26] Ch. Ch. MS Wake 21, fo. 104, Bate to Wake, 10 Feb. 1719.
[27] Ibid., fo. 108, 16 Feb. 1719. [28] Ch. Ch. MS Wake 10, fo. 166, 20 Apr. 1726.
[29] *Canterbury, 27th October, 1749, Sir the Hop-Planters in the City* [BL., Cup. 645. e. 1 (3)]. See also LPL MS Gibson 1742, fo. 43, 'Reasons humbly offered to the Archbishop of Canterbury against the Bill'.
[30] LPL MS Moore 2, fo. 98, 26 Apr. 1792.
[31] Surveys include: LPL MSS 923, 1126, 1134, VG 2/5 and Bodl. MSS Tanner 99 and 122.

offset the benefit, and not all parishes had houses, on account of their monastic foundation. Perhaps this is why Wake received the curious statement in 1720 from the vicar of Preston: 'I board in my parish church.'[32] At the Restoration a number of houses were declared unfit; some incumbents complained of houses being 'destroyed' during the Civil War.[33] Giles Hinton moaned about the house in his parish of Biddenden in 1683, on which he himself had already laid out £200: 'I was not born in a Hog-sty, though I may dye in a worst place.'[34] Since the parsonage was one of the hidden benefits of the parish, new incumbents might sue the previous minister if the house had been allowed to fall into disrepair. In 1684 the Church court ordered Nathaniel Collington to pay £110 to Samuel Pratt, his successor, for dilapidations; Collington had then taken the case to the court of Arches, knowing that Pratt did not have much money.[35] Archbishop Sancroft was particularly careful to enquire into the state of the vicarages. In 1682 Henry Gerrard, the vicar of Lydd, was surprised by the complaints about his house, claiming that it was in as good repair as other houses in the diocese and that he had spent over £500 on it.[36]

Any account of the economics of the parish should take note of the character of the incumbent. Too often analyses of clerical incomes eschew mention of individual personalities, probably because such factors are seen as unscientific. But in the case of the eighteenth-century clergy, who were not like modern salaried functionaries, who are only marginally dependent on fees, personal relations could be, and often were, a decisive factor in determining a clergyman's income. Anthony Russell has claimed that tithes gave the clergy a measure of 'role autonomy', giving beneficed clergy an economic security and independence unique among eighteenth-century occupations,[37] but this is to leave out of the equation the real and personal difficulties which might lie embedded in the system. Mere lists of figures of

---

[32] Ch. Ch. MS Wake Visitation Returns B, fo. 630. See also Hasted's comments on the 'hovel' at Bicknor 'with a room projecting across the Isle': *History of Kent*, v. 568.

[33] For example, LPL MS 1126, fos. 10, 36, 47.   [34] Bodl. MS Tanner 124, fo. 60.

[35] Ibid., fo. 43, 'Case between Pratt and Collington'. In 1678 Archdeacon Parker claimed that the charges of suing predecessors make 'present incumbents less carefull of their repairs and the successors unwilling to sue for dilapidations': ibid., fo. 99, 5 Dec. 1678.

[36] Ibid., fo. 49, Gerrard to Thorp, 1 Aug. 1682. Evidence of clergy putting their houses into repair can be found in LPL Registers, for example: Wake Register I, fo. 379. Secker Register II, fo. 382; CCAL, U3/132/1/1, fo. 39: Ripple; Crundale: MS 1125. Houses new built in 1806: Acris, Aldington, Chilham: LPL, VG 3/2. In 1768 the dean and chapter suggested to Archbishop Cornwallis that vicarage houses were not kept up because they were only held for life and that something ought to be done for them 'like in Ireland': CCAL, Chapter Act Book, 1761–75, fo. 103. In his will Secker left money for poor parsonages in the diocese: LPL MS Secker 7, fo. 368. For rebuilding at Saltwood: Hasted, *History of Kent*, viii. 228.

[37] Russell, *Clerical Profession*, 28.

the values of livings do not in themselves tell us anything about the complex network of relationships within the parish which powerfully affected the actual size of clerical incomes. The case of Michael Bookey, for instance, vicar of St Lawrence in Thanet, shows that rapport between clergy and parishioners required careful handling. Wake was advised to 'remove him to a less populous place where he'll do less mischief than he does here', having been informed that 'there was no likelihood of there being any good understanding betwixt him and his neighbours, whom he has very thoroughly provoked'.[38] The archbishop was told: 'was there a more agreeable person, the Easter Book and perquisites might be of more value, as they have in times past to the present incumbent. The house new built by the present incumbent about 1700 with assistance of the parishioners, who were very generous and gave him above £70.' The crux of the matter was baldly stated: 'the inhabitants of the island are generally well disposed and affected towards their ministers . . . but they will not be insulted and trampled upon, they neither can, nor will be treated with insolence or contempt.'

One mid-eighteenth century dispute concerned the parish of St Paul's, Canterbury, and indicates the consequences which clergy faced in falling out with leading members of the parish. The rector, Thomas Lamprey, was engaged in a controversy over tithes with the Honourable Frances Rook, daughter-in-law of the celebrated Captain Rook, who had captured Gibraltar. The case went through the courts and in 1757 the Chief Justice found in favour of Rook. Lamprey complained to the dean and chapter, who were patrons of the living, that she had browbeaten the other parishioners into non-payment.[39] Christopher Hill has characterized this relationship as one in which the clergy were economically dependent on the laity,[40] but this needs qualification, for our knowledge of tithing practices usually comes through judicial records which illuminate the system at the points at which it broke down and ignores its long periods of comparatively untroubled operation. We should thus not exaggerate the fractiousness involved in collecting the 'contentious tithe',[41] for the norm was the peaceful extraction of tithes. Of course there were local tensions, but they were aroused by individuals rather than the institution and were occasional rather than endemic. Tithe books show that regular payments were normally made by the majority of the parish with only one or two refractory dissentients.[42]

---

[38] Quoted in Ch. Ch. MS Wake 9, fo. 264, Lewis to Wake, 30 July 1723.
[39] LPL, Secker, 3, fo. 139, Lamprey to Secker, 29 Nov. 1758.
[40] Hill, *Economic Problems of the Church*, 351.
[41] Evans, *Contentious Tithe*, esp. pp. 44–93.   [42] For example, KAO, U 194/Q/3/1.

When harmony was achieved, this was often the result of negotiation and bargaining between incumbent and parishioners. In 1786 Robert Phillips, the vicar of Bekesbourne, informed Archbishop Moore that his successor could no doubt get more than £90 from the living: as for himself

> ye only means I could devise of bringing my parishioners to terms was to grant them a permanent lease, with full power to do whatever they pleased with their lands, w'out any add. tithes from them, which will be a considerable inducement for them to lay down more land in pasture, and to increase their Hop plantations. This they do.[43]

New incumbents could find the situation particularly difficult, for they had not yet earned the respect of the parish. In 1798 Edward Nares was collated to Biddenden. He immediately attempted a new valuation of the tithes to keep up with the increased wartime prices. This met with hostility:

> Threats were thrown out that many would desert the Church. Many would plough no more, but avail themselves of the modus upon grass. Many would make me take my tithes in kind and would make me wipe my waggon wheels before they enter'd their fields. I bore it all with patience, but deeply lamented the angry manner in which they were dispos'd to receive their new rector. I met them publickly but once. I then told them my full sentiments. I explain'd to them that I knew nothing myself about it; that I had employ'd a surveyor, and had made a demand below his estimate; that I did it not for myself personally but to ascertain the proper amount of the rector's claims, and wish'd to give them all the opportunity of making a reasonable composition. That it was my wish to settle matters amicably, but that if I heard a word more of threats I would go to extremities.[44]

In dealing with parishioners, Secker stressed the duty of incumbents to preserve, and if necessary regain, the financial rights of the Church, but at the same time not to appear contentious.[45] Law suits were costly and taking parishioners to court could create further disaffection, ruining any chance of an amicable relationship between clergy and their flock. As Charles Bean confided to Wake in 1719, his parishioners never forgave him for taking them to court.[46] Many potential disputes may have been settled before they reached the courts. In any case, tithe suits could end up in favour of the clergy even against influential landowners. A dispute in 1730 at Great Mongeham ended with the incumbent defeating the D'aeth family.[47]

---

[43] LPL MS Moore 3, fo. 14, Phillips to Moore, 20 Mar. 1786.
[44] Quoted in G. Cecil White, *A Versatile Professor. Reminiscences of the Rev. Edward Nares, D.D.* (1903), 143.
[45] Secker, *Charges*, 123–61.
[46] Ch. Ch. MS Wake 20, fo. 175, Bean to Wake, 9 Oct. 1719.
[47] CCAL, Z.4.15, fo. 84v.

The Quakers were the most obstinate group of the community who refused to pay tithes. A crisis situation developed during the 1730s when the Quaker Tithe Bill, which would have enabled Quakers to be relieved from paying tithes, threatened to go through Parliament.[48] Along with the bishops and other clergy from the rest of the country, the clergy of the Canterbury diocese petitioned against the Bill.[49] Yet visitation returns indicate that even between this section of the parish and the incumbent some measure of consensus could be reached. In 1738 one investigation into the relationship between clergy and Quakers in the diocese claimed that Quaker complaints of oppression by the clergy were ill-founded and that 'most of the same sect in the neighbouring parishes pay their tithes pretty orderly'.[50] Some ministers reported that Quakers paid their dues without causing trouble, one clergyman suggesting that the reason for this was the 'inoffensive and friendly manner of the clergy'.[51] The rector of Deal, in 1758, congratulated himself on the fact that Quakers in the parish paid tithes and remarked that he let the poorer ones off their dues, allowing them to work them off in his garden.[52] And, perhaps charitably, the vicar of Biddenden in 1758, with regard to the Quakers in his parish, pronounced himself 'willing to believe the little difficulties I have met with in collecting my dues owing as much to their poverty as to their obstinacy'.[53]

The difficulties associated with the tithe system ensured that clergy were forced into an intimate knowledge of the agricultural life of their parish, which may have helped them in their pastoral task. They needed detailed information of farming activities and current prices, and had to be astute men of agricultural business, if they were not to lose out through ignorance. Sometimes this interest in farming matters could become an obsession, as in the 1680s in the case of Dr Eve, the rector of Lynstead, who was nicknamed 'the farming Doctor'.[54] The tithe books which survive belonging to the incumbents of Great Chart show that some clergy kept records of the acreage belonging to each landowner in the parish and noted carefully what kinds of crops were sown.[55] Collecting tithes could be even more

---

[48] Taylor, 'Walpole, the Church and the Quakers', 51–77.
[49] *The Political State of Great Britain*, 52 (1736), 440, 'Petition of several of the Clergy of the County of Kent and Diocese of Canterbury on behalf of themselves and their Brethren of the Church of England'.
[50] *An Examination of a Book, lately printed by the Quakers; intitled, A Brief Account . . . so far as the Clergy of the Diocese of Canterbury are concern'd in it* (1738), 122. The book in question was *A Brief Account of the Many Prosecutions of the People Call'd Quakers in the Exchequer, Ecclesiastical and other Courts* (1736).
[51] LPL MS 1134/1, fo. 273.   [52] Ibid., /2, fo. 5.   [53] Ibid., /1, fo. 77.
[54] Bodl. MS Tanner 124, fo. 182, William Wickens to Sancroft, 4 Apr. 1684.
[55] CCAL, U3/43/3/1–2 (Tithe Books 1758–69 and 1787–1808).

time-consuming. In 1680 the vicar of Chislet informed Sancroft that tithes were paid by 122 separate individuals, of whom 71 did not reside in the parish, but elsewhere in Kent, Essex, or London: 'I being forced to go 200 miles circuit . . . for ye gathering it in, but also to ye further impairing of ye revenues, ye sea lately broke in and hath drowned a considerable quantity of land.'[56] In 1681 the incumbent of St Mary's in the Marsh complained that the occupiers had frequently pulled the wool over the eyes of his predecessors by pretending that their lands lay in neighbouring parishes.[57] Johnson of Cranbrook's *Clergyman's Vade Mecum* (1706) pointed out that in some places 'a gentleman received thousands from fewer hands than a cleric 3 or 4 score from as many as 500 different people'.[58]

It was a common theme of archiepiscopal charges and correspondence that the clergy should be more vigorous in asserting their rights. In this they were assisted by the existence of terriers—lists of the assets with which the livings were endowed, which could be consulted when trying to safeguard the incumbent's income. Sometimes the terriers could be used against what were claimed as customary rights by those who obstinately held to a conception of property rights which was now being rapidly pushed aside.[59] What was at stake here essentially were two differing conceptions of property rights.[60] In 1720 Wake reminded clergy of the importance of making terriers and tending to their incomes.[61] By the mid-century Andrew Ducarel, librarian at Lambeth, published a list of the terriers relating to the parishes in the diocese which were stored in the registry of the consistory court at Canterbury.[62] Most of them dated from the 1630s—during the Laudian attempt to put clerical incomes on a sounder footing—but several were drawn up in the 1740s and 50s, indicating more recent campaigns to preserve such rights.

[56] Bodl. MS Rawl. lett. 59, fo. 132, Richard Howard to Sancroft. In 1771 the incumbent of Bethersden complained of the 120 separate landowners and tenants who paid tithes: LPL MS Cornwallis, fo. 68.

[57] Bodl. MS Tanner 124, fo. 54, Henry Hunt to Thorp, 9 Apr. 1681.

[58] Johnson, *Vade Mecum*, A5v. Johnson's rival in the diocese, John Lewis, predictably attacked the tenor of Johnson's book: 'A Supplement to the fourth edition of the first part of the Clergyman's Vade Mecum. By Constantine Richerius, April 28 1716', in Bodl. MS Rawl. c. 412, fo. 11.

[59] As at Tenterden in the 1680s: Bodl. MS Tanner 126, fo. 91: 'I desire to know whether ye terrier and ye book of my predecessors be a sufficient evidence against ye custom'. On the importance of terriers more generally see *Ecclesiastical Terriers of Warwickshire Parishes*, ed. D. M. Barratt, 2 vols. (Oxford, 1955-71).

[60] See the discussion of the role of custom in Bushaway, *By Rite*, 5-27.

[61] Draft charge of 1720: Ch. Ch. MS Wake 8, fo. 269.

[62] A. C. Ducarel, *A Repertory of the Endowments of Vicarages in the Diocese of Canterbury* (1763).

Part of the problem for the cleric in collecting his dues was the difficulty in knowing exactly the legal rights of the parish. To help them in this task Canterbury incumbents made use of John Johnson of Cranbrook's *Vade Mecum* in which he observed that

it would be much for the benefit of the Church if the clergymen knew more of the law than they generally do . . . they would find it more useful to them than several of those sciences which they are taught in the universities . . . it would save them many a counsel's fee and secure them from being imposed upon.[63]

As a High-Churchman, Johnson was a vigorous supporter of the independence and spiritual nature of the Church; for him the economic independence of the clergy was part of his wider view of the clerical function.

The parochial income could only be properly collected if the incumbent had a good grasp of local history. As a result, not a few clergy in this period were local historians through necessity, rummaging through papers to ascertain their rights. In 1763 George Hearne claimed the small tithes of St Gregory's Priory for his parish of St Mary's Northgate since the Priory was situated in the parish. None of his last predecessors had received them, 'but then', he noted, 'my predecessors, as far as it appears, never examined the papers left by Mr Stockar, and most of them had either a fortune or other good preferments, so that they were under no necessity of inquiring after such small things'.[64] Other incumbents left notes for their successors.[65] John Duncombe, the vicar of St Andrew's, Canterbury, researched into local history, publishing *The History and Antiquities of the two parishes of Reculver and Hearne* (1784) and *The History and Antiquities of the Three Archiepiscopal Hospitals* (1785). The most distinguished work of local history produced in the period, Edward Hasted's exhaustive *History of the County of Kent* (1778–99) was not only written with the help of local clergy, but at times was also used by clergy to find out about tithing practices.[66] A. C. Ducarel, the Lambeth librarian, supported by Archbishop Secker, published his *Repertory of the Endowments of Vicarages in the Diocese of*

---

[63] Johnson, *Vade Mecum*, 6.

[64] LPL., TR 12, fo. 117, George Hearne to Secker, 1 Oct. 1763.

[65] KAO, U194/Q3/1 Langley Tithe book; ibid., U41/3/1/ Brabourne, 7–9, 'Hints and memorandum concerning tithes'.

[66] John Duncombe, *The History and Antiquities of the two parishes of Reculver and Hearne* (1784) and id., *The History and Antiquities of the Three Archiepiscopal Hospitals at and near Canterbury* (1785). See also John Lewis, *The History and Antiquities of the Abbey and Church of Faversham* (1727); id., *The History and Antiquities as well Ecclesiastical as Civil of the Isle of Tenet in Kent* (2nd edn., 1736); J. Boyle, *In Quest of Hasted* (Chichester, 1984). Hasted dedicated his fourth volume to Dean Brownlow North. For evidence of clergy consulting Hasted: LPL., TR 9, fo. 93; LPL., 1806.

Canterbury in 1763 (reprinted in 1782). He hoped that this would solve the problem of disputed tithes and mean that clergy would not have to turn to the law. He saw his work as of use both to parishioners and to clergy, especially new incumbents who often found it hard to stand up against the local inhabitants. He planned to do the same for every diocese in the country.[67] Ducarel helped diocesan clergy in their disputes, searching through documents at Lambeth, and even writing to Rome in case any relevant pre-Reformation material survived. And it was not always a case of sorting out potential disagreements between clergy and parishioners. Uncertainty over matters such as parish boundaries could lead to disputes between clergy, and this is one reason why certain incumbents maintained the tradition of 'beating the bounds' of the parish.[68] One bemoaned that 'it being my misfortune to have never an ancient man left in ye parish to give a true account of ye ancient Bounds'.[69]

Secker warned his clergy against the *modus decimandi*, a method whereby tithes were exchanged for a monetary payment. In doing this the clergy were betraying their trust for their successors, 'and thus what was given for the support of the clergy in all future times, is decreasing continually and becoming less sufficient'.[70] By agreeing to a modus clergy could avoid the effort of collecting tithes in kind and could evade tithe disputes with parishioners, but this practice had the attendant danger that income did not keep in line with inflation, thereby reducing the clergy's real income. The incumbent of Chislet told Wake in 1723 that he had attempted to break the modus and 'resolved to have ye tithes in kind or a payment for them in some measure proportional to ye value' but the 'very low and scanty price every produce bears, will not permit me to make such an immediate advance as might have been done some years ago'.[71] One way by which the clergy could keep the convenience of the modus without losing out in times of inflation was to negotiate temporary tithe compositions whereby the clergyman could resume taking tithes in kind or reach a new composition. Thus a new agreement was made at Smarden in 1782 as a result of which the tithes increased in value.[72] One of John Boys' correspondents, after looking at the variety of moduses in the diocese, was driven to write: 'what is meant by a fair commutation of tithes I know not. An equivalent or commutation that

---

[67] Ducarel, *Repertory*, preface. For his plan for every diocese: Bodl. MS Eng. Misc. b. 46, fos. 29–35.

[68] LPL MS 1163, fos. 108, 9, 140, 156; Bodl. MS Eng. Misc. b. 46, fo. 39: 'copy of a letter from Mr James Byres, antiquarian at Rome, to Revd Mr Vyse'. KAO, U/25/27/1: 'Map of Benenden Parish by Joseph Hodskinson as a result of a bounds perambulation in 1777'.

[69] Bodl. MS Tanner 126, fo. 90.   [70] Secker, *Charges*, 125.

[71] Ch. Ch. MS Wake 22, fo. 57, 10 Oct. 1723.   [72] Hasted, *History of Kent*, vii. 483.

would satisfy all parties is perhaps impossible.'[73] Archbishops even frowned on incumbents who leased their tithes to a tenant who would then assume the task of collecting the tithes, while the clergymen received a cash rent. The rent was always somewhat less than the full value of the tithes, for tenants charged a commission for their labours. Potentially perhaps even more damaging, the tithe collector might sour the personal relationship between incumbent and parishioners. Archbishop Moore wrote in 1792 to the rector of Lydd on what he held to be a 'matter of considerable importance. It is said that you have let . . . the Rectorial and vicarial tithes of Lydd to a person not of the parish . . . and this without having had any dispute'.[74]

Secker also argued that lay encroachments on Church property did not, in the end, benefit the laity:

For probably few of them in Proportion will be gainers by what we lose but the whole Body of them, wherever the Provision for us becomes incompetent, must either make another at their own Expense, or be deprived in a great measure of the good Influence of our office, with respect to this world and the next.[75]

This point was also made by Dean Sydall in 1716. He warned that the laity would be deprived of the means to salvation if the clergy were not supported. If the clergy were not maintained all they would lose would be 'a little present Comfort', whereas the laity 'must lose all the Benefit which God design'd by the Institution of our Ministry, and may thereby endanger their own Eternal Salvation'.[76]

Although there were clear problems over the collection of tithes, such disputes as there were decreased during the eighteenth century, rather than building up steadily into the rural outburst of the Swing riots of the 1830s. Significantly, the greatest number of confrontations between parishioners and clergy which reached the Court of Arches was in the late seventeenth and early eighteenth centuries, suggesting that after this period in many parishes tithe disputes had ended and a state of comparative equilibrium reached.[77] One explanation for this is that for most of the period the clergy

---

[73] John Boys, *General View of the Agriculture of the County of Kent, with Observations on the Means of its Improvement* (1794), 37.

[74] LPL, MS Moore 2, fo. 128, Moore to Huddersford, 9 Feb. 1792.

[75] Secker, *Charges*, 126.

[76] Elias Sydall, *The Clergy Farther Vindicated. A Sermon Preach'd in the Cathedral-Church of Canterbury, at the Primary Visitation of William Ld Archbishop of Canterbury, on Saturday June 16th 1716* (1716), 27.

[77] Certainly the evidence left by those cases which reached the Court of Arches would suggest that the highest number of tithe disputes was in the late seventeenth and early eighteenth centuries: J. Houston (ed.), *Index of Cases in the Records of the Court of Arches, 1660–1913*, British Record Society (1972), 618–19. A similar decline in cases has been noted in Norfolk: Jacob, 'Norfolk', 133–4.

could take advantage of a fairly stable economic situation.[78] From the late eighteenth century, however, there were signs of renewed tension. It was then that James Gambier, the rector of Langley, felt moved to write a defence of the right to tithes, resting his case on the public service given by the clergy. He argued that the question of tithes 'involves the rights of a large and respectable body of gentlemen', and that it was 'a question in which the conduct of the greater part of the community is concerned. For most people either pay or receive tithes'.[79] It was now too that Pitt talked with Archbishop Moore about the possibilities of a general commutation of tithes.[80]

THE VALUE OF LIVINGS

Despite the difficulties facing an incumbent in collecting his tithe, the general value of clerical incomes rose during the century (see Table 3). Many of the inequalities in income were mitigated by plurality, so that, even in the Restoration period, few incumbents were really poor. Sheldon's survey shows that by uniting benefices most incumbents were able to receive between £80 and £100 p.a., and only a few, often connected to the cathedral, received much more.[81] There were other ways of improving the incomes of clergy, among them the union of parishes, windfalls derived from donations, and voluntary augmentations. At the Restoration, a serious attempt was made to augment poorer livings and several Canterbury parishes were augmented by Juxon. In 1695 Archbishop Tenison and the Bishop of Ely were left a bequest of £100 p.a. to be divided among twenty poor vicars, ten from each diocese.[82] The Canterbury city parishes were united under an Act of 1681. The fifteen parishes had for a long time been notoriously poor, and uniting them was one way of providing the minister with a realistic income. Such unions were, however, fraught with difficulties as they

[78] Evans, *Contentious Tithe*, 43, 59. Also, id., 'Tithes' in J. Thirsk (ed.), *Agrarian History of England and Wales*, v. *1640–1750*, ii. (Cambridge, 1985), 405.

[79] KAO, U 194/F 12/1 'A Please for the Clergy or a Defence of the Right to Tithes on Principles of Equity'.

[80] CUL Add. MS 6958, letter 1033, Pitt to Moore, 16 Dec. 1791. Nevertheless in 1793 the bishop of Bangor told Moore that 'I am of the opinion that things were never more quiet with respect to tithes than at present': LPL MS Moore 9, fo. 1, 23 Jan. 1793.

[81] LPL MS 1126.

[82] Bodl. MS Tanner 141, fo. 100. A list of Juxon's augmentations to 25 Canterbury livings is in Kennett, *Case of Impropriations*, 256. See ibid., 257 and 306 for Sheldon and Sancroft's augmentations. For Tenison's augmentations: LPL MS 1153, fos. 1–3. The cathedral augmented 45 poor livings at the Restoration: Bodl. MS Tanner 126*, fo. 76.

TABLE 3. *Parochial Revenues According to Status of Parish (Numbers)*

	1663	c.1688	1736	1758	c.1830
Under £50					
Rectory	51	43	32	22	2
Vicarage	70	62	41	20	2
Curacy	25	25	21	20	4
£51–100					
Rectory	39	40		35	5
Vicarage	32	44		60	2
Curacy	2	3		4	13
£101–50					
Rectory	18	17		30	11
Vicarage	3	3		20	11
Curacy				1	10
£151–200					
Rectory	6	4		9	17
Vicarage				3	18
Curacy					4
£201–50					
Rectory	3	9		8	15
Vicarage		2			20
Curacy					1
£251–300					
Rectory				4	4
Vicarage					10
Curacy					1
£301–50					
Rectory	1	1		2	6
Vicarage					7
£351–400					
Rectory					9
Vicarage					9
£401–50					
Rectory					6
Vicarage				1	6
£451–500					
Rectory					3
Vicarage					1
£501–50					
Rectory					5
Vicarage					2
Curacy					1

TABLE 3 *cont.*

	1663	*c.*1688	1736	1758	*c.*1830
£551–600					
Rectory					5
Vicarage					2
£601–50					
Rectory					2
Vicarage					2
£651–700					
Rectory					4
Vicarage					1
£701–50					
Rectory					3
Vicarage					2
£751–800					
Rectory					2
Vicarage					2
Curacy					1
£801–50					
Rectory					
Vicarage					
£851–900					
Rectory					
Vicarage					1
£901–50					
Rectory					
Vicarage					
£951–1,000					
Rectory					1
Vicarage					
£1,000–500					
Rectory					6
Vicarage					
£1,501–2,000					
Rectory					2
£2,001–500					
Rectory					1

Figures compiled from: LPL MS 1126; Bodl. MS Tanner 122; *The Return Made by the Governors of the Bounty of Queen Anne* (1736); LPL, VG 2/5; *Parliamentary Papers*, 1835, XXII, *Report of the Commissioners . . . Ecclesiastical Revenues*, 186–213.

interfered with patronage rights. The union of Faversham and Preston was proposed by Sancroft but opposed by the corporation of Faversham, which did not want to make the joint income a legal right of the incumbent, but wished to be able to bestow it at will.[83] This was perhaps the legacy of earlier seventeenth century radical thinking in the diocese, which had wanted to solve the problem of clerical maintenance by making the incumbent dependent on the voluntary contributions of his congregation.[84] Faversham itself was noted as a centre of nonconformity and Sancroft hoped that the changes in the membership of the corporation in 1686 would help the plan. Preston was not in favour of the union either: proud of its independence, it strongly resented the idea of being submerged into Faversham. Sancroft suspected that the petitions signed by the parishioners of Preston were got up by the incumbent's father-in-law.[85] The union came to nothing and illustrates the problems which the Church hierarchy encountered. Institutional change was often hindered by forces outside the Church's control.

The most sustained attempt at augmentation was Queen Anne's Bounty. In 1704 the Bounty placed £50 as the poverty line; in 1736 94 of the Canterbury livings were under this, in 1758 62, and by 1809 only 15 were valued at less than £50.[86] The Bounty has often been contrasted unfavourably with the Ecclesiastical Commission in its ability to solve the financial problems of the parish clergy, but the difference was not so much an unwillingness on behalf of the Church to admit the problem as the administrative difficulty of putting the scheme into operation. The principles of the scheme have been documented elsewhere and need not be gone into here: suffice it to say that the money was raised by the Crown returning first fruits and tenths for the use of the Church. Livings were augmented by lot over the whole country, but if £200 was donated towards any living, the Bounty would match it. If the rate of return can be estimated at 3 or 4 per cent, this would mean that a benefice's income could be expected to increase by £6–8 p.a. as a result of a £200 donation. There were sometimes delays in achieving this, such as those caused by the unavailability of land for purchase, which clergy were often expected to find. The Bounty offered a low rate of interest—only

[83] For the union of the Canterbury city parishes see LPL, Cartae Miscellenae I, fos. 454 and ibid., Sancroft Register II, 343; Bodl. MS Tanner 33, fos. 254–7; Bodl. MS Tanner 36, fo. 253. The full story of Faversham is in Bodl. MS Tanner 33, fos. 242–4, 249, 277 and Bodl. MS Tanner 125, fos. 19, 40–2, 46, 65.

[84] See Hill, *Economic Problems*, 184–5, 297–8.   [85] Bodl. MS Tanner 33, fo. 249.

[86] Figures from: I. Green, 'The First Years of Queen Anne's Bounty', in O'Day and Heal, *Princes and Paupers*, 243; LPL, VG 2/5; ibid., VG 2/7. See also: Parliamentary Papers, 1835, 22, *Report of the Commissioners appointed by His Majesty to inquire into the Ecclesiastical Revenues of England and Wales*, 186–213.

about 2 per cent—and thus the benefactor might lose money.[87] Sometimes clergy themselves contributed to this scheme. In 1724 the dean and chapter gave money towards the augmentation of Brook. Henry Godolphin, the dean of St Paul's, had given £3,000 to the Bounty, to be given as he directed. He was known to the minor canon John Gostling, who persuaded him to give £100 and the dean and chapter made up the rest.[88] John Smith (d. 1732), the rector of Chart Sutton, left £200 in his will for the parish, and with the money donated by the Bounty a small farm of £20 p.a. was purchased.[89] More significant for the relationship between the Church and the wider community were the contributions made by the laity. In 1718 Sir Thomas Dunk, of Hawkhurst, gave £200 to the parish.[90] Whilst Secker was on the Board, poor livings in the Canterbury diocese received augmentations from Sir Philip Boteler's fund. £14,000 was left to Boteler by his aunt and, as he lived in Kent, Secker was able to persuade him to augment 38 parishes. In all, 67 Canterbury livings were augmented with gifts from the laity by 1828. It is indicative of the relations between Church and society in Kent that over two-thirds of the diocesan livings receiving augmentation in the eighteenth century did so to match gifts of money and land given by the laity, as opposed to receiving augmentation by lot.[91]

It has become almost a historical truism that increases in the wealth of the parish clergy, especially after the mid-eighteenth century, were a direct result of the enclosure acts and the agricultural revolution. This is not true of the Canterbury diocese, where enclosure had occurred long before 1660.[92] Changes in Kent were more gradual. Yet between 1660 and the early nineteenth century there was a transformation in the values of the poorer livings.[93] The position of the poorer incumbents and curates (who were usually younger men who would 'progress' to their own livings)

---

[87] A. Savidge, *The Foundation and Early Years of Queen Anne's Bounty* (1955) and Best, *Temporal Pillars*, 78–136. See also S. Harrat, 'Queen Anne's Bounty and the Augmentation of Livings in the Age of Reform', *Transactions of the Leicestershire Archaeological and Historical Society*, 61 (1987), 8–18.

[88] Hasted, *History of Kent*, vii. 155. Tenison left £1,000 for the augmentation of 5 poor benefices on condition that the Bounty matched this: LPL MS 952, fo. 92. Secker left £1,000 to augment 5 poor livings in the diocese and £1,000 to repair houses: LPL MS Secker 7, fo. 371.

[89] Hasted, *History of Kent*, vii. 383.   [90] Ibid., v. 332.

[91] LPL MS 1120, fo. 95, Secker to Boteler, 5 Nov. 1765. For a list of the Canterbury livings augmented during the long eighteenth century see C. Hodgson, *An Account of the Augmentation of Small Livings by the Governors of the Bounty of Queen Anne, by the Augmentation of the Maintenance of the Poor Clergy* (1826), 237.

[92] Virgin, *Church in Age of Negligence*, 44; J. Thirsk, 'Enclosing and Engrossing', in id. (ed.), *Agrarian History*, v. 246.

[93] Virgin, *Church in Age of Negligence*, 254.

contrasts favourably with the lot of poor clergy in France and America.[94] Figures for the mid-eighteenth century show curates receiving between £40 and £50, on top of which they often received free lodging and surplice fees.[95] Those obtaining less were frequently beneficed clergymen as well, whose salary would be increased by their own income. Much of the initial support for the French Revolution came from curés battling against the wealthy dignitaries, and in 1789 they supported the sale of Church property to pay off the national debt.[96] In England there was no such revolt of the lower clergy on class lines, and in the early nineteenth century curates in the diocese were receiving on average £75 to £80, with lodging.[97]

THE CHURCH AND THE POOR

As far as the poor were concerned, the restoration of the Anglican Church may have been advantageous.[98] They might well receive money and gifts of food through the auspices of the parish church, for incumbents were often the trustees of local charities and benefactions. Visitation queries asked about these benefits, urging the clergy to ensure that the poor were not robbed of them. Clergy were held responsible for conserving the charitable gifts which had been left to the parish, for the support of the poor. These came usually in the form of income from a block of land. Sancroft encouraged the resumption of such gifts by instigating a Charitable Commission in the diocese.[99] Bequests, relating to money given for the maintenance and education of the poor (or the upkeep of churches), were recovered for several parishes: Seasalter, Elham, Marden, Bearsted, St Margaret's-at-cliffe, East Sutton, Canterbury, Newington, Harrietsham, Headcorn, Sandwich, Hythe, Boughton Blean, Leeds, Hollingbourne, Ospringe, and Faversham.[100] In 1683 Giles Hinton informed Sancroft that the charity of bread to the poor was observed at Biddenden, but was dispensed with much 'disorder and indecency' and needed regulation.[101]

[94] F. G. James, 'Clerical Incomes in Eighteenth-Century England', *Historical Magazine of the Protestant Episcopal Church*, 18 (1949), 311–25.

[95] See curates' salaries in LPL, VG 2/5.

[96] McManners, *French Ecclesiastical Society*, 280.   [97] LPL, VB 1/13–14.

[98] This perhaps helps explain the popularity of the Restoration: J. S. Morrill, 'The Church in England, 1642–9', in id. (ed.), *Reactions to the English Civil War* (1982), 91, 113.

[99] Bodl. MS Tanner 126, fo. 124, 4 Sept. 1683.

[100] *List of the Proceedings of Commissioners for Charitable Uses*, Public Record Office (1899), 48.

[101] Bodl. MS Tanner, fo. 243. John Lewis provided a list of 'pious and charitable' benefactions to show that the Church of England exceeded the Church of Rome in charity: *History of the Abbey and Church of Faversham* (1727), 190.

An analysis of the visitation returns for 1716, 1758, and 1806 shows that, besides benefactions to the poor, over which the incumbent usually had administrative oversight, many parishes expressly mention use of the offertory money for the poor and needy.[102] This was usually given to 'poor communicants', an indication of the way in which active Church membership had wider repercussions. Such use of poor relief was a clear attempt to control the lower orders, by obliging them to attend church. In several parishes, however, incumbents stated that such money was not restricted to communicants, perhaps in an attempt to win over people to the Church. At St Peter's, Sandwich the vicar reported that 'the sacrament money is reserved to winters . . . when I distribute meals and boiled peas, so that in the severest seasons any parishioner is served 2 or 3 very comfortable meals a week'.[103] The vicar of Chilham warned of the need to hand out actual gifts of food, since if money was given, the poor would waste it in the alehouse.[104] Examples like these are suggestive of the crucial role which clergy could play in the moral economy of the parish. Whilst it would certainly be foolish to ignore the ways in which such doles could reinforce the cause of social order and hierarchy, this does not mean that they did not provide necessary nourishment and subsistence. In a long-enclosed county like Kent where common grounds were scarce, the significance of such gifts and the distribution of bread should not be underestimated, especially in times of distress. In 1789 the sacrament money at Bishopsbourne was used for a whole range of poor relief: for clothing, for assistance when a parishioner lost his cow, paying for the treatment of a broken arm, and distributing bread.[105] Hasted was concerned to convey the impression that clergy were benevolent and caring to the poor. At Kingsnorth he recorded that Philip Hawkins was 'a most worthy clergyman, having the blessings of the poor especially, for his goodness and benevolence to them'.[106] Much has been written in recent years about the resurgence of paternalist ideals in the decades after 1770 as a way of maintaining order within rural society.[107] Faced by a range of political, economic, and social tensions which were exacerbated by the war with France, it is not surprising to find clergy in Kent preaching the need to look after the lower orders. In 1795—a crisis year in

---

[102] Analysis of Ch. Ch. MS Wake Visitation Returns A; LPL., MS 1134/1–4; ibid., MS VG 3/2/a–d.

[103] LPL, VG 3/1/c, fo. 217.

[104] Ibid., /a, fo. 73. For examples of giving to those not present: LPL MS 1134/1, fos. 115, 116.

[105] CCAL, U 3/166/11/5.   [106] Hasted, *History of Kent*, v. 592.

[107] D. Roberts, *Paternalism in Early Victorian England* (1979). See also Langford, *Propertied Englishman*, 367–436.

southern England on account of a disastrous harvest—clergy were in the forefront of those who expressed concern for the labourers' position.[108] An anonymous 'clergyman in the diocese of Canterbury' argued that the stability of the country depended on the fidelity of the lower orders, stressing the utmost importance of poor relief.[109] However, the ability to perform this charitable function fluctuated with circumstance. In 1803 John Gostling complained that the heavy taxes he was obliged to pay were damaging to the poor:

From the numerous poor in each parish, I lose a part of my tithe and the cesses for the maintenance of them, the enormous taxes unfortunately now required for the support of our King and our Country, put it absolutely out of my power to do more than keep them wind-tight and water-tight.[110]

MAINTAINING THE CLERICAL FAMILY

The zeal with which incumbents collected their tithes has embarrassed ecclesiastical historians, to whom it has often appeared rather unseemly.[111] Yet it is possible to argue that the necessity of exacting their just dues was more urgent for the clergy of the eighteenth than for those of the sixteenth century. Income through tithes was often crucial in the clergyman's task of providing for his family. The need to support their families, it has been suggested, may have led many 'sufferers' during the 1640s and 50s eventually to comply with the new regime.[112] This necessity remained one of the most pressing concerns of clergy after 1660. A catalogue of Canterbury benefices, which was annotated by Sancroft, records, apart from the values of livings, whether the incumbents were married and how many children they

---

[108] David Davies, *The Case of Labourers in Husbandry* (1795).

[109] [Anon.], *Personal the Best Pledge of Public Reform. Addressed to Inferiors. In which their Duty to the Country is ascertained by the Care she takes of them. By a Clergyman in the Diocese of Canterbury* (1795).

[110] LPL, Moore 2, fo. 234, Gostling to Moore, 11 Dec. 1803.

[111] Cf. Russell, *Clerical Profession*, 128, 167.

[112] I. M. Green, 'Career Prospects and Clerical Conformity in Early Stuart England', *Past and Present*, 90 (1981), 79 suggests that one-quarter of the clergy remained unmarried. For the reluctance of clergy to marry in sixteenth-century Kent see P. Collinson, *The Birthpangs of Protestant England. Religious and Cultural Change in the Sixteenth and Seventeenth Centuries* (1988), 76–8. Bodl. MS. Eng. Lett. c. 43, fo. 114: in the 1570s 129 of the parish clergy were married. Green, 'The Persecution of "Scandalous" and "Malignant" Parish Clergy During the English Civil War', *EHR*, 104 (1979), 527. For the need to support a family see also P. Collinson, 'Shepherds, Sheepdogs and Hirelings: The Pastoral Ministry in Post-Reformation England', *SCH*, 26 (1989), 214–15.

had. The great majority (82 per cent) were married and had children.[113] This was bound to have consequences for the economics of the benefice. Incumbents often petitioned archbishops for richer livings so that they might maintain their families better and educate their children.

Few people suffered more severely from a change in circumstances than clergy's widows, since they had nothing to fall back on. When Thomas Patten was collated to Bethersden in 1764 he was peeved to find that 'the daughters of the late vicar, taking advantage of the badness of the roads, have staid so long in the house as to put me to great inconvenience'.[114] Some incumbents took pity on their predecessor's wives: in 1806 Thomas Morphet declined to sue for dilapidations because the widow was so distressed.[115] Other widows earned an income by teaching the catechism for their husband's successor. The problem faced by clergy-widows was highlighted in a letter sent to Secker requesting him to promote a bill in the House of Lords to make the profits of a vicarage available to the relatives of the last incumbent until after harvest: 'for as the law now stands, it surely can't be equal—viz, that, as it may happen, a few weeks before the harvest the present incumbent's successor shall be entitled to fruits which have been growing a great part of the year without his having done any duty at all during the whole time.'[116]

After the Restoration various charities were established to help the plight of the families of the clergy. Some of these had been anticipated in the Interregnum. In 1658 John Cogan had left money for a hospital to look after Canterbury clergy-widows, but the bulk of Cogan's property consisted of lands expropriated from the archbishop's estates by the committee of sequestrators, of which he had been chairman, and these were restored to Juxon in 1660. Though the hospital remained in use because in 1670 more money was given, with no funds to maintain it, it fell down. In 1771 the dean and chapter provided 20 guineas towards its repair.[117] At the national level, the most significant of these charities was the Corporation of the Sons of the Clergy, which had its roots in the 1650s, but was made into a Corporation in 1678.[118] Several clergy connected to the Canterbury diocese were invited to preach at the annual charity meeting in London, as part

---

[113] Bodl. MS Tanner 122.

[114] BL MS 39311, fo. 160, Patten to George Berkeley, 4 June 1764.

[115] LPL MS VG 3/2/c, fo. 105.

[116] LPL MS Secker 7, fo. 152v, 'Anonymous' to Secker, Oct. 1765.

[117] For Cogan's Hospital see N. Cox, *Bridging the Gap. A History of the Corporation of the Sons of the Clergy over 300 years, 1655–1978* (Oxford, 1978), 46; CCAL, Chapter Act Book, 1761–75, fo. 45.

[118] Cox, *Bridging the Gap, passim.*

of the effort to raise money. In 1697, in a charity sermon, the future Dean Stanhope made the connection between the cleric as father to his flock and father to his family and pointed to the need to look after clergy families: 'the Care and Abilities of such a Person to instruct and oversee the House of God as a Spiritual Father, would best be measured by the condition of his own Family at Home.'[119] The link between the well-being of the family and that of the clerical profession was such that several preachers worried lest the unfortunate circumstances of destitute clerical families became a slur on their calling. In 1699 William Assheton, the rector of Beckenham, argued that the sons of the clergy were 'an ample vindication of the Marriage of the Clergy', and had 'furnished the Publick with men of the best Figure'. They were 'the Envy of Rome and the Glory of the Reformation'.[120] Assheton established a rudimentary life insurance policy for the benefit of these families. Clubbing together to form mutual insurance policies was one way to avoid the prospect of leaving families in penury, and it is not surprising that clergy were in the forefront of such developments.[121] In 1762 George Horne observed that the case of the parish clergy in England was harder than elsewhere because of the lack of security for their dependants. He thought that it was 'a pernicious remnant of popery' that a clergyman's widow, whose husband 'had done no crime but being separated to the service of God', should be left destitute of any provision.[122]

The Corporation was a nationally organized institution, but by the mid-century initiatives had sprung up at the diocesan level too. Although tensions between the Corporation and the local societies existed—since both were competing for the same funds—a society was established in Canterbury on 20 August 1751.[123] Between 1751 and 1781 a total of £6,664 was

[119] George Stanhope, *A Sermon Preached at the Annual Meeting of the Sons of the Clergy 7 December 1697* (1698), 3. By the end of the period it was providing for 400 English and 100 Welsh widows: LPL MS Moore 6, fo. 233.

[120] William Assheton, *A Sermon Preached at the Anniversary Meeting of the Sons of the Clergymen in St Paul's Cathedral, 5 December 1699* (1700), 34. At the end of the sermon was 'A First Account of the Rise, Progress and Advantages of Dr Assheton's Proposal, as now Improved and Managed by the Company of Mercers'.

[121] L. Davidoff and C. Hall, *Family Fortunes. Men and Women of the English Middle Class, 1780–1850* (1987), 213. For a European context see D. Gugerli, 'Protestant Pastors in Late Eighteenth-Century Zurich: Their Families and Society', *Journal of Interdisciplinary History*, 22 (1992), 369–85.

[122] George Horne, *A Sermon Preached Before the Sons of the Clergy, in the Cathedral Church of St Paul, Thursday 6 May 1762* (1762), 14.

[123] In 1722 Dean Sydall wanted to set up a diocesan scheme: Ch. Ch. MS Wake 22, fo. 112, Sydall to Wake, 24 Feb. 1722. See *An Account of the Rules of the Society for the Relief of the Widows and Orphans of Poor Clergymen, Canterbury, 20 August, 1751* and Cox, *Bridging the Gap*, 41. More informal schemes were also adopted. A subscription was set up in 1784 for the

raised and in 1770 the charity was maintaining 5 widows and 19 children in the diocese.[124] Another charity in the Canterbury diocese was established by George Sykes, the vicar of Preston, who in 1765 left a benefaction of £1,000 to maintain six poor clergy widows 'of sober life and good conversation'.[125] For some, of course, marriage was not an economic burden. Elias Sydall informed Wake that Richard Kellway, the incumbent of St Mary's in the Marsh, had increased his fortune by his two wives.[126]

Marriage could also affect the position of the incumbent in other ways. The pastoral and social role of the clergy was often aided by the presence of his family, who could act in some cases as assistants, providing and distributing charity and hospitality. The ways in which the Church of England depended on these unpaid helpers has not perhaps been sufficiently realized. At the local level the wives and families of clergy were often invaluable in developing a close relationship between clergy and parishioners.[127]

An added expense for clergy in the period after the Restoration was the payment of taxes. Since 1664 the Church had lost the right to tax itself and this seems to have been especially regretted during the 1690s when the clergy had to contribute to William III's wars.[128] The incumbent of Throwley complained to Wake in 1716 of being 'spitefully tax'd to ye King, Church and poor beyond what the living is worth'.[129] Such taxes may have initially helped to keep many clergy hostile to the new Whig regime. Archdeacon Battely lamented the heavy burden of these new impositions, arguing that most clergy in the diocese were charitable and should not have to pay extra taxes.[130]

family of John Smith (late incumbent of St Cosmus and St Damien, Canterbury): see advertisement at end of the sermon by William Backhouse, *God the Author of Peace and Lover of Concord. A Sermon preached at the Parish Church of Deal, on Thursday, July 29 1784* (Canterbury, 1784).

[124] CCAL, Dean's Book, 1761–70, fo. 198.

[125] CCAL, Chapter Act Book, 1760–1775, fo. 105.

[126] Ch. Ch. MS Wake 9, fo. 238, Sydall to Wake, 31 Jan. 1723.

[127] As early as the 1570s William Harrison had become convinced that it was the support of a wife which made it possible for ordinary incumbents to do their duty: Heal, *Hospitality*, 252. For some indication of the ways in which wives gave clergy intellectual companionship see *A Parson in the Vale of the White Horse: George Woodward's Letters from East Hendred, 1753–61*, ed. D. Gibson (Gloucester, 1982), 62. William Jones wished that his wife was a preacher, 'but the use of her voice is reserved for the Church Triumphant': Magdalen College, Oxford, MS Horne 471 fo. 31, Jones to Horne, 15 Nov. 1791.

[128] Bennett, *Crisis*, 16.

[129] Ch. Ch. MS Wake Visitation Returns A, fo. 285.

[130] Bodl. MS Tanner 288, 'On Vicars', fo. 79. There was also some controversy as to whether clergy should pay tenths to the archbishop: LPL MS 953, fo. 101, John Cotton to Tenison, 2 Nov. 1715.

PLURALISM

One of the most common justifications of pluralism and non-residence was the claim that the maintenance of wives and families made such practices inevitable, often because the parsonage was too small. Though scandalous in days of popish celibacy, pluralism was now often necessary.[131] Two clergy connected with the diocese, Henry Wharton and George Stanhope, published a vindication of pluralism, arguing that it did not harm the Church in its pastoral function, but enabled clergy to live in an appropriately learned and educated manner.[132] 'It is certain', they claimed, 'that it is not so much the force of reason, or the sense of duty which maintains religion among many of the meaner and unlearned sort, as the opinion which they have of their pastor'.[133]

The main grounds for the attack on pluralism lay in the pastoral sphere: it allegedly made the incumbent non-resident, took the clergyman away from his flock, and left parishioners abandoned. The compact parishes of most of the Canterbury diocese, however, made it possible for clergy to serve two cures. This was the eighteenth-century equivalent of the modern union of parishes and provided a partial remedy for the poverty of some of the livings. Parishes with small populations yielded little income, and an incumbent was justified in holding two or three, if they were contiguous. In 1674 Sheldon was informed of 22 livings in the diocese which were so poor that no clergyman could subsist on them, and which had to be served by neighbouring clergy.[134] Pluralism enabled the Church to stretch its limited resources to provide at any rate a minimum pastoral oversight throughout the diocese. However, not all pluralism in the Canterbury diocese conformed to this model. Less justifiable on these grounds was the combination of rich livings, such as the holding of a wealthy benefice with a cathedral prebend. This could account for some spectacular incomes, such

---

[131] Ferdinando Warner, *The Ecclesiastical History of England to the Eighteenth Century*, 2 vols. (1756–7), ii. 659.

[132] George Stanhope and Henry Wharton, *A Defence of Pluralities* (1691). John Johnson answered this with *The Case of Pluralities and Non Residence Rightly Stated* (1694).

[133] Stanhope and Wharton, *Defence*, 203.

[134] Bodl. MS Tanner 124, fo. 73: 'List of livings so small that no man could subsist on them', 20 Oct. 1674. Cf. ibid., fo. 84, 4 Apr. 1683, in which Henry Ullock explained to Sancroft why clergy were non-resident. Yet in 1675 the parishioners of Aldington petitioned Sheldon for a resident minister who would visit sick parishioners and be someone to whom they could resort for 'Ghostly Counsell and Advice': Bodl. MS Tanner 124, fo. 55, 21 Dec. 1675. In 1681 John Sidway was deprived for non-residence: Bodl. MS Tanner 125, fo. 62, Thorp to Lukin, 11 Jan. 1681. Of course, non-residence was by no means a peculiarly eighteenth-century problem: see J. I. Daeley, 'Pluralism in the Diocese of Canterbury, During the Administration of Archbishop Parker, 1559–75', *JEH*, 18 (1967), 33–49.

as the £2,000 obtained by Robert Moore in 1805. But figures for the early nineteenth century suggest that this type of fortune gained through pluralism was not as common as some contemporaries feared. In 1810, for example, less than 18 per cent of the pluralists in the diocese fell into this category.[135]

The hierarchy was aware of the dangers of non-residence—often associated with pluralism—and tried to monitor the situation. Secker warned the incumbent of Woodnesborough in 1758 that it would be 'better for you another day, Sir, to have brought up your family with the strictest frugality, than to have deprived a flock of Christ, put under your care, through the course of years, of one of the religious offices, which ought to have been performed amongst them'. This theme was repeated in his 1758 charge to the Canterbury clergy: 'it is only living amongst your People and knowing them thoroughly that can show you what is Level to their Capacities and suited to their Circumstances and what will reform their Faults and improve their hearts in true Goodness. Yet unless this is your Business with them and unless you perform it Everything else is Nothing.'[136]

A real attempt to come to grips with the problem was made in the 1803 Act, which gave a very strict definition of non-residence, applying this to incumbents even if they lived in the parish but did not reside in the vicarage itself. The figures for non-residence collected as a result do not indicate the reality of pastoral provision provided in most parishes. John Gostling was non-resident at St Peter's, Canterbury, but this did not mean he neglected his cure: 'I generally walk to them once every day,' he reported, 'sometimes oftener to enquire whether I am wanted.'[137] The most common excuse offered by offending clergy was that houses were unfit for habitation. At Sheldwich the house was described as a 'thatched cottage',[138] and at Sevington the incumbent informed Archbishop Moore that there was no house for the clergy: 'it is now and has been tenanted for these last forty

---

[135] Parliamentary Papers, 1810, X, *Returns on the Residence of the Beneficed Clergy*, 160–1.

[136] LPL MS Secker 3, fo. 176, Secker to Norris, 24 Aug. 1758; *Charges*, 208. He also recommended that bishops should make a list of resident and non-resident clergy: LPL MS 2598, fo. 93. Other pressures included writing conditions of residence into leases: CCAL, Dr Potter's Book, 1729. Such caution indicates that Geoffrey Best rather overstated the case by suggesting that by the early nineteenth century pluralism was seen as 'the hidden hand of divine wisdom'; *Temporal Pillars*, pp. 74–5. It also suggests a marked difference from the situation in the diocese of Durham where the problem of pluralism was not tackled until the late 1830s: W. R. Maynard, 'Pluralism and Non-Residence in the Archdeaconry of Durham, 1774–1856: The Bishop and Chapter as Patrons', *Northern History*, 26 (1990), 103–30. Also R. Mitchison, 'Pluralities and the Poorer Benefices in Eighteenth-Century England', *HJ*, 5 (1962), 188–90.

[137] LPL MS Moore 3, fo. 234, Gostling to Moore, 11 Dec. 1803.   [138] Ibid., fo. 264.

years by Mr Willes by trade a brick-layer who keeps the premises in good repair, and I reserve 1 room for my own house.'[139] Moore often granted licences for one year only, to encourage incumbents to put such defects to rights.[140] In 1804 140 clergy in the diocese were classified as resident, 111 were exempt, and 98 had licences for non-residence, of which 42 lived in the neighbourhood.[141] In 1810, it was recorded that out of a total of 349 benefices 144 had a resident cleric, and 205 a non-resident.[142] But this obscured the point made in the 1806 visitation returns that many of the technically non-resident clergy lived nearby, even in the parish itself, and thus were in easy reach of their flocks. Many of the non-resident clergy chose to live in neighbouring towns and their parishes may have benefited by the stimulus which clergy could gain from urban residence, and the chance it provided for meeting others. Non-residence did not necessarily mean that the parish was poorly served. Duty could be done even if the clergyman resided outside the parish, and this reduced the supposedly malign impact of non-residence on the workings of the Church.[143] Nevertheless, the diocesan authorities continued to monitor the situation, and Manners Sutton introduced a renewed campaign against non-residence: disciplining and fining those clergy who were absent without permission.[144]

GIFTS TO THE CHURCH

A significant feature of the period, indicative of the wider economic relationship between the clergy and their parishioners, was the ability of many incumbents to persuade the laity to contribute towards the costs of the repair, improvement, and building of parish churches. The power of Anglican projects to extract money from the laity is worth remembering as a corrective to the view that the social hold of religion was increasingly marginal.[145] Of course, this depended on parochial goodwill, and in the Restoration period, the strength of nonconformity in many parishes made it difficult to obtain funding to effect such repairs. In 1679 Thomas Paramour reported that Goodnestone church had been recently rebuilt, but was not in good order:

---

[139] Ibid., fo. 256.   [140] For example, ibid., fo. 258: Petition of Montagu Pennington.
[141] Ibid., fo. 291.   [142] LPL, VG 2/7.
[143] For a similar situation in the diocese of Norwich see W. M. Jacob, 'A Practice of a Very Hurtful Tendency', *SCH*, 16 (1979), 315–26, where 147 of the 362 technically non-resident clergy lived within 4 miles of their parish.
[144] LPL, VB 1/15, p. 23.
[145] For instance, W. K. Jordan, 'Social Institutions in Kent, 1480–1660. A Study of the Changing Pattern of Social Aspirations', *AC*, 75 (1961), 124.

the parishioners being all (within some 2 or 3 families) dissenters from our Church, as Anabaptists chiefly and some Quakers, there is no pulpit cushion, nor pulpit cloth, no surplice, no common prayer book, the Bible out of the covers and imperfect, and . . . no communion table, neither have they any churchwarden, nor a clark, so . . . I am forced to carry our Publick Liturgy in my pocket, and to give my own clark his dinner to accompany me in the afternoon.[146]

However, there were indications of improvement. In 1671, for instance, major repairs were carried out to the church at Godmersham and a petition to the archbishop from the parishioners asked whether they might be allowed to make use of the Great Hall in the parsonage house 'by reason of the great repairs of our church which are now going about, for the publick service of God, until the repairs are finished'.[147] The affection shown by certain sections of the laity for the Church revealed in donations of church plate and contributions to church repair has been demonstrated for several dioceses in the late seventeenth century; it was clearly shared by a great many eighteenth-century laymen as well.[148] Linda Colley has claimed that such donations are a litmus test for discovering Tory gentry, for these were keenest to sponsor refurbishment programmes.[149] This is not surprising, since the Tory party, as long as it continued after 1714, claimed to be the party of the Church. The Earl of Thanet, a prominent Tory in the diocese, gave an altarpiece and new pews to Hothfield in the 1720s, thus conforming to Colley's model. But it is equally important to remember that Whigs too could claim to be supporters of the Church, and Whig laymen contributed generously to the upkeep of many parish churches. In 1695 the Whig MP of Queenborough, Colonel King, took on the expense of repairing the church there,[150] and in 1700 Maidstone was neatly pewed by the Whig MP Sir Robert Marsham.[151] That High-Church Tory, John Johnson, complained

---

[146] Bodl. MS Tanner 124, fo. 224, T. Paramour to R. Thompson, 16 July 1679. Similar comments had been made of the same parish in 1666: LPL, C.M. VI, fo. 22. The repairs had been paid for by Sir Leoline Jenkins: ibid., TS 2, fo. 8.

[147] Quoted in C. E. Woodruff, 'The Records of the Courts of the Archdeaconry and Consistory Court of Canterbury', *AC*, 40 (1929), 102–3.

[148] For example, R. A. Beddard, 'Cathedral Furnishings of the Restoration Period: A Salisbury Inventory of 1685', *Wiltshire Archaeological Magazine*, 66 (1971), 147–55. Hollingbourne had an altar frontal worked by the ladies of the Culpepper family during the Interregnum and given to the church at the Restoration: G. W. O. Addleshaw and F. Etchells, *The Architectural Setting of Anglican Worship. An Inquiry into the Arrangements for Public Worship in the Church of England from the Reformation to the Present Day* (1948), 147.

[149] Colley, *Defiance of Oligarchy*, 117.

[150] For Thanet's benefactions: Bodl. MS Eng. Th. c. 24, fo. 395; Hasted, *History of Kent*, vii. 523. For King: ibid., vi. 244.

[151] Hasted, *History of Kent*, iv. 317. For Marsham's staunch Whig credentials: Sedgewick (ed.), *House of Commons, 1715–1754*, ii. 243.

in 1709 that the churches in the diocese were 'scarce . . . furnished with the necessary ornaments, 'tho many of them are very noble shells, and with some expense might be made equal to most parish churches in England',[152] but he later found reasons for thinking that Whigs would give to such projects. He wrote to Charlett after the South-Sea Bubble:

I am told the traders and monied men begin to find themselves pinched; if so, I will not think our case desperate. For they who are most indolent, as to the concerns of Religion, yet may feel an uneasiness at the decay of their stock or profit. And I am so far a Lockist as to believe that uneasiness is the first motive to all noble efforts and enterprises. God give all a sense of their misery that they might find out the means of relief.[153]

Individual members of the laity gave ornaments and plate to their local church, and many of these donations were faithfully recorded in Hasted's survey. In 1687, for instance, Mrs Lovejoy gave a chalice to St Peter's, Thanet, after the original had been stolen. In 1722 Frances Campion, the wife of Sir William, a Whig MP, gave two silver flagons for the sacrament.[154] In the early eighteenth century Leeds church was described as 'greatly ruinous'; in 1753 it was completely rebuilt thanks to the generosity of Lady Highmore.[155] Sometimes the desire of the gentry to leave their mark on the interior of a church could prove disastrous. At Boughton Malherbe, for example, the monument for Lord Stanhope and Countess Chesterfield 'was injudiciously placed inside the altar rails, and filled almost the whole space . . . but it has lately been taken down [1780s] to make room for an altar and railing'.[156] At Hythe the parish took on the responsibility of repairing the high chancel because the rector—the incumbent—could not afford to do so.[157] Extensive repairs were carried out at St Peter's, Thanet in 1758. The vicar, Charles Willis, noted that 'the parishioners, zealous for the honour of God and willing to give an example of true Christian piety in their Neighbourhood condescended to an assessment of six-pence in the pound rent for carrying out those laudable designs'.[158] Another method of raising finance for repairs was through a general subscription. The method of effecting this was for a brief to be issued. Lists of briefs can be found in parish records and it is clear that people were more

[152] Bodl. MS Ballard 15, fo. 89, Johnson to Charlett, 28 Sept. 1709.

[153] Ibid., fo. 148, 29 Apr. 1721.   [154] CCAL, U3/120/1/3.

[155] Hasted, *History of Kent*, v. 499. Otterden was rebuilt in 1753 with the financial backing of Lady Hastings: ibid., 542.

[156] Ibid., 411. The nave of Godmersham Church fell down in 1761 because local gentry were busy digging up graves to make room for their own: ibid., vii. 60. Similar damage occurred at Bredgar: ibid, vi. 99.

[157] Ibid., v. 411.   [158] CCAL, U3/120/1/3.

willing to contribute to repairs (especially when a church had suffered some calamity like being struck by lightning) if the cause was a local one. In 1754 £2,300 was raised in this way for the rebuilding of Faversham church and £400 for an organ. Secker sent a letter to the clergy of the diocese in 1763, urging them to exhort their parishioners to contribute to the repairs of Sittingbourne church.[159] It was, he explained, part of their duty to support such causes. In 1779 Chart Sutton was much damaged by lightning and £1,810 was raised by a brief throughout the county.[160] Money was also raised, through subscription, for the rebuilding of St Andrew's, Canterbury between 1765 and 1780. At the opening ceremony, the incumbent, John Duncombe, spoke of the importance of subscribing to this, the first church built in the city of Canterbury which was not popish in origin. On the subscription list were the MPs for the city, Thomas Best and Richard Milles (who each gave a £100), the mayor, and the dean and chapter.[161]

Lay finance was usually necessary for the building of new churches. The eighteenth century is not usually seen as a century of church building and certainly it fell far behind its successor. Part of the explanation, for a southern diocese like Canterbury, was that there was already a proliferation of churches and so little need to build any more. Indeed, the size of the parish churches in some of the Kent villages in the early nineteenth century made Cobbett believe that the population was declining, since they were far larger than the number of inhabitants would require.[162] Nevertheless, certain areas of the diocese saw a marked growth in population, which, although it did not compare with the huge upswing after 1800, forced the Church to build new places of worship. The administrative costs of creating new parishes were heavy, since it required an act of Parliament, with the result that most of the church building in this period consisted of the erection of chapels of ease in existing parishes. In 1673 a chapel of ease was built by the government for the dockyards at Sheerness in the parish of Queenborough.[163] In 1716 Wake consecrated a chapel to serve the parishioners of

---

[159] Hasted, *History of Kent*, xi. 363. For Sittingbourne: ibid., vi. 160. Secker's letter was reprinted in GM, 1763, 372. For a study of briefs see W. A. Bewes, *Church Briefs, or Royal Warrants for Collections for Charitable Objects* (1896).

[160] Hasted, *History of Kent*, v. 352.

[161] John Duncombe, *A Sermon Preached at the Consecration of the Parish-Church of St Andrew in the City of Canterbury, Monday July 4 1774* (Canterbury, 1774), 18; CCAL, U/3/5/6/1, fo. 1.

[162] See C. W. Chalklin, 'The Funding of Church Building in the Provincial Towns of Eighteenth-Century England', in P. Clark (eds.), *The Transformation of English Provincial Towns* (1984), 284–310; Cobbett, *Rural Rides*, 186 (Goudhurst), 189 (Appledore), 191 (Brenzett).

[163] Hasted, *History of Kent*, vi. 233.

Lower Deal. Its financing indicates how such a cost could be spread over a wide range of inhabitants and did not depend on a single large family. In 1707 the parish bought the ground and in 1712 procured an Act to put a duty on all the coals landed at Deal harbour. In this way, together with donations from the archbishop and the cathedral, £2,500 was raised.[164] A similar method was employed in the building of chapels of ease at Ramsgate, in the parish of St Lawrence, Thanet between 1789 and 1791, as a response to the large increase in the population.[165] In 1822 a new chapel was consecrated at Sandgate in the parish of Folkestone, funded by the parliamentary grant of 1818 for the building of new churches.[166]

The raising of money for the building and refurbishment of parish churches is symptomatic of the ways in which parishioners were able to demonstrate loyalty to the Church and to their minister. Of course there were times when individual incumbents found sections of the parish reluctant to accept their economic demands. In these circumstances the outcome was, as often as not, friction and conflict. But, given the enormous difficulties entailed in the collection and administration of the tithing system, it is remarkable that evidence of hostility and non-payment is not more forthcoming. Indeed, as far as the economy of the parish was concerned, the diocese of Canterbury suggests that a model of consensus, and at times positive co-operation, may be more applicable for the ways in which parishioners related to the clergy. How far this model might be applied to other areas of the Church's involvement with society will be explored in the next two chapters.

[164] CCAL, U3/67/28/3; LPL, Act Book.   [165] Hasted, *History of Kent*, x. 346.
[166] LPL, VB 1/14, 418.

III. The Church and Society

5

The Church and the Problem of Nonconformity

This chapter examines the responses of Anglican clergy towards non-conformity in their parishes. The conventional view, propagated by dissenters, Methodists, and Evangelicals, is that the Church of England in this period was a static institution with a limited capacity to absorb new religious impulses. Denominational histories have attempted to define clear-cut differences between such groups and mainstream Anglicanism, often explaining their growth in terms of a necessary reaction to the limitations of a hidebound Church of England. Thomas Timpson, in his *Church History of Kent* (1859), for example, praised an evangelical tradition which had constantly stood outside and had justly criticized the Anglican Church: claiming that 'nonconformists and dissenters, from age to age, in all their chief denominations, have held substantially the same doctrines of sound evangelical Protestantism'.[1] Indeed, the development of Methodism was for R. C. Jenkins, the nineteenth-century historian of the Canterbury diocese, the witness *par excellence* to the shortcomings of the eighteenth-century Church: proof of 'the utter secularity and deadness of religious sentiment and conduct which brought this great reaction'.[2]

Recent historians, however, have emphasized that dissent cannot be seen in terms of a simple reaction to the Established Church. Alan Everitt, paying particular attention to the Kentish experience, analysed the mixture of topographical, socio-economic, geographic, and personal factors which explain the existence of religious nonconformity; factors which go beyond hostile reaction to the Church.[3] In any case, Ian Green has demonstrated that the Restoration Church, in Canterbury and elsewhere, far from being an intolerant institution staffed by bloodthirsty Laudians, had its origins in a Church of moderation and latitude, willing to make overtures to

---

[1] T. Timpson, *Church History of Kent. From the Earliest Period to the Year MDCCCLVIII* (1859), 223.

[2] Jenkins, *Canterbury*, 388.

[3] A. Everitt, *The Pattern of Rural Dissent: The Nineteenth Century*, University of Leicester, Department of Local History, Occasional Papers, 4 (1972).

nonconformists, before being pushed aside by a Cavalier and largely intolerant laity.[4] Despite the rigorous attitude of Sheldon and some of his fellow
bishops in the years after the Restoration, the views of the parish clergy and
the de facto toleration that emerged in the parishes even before the
Toleration Act of 1689, suggest that moderation lived on. In their dealings
with both Old and New Dissent, clergy often found consensus more useful
than confrontation. Such tactics have distinct similarities to those of
Elizabethan and Jacobean clergy towards Puritans and 'semi-separatists'.[5]
It may be that this strategy of compromise, and sometimes grudging approval, towards 'dissenting' communities, whose members might attend
Church services, has been one of the most enduring features of the Church
of England's position within local society and far more typical than the
monochrome uniformity insisted on with such disastrous consequences by
Archbishop Laud in the 1630s.[6]

THE RESTORATION RELIGIOUS SETTLEMENT, 1660–1688

Tolerationist schemes emerged in the Restoration period itself. Much has
been made of this as the age of the 'great persecution', but historians have
concentrated too readily on the official policies, on the so-called Clarendon
code, and not on the problems of implementing these statutes in the
parishes.[7] Even Sheldon, who has been seen as 'the inexorable opponent of
any compromise with dissenters', who, in the view of the first historian of
the diocese 'ruled by an arbitrary and impolitic government', and who, according to Pepys, enjoyed making fun of dissenters as part of his after dinner entertainment at Lambeth,[8] was unable to achieve, and indeed did not
attempt, a continual purge of dissenters, either in his diocese or in the country at large. In this he fell short of the Laudian ideals which are supposed to
have been revived at the Restoration. In the summer of 1660, whilst bishop
of London, he preached of the need to 'strip ourselves of all unruly

⁴ Green, *Re-establishment of Church of England*, esp. ch. 1. See also C. Cross, *Church and
People, 1450–1660* (1976), 233. Sheldon's intolerance is discussed in Bosher, *Restoration
Settlement*, 265. It is significant that Matthew Wren (who was more Laudian than Laud) was
passed over for the post of archbishop in 1663.

⁵ Collinson, *Religion of Protestants*, 89 and Fincham, *Prelate as Pastor*, 212.

⁶ Clark, *English Provincial Society*, 361–71.

⁷ G. R. Cragg, *Puritanism in the Period of the Great Persecution, 1660–1688* (Cambridge,
1957), 66–127.

⁸ Jenkins, *Canterbury*, 365; *The Diary of Samuel Pepys*, ed. R. Latham and W. Matthews, 11
vols. (1970–83), xi. 554, 14 May 1669.

passions' in order that we should not be 'at enmity among ourselves for trifles'.[9] In the initial stages of the Restoration, at least, he treated the Presbyterian leaders with respect. A more aggressive outlook developed in response to the subversive behaviour of some dissenters. The Anglican hierarchy and the Cavalier gentry feared the possibility that nonconformists might yet usher in another Civil War. Clergy were fully alive to the radical connections of dissent in Kent and the fear of extreme groups such as the Quakers had alarmed many Presbyterians into supporting the Restoration and conforming to the Anglican Church, in the belief that the threat of the sectaries was far worse than the abuses of an unreformed Church.[10] The fierce self-identification of the Kentish Quakers with Old Testament prophets seemed calculated to perturb the Establishment.[11] The conduct of the two women who rode through Canterbury with flaming torches in 1660 was frightening in the context of fears of plots to overthrow the new order; so too were the actions of Quaker preachers who, before assemblies of over seven hundred people, 'banged' the bishops.[12]

But the Church authorities' response to dissent was rarely monolithic; they were aware of the differences, both religious and political, between various groups, fearing the radical sects more than moderate Presbyterians. The dean and chapter wrote to the Kentish gentry in 1660, proposing to raise funds 'for persecuting some of the more *factious* dissenters'.[13] Intolerance was reserved for those who, it was feared, might be a political and social, and thereby an ecclesiastical threat. As long as the Civil War was remembered, any activity which seemed to smack of disorder met the same reaction—lest it foreshadowed a revival of those horrors which had only just been contained.[14] The city had long had a reputation for harbouring religious and political dissidents: Canterbury had sheltered radicals who had been forward in petitioning for the king's death in 1649 and it remained a centre for dissent and subversion through the 1660s and 70s. The nonconformist plots against the restored Establishment were not chimerical in the eyes of the clergy. In 1660, for example, the cathedral chapter encouraged servants to keep 'arms in the Church on the arrival of the King'

[9] Gilbert Sheldon, *David's Day of Deliverance and Thanksgiving. A Sermon Preached before the King at Whitehall, 28 June 1660, being the Day of Solemn Thanksgiving for the Happy Return of His Majesty* (1660), 47.

[10] B. Reay, 'The Quakers, 1659 and the Restoration of the Monarchy', *History*, 63 (1978), 193–213.

[11] R. J. Acheson, 'The Development of Religious Separatism in the Diocese of Canterbury, 1590–1660', unpub. University of Kent Ph.D. thesis, 1983, 266.

[12] *CSPD*, 1660–1, 539, 19 Mar. 1661.   [13] HMC, *9th Report*, 121.

[14] P. Seaward, *The Restoration, 1660–1688* (1991), 2–3.

in case of any trouble.[15] In 1661 Henry Oxinden informed his cousin at Barham:

if you know not the newes already, then know that there are very strict letters from the council to secure such as have been active under the late usurp'd and tirannical power and that there is a cause to suspect retaine their principles. In order thereto the Canterbury Deputy Lieutenants have silenced John Durant and some think Ventris and Blind Taylor were so served yesterday.[16]

The Secretary of State, Sir Henry Bennet, received a letter from Colonel Thomas Culpepper in 1662 concerning the arrest of Thomas Palmer, an itinerant nonconformist preacher: 'Your preacher I found in a disguize intending to have passed my men, and being discovered made some persistence. I had taken about 200 of his Auditors and set sentries on them in the church.' He also noted that 'the wild of Kent is a receptacle for the distressed running parsons and I heare they have ventured abundance of seditious practices'.[17] Complaints were made in 1663 of fanatics with cudgels who 'frightened the countryside' in and around Canterbury.[18] This fear lay behind Sheldon's attempt on his elevation in 1663 to discover what had happened to those who had played an active role in the Cromwellian regime in his own diocese. In this context Burnet's harsh comments on Sheldon's religious attitude become more understandable: 'He seemed not to have a deep sense of religion, if any at all, and spoke of it more commonly as an engine of government and as a matter of policy.'[19] For it was precisely the interconnection between religion and politics which induced such a mentality.

What appeared so threatening about the sects which had flourished during the Civil War and after was the fact that they had gentry and even aristocratic championship. Patrick Collinson has pointed out that much of the strength of early-seventeenth century Puritanism lay in its ability to win gentry backing and thus political leverage.[20] As the Anglican authorities found out, such support was by no means over at the Restoration. The hierarchy was also keen to monitor the activities of the ministers who nurtured dissenting congregations. At times the authorities blamed them entirely

---

[15] CCAL., Petition 231. For Baptist plotting see W. T. Whitley, 'Militant Baptists, 1660-1672', *Transactions of the Baptist Historical Society*, 1 (1909), 148-55.

[16] BL Add. MS 28004, fo. 259, Aug. 1661: quoted in Acheson, 'Religious Separatism', 190.

[17] Quoted in *VCH, Kent*, ii. 100.

[18] *CSPD*, 1663-4, 72, W. Kingsley to Secretary Bennet, 20 June 1663.

[19] Burnet, *History of Own Time*, i. 320.

[20] P. Collinson, *The Elizabethan Puritan Movement* (Berkeley, Calif., 1967), 54.

for the existence of nonconformity. They were the 'great poisoners' of the people,[21] and without them it was hoped the problem would fade away.

In fact, as Geoffrey Nuttall has shown, although several ejected clergy did play a part in sustaining post-Restoration dissent in the Canterbury diocese, they did not create it.[22] Nonconformity in the diocese, as in Kent as a whole, had long roots. John Lewis, the incumbent of Margate and a keen researcher into the Protestant past, could declare in his *Brief History of the Rise and Progress of Anabaptism in England* (1738) that from his enquiries into Kentish history, 'the religion of the Protestants is no novelty'.[23] Lewis also wrote a defence of John Wycliffe and John Foxe and a Life of Caxton, the early Protestant printer and a Kentish man.[24] His assumption of a long Protestant pedigree anticipated the agenda of modern historical scholarship with its interest in an underground tradition of dissent and nonconformity in England as a whole and Kent in particular.[25] Peter Clark has claimed that in Kent: 'there was an element of hereditary separatism, whose fragile thread, part myth and part reality, ran back through the mediation of Marian martyrdoms, and Edwardian Anabaptists, as far as the Lollards.'[26] David Underdown has suggested that the incidence of biblical first names in the region may have been a sign of a long-standing Puritan subculture.[27] Christopher Hill has found that the doctrines of mortalism, millenarianism, and the perfectibility of man were still being discussed in Kentish General Baptist congregations in the mid-eighteenth century.[28] The Weald especially has been noted as a centre of both Lollardy and early Protestantism as well as of semi-separatist groups at the end of the sixteenth century.[29] It is not clear why this region was so attractive to such groups. Some historians have cited the size of the parishes in the area, and the fact that large numbers of the population lived in outlying hamlets, several miles away from the parish church; others stress the links between

---

[21] Cf. LPL, MS 1126, fos. 35, 37, 38.

[22] G. F. Nuttall, 'Dissenting Churches in Kent before 1700', *JEH*, 54 (1963), 187.

[23] John Lewis, *A Brief History of the Rise and Progress of Anabaptism in England* (1738). Quotation from the draft version in Bodl. MS Rawlinson. c. 441, fo. 130.

[24] Lewis, *The History of the Life and Sufferings of the Reverend and Learned John Wicliffe, D.D.* (1720), id., *The Life of Mayster Wyllyam Caxton* (1737). See also his *A Specimen of the Gross Errors in the Second Volume of Mr Collier's Ecclesiastical History: being a Vindication of the Right Reverend and Learned Dr Gilbert Burnet, late Bishop of Sarum* (1724). For his attitude to Elizabeth Barton: LPL MS 1125, fo. 5.

[25] J. A. F. Thompson, *The Later Lollards* (Oxford, 1977); J. F. Davis, *Heresy and Reformation in the South East of England, 1520–1559* (1983); C. Hill, 'From Lollards to Levellers', in *Religion and Politics in Seventeenth-Century England* (Brighton, 1986), 189.

[26] Clark, *English Provincial Society*, 171.

[27] Underdown, *Revel, Riot and Rebellion*, 74.   [28] Hill, 'Lollards to Levellers', 189.

[29] William Laud, *Works*, v. 361.

nonconformity and the presence of industry.[30] In 1683 Giles Hinton, the rural dean of Charing, reported that dissenters were not so numerous in Biddenden as they had been when the cloth industry was more active.[31]

The Sheldon Catalogue of 1663 was the first major enquiry into the distribution of dissent and shows that the Weald, the major towns, Canterbury, Sandwich, Dover, and Ashford, and the sailing communities around the north Kent dockyards were the main centres for nonconformity, presenting the most obvious problems for Anglican clergy in their attempt to resurrect the dominance of the Church in the parishes.[32] Ashford, for instance, provides a good indication of the pressures faced by an Anglican minister in a parish where the presence of the nonconformist tradition was strong. It was reported that 'for his asserting and maintaining the ceremonies of the Church of England', Richard Whitelocke was 'hated by his parishioners, who are generally still Presbyterians'.[33] The Catalogue also indicates some of the assumptions which the Church hierarchy held about dissent, showing how far the Church valued the support of leading gentry in curbing it. Not all gentry in the Canterbury diocese were, the Catalogue revealed, 'friends of the Church'. Mr Watts, the patron of Benenden, was a 'fanatic'; Tenterden had 'not one honest justice in it'; at Bekesbourne the Independents were 'led by gentry' and the younger son of the Honeywood family was observed to be a 'roundhead'; at Wittersham Henry Beane aroused concern because he 'went about with a petition against Monarchy'. At Ashford the patron of the dissenters was Nailor, 'one of Oliver's justices'.[34] At Langley it was recorded that 'the chief man of the parish', Abel Beeching, 'was a Brownist and a very troublesome man'. The diocesan officials were relieved that at Westbere there were no dissenters, and that there 'was no gentleman in it but Culmer's son, whose father was an independent preacher, Anabaptist, Quaker, anything, now dead. This Culmer comes to church'.[35]

The Anglican Church aimed not to eliminate dissent so much as to limit its potential as a political force. The 1662/3 Returns for the lathe of St Augustine recorded only the more extreme groups: the Independents,

---

[30] Collinson, 'Cranbrook and the Fletchers'; J. F. Davis, 'Lollard Survival and the Textile Industry in the South-East of England', *SCH*, 3 (1966), 191–201.

[31] Bodl. MS Tanner 124, fo. 61, Hinton to Sancroft, 1683. For the decline in the Wealden cloth and iron industries by the late seventeenth century see B. M. Short, 'The South East', 307–8.

[32] For the sailing communities see B. Capp, *Cromwell's Navy* (Oxford, 1990), 295.

[33] LPL MS 1126, fo. 35. On Whitelocke see also CCAL Add. MS 91, p. 91.

[34] LPL MS 1126, fo. 35 (s.v. 'Benenden'), fo. 38 (s.v. 'Tenterden'), fo. 9 (s.v. 'Beakesbourne'), fo. 33 (s.v. 'Wittresham' and 'Ashford').

[35] Ibid., fo. 42.

Anabaptists, and Quakers, but paid no attention to Presbyterians.[36] It also emphasized the number of female nonconformists, another indication of the perceived social threat of dissent. Keith Thomas has shown the central role women played in the Civil War sects, and Thomas Edwards' *Gangraena* (1646) remarked on the number of women preachers in Kent.[37] In the Restoration era the attraction of women to dissent underscored the challenge some groups seemed to present to patriarchal society, confirming the impression of radicalism. Research has examined the contrasting ways in which male and female converts to sectarian congregations were depicted: women were more likely to be accused of emotional volatility, immorality, and insanity.[38] In Maidstone the diocesan officials found that 'none was worse than the Gaoler's wife and her undervarlets'.[39] It is unlikely that women actually played a disproportionate part in dissenting activity, although they were prominent in providing hospitality for nonconformist clergy, yet such was the Anglican perception.

The dilemma for the Crown at the Restoration was how to reward those clergy who had suffered for the royal cause without alienating those who had aquiesced in some measure in the Puritan regime but who would be likely to support the restored Church. The Act of 13 September 1660, 'For the confirming and restoring ministers', was an attempt to maintain the balance, by reinstating surviving ejected loyalists and installing those presented during the Interregnum by the lawful patron but who had been refused admission by the parliamentary committees. Other incumbents were allowed to remain in their livings provided they had not petitioned for the death of Charles I, or denied the validity of infant baptism. The Act was a moderate attempt to satisfy as many as possible, and in the diocese of Canterbury it does not seem to have provoked much hostility. Since so much patronage in the diocese had devolved to the Crown through lapse, the king was besieged by petitioners, in some cases even before he left Breda. But most of those whom Charles presented to Canterbury livings before the implementation of the Act were clergy appointed to vacant benefices, and so there were no problems of ejection.[40] While in Leicestershire the Act brought ejections to nearly a quarter of the parishes, in the

---

[36] Bodl. MS Tanner 124, fo. 108.

[37] K. V. Thomas, 'Women and the Civil War Sects', *Past and Present*, 13 (1958), 42–57; Thomas Edwards, *Gangraena* (1646), 8–9.

[38] Quoted in R. L. Greaves, 'The Role of Women in Early English Nonconformity', *Church History*, 52 (1983), 299–311. A similar identification has been found in D. M. Valenze, *Prophetic Sons and Daughters: Female Preaching and Popular Religion in Industrial England* (Princeton, NJ, 1981).

[39] LPL MS 1126, fos. 43, 7.   [40] Green, *Re-establishment of Church of England*, 44.

Canterbury diocese only nineteen clergy were removed.[41] Among those restored were John Warner, bishop of Rochester. He had held Bishopsbourne since 1619 and was an early petitioner to be restored. He remained at Bishopsbourne until 1662. Not all those ejected in 1660 became nonconformists. Joseph Hemmings, who had been presented to Lydd on the sequestration of Edward Wilsford, had to give up the living at the Restoration. He conformed to the Anglican Church in 1662, but was unable to find a benefice in the diocese and became rector of Swineshead in Huntingdonshire in 1666.[42]

Some, however, were ejected where there was no evicted loyalist to be restored. They included the most overt extremists who had held city parishes during the Interregnum and who had led the attack on the cathedral. John Durant, for example, was rector of St George's (1649–60) and had taken the place of a six-preacher. The Church found it relatively easy to detect and identify the extremists, but Presbyterians, who were more likely to participate in both Church and nonconformist activities, presented more of a difficulty. This was especially the case when the incumbent took the oaths in 1662 after the Act of Uniformity but remained Presbyterian in outlook. Under the terms of this Act only episcopal ordination was recognized as valid and clergy had to 'declare their unfeigned assent and consent' to everything in the revised Book of Common Prayer, and subscribe to the Thirty-nine Articles. Forty-one clergy were ejected from Canterbury livings between 1660 and 1662, representing just under 20 per cent of Canterbury ministers, not far from the national average.[43]

Some gentry in Kent continued to give support to nonconformist clergy within the diocese, even after the ejections. MPs such as John Boys, John Dixwell, and Henry Oxinden joined in the 'nonconformist' religious meetings at Barham:

They met at first once a fortnight on Fridays, and afterwards once in every month, on a week day. Upon a Lord's day, they received the Lord's supper together, after hearing a sermon in the Church, the three ministers taking turns. They also kept together many days of fasting and prayer; and held on to this course for some years very comfortably and profitably.[44]

At Chilham Samsom Horne was supported by Sir John Fagg at his house at Mystole after eviction. Some nonconformists received kindly treatment

[41] Pruett, *Parish Clergy*, 17; Green, *Re-establishment of Church of England*, 58–9.

[42] A. G. Matthews, *Walker Revised* (1947), 226; id., *Calamy Revised* (1934), 256.

[43] Ibid., pp. xii–xiii.

[44] *The Nonconformist's Memorial; Being An Account of the Lives, Sufferings and Printed Works of the Two Thousand Ministers Ejected from the Church of England . . . Originally Written by Edward Calamy*, ed. Samuel Palmer, 3 vols. (2nd edn., 1803), ii. 319.

from the clergy. John Osbourne was begged by the patron of Benenden, Sir John Hendon, to conform, and the dean of Rochester offered him a better living if he would do so. Although he declined, Osbourne 'continued to live in friendship' with the Established clergy.[45] The case is illustrative of the relationship between some nonconformists and the Church. Through concentration on the extremists, such amicable relations have been ignored. Others were allowed to preach in parish churches. Daniel Poyntel, ejected for not conforming at Staplehurst, appears to have known Archbishop Juxon, who licensed him to preach in his former pulpit if the new incumbent permitted; according to Calamy,

the weighty sense he had of his ordination vow, the desire of doing good, by preaching the gospel, and the woe which he was persuaded would follow if he preached it not, drew him to comply farther with the Church than some of the narrowest principles thought he could and brought him sometimes within his own pulpit . . . after Bartholomew Day.[46]

This kind of behaviour irritated more adamant nonconformists, such as the Quakers who posted a message on the 'steeple-house' door in Cranbrook: 'You that are called Presbyterians, if you join with [Anglicans] to read or hear read the common prayer book in any way of worship, then you be found hypocrites and dissemblers.'[47] This suggests that the differences between dissenters caused tensions, as well as simple divisions between dissent and the Church.

To make matters more difficult some Anglican clergy in the diocese had Presbyterian leanings, and ideological, familial, and educational ties, even after the ejections of late 1662 complicated the matter of defining nonconformity. Those who conformed in 1662 but remained Presbyterian at heart caused some concern. At Kingston the compiler of the Sheldon catalogue was perturbed to find that the vicar 'acknowledges one Anabaptist and one Quaker but says nothing about Presbyterians'.[48] Obviously such incumbents were not going to report those with whom they sympathized. The authorities were also troubled by some of those clergy who had ministered

---

[45] Ibid., 319–20.   [46] Ibid., 336.

[47] Quoted in D. R. Lacey, *Dissent and Parliamentary Politics in England, 1661–1689* (New Brunswick, NJ, 1969), 16.

[48] LPL MS 1126, fo. 11. Prayer Books were requested for the Canterbury diocese so 'that the services may be performed within the time limited': CCAL, W/Z/2, R. Aldworth to the commissary general, 3 July 1662. Burnet claimed that not enough books were printed, which meant that some had to resign their livings because they were too conscientious to subscribe to what they had not seen: *History of Own Time*, i. 330. Juxon gave a dispensation to Francis Porter (vicar of Eynesford) to defer making the public declaration of his assent to the Book of Common Prayer in Church until 21 Nov. 1662: Bodl. MS Tanner 125, fo. 51.

under the Cromwellian regime and had now taken the oaths. The incumbent of St Mildred's, Canterbury was 'followed by Presbyterians and Schismatics and proud of his popularity'.[49] Edward Aldey, rector of St Andrew's, Canterbury (1624–73), was called, 'a soft man, of weak resolutions, and heretofore a little inclining to Presbyt . . .'. This particular judgement may have been a little unfair. After all, Aldey had preached a sermon in defence of Christmas Day services in December 1647, a stand widely believed to have been instrumental in rallying support for Charles I in Kent during the second Civil War of 1648. He was rewarded for his attempt to maintain Anglican orthodoxy by being made a canon of the cathedral in 1660. Robert Clarke was 'somewhat suspected, because he hath kept in for 17 years together during all the troubles and changes'.[50]

The diocesan authorities found the same worries later in the decade. As archdeacon, Sancroft conducted a survey of incumbents in 1668. Thomas Hayes, vicar of Boxley, was found to have 'reform'd from Nonconformity'. He had obviously improved in the officials' eyes since 1663 when he had been criticized for not being licensed, and for the fact that 'in many things he doeth too much participize'.[51] But the survey showed that incumbents appointed even after 1662 might be questionable in their orthodoxy. John Cooper, for example, was presented to Cranbrook in late 1662 and in 1668 was found 'resident but . . . not of the strictest conversion'. John Edwards of Barfreston was characterized as a 'slight preacher and still leavened by ye old unconf[ormity] . . .'.[52] There may have been a certain amount of collusion between clergy and parishioners against the Church's detection mechanisms, and some clergy who were suspected to have had nonconformist connections were defended by their parishioners. In 1663, for example, John Young, the vicar of St Lawrence, Thanet, was supported by the churchwardens and eighty-nine parishioners against the imputation of nonconformity.[53] Even those who conformed to the Church of England may have carried with them preaching styles and techniques similar to those adopted by dissenters. John Stockar, for instance, was noted as being conformable to the Church but one who 'preaches after ye Presbyterian model'.[54]

Ejected ministers presented a particular challenge to the Anglican authorities. Despite the fact that only a few remained active in the diocese

---

[49] LPL MS 1126, fo. 3.   [50] Ibid., fos. 1, 17.
[51] Bodl. MS Sancroft 99, fo. 29; LPL MS 1126, fo. 40.
[52] Bodl. MS Sancroft 99, fo. 54; Bodl. MS Rawl. lett. 106, fo. 91.
[53] LPL MS 2686, fos. 50–1, Petition of Churchwardens and inhabitants of St Lawrence, Thanet, 17 Nov. 1663.
[54] LPL MS 1126, fo. 3.

during the 1660s, the Church, in keeping with its policy of pinpointing the chief ringleaders and supporters, sought to keep track of their whereabouts. George Hammond, for one, appears to have been very active in parishes between Cranbrook and Ashford; and the fact that he was reported as encouraging several dissenting congregations may have given the impression of greater co-ordination amongst nonconformist groups than in fact existed.[55] Attempts to stop such behaviour, such as the First Conventicle Act of 1664 and the Five Mile Act of 1665, depended on the co-operation of the secular authorities. This was not always forthcoming. In Canterbury, the presence of a mayor who was sympathetic to Presbyterianism ensured that several ejected ministers would find some sustenance even in the heart of the restored Church.[56] The corporation could control juries so that on several occasions during the 1660s dissenters were not convicted.[57] A report to the privy council in 1665 declared that most of the grand jury in Canterbury were 'fanatics'.[58] After the lapsing of the 1664 Conventicle Act, JPs in the Canterbury area found themselves powerless. In 1667 they complained:

We finding in this city of late several conventicles in great numbers . . . did by ourselves without any number of soldiers go to the place of meeting, and there we found one Robert Beake amongst 1000 people . . . in a conventicle preaching and exercising under pretence of Religion . . . and when we desired them to depart and dissipate they obstinately refused and bid their preacher stand fast and go on . . . and having not power sufficient we did depart, finding that by their great number and interest in that place we could not effect what we desired . . . for their insolences are so high, and boldness already such that we fear, it may not be in our power to suppress them . . .[59]

This is an indication that the JPs were pressing the government to promote legislation: it supports other evidence that policy was often the product of pressure from the localities, the outcome of a symbiotic relationship between central and local government.[60]

In 1665 Sheldon ordered an enquiry concerning the ejected clergy, 'where and how and in what profession of life they now do live', and 'how

---

[55] Ibid., fo. 35 (s.v. 'Benenden', 'Bethersden', 'Biddenden'); fo. 36 (s.v. 'Cranbrook'); fo. 37 (s.v. 'High Halden', 'Hawkhurst'); fo. 38 (s.v. 'Smarden'); fo. 42 (s.v. 'Lenham').

[56] Bodl. MS Tanner 48, fo. 26, Turner to Barwick, 18 Aug. 1662.

[57] M. V. Jones, 'The Divine Durant: A Seventeenth-Century Independent', *AC*, 83 (1968), 202.

[58] *CSPD*, 1665–6, 102, Anthony Cooley to Henry Muddiman, 15 Oct. 1665.

[59] Bodl. MS Tanner 45, fo. 243, The deputy-lieutenants and Justices of the Peace of Canterbury to the Hon. Sir Wm Morice, Secretary of State, 29 Dec. 1667.

[60] This theme has been studied by Fletcher, *Reform in Provinces* and A. M. Coleby, *Central Government and the Localities: Hampshire, 1646–1689* (Cambridge, 1987).

they behave themselves in relation to the peace and quiet as well of the Church as of the State'.[61] Similar enquiries were issued again in 1669.[62] He hinted that one of the problems the Church faced in dealing with dissenters was the inconsistency in royal policy, in its vacillation between indulgence and repression: 'His Majesty . . . lately speaking much against these disorderly meetings and expressing an indignation of all reports of him, as if he either favoured, or connived at them'.[63] Sheldon demanded information not only concerning the ministers but also the size and 'quality' of their congregations. The connection between dissenting activity and the Civil War was again brought out, and in his visitation articles to the diocese in 1667 the archbishop asked if there were any in the parish who denied the King's Supremacy.[64] In Canterbury a good deal of gentry backing for the dissenting cause remained. Thomas Scott was 'a ringleader of Petitioners for the King's trial'; other supporters included John Jacob, Edward Hirst, the attorney, and Sir William Brodnax, a JP. Brodnax also patronized Nathaniel Wilmot, who had been ejected from Faversham and was reported as being an itinerant preacher at conventicles in the Isle of Sheppey.[65] The existence of continuing gentry participation in dissent should be stressed against those historians who depict the Restoration gentry *en masse* as Cavalier ultras.[66] Sheldon wanted his officials to report any justice who 'do not his duty'.[67] In 1666 he heard that a Mr Barry, a nonconformist leader who after the Five Mile Act ought not to have been living in Dover, was continuing to hold meetings there 'wherein he scatters his seditious Doctrines and principles among ye people'.[68] He wanted Colonel Strode to enquire into the matter and make use of his authority to put the penalties into effect, which would be not only a public service to the town but enhance 'good order and government'.[69] In 1669 it was found that at Nonington the Anabaptists met at the house of Richard Kingsford, 'a rich surly sectary'.[70] He had been presented to the Church court during the previous year, 'least he, by example, spoils the whole parish'.[71] The Conventicle Act of 1670

---

[61] LPL, MS 639, fo. 152.

[62] Ibid., Sheldon Register II, 205, Sheldon to the bishop of London, 7 July 1665. See also Bodl. MS Tanner 44, fo. 131, Leoline Jenkins to Sancroft, 20 July 1669.

[63] Bodl. MS Tanner 282, fo. 60, Sheldon to the commissary, dean, and archdeacon of Canterbury, 7 May 1669. The information collected was used to argue for the Conventicle Act; Spurr, *Restoration Church of England*, 72.

[64] Bodl. MS Tanner 125, fo. 33.   [65] LPL MS 639, fos. 152, 154.

[66] Green, *Re-establishment of Church of England*, 200.

[67] Bodl. MS Tanner 282, fo. 60. See A. Fletcher, 'The Enforcement of the Conventicle Acts, 1664–1679', *SCH*, 21 (1984), 234–7.

[68] Bodl. Add. MS c. 308, fo. 66, Sheldon to Strode, 18 June 1666.

[69] Ibid.   [70] LPL, MS 639, fo. 155.   [71] CCAL, X. 7. 10, fo. 101.

placed harsher penalties on the ringleaders (and it now only needed one JP to arrest them) whilst fines were reduced for ordinary offenders. In practice this attitude towards the more humble offenders had been employed during the 1660s. It was, after all, impractical to send them to prison and fines were more common. In Cranbrook in 1665 the fines taken at the conventicle was handed over by the justices to the churchwardens and distributed to the poor.[72] It is also clear that the itinerancy of the nonconformist ministers had not been curbed. Charles Nichols was found to be preaching at Adisham, Ash, Dover, Nonington, Sandwich, Staple, Wingham, and Womenswold.[73] Goudhurst, situated on the border with the diocese of Rochester, had many 'conventiclers' with teachers coming down from London.[74] In several parishes the congregations are described as 'mean', but the leaders as 'good'.[75]

For eleven months in 1672, dissenting ministers within the diocese were given some respite through the Declaration of Indulgence. The licences which were taken out in response to the Declaration are by themselves an unsatisfactory indicator of the size of dissent in the diocese, for they tell us nothing about the congregations and reveal the names of only some of the ministers (Quakers, for example, did not take out licences, since they did not think that the king had the right to take away religious freedom). Thirty-seven individuals in the diocese petitioned for a licence, and only nine of these had been ejected clergy.[76] These petitioners were mainly registered in the larger towns: Canterbury, Sandwich, and Dover, and in parishes in the Weald. In Canterbury, the hall of Mr Roper at St Dunstan's was licensed for Robert Beake and Thomas Ventriss.[77] Besides licences for persons, twenty-three licences were taken out for places in the diocese. These included the house of Lady Taylor at Maidstone, and Wotton Court.[78] It would be wrong to argue that the Declaration 'saved' dissent in the diocese, for the legislation of the 1660s had only been sporadically enforced. However, it encouraged less-committed members of dissenting congregations to play a more sustained role in support of nonconformity and allowed them to grow. Legislation in the 1660s had been unable to crush the activities of the hard-core dissenting leaders, but it may well have dissuaded fringe members from attending meetings. This attitude changed in 1672. Archdeacon Parker had no doubt on this point. Writing in 1676 he

---

[72] LPL, MS 639, fo. 156.   [73] Ibid., fo. 155.   [74] Ibid., fo. 154.   [75] Ibid.

[76] Ejected clergy: Robert Beake, John Durant, Charles Nichols, Francis Taylor, Nicholas Thoroughgood, Thomas Ventris, Nathaniel Wilmot, Samuel Hieron, Daniel Poyntel. Names in F. Bate, *The Declaration of Indulgence 1672: A Study in the Rise of Organised Dissent* (1908), Appendix xxxii.

[77] Ibid.   [78] Ibid.

lamented that 'many left the Church upon the Indulgence who before did frequent it'.[79]

Parker's comment was written at the end of his own return to the Compton Census of 1676. The Census has been much used by historians as a tool to measure the relative strengths of Anglicanism, Protestant non-conformity, and Roman Catholicism in this period, as well as being a source for demographic historians.[80] The shortcomings of the Census as a document are well known: confusion amongst incumbents over the exact meaning of the questions; the fact that most replies only dealt with inhabitants over the age of sixteen; the political reasons behind calling the Census, all of which negate its utility as a 'scientific instrument'.[81] It has been conjectured that the returns for the Canterbury diocese were particularly suspect and that Archdeacon Parker was guilty of manipulating the figures: by magnifying the numbers of inhabitants in the diocese he may have decreased the proportion of dissenters to conformists, thereby giving the impression that the clergy in the diocese had done well to keep the numbers of dissenters down.[82] Parker increased the total number of inhabitants to 59,596, whereas the true total was not more than 53,414. It seems more likely, however, that the discrepancies between the totals for the deaneries and the figures for individual parishes were caused by carelessness and copying errors, rather than by wilful manipulation.

The number of dissenters in the Canterbury diocese as revealed by the Census was rather higher than the national average.[83] Even so, historians of nonconformity have criticized it for being a measure only of the hardline dissenters, underestimating those who might occasionally have attended

---

[79] LPL MS 639 fo. 166, Parker to Sheldon, 13 Apr. 1676.

[80] The most thorough treatment is *The Compton Census of 1676: A Critical Edition*, ed. A. Whiteman, British Academy Records of Social and Economic History, new series, X (1986), 2–35. See, too, C. W. Chalklin, 'The Compton Census of 1676: The Dioceses of Canterbury and Rochester', *A Seventeenth Century Miscellany*, Kent Records, 17 (1960), 153–74. Sources for the Canterbury returns are LPL MS 639, fos. 163–8 and in CCAL there are the original returns from the incumbents to the diocesan officials: CCAL, H/Z.

[81] See the discussion in Chalklin, 'Compton Census', 153–7.

[82] Overstated deaneries:

	Parker's totals	Totals by Parishes
Sandwich	2,774	2,694
Bridge	3,422	3,339
Lympne	1,735	1,734
Sutton	10,666	4,666
Ospringe	3,437	3,359

[83] Chalklin, 'Compton Census', 157.

nonconformist meetings, especially Presbyterian, but who were also regular in their attendance at the parish church. But this is as it should be. To expect that the Census should call any who attended a nonconformist meeting a dissenter misses the true nature of dissent in this period, and the fluidity which allowed parishioners to attend both the parish church and a nonconformist meeting. The returns show that several incumbents struggled with problems of definition in drawing up their answers: did dissenter mean those who did not take Holy Communion or those who did not attend church at all? The vicar of St Lawrence, Thanet gave several possible answers to the question, remarking that of the 1,200 inhabitants, 'about 50 persons are wholly absent' but that fewer than 200 took Communion once a year, and fewer than 100 took it three times, 'for though the most part of the 1,200 come constantly to the church to prayers and sermon, yet few of them will be induced to receive the Communion by any arguments or perswasions'.[84] Some incumbents were well aware that even those who were absent from church services might have other reasons than the fact that they were dissenters. Francis Nicholson, the curate of Goodnestone-by-Wingham, listed parishioners who were sick or away in London. Others complained of absentees, although there was no sect in the parish.[85] The parishioners of Ash were described as neglecting communion, 'some out of obstinacy, and others out of careless and atheistical presumptions wilfully absenting themselves from the public service and communion of the Church, so in times of liberty turn deaf ears to all exhortations and instruction to the contrary'.[86] The rector of Frittenden indicated that it was simplistic to divide inhabitants into Anglican, Nonconformist, and Catholic. He listed other more nuanced categories: 'professed Presbyterians wholly refusing society with the Church of England—not above 2 or 3; Anabaptists 31; Quakers 2; Brownists 2; Neutralists between Presbyterians and Conformists 30–40; Licentiers, or no kind of religion, 11; unfrequent resorters to parish church 30–40.'[87]

The fact that many who were Presbyterians also attended the parish church indicates that the aversion to separatism displayed by Anglican clergy was shared by some dissenting groups themselves. Patrick Collinson has shown how this attitude in the pre-Civil War era led to 'semi-separatism', a kind of halfway house between acceptance of the Church and breaking away from it, and clearly this attitude continued to determine the behaviour of many post-Restoration dissenters.[88] There was always a large body of occasional conformists, attending both the parish church and the

---

[84] CCAL, H/Z, fo. 195.   [85] Ibid., fo. 82.   [86] Ibid., fo. 17.
[87] Ibid., fo. 79.   [88] Collinson, *Religion of Protestants*, 274–83.

dissenting meeting house, who perhaps should be classified as 'occasional dissenters'. A good many people who were otherwise uncommitted to dissent may have gone along to a meeting to hear preachers, blurring any notion of confessional boundaries. They took their children to the Anglican clergyman for baptism and may well have attended the parish church after the meeting. Others might have cut sufficiently loose of the Established Church to have their children baptized in the meeting, but nevertheless did not engage in full communion.

What the Census can show, confirming other records, is the geographic distribution of dissent. A large area of the diocese, towards the north coastal area, especially the deaneries of Sittingbourne and Ospringe, recorded very few dissenters; interestingly this was to be the main area of Methodist influence in the diocese in the next century. The areas of nonconformist strength were the major towns to the east and the Weald. This comes out clearly in the map of parishes where the proportion of dissenters to the number of inhabitants was 1 : 15 or more (Map 2). Towns with this proportion of nonconformists were Canterbury, Cranbrook, Tenterden, Ashford, Sandwich, Deal, Folkstone, Hythe, and Dover. Their influence spread into the rural hinterland and reinforces the conclusions of Bebb and Hurwich that by this date dissent was migrating into the towns and drawing its membership mainly from the urban sector.[89] Incumbents who attempted to distinguish between the different types of dissenter found this easier in towns than in rural districts where they resorted to blanket descriptions. It would have been more difficult in a rural parish to maintain meetings of different dissenting groups: it is more likely that the congregations that did survive contained members of various sects. Only in the towns could incumbents differentiate more rigidly between denominations, for here distinctions were sharpened by rivalry between dissenting groups.

The Weald contained a large proportion of Anabaptists and Quakers; in Staplehurst, for instance, the incumbent recorded 160 Quakers, Anabaptists, and Brownists.[90] The last group are a survival from an earlier period, and show the continuity of radical dissenting traditions, or at least nomenclature, in the region. In 1716 Brownists were reported living at Egerton, Bethersden, Boughton Malherbe, and Cranbrook, where the Brownist had 'a concubine'.[91] It is difficult to know how far such congregations after

---

[89] E. R. Bebb, *Nonconformity and Social and Economic Life 1600–1800* (1935); J. J. Hurwich, 'Dissent and Catholicism in English Society: A Study of Warwickshire, 1660–1720', *JBS*, 16 (1976), 24–58.

[90] CCAL, H/Z, fo. 181.

[91] Ch. Ch. MS Wake Visitation Returns A, fos. 93, 96, 103, 105.

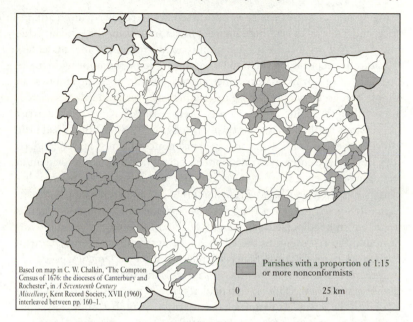

Based on map in C. W. Chalkin, 'The Compton
Census of 1676: the dioceses of Canterbury and
Rochester', in *A Seventeenth Century
Miscellany*, Kent Record Society, XVII (1960)
interleaved between pp. 160–1.

Parishes with a proportion of 1:15
or more nonconformists

0   25 km

MAP 2. The Distribution of Nonconformity in the Diocese of Canterbury, 1676

1660 had direct continuity with their Tudor forebears.[92] Indeed, it may be that the Anglican clergy themselves created the idea of a tradition of dissent, to impose a kind of pattern on their opponents. Archdeacon Parker, for example, believed that 'the leaders and preachers of the several factions are such as had a great share in the Rebellion'.[93] Of especial concern were the 300 Muggletonians living in the diocese, a sharp reminder of those groups who had played such a prominent part when the world had been turned upside down. As late as 1786 Archbishop Moore was told of six Muggletonians living in Faversham who 'never attend Church, and whose tenets are so absurd and fanatical, that reason and argument have not the least influence on them'.[94]

The fluctuating membership of dissenting congregations, especially in smaller rural parishes, could be affected by the efforts of individual incumbents, who by their personal exertions and initiatives might win them back. Francis Nicholson was successful, at Goodnestone, during the 1670s, in

[92] Acheson, 'Religious Separatism', 204.
[93] LPL MS 639, fo. 168.   [94] Ibid., VG 3/1/c, fo. 57.

bringing all but one of the erstwhile dissenters to regular church attendance, and achieved a very high turn out of communicants.[95] William Cade told Thorp of his success at Bicknor in 1680 in bringing former dissenters to Church, encouraging them to be baptized. He hoped to provide 'more instances of this or like nature which are too many to be found amongst an almost barbarous people, whose carelessness of everything that is sacred, argues that the pains of my worthy predecessors have made but weak impressions on them in the concerns of Religion'.[96] Such efforts had little effect on the more radical groups or against nonconformist leaders; indeed they might have confirmed them in their convictions. This was evident in the diocese when a more concerted policy of harrassment towards dissenters was attempted between 1678 and 1686, under Archbishop Sancroft. Sancroft's programme has been described as one of 'thorough',[97] yet it is clear that in his diocese he was aware of the difficulties and even the undesirablility of presenting the Church as a persecutor. Within a general framework of proselytism, Sancroft's policy was one of leniency, especially in attempting to woo influential dissenters, who might bring over large numbers with them. This was particularly true of his attitude to dissenting leaders in the towns. At Sandwich the mayor, Mr Combes, supported nonconformists, and in 1682 was presented to the ecclesiastical court in Canterbury for not receiving the sacrament. Andrew Mills, the vicar of St Clement, Sandwich, complained that Combes had been chosen mayor illegally since he had not fulfilled the requirements of the Test Act.[98] Combes had appealed against this to the court of Arches. Mills urged Sancroft to stop his appeal, otherwise there would be 'no managing of him'.[99] George Thorp wanted to deal harshly with him, 'but in obedience to your Grace's former commands, I thought I could not more than admonish him to do it at Xmas . . .'.[100] The mayor's influence in the town was such that St Bartholomew's hospital had become 'a common sanctuary and refuge for several persons notoriously disaffected to the government both of Church and State'. Its inmates refused to attend church services and take the sacrament, and included Francis Hooke, 'his name being found among those in this county which signed the black petition for the murder of the late king'.[101] Furthermore, the female Quaker preacher, Joan Vokins, was protected by the mayor when she confronted Mills. Her account of the

[95] CCAL, H/Z, fo. 82.
[96] Bodl. MS Rawl. lett. 59, fo. 52, William Cade to Thorp, 20 Dec. 1680.
[97] G. V. Bennett, 'The Seven Bishops: A Reconsideration', *SCH*, 15 (1978), 270.
[98] Bodl. MS Tanner 126, fo. 116, Mills to Sancroft, 24 Jan. 1683.   [99] Ibid.
[100] Bodl. MS Tanner 33, fo. 221, Thorp to Sancroft, 23 Nov. 1682.
[101] Bodl. MS Tanner 126*, fo. 115, 1 May 1684.

incident in her spiritual autobiography, *God's Mighty Power Magnified*, is worth quoting as an example of the behaviour which so perturbed the Anglican authorities:

And on the first day, being the 5th of the 4th month, 1681, I went to the steeple-house, as it was before me . . . and in the strength of the almighty power I delivered that message which I received of the Lord Jesus . . . and I exhorted them, both priest and people, to take heed to a measure or manifestation thereof in their own hearts, and leave off their idolatry, and come to be true spiritual worshippers. And I laid before them the danger of the one and the benefit of the other, till the priest caused me to be hauled out. And when I came forth, many of his hearers followed me, and I had a good opportunity with them . . . but the priest put off his hat to us and bustled away, and endeavoured to send me to prison. But the God of power, who preserved me when much evil hath been intended, prevented him, that he could not prevail with the mayor . . . I was informed that the priest above specified did do his endeavour to stir up persecution against Friends and put the mayor to some trouble for not punishing me. But therein he did, nor could do, no more than manifest his own malice and what birth he was of. The Lord hath set his bounds.[102]

The Church supported royal efforts to remodel borough and corporation charters since this was a way of changing the religious complexion of the mayor and jurats.[103]

There is some evidence to suggest that harsher policies towards dissenters were forced on Sancroft by his diocesan officials, in the same way that pressure from the localities affected the policy of central government. He was, after all, later to back plans for comprehension concerning liturgical reforms in 1688–9 in order to win over the moderate nonconformists.[104] Sancroft's correspondents in the diocese understood the need to work slowly against dissenters, but they were also aware of the danger if the Church appeared powerless. George Thorp wrote a charitable petition on behalf of Basil Harrison, 'a reformed Anabaptist', who had suffered unusually heavy fines through duplicate prosecutions, but who was now loyal to the Church, yet concerning dissenters at Chislet he was more severe: 'I know your Grace would not have us proceed to extremities, but if

[102] [Joan Vokins], *God's Mighty Power Magnified: as Manifested and Revealed in his Faithful Handmaid Joan Vokins* (1691), 38–42, quoted in *Her Own Life. Autobiographical Writings by Seventeenth-Century Englishwomen*, ed. E. Graham, H. Hind, E. Hobby, and H. Wilcox (1989), 222–3; Mills mentioned the incident: Bodl. MS Tanner 126, fo. 117, Mills to Robert Thompson, 26 Nov. 1681.
[103] C. Lee, '"Fanatic Magistrates": Religious and Political Conflict in Three Kent Boroughs, 1680–1684', *HJ*, 35 (1991), 43–61.
[104] Sykes, *From Sheldon to Secker*, 85.

any obstinate persons remain, they must be given over as incorrigible'.[105] Edward Hirst, an influential dissenter around Canterbury, was cited to appear before the Church court but pleaded that since he had been convicted in the secular courts he was exempt from ecclesiastical jurisdiction. This provides an example of the practice of flouting ecclesiastical courts by getting a prohibition, so that the case could only be dealt with in secular courts. This had long been a problem for the Church authorities, and post-Restoration clergy, in keeping with the general desire to maintain Church privileges, vigorously defended the independence of their own courts. Sancroft, in his regulations for ecclesiastical courts, ordered that there should be no prohibitions or commutations of penance for money.[106] Archdeacon Parker complained to Thorp, 'if it be not gone through with, we are utterly blown up here, for this is a leading case, and Hirst is a leading man, so that if we can hinder him, the people will not be so obstinate at appeals . . . but if he be not mastered, we are baffled forever'.[107] Indeed, Parker and Sancroft fell out over the treatment of dissenters in the diocese. Parker, who has been called a 'neurotic royalist and disgruntled careerist',[108] accused Sancroft of being too indulgent towards them, especially Hirst and Durant, and called him a Whig. He claimed that the archbishop had stood in the way of one Captain Roberts, who, according to Parker, was known as 'Bishop Bonner' and had been so zealous in prosecuting nonconformists that some of the local gentry had wanted to club together to give him money for his pains.[109]

In dealing with dissenters, threats of excommunication in this period had some weight, by pushing the less committed back within the Church.[110] The social penalties of excommunication, especially in a close-knit rural community, were still potentially horrific. Excommunicates were not supposed to sit on a jury, receive any legacy, or converse with others in the community. Sancroft asked incumbents and churchwardens in his visitation articles of 1682 whether any parishioners talked to excommunicates or schismatics.[111] Despite such efforts to uphold the separate powers of Church jurisdiction, it was obvious to clergy that the Church could do little without the support of the temporal authority. Against moderate dissenters

[105] Bodl. MS Tanner 34, fo. 165, Thorp to Sancroft, 9 Oct. 1682; MS Tanner 33, fo. 228, Thorp to Sancroft, 25 Jan. 1683.

[106] Bodl. MS Tanner 280, fo. 117, 'A Paper against Prohibitions in Ecclesiastical Courts', by Robert Thompson (n.d.); MS Tanner 300, fo. 143, Sancroft's regulations.

[107] Bodl. MS Tanner 36, fo. 223, Parker to Thorp, 27 Jan. 1682.

[108] R. A. Beddard, 'The Church of Salisbury and the Accession of James II', *Wiltshire Archaeological Magazine*, 67 (1972), 141. On the rift between Sancroft and Parker: Bodl. MS Tanner 31, fos. 166, *et seq.*

[109] Ibid., fo. 166.   [110] Bennett, *Crisis*, 7.   [111] Bodl., MS Tanner 124, fo. 9.

the threat of excommunication held some force, yet Quakers were seldom frightened by such penalties, and against these the Church relied on lay assistance. An account of the court proceedings at the 1682 visitation showed that the ecclesiastical courts found that 'the greater part being either poor or Quakers, have not paid one farthing of fees to judge, registrar or apparitor'.[112] James Wilson, the rural dean of Sutton, grieved that the

dissenters in these parts tho they must not so publickly as heretofore, yet refuse to join in communion with ye Church, ye laws unless it be in great towns not being put in execution against them. Upon application made to ye Justices of Peace, they have now issued out their warrants to ye constables, to warm up ye churchwardens in every parish to bring in ye names of all felons.

He hoped that

if they put the 12d act in execution [this would] reduce great numbers from their neglect and nonconformity; for it is very certain that the common sort of people are more afraid of the penalty of 12d weekly than of the sentence of excommunication which is now accounted by them but brutus fulmen without the writ de excommunicate capiendo follow it, which is so very rare in the country that the common people know it not.[113]

The 12d. Act was first established in 1559, fining parishioners who were absent from church services, and used against Catholics. That it could also be employed against Protestant dissenters shows the flexibility of legislation in the early modern period. In 1606 a £20 penalty was introduced for those not receiving the sacrament once a year. Archdeacon Parker explained to Sancroft why this harsher act was resorted to. Some Quakers and Anabaptists would not promise conformity, and although the 12d. Act had been used against them, this had not worked, 'because the lawyers tell both the constables and the people, that there can be no breaking open of doors to distrain, so that when they come to demand it, it is but clapping to the shop door, and the whole business is made a mock, and it was the battle that was given us this way that put us upon the £20 Act'.[114]

The combined use of the threat of religious and temporal penalties saw an impressive shrinkage in the dissenting congregations. There is some indication that the actual penalty of excommunication was only used against the 'stiffer' dissenters, but that the threat was enough to bring over the others. Thorp informed Sancroft in 1682 that the courts were discovering people who had not received the sacrament for several years, 'and I doubt

---

[112] Bodl. MS Tanner 125, fo. 76.
[113] Bodl. MS Tanner 124, fo. 47, Wilson to Sancroft, 11 Sept. 1682; MS Rawl lett 59, fo. 481, Wilson to Sancroft.
[114] Bodl. MS Tanner 123, fo. 177, Parker to Sancroft, 23 Sept. 1682.

whether some at all'.[115] The Sancroftian regime was, after all, not merely concerned to detect the nonconformist leaders and force people to attend church services; it was, as G. V. Bennett has suggested, an attempt to plant the distinctive features of Anglican worship in the hearts and minds of ordinary people.[116] Giles Hinton thought that this might be possible in the Weald where the 'generality of dissenters are not so much by their own choices, as by the ignorance or error of their education, for they are as much to[o] weke in the constitution and usages of the Church of England, as the disciples of Ephesus were all of the Holy Ghost'.[117]

It is a consequence of the type of records left by the Church in this period that our impression is of a largely intolerant and persecuting institution. By their very nature, visitation records and court books only deal with the harsher aspects of Anglican policy. But there were more positive ways of dealing with dissenters in the parish, through persuasion and pastoral work. James Haydock, the curate of Nockholt, explained to Sancroft in 1680:

> I have done his Majesty and the Church of England more services than most clergy in my capacity. I have discoursed with Anabaptists, and so far convinced them that I have baptized 7 children, and persuaded the whole company to take oaths of supremacy. I have persuaded with many dissenters not only to hear, but I trust, to approve the common prayers of the Church . . .[118]

An indication of the tolerance shown to nonconformists can be seen in the treatment of the Walloon and Huguenot settlers who had established themselves in Kent, fleeing from persecution on the Continent.[119] They had been permitted to set up places of worship in the diocese: in Sandwich (1561), Maidstone (1567), and Canterbury (1564). Elizabeth I had granted them freedom of worship; but they became the objects of Laud's hostility during the 1630s. Peter Clark claims that 'the most unpopular manifestation of the new Laudian temper in the Kentish Church was his treatment of the Stranger community'.[120] Post-Restoration clergy did not resume this aspect of Laudian policy and both Sheldon and Sancroft showed considerable sympathy towards them. Sheldon, so often seen as a Laudian, did

---

[115] Bodl. MS Tanner 33, fo. 223, Thorp to Sancroft, 8 Mar. 1682.

[116] Bennett, *Crisis*, 6. See also his 'The Seven Bishops: A Reconsideration', *SCH*, 15 (1978), 267–87.

[117] Bodl. MS Tanner 124, fo. 61, Hinton to Thorp, 1683.

[118] Ibid., fo. 102, James Haydock to Sancroft, 25 May 1680.

[119] On the broader relationship see O. P. Grell, J. I. Israel, and N. Tyacke (eds.), *From Persecution to Toleration. The Glorious Revolution and Religion in England* (Oxford, 1991).

[120] Clark, *English Provincial Society*, 365. See also, J[ean] B[ulteel], *A Relation of the Troubles of the three forraign Churches in Kent. Caused by the Injunctions of William Laud* (1645). On the more general problem see F. W. Cross, *History of the Walloon and Huguenot Church at Canterbury* (Canterbury, 1898).

nothing to hinder their worship. The ecclesiastical courts in Canterbury had suspended Vital Delon for marrying John Six and Mary Hooke without publishing the banns in the parish church; Sheldon let him off the sentence.[121] Louis Herault, later a prebendary of Canterbury Cathedral (stall IX, 1671–82), expressed the gratitude felt by the foreign Protestant community in England in his *Remercient facit ay Roy* (1666). There is some indication that the authorities in the first years of the Restoration were wary about the potentially divisive aspects of the Huguenots in Canterbury. When splits developed amongst the Canterbury congregation, the cathedral chapter favoured M. Jannon's party which conformed to Anglican liturgy.[122] But the Huguenot communities flourished, establishing themselves in several Canterbury parishes: St Alphege's, St Mary Northgate, St Peter's, Holy Cross, and St Mildred's. Not surprisingly, some of these parishes returned a majority of nonconformists in the Compton Census.[123] Relations between the foreign and Anglican communities were amicable and the JPs in 1676 spoke favourably of their good behaviour and of the credit they brought to the city.[124] During the 1680s the number of Huguenot immigrants increased as a result of renewed persecution in France under Louis XIV which culminated in the revocation of the Edict of Nantes in 1685. In response, Sancroft urged Archdeacon Parker in 1681 to

use your utmost endeavours to promote and encourage the charitable contributions of all persons of ability within your jurisdiction; and that as well by your example of your own more than usual liberality as also by strictly encouraging the clergy everywhere . . . to stir up their parishioners freely and cheerfully to extend the bowels of their compassion to these new poor persecuted brethren.[125]

Parker may have been out of sympathy with such charity. He had, after all, received promotion for his trenchant call for legislation demanding complete conformity in his *Discourse of Ecclesiastical Politie* (1670). Nevertheless, a brief was issued to raise money for the Huguenots. Parker pointed out to Thorp that despite some confusion about the ecclesiastical identity of the French Protestants, although the initiative was opposed, it was successful: 'people have been waylaid both ways, with the fanatiques that they are papists, and with the honest people that they are fanatiques, and yet

---

[121] Bodl. MS Tanner 92, fo. 152.

[122] *CSPD*, 1661–2, 315, 20 Mar. 1662. Cf. BL Add. MS 29,587, fo. 43: 'Instructions Concerning the Walloons, 1670'.

[123] See parishes in CCAL, H/Z: esp. Canterbury, Sandwich, Maidstone, and Dover.

[124] Bodl. MS Tanner 92, fo. 169: Certificate of the Justices of the Peace, 11 May 1676.

[125] Bodl. MS Tanner 36, fo. 152, Sancroft to Parker (draft) 1681. It was also hoped that such charitable behaviour would encourage Huguenots to conform to the Church of England: Bodl. MS Tanner 31, fo. 247, Tillotson to Henry Maurice, 19 Jan. 1686.

non-withstanding as far as I can guess from those collections that have been brought in, the contribution will be considerable.'[126]

A community of French Protestants, led by the Marquis of Venours, settled in Boughton Malherbe. Sancroft instructed Michael Stanhope, the rector, to treat them well, calling them 'not only professors of the Protestant religion, but confessors, and sufferers, for the same'.[127] The archbishop had written to Dr Cowel Hage in 1684 in a similar vein: 'I can by no means as our brethren seem to do give up the whole Protestant cause as lost and desperate and ready to breathe its last. No! God hath by the Reformation kindled and set up a light in Christendom which I am fully persuaded shall never be extinguished.'[128]

The clergy's response to the plight of the Huguenots is an indication of the growing rift between the Church and James II. In 1685 the new king, echoing Laudian policy, ordered Colonel Strode, the lieutenant of Dover castle, to make the French congregation use the liturgy of the Church of England, 'wherein if they fail, we do authorize, and require you . . . to shut up the church doors and suffer them to meet no more'.[129] During 1686 Sancroft prepared a circular letter on behalf of the Huguenots which was heavily censored by James, who objected to its anti-Catholic sentiment. The Anglican clergy had used the opportunity, in encouraging charity to the exiled Huguenots, to contrast the benevolence of the Church of England with the intolerance of popery, and the popular response to the series of briefs for French Protestant assistance from 1681 to 1703 was impressive.[130] James also forbade Anglican clergy to preach on the topic, since this was a principal opportunity to attack Catholicism.[131]

The sufferings of the Huguenots, who streamed into Kent during the 1680s, could be portrayed as what might happen to Protestants under a Catholic monarch. Lay suspicion of James was widespread. In 1684 a Kent labourer, William Burnam, was found guilty of claiming that 'the Duke of York is a wizard. I pray he may be consumed in Brimstone and Hell Fire. He rides about at night in fiery chariots to torment souls and he is preparing for a field of blood. His witchcraft will lay the nation in blood and Popish

---

[126] Bodl. MS Tanner 36, fo. 223, Parker to Thorp, 27 Jan. 1682. The diocese raised £100 for this: BL MS Harleian 3790, fo. 23.

[127] Bodl. MS Tanner 36, fo. 239, Sancroft to Stanhope, 27 Feb. 1682.

[128] Quoted in E. G. Rupp, *Religion in England, 1688–1791* (Oxford, 1986), 72.

[129] Bodl. MS Tanner 125, fo. 64, James II to Colonel John Strode, Lieutenant Dover Castle, 30 July 1685 (copy).

[130] Bodl. MS Tanner 33, fo. 291, 17 Mar. 1686; MS Tanner 37, fo. 154; MS Tanner 31, fo. 279[R].

[131] *CSPD*, 1686–7, 56–7, king to the archbishops of Canterbury and York, 5 Mar. 1686.

slavery'.[132] It has been claimed that the presence of the refugees contributed to the unanimity with which James was expelled in 1688.[133] The Huguenots' distrust of James was so strong that they kept alive anti-Stuart sentiment. John Deffray, who became ordained as an Anglican clergyman and served at New Romney from 1690 to 1738, told Archbishop Wake in 1716:

I was one of those French refugees who in 1685 escaped from the Great Tribulation and found a most kind refuge and adoption . . . and since that time have shared in all the troubles and deliverances of this nation . . . and promoted its true interest . . . I have in these parts opposed that Popish interest, which a rebellious faction is now by perjuries, infidelities, atheism and immorality, to force upon us.[134]

Treatment of the Huguenots shows how far the spirit of the Restoration Church differed from Laudian policy; it was here more akin to that of the Elizabethan and Jacobean Church.

THE CHURCH AND CATHOLICS, 1660–1688

Attitudes towards Catholics in the diocese provide a counterpoint to the problem of Protestant nonconformity.[135] Concentration on one group or the other as being the greater enemy to Anglican hegemony depended on time and circumstance. In the period immediately following the Restoration, Catholics were not seen as much of a menace in the diocese. Although members of the dean and chapter and some of the parish clergy published against the Catholic threat, the Church authorities appear to have been far more preoccupied with gathering information about Protestant dissenters. This was probably because the number of Catholics in the diocese was extremely small. Even when the diocesan mechanisms for detection came across Catholics the authorities do not seem to have been too perturbed. The Sheldon Catalogue of 1663 reported a M. Poulage, 'a popish recusant parson' at Rodmersham, but he was described as being 'a gentleman of fair carriage'.[136] Although the popular imagination was fired by anti-

[132] Quoted in B. Sharp, 'Popular Political Opinion in England, 1660–1685', *History of European Ideas*, 10 (1989), 22.
[133] R. D. Gwyn, 'James II in the Light of his Treatment of Huguenot Refugees in England, 1685–1688', *EHR*, 92 (1977), 833.
[134] Ch. Ch. MS Wake 7, fo. 100, Deffray to Wake, 29 Jan. 1716.
[135] J. Bossy, *The English Catholic Community, 1570–1850* (1975).
[136] LPL MS 1126, fo. 48.

Catholicism, there was little in the Canterbury diocese to be afraid of. In the sixteenth century Kent had been in the vanguard of the Reformation, and the few remaining pockets of Catholics in the diocese conformed to John Bossy's model of seigneurial leadership.[137] The presence of individual gentry families such as the Hales and Teynhams was crucial in maintaining the Catholic cause in the diocese, and so the distribution of Catholics in the post-Restoration period was far less diffuse than that of Protestant dissent. Whilst Protestant nonconformity, or at least its organization, was increasingly urbanized, Catholics remained rooted in the rural parishes. The Compton Census noted that there were about 111 Catholics in the diocese in 1676,[138] and a Catholic source for 1678 revealed that there were 148 Catholics in the whole of Kent, the main centres of Catholic practice being Boughton Blean, Benenden, Hackington, and Dover. Thirty-one per cent of these were styled 'gentry', showing that Catholicism was socially more top-heavy and more reliant on gentry support in Kent than in Lancashire where there were a number of large independent plebeian Catholic communities.[139] But despite the low numbers, the fears of Catholicism were resurrected during the Popish plot, in part, perhaps, since Titus Oates had been the incumbent of Bobbing in the 1670s. Anxiety escalated during James' reign. The elevation of Sir Edward Hales to the bench was seen as part of the king's romanizing policy. George Thorp complained to Sancroft in 1687 that Boughton Blean, where Hales lived, was 'the chief nest of Romanists' in the diocese, the chapel there being the 'centre for proselytites'.[140] To make matters worse for the Church in Canterbury, Archdeacon Parker himself was suspected of being a crypto-papist.[141] Certainly, he objected to Sancroft's anti-Catholic stance, and he was friendly with Lord Strangford's family.[142] During James' abortive first flight from England, he was arrested disguised as a cleric when he arrived at Neat Court in the Isle of Sheppey. He was apprehended by some fishermen and brought to Faversham. On his second escape, Hales and other Catholics in the area provided help.[143]

[137] Bossy, *Catholic Community*, 149–81.   [138] LPL MS 639, fo. 166.

[139] B. G. Blackwood, 'Plebeian Catholics in Later Stuart Lancashire', *Northern History*, 25 (1991), 160–73.

[140] Bodl. MS Tanner 30, fo. 230, Thorp to Sancroft, 5 July 1687. For this reason it was recognized that a well-qualified candidate needed to be the incumbent there: MS Tanner 124, fo. 236, Gamlyn to Needham, 4 July 1687.

[141] Bodl. MS Tanner 31, fo. 113, Parker to Maurice, 2 June 1685.

[142] Ibid., fo. 166: complaint of Parker against Sancroft.

[143] A. A. Daley, *History of the Isle of Sheppey* (1904), 137.

ANGLICANS AND DISSENTERS, 1689–1828

In legal terms the Toleration Act of 1689 marked a definite break in the relationship between Anglican clergy and nonconformity, but at the parish level the distinctions between Anglicans and dissenters remained blurred. The ideal of a national Church continued in the minds of many parish clergy throughout the eighteenth century, ensuring that they never gave up their claim that they were responsible for the pastoral care of the whole parish. What worried some clergy, however, was the schismatic nature of dissent. John Spurr has recently argued that comprehension was abandoned in 1689 largely because of a deep-seated Anglican fear of schism within the Church.[144] Like many Churchmen, John Bowtell, the vicar of Patrixbourne, remained convinced that despite the Toleration Act, the practice of schism, so firmly condemned by the Fathers, still remained a heinous sin.[145] In this context, where persecution had failed, dissent might be won over through the exertions of individual clergy, or through the subtle social pressures given by gentry and leading members of the parish. In one way the more repressive policies of the Restoration period had been successful: the gradual waning of support for dissent amongst the gentry classes meant that its overt political threat had lessened. John Johnson, for one, gave help to a dissenting gentlewoman in 1720 who had conformed to the Church.[146] Of course, this transfer of allegiance was never complete. For most of the eighteenth century the area around Cranbrook was dominated by the Tempests, a leading gentry family who remained nonconformists. One incumbent claimed that 'Mr Tempest is set against the whole body of the clergy, against the episcopal worship, and by consequences of the most renowned Church of England'.[147] Anglican clergy perceived that such support for nonconformity greatly impeded their work. After John Johnson's death, John Cook told Wake that the presence of the Tempest family in the area meant that the new vicar of Cranbrook needed to be strong enough to withstand them.[148]

Nonconformist records show how far they themselves continued to value gentry backing. The Evans list (1715) recorded the number of

---

[144] J. Spurr, 'The Church of England, Comprehension and the Toleration Act of 1689', *EHR*, 104 (1989), 927–46.

[145] J. Bowtell, *A Sermon Preach'd at Patrixbourne . . . to prove the dissenters are impos'd upon by their Teachers and Ought to Conform to the Church of England, as by Law established* (1711), 15.

[146] Ch. Ch. MS Wake 7, fo. 311, 24 Nov. 1720.

[147] CCAL, Christ Church Letters, no. 205, Tilden to Ayerst, 29 June 1737.

[148] Ch. Ch. MS Wake 10, fo. 240, John Cooke to Wake, 10 Dec. 1725.

'gentlemen hearers' in their congregations. There were 11 gentlemen and 23 tradesmen 'hearers' at Cranbrook; Staplehurst had 10 gentlemen; Tenterden had 20.[149] The term 'hearers' was rather vague; it did not mean that they were committed dissenters, for they may well have attended both the meeting house and the parish church. John Johnson suggested that the number of dedicated dissenters was rather less than the Evans list implied. He reckoned that there was only one gentleman and the wife of a JP amongst the dissenters in his parish of Cranbrook.[150] The gradual decline of upper-class interest in nonconformity presents a contrast to the fate of Catholicism where gentry support was vital for its survival.[151]

The divisions that developed between High and Low clergy in the years immediately after 1689 hinged on the issue of dissent. How one viewed dissent largely determined one's Churchmanship. What was at stake was the whole vision of society; the position of the Church within that society; and the relationship between the Church and nonconformists.[152] Differing attitudes towards dissent inflamed party strife within the diocese. High Churchmen pointed to the errors of schism, while Low Churchmen argued that such a rigoristic view of religious variation was an innovation. John Lewis attacked Thomas Brett's contribution to the Lay-Baptism controversy, arguing that if Brett's denunciation of this practice was taken to its logical conclusion it 'must very near affect multitudes of people in our kingdom'.[153] In 1712 Arthur Ashley Sykes, the vicar of Godmersham, and a vigorous Low-Church publicist, remarked that

I little imagined that our pulpits would sound with such doctrines as would confound our own auditors and expose ourselves . . . to the contempt of all the judicious persons of the Reform'd world. We have hitherto believed the differences between us and the dissenters to have been about ceremonies and not about the first principles of Christianity. But now those men who have justly deserved the commendations they have received from all the Divines of our Church, are prov'd by our discoveries, not to have so much as understood the great and substantial difference between us. For no one can believe, that they would have insisted on the comparatively trifling circumstances, the kneeling at the communion, the wearing a surplice, the cross in Baptism . . . and have omitted the more material question, whether they were Christians or not.[154]

[149] Dr Williams's Library, MS 34/4, fo. 53.
[150] Ch. Ch. MS Wake Visitation Returns A, fo. 103.
[151] Bossy, *Catholic Community*.   [152] Bennett, *Crisis*, 20–2.
[153] Bodl. MS Eng. Th. e. 30, fo. 73, Lewis to Brett, 23 Oct. 1713.
[154] Arthur Ashley Sykes, *An Answer to that part of Dr Brett's Sermon which relates to the Incapacity of persons not episcopally ordained to administer Christian Baptism* (1712), 1. See also Bennett, *Crisis*, 151–4.

Hostility was shown by some of the High-Church clergy towards Archbishop Tenison because he had supposedly discouraged 'a lecture intended
by ten or a dozen clergymen to be set up at Maidstone in opposition to the
dissenters.'[155] One of the most prolific writers against the dissenting position was Theophilus Dorrington, himself a former dissenter, and now rector of Wittersham (1699–1715).[156] Wittersham was in the Weald, 'in the
midst of Dissenters', and Dorrington urged his neighbouring clergy to join
him in writing against nonconformity. He criticized the dissenters for the
invalidity of their orders, their doctrinal inconsistency, and their volatility;
in his view they were 'giddy, various and inconsistent in their opinions,
often changing them from bad to worse'.[157] Living in an area where many
of the nonconformists were Anabaptists, he was particularly anxious to win
over the more moderate dissenters, especially the Presbyterians, to Anglican worship. 'It must grieve us,' he wrote, 'to see those who are most cap-
able to be members of the Church of England to lose ground to those who
are less so'.[158] He also feared that nonconformists were vulnerable to
seduction by papists:

I have set myself as bound to cure the dissension, if I can, by justifying our baptising of infants in my morning sermons and in private conferences. I have also
endeavoured to bring my parish in the management of their affairs to the order
established by law, that I might relieve the small ones from being influenced by the
favour or displeasure of the greatest who are dissenters. I have set myself by order of
the justices of our division, to enquire into the licences of the many teachers that
hold meetings in my parish which is haunted . . . by a great number of them, and
they have three or four several meetings in a day. This is thought requisite to secure
if possible the wretched people in this obscure corner of the world from being
seduced altogether from the Protestant religion . . . And it must be observed that
this is a corner which by its nearness to Romney Marsh, and by virtue of the acces-
sibleness of our coast lies but too conveniently to hold a correspondence with
France, which also they have been accused of.[159]

If conflicting attitudes towards nonconformity could produce tensions between clergy, it could also form part of the reason for differences between
clergy and their parishioners. Complaints were made against Charles Bean

[155] Bodl. MS Ballard 6, fo. 87, Gibson to Charlett, 4 Dec. 1703.
[156] Theophilus Dorrington, rector of Wittersham, 1699–1715. As an erstwhile dissenter,
he made extra efforts to demonstrate his loyalty. See his *The True Foundation of Obedience and
Submission to His Majesty King George* (1714).
[157] Id., *The Dissenting Ministry in Religion, Censur'd and Condemn'd from the Holy Scriptures*
(1703), 3.
[158] Id., *A Vindication of the Christian Church in the Baptizing of Infants* (1701), preface.
[159] LPL MS 942, fo. 163, Dorrington to Dr Hody, 14 Sept. 1700.

for his Low-Church attitude, and Astley Cressner, the incumbent of Eastry, had the windows of his house smashed in because it was 'hereditary in a certain family to . . . beat their minister when he did not happen to be of their own stamp'.[160]

In dealing with nonconformists, weight was placed on pastoral efforts. Much of the force behind the increased pastoral emphasis after 1689 was the belief that this was the way to win over dissenters. A campaign of this sort could appeal to different styles of Churchmanship. After the failure of the persecutions of the previous years, even High Churchmen could support it as a way of persuading dissenters back into the Church. In 1716 Charles Bean informed the clergy of the diocese that the role of the clergy in the new regime was to heal wider social and political divisions, and in this task winning over dissenters would be paramount. But, he warned, 'loading them with opprobious characters, and contumelious language will not one whit incline them either to us or our disciples'. The best method was for the clergy to prove themselves more devout and better qualified than the nonconformist leaders.[161] After the Toleration Act rivalry replaced persecution. William Birch, a dissenting minister, came before the archdeacon's court in 1698 for preaching in Egerton church. He claimed that 'he being a dissenting minister was desired to preach at the funeral of a young man who died at Faversham . . . he was going to do it in the meeting house, but the company being great and many more expected, he did it in the church, very unwillingly'.[162] Such battles over space were part of a wider competition between the Church and its opponents which resulted in an attempt to strengthen the Anglican commitment of parishioners through education and catechism. For, as Dorrington explained, clergy must enable their parishioners to confound nonconformists in argument. 'By virtue of trade and business in the world [they] do often meet these people while they shun us, and can make them hear what is necessary to rectify and inform them when we cannot'.[163]

Overt High-Church antagonism to dissent had declined by the 1730s, partly as a result of the change in the political affiliation of the diocesan clergy as shown in Chapter 2. By now archbishops were able to persuade the majority of the clergy in their diocese that the Church had little to fear from dissent. In large measure the more relaxed attitude to nonconformity was

[160] Ch. Ch., MS Wake 9, fo. 184, 14 Apr. 1722.

[161] Charles Bean, *The Obligations of the Clergy to Promote a Legal Subjection to His Majesty, and Mutual Charity among their Fellow Subjects. Considered in a Sermon Preach'd at Ashford in Kent on June 22, 1716* (1716), 24.

[162] CCAL, X.7.9, fo. 35.   [163] Dorrington, *Dissenting Ministry*, 135.

encouraged by the belief that Old Dissent was static and provided little challenge to the Anglican hegemony. A distinctive characteristic of several eighteenth-century archbishops was their ability to be good Churchmen yet remain on friendly terms with the dissenters. It is this fusion of attitudes that was the main defining feature of 'latitudinarian Churchmanship', a term which had little doctrinal significance, but rather suggested the willingness of the clergy to get on with dissenters.[164] Tillotson had asserted firmly that,

I am still of the old opinion, that moderation is a virtue and one of the peculiar ornaments and advantages of the excellent institution of our Church, and must at last be the temper of her members, especially the clergy, if ever we seriously intend the firm establishment of the Church, and do not . . . design creating heats and divisions . . .[165]

Succeeding archbishops followed this premiss, and exhorted their clergy to do the same.

In this context, clergy wrote to the archbishops asking their advice on how to deal with dissenters in their parishes. Their problems were wide-ranging: how should dissenters be received back into the Church; how should they be treated socially; could the clergy give them rites of a church burial? John Clough, the vicar of Ashford, informed Wake in 1722,

My predecessor, Mr Warren, I find, made no scruple to bury ym, not even in the church when desired. But how to reconcile that practice with some of doctrines and canons of our Church, particularly ye 9th canon, which declares ym excommunicate, or with ye rubric before ye burial office; it is a difficulty . . . the business of episcopal ordination seems to be given up if we allow their burial . . .[166]

George Shocklidge developed the problem,

whether or not I am to consider Anabaptists, who have received baptism in their own way, as unbaptized persons and to be excluded from the office of burial. If so, why? Not, I suppose because it has been admitted to adults and by total immersion, our Church does not condemn this. If because of want of episcopal ordination, am I to deny equally the office of burial to all, who have received baptism among Presbyterians and Independents.

He called the matter a 'perplexed dilemma'.[167]

[164] See above, pp. 97–99. For problems of definition see J. Spurr, '"Latitudinarianism" and the Restoration Church', *HJ*, 31 (1988), 61–82.

[165] Quoted in Birch, *Tillotson*, 103.

[166] Ch. Ch. MS Wake 22, fo. 191, John Clough to Wake, 19 Feb. 1722.

[167] Ch. Ch. MS Wake 9, fo. 3, George Shocklidge to Wake, 30 Apr. 1721. The issue caused some controversy in the diocese as a result of Thomas Brett's sermon *The Extent of Christ's Commission to Baptise* (1712).

Archbishops gave their clergy permission to baptize dissenting adults into the Church and visitation returns list those adults recently baptized. In 1728 the vicar of Tenterden noted with some pride that he had baptized twelve adults since 1724.[168] Some clergy pointed to difficulties in carrying out these baptisms in church. The vicar of St Peter's, Sandwich reported that he had privately baptized a twenty-seven-year-old man, 'which was done before selected witnesses, because the public performance might prove prejudicial to him; his relations being Anabaptists and enemies to our Church'.[169] Even the High Churchman John Johnson could go some way to meet the sensitivities of nonconformists who wished to conform. In 1716 he informed Wake that the main obstacle to receiving some erstwhile dissenters into the Church was their embarrassment at having to be baptized at the font in front of the congregation. In 1725 he had a baptistry built in Cranbrook church so that Anabaptists desiring to become Anglicans could be fully dipped. Johnson's detailed reports to Wake concerning the range of dissenting beliefs in his parish suggest that he knew the nonconformists in his parish and discussed their beliefs with them.[170]

In part, the increasingly tolerant attitude can be explained by changes within dissent itself. Its loss of gentry support made it seem less of a threat. In rural parishes, at least, clergy reported that the majority of dissenters were 'poor and mean' and thus found it difficult to influence others. It is clear that the thesis that eighteenth-century dissent was becoming increasingly wealthy and respectable can be overstated. The clergy's attitudes to dissenting ministers also altered during the eighteenth century. They were no longer seen as the 'seditious' and 'factious' leaders of the Restoration period, but as 'sober' men. In large measure this perception was a consequence of the changed face of some dissenting groups who had disavowed any revolutionary intentions. In 1741 Benjamin Wills, the dissenting leader at Maidstone, stressed the 'charitable' and 'sober spirit' of Kentish nonconformity, distancing them from the dissenters of the seventeenth century: 'As for the first nonconformists or Puritans . . . [they are] no rule to us'.[171] In some cases the decline in the dissenting threat made it possible for Anglican clergy to hold a juster appreciation of nonconformist piety. The rapprochement between dissent and Anglican clergy owed something

---

[168] Ch. Ch. MS Wake Visitation Returns D, fo. 135.

[169] Ch. Ch. MS Wake Visitation Returns A, fo. 309.

[170] Hasted noted, however, that it had only been used twice 'in seventy years': *History of Kent*, v. 100; Ch. Ch. MS Wake Visitation Returns A, fos. 103–4.

[171] Benjamin Mills, *An Examination of the Remarks made by a Curate of the Diocese of Canterbury. On the Account of A Controversy between the author of The Trial of Mr Whitefield's Spirit, and Benjamin Mills* (1741), 19.

to the recognition that many of the dissenting congregations were at least orthodox in their belief. Nathaniel Lardner, the well known literary defender of Revelation against the Deists, spent the last years of his life at Hawkhurst, and, as a conservative in theology, helped to allay fears about the radicalism of nonconformity.[172]

In 1758 the rector of Wittersham acknowledged that although some families in his parish were

> partly members of the Church of England, and partly Anabaptists; the rest of the dissenters here, I believe to be the serious professors of Christ's religion in their own way, and [he hoped], as we live together in a peaceable and friendly manner, I don't despair, through the blessings of God, of being successful in my application to them.[173]

However, as dissent became less of a dynamic movement and more of a dynastic tradition, it became harder for Anglican clergy to win nonconformists over. In some parishes, at least, though a tolerant modus vivendi developed between Anglicans and dissenters, the clergy found the dissenters religiously immune to their teachings. In 1716 the rector of Frittenden admitted that he knew little about the nonconformists in his parish, and, moreover, that he did not know of any way to find out about them.[174] The emergence of nonconformity as a distinctive cultural tradition ensured that a new and different pattern of religious life was emerging within the parishes of rural England. The incumbent of Sellinge recognized that 'since I have been the vicar of the place, I have received three of the same sect into the Church, and have done my utmost endeavour to prevail upon the rest, but find the prejudice of education too strong for argument'.[175]

In their visitation replies, eighteenth-century incumbents measured dissent in terms of families, an index of familial religious solidarity. This is a marked development from the situation in the decades immediately following the Restoration where clergy were more concerned to pinpoint individuals who were considered dangerous to the regime. An inward-looking dissent had evolved its own distinctive familial culture in which endogamy was common and children were reared within their own communities. As a result, however, it had lost its ability to recruit new members. Richard Vann has noted that 'by the end of the first century of Quakerism, 90% of Quakers were the children of Quakers'.[176] The vicar of Folkestone thought that Quakers were less prone to expansion than other dissenters; 'so far as I

---

[172] For Lardner see *DNB* (He is buried in Hawkhurst Church).
[173] LPL MS 1134/4, fo. 232.
[174] Ch. Ch. MS Wake Visitation Returns A, fo. 109.   [175] Ibid., fo. 33.
[176] Vann, *English Quakerism*, 167.

have observed (and I have had manifold experience among Baptists and others) the Quakers are not so industrious to make proselytes as others are'.[177] It seems to have been easier to inculcate the rigours of Quaker discipline in the family than to spread it to outsiders. One result of this, as an incumbent in the diocese observed, was that the Quakers 'seem extremely bigotted in their opinions and hold their neighbours in great contempt, as if for want of their light everybody else was in the dark'.[178] Visitation returns show that there was not so much a decline in dissenting congregations as a growth of stability; familial solidarity seems now to have become crucial in maintaining these communities.[179]

The years after the Toleration Act saw many meeting houses established in the diocese; by 1715 53 meeting houses were registered, the great majority being in the towns, an indication of the way in which rural nonconformist centres were losing out to urban centres [Map 3]. In 1720 it was noted that at West Langdon there was no meeting house, nonconformists instead going to Deal or Dover for public worship.[180] The Thompson Census of 1773 shows that there was no decline in the number of licensed houses, although there may have been a reduction in the numbers attending.[181] Dissenting fortunes could fluctuate, depending often on the relationship between the congregations and the dissenting minister. A new meeting house was erected in St Alphege's, Canterbury in 1724, but the congregation disappeared for want of a minister.[182] In 1758 it was reported that at St Clement's, Sandwich 'the meeting house is lately sold to one of our brewers and converted to a beer cellar'.[183]

Dissenting congregations suffered if their ministers took orders within the Church. Anglican clergy encouraged this since it might be a way of bringing other members of the congregation over to the Church. In 1725 Samuel Weller, the curate of Maidstone, informed Wake that William Jacomb, the Presbyterian minister in the town, sought Anglican orders, and hoped that other leading members of the dissenting community would follow his example.[184] Since dissent was now seen in terms of families, incumbents explained that decline in numbers of dissenters in some parishes was 'owing in part to women marrying Churchmen, who generally attend

---

[177] LPL MS 1134/2, f. 100.

[178] Ch. Ch., MS Wake 22, fo. 254, John Lewis to Wake, 4 Mar. 1725.

[179] Obelkevich, *Religion and Rural Society*, 313.

[180] Dr Williams's Library MS 34/4, fos. 53–4; Ch. Ch. MS Wake Visitation Returns B, fo. 684.

[181] Dr Williams's Library MS 38/6 (Thompson MS), fo. 18[R–V].

[182] Ch. Ch. MS Wake Visitation Returns C, fo. 55.					[183] LPL MS 1134/4, fo. 13.

[184] Ch. Ch. MS Wake 10, fo. 250, Samuel Weller to Wake, 18 Jan. 1726.

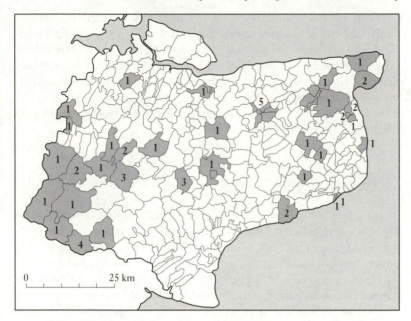

MAP 3. The Distribution of Nonconformist Meeting Houses in 1715

their husbands to the Established Church'.[185] Clergy also liked to believe
that their own tactics and piety contributed to the decline. The rector of
St Andrew's, Canterbury boasted in 1758 that the number of 'sectaries has
much lessened, chiefly, I believe, owing to the moderation with which they
are treated'.[186]

Dissent could, of course, still be divisive. This was especially true in the
towns. In 1778 Hasted observed that in Maidstone 'dissension in matters of
religion unhappily destroys much of that social intercourse and harmony
which would otherwise unite the inhabitants of this flourishing town'.[187]
At election times urban politics in Maidstone were exacerbated by religious
divisions between the Tory mayor and corporation and the large numbers
of dissenters and Whig supporters.[188] But this is an example not of clerical
but of lay hostility towards dissent. It is no longer possible to accept the
view that religious issues disappeared during eighteenth-century political

[185] LPL MS 1134/3, fo. 9.   [186] LPL MS 1134/1, fo. 175.
[187] Hasted, *History of Kent*, iv. 263.
[188] J. A. Phillips, *Electoral Behaviour in Unreformed England: Plumpers, Splitters and
Straights* (Princeton, NJ, 1982), 159.

elections, but the clerical role in leading antagonism towards dissent certainly lessened. It has been shown that in Kent after 1715 election propaganda did not stress the political part played by the clergy; there is little evidence of clergy heading riots against dissenters.[189] Colley maintains that the 'Tory party would have found it difficult to moderate its attitude towards dissent: assertive Anglicanism was too crucial to its ideology'.[190] This may have been true of lay society, but it was not true of the clergy in the diocese of Canterbury.

ANGLICANS AND CATHOLICS, 1689–1829

Anti-Catholic sentiment was still fervent after the Revolution of 1688; Catholics were associated with Jacobitism and were thus seen as threats to the new regime. That High Churchman John Johnson, often suspected of popery himself, was concerned that the leading families in Boughton Blean who were papists might influence his own parishioners at Cranbrook. Thus, in the years immediately after the Glorious Revolution he was 'very zealous' for William and Mary, 'in so much that he afterwards blamed himself for being too much a Williamite'.[191] Vigilance was shown in the detection of 'popish emissaries'. In 1689 one Vincent Taffe, an Irishman, was arrested for having administered mass in a private house in Dover,[192] and the Privy Council received a report of a 'considerable quantity of arms hidden in the house of Sir Robert Guildford at Biddenden or in the ponds thereabouts'.[193] Non-jurors and some of their High-Church allies were also treated with suspicion. The draft of an address by Tenison to the diocesan clergy stressed the need for vigilance against popery, pointing out the ways in which popish tenets were creeping into the Church—a process which in his opinion Archbishop Laud had inaugurated.[194] John Lewis accused Thomas Brett and the High Churchmen in the diocese of trying to impose Catholicism on the nation. He criticized them for using 'Catholic' terminology such as 'extreme unction', for although they claimed not to interpret them in a Roman sense, he feared that the only reason for their use was

to pave the way to a political design. The common people are often governed by sounds. And so it was thought expedient to make these terms useful and familiar to

[189] Newman, 'Elections in Kent', 36.   [190] Colley, *Defiance of Oligarchy*, 172.
[191] BL Add. MS 28651, fo. 9.   [192] LPL MS 1029, fo. 4, 24 Apr. 1689.
[193] *CSPD*, 1689, 116, 23 Sept. 1689.   [194] LPL MS 1037, fo. 17.

them that they might not be shocked when they heard them used by Popish priests, and might be brought to think Popery not so formidable as is represented.

High Churchmen, he insisted, were trying 'to cool men's zeal for a Protestant succession'.[195]

In fact, non-jurors in the diocese were reluctant to form separate flocks. Only Thomas Brett, who became a non-juror in 1716, established any distinct type of congregation, in Wye, where the patron was the non-juring Earl of Winchilsea, though he was reported also to have some followers at Faversham.[196] He was presented to the Assize court in 1717 for keeping a conventicle, but the case was dropped after the Act of Idemnity, which was passed in that year. In 1719 Archdeacon Green advised Wake that it was better to ignore Brett's ministrations, arguing that if he was prosecuted he 'might gain advantage through pity'.[197] In 1729 John Simpson, the vicar of Norton, was accused of Jacobitism for allowing Brett to preach at the funeral of Mrs Smith, the wife of a non-juring linen-draper at Faversham. Archdeacon Lisle complained that 'as Dr. Brett is a busy man I wish something could be done to restrain his zeal, which may be of mischievous consequences in those parts where he lives'.[198] Nevertheless, the authorities left Brett alone. It was reported in 1758 that there was still a non-juring family at Wye, and as late as 1806 a non-juring family was found at Tenterden.[199]

The fact that few of the Canterbury clergy met Catholics in the course of their careers meant that they were willing to believe in rumours about them. Wake was informed in 1720 by the incumbent of Sittingbourne that a woman who 'seemed very sober and modest' was abducted by a priest

in scarlet wolf clothing ... I am told several coaches full of such poor victims have been through this town ... I think every good man should be assisting in ye identification and punishment of such damning villanies. I am ignorant of ye severity of our laws against such offenders, but have sent for a book treating of them.[200]

This belief was nourished by a long tradition of Protestant pornography which feasted on the sexual nature of Catholicism, and strove to link popery with debauchery. It is worth noting, in contrast, that a number of clergy also possessed Catholic devotional manuals, which, if suitably edited for

---

[195] Bodl. MS Eng. lett. c. 30, fo. 61, Lewis to Brett, 'St. Bartholomew's day', 1715, 14.
[196] Ch. Ch., MS Wake Visitation Returns B, fo. 588.
[197] Ch. Ch. MS Wake 8, fo. 141, Green to Wake, 17 Aug. 1719.
[198] PRO, 1729 SP 36/16, fo. 32, Lisle to Wake, 25 Nov. 1729.
[199] LPL, MS 1134/4, fo. 260; ibid., VG 3/2/d, fo. 92.
[200] Ch. Ch., MS Wake 8, fo. 313, Swann to Wake, 28 Nov. 1720.

Protestant eyes, were regarded as valuable auxiliary aids to Anglican worship.[201]

The incumbents who served in the few parishes in the diocese which
contained Catholic families indicated that they managed to get on fairly
well with them, which supports Colin Haydon's contention that clerical
animosity towards Catholics softened during the century.[202] In 1720 the
vicar of St Cosmus Blean observed that a popish widow, Mrs Curd, was 'not
bigoted, but very civil in her carriage, both to me, who has often used gospel
means to convert her, and to her neighbours'.[203] The Hales family kept a
popish priest at Hackington and the vicar complained that because the
management of the parish almshouse was in the hands of the lord of the
manor it was filled with Catholics, though otherwise 'Sir Edward is very
obliging'.[204] Most Catholics lived in closely grouped parishes, towards the
north-west of the diocese. At Lynsted, where the Teynhams were the chief
Catholic family, the incumbent noted with relief in 1758 that Sir Charles
Mallory resided in the parish for some of the year. 'It is a very happy
circumstance for us that he is a J.P. as upon that account, the papists keep
themselves more within the bounds than I believe they would do otherwise.'[205] Their chapel became the focus for Catholics in the area. In 1765
it was reported that they had forty dependants in the parish.[206] The incumbent of nearby Newnham told Secker in 1758 that, 'I have at different times
given to the children some familiar expositions against popery, being here
near our enemies head-quarters'.[207] At Doddington the Thornycroft
family were deemed by the incumbent to be peaceful, 'but though they have
not perverted one of my flock, that this parish should always be with a
papist, the lord of the manor settled his game-keeper and his wife in it,
which he or his agent had before reduced'.[208] The Darells of Calehill, near
Goudhurst, were recusant from 1694. During the eighteenth century the
numbers attending the chapel in Calehill House were between forty and
fifty.[209]

Yet if there was no overt hostility, suspicion remained. In 1716 Archdeacon Green advised Wake of the need to have a good man at Little Chart

---

[201] Translation of Catholic works included G. Stanhope's edition of *Parsons. His Christian
Directory* (1699); id., *The Christian's Pattern; or a Treatise on the Imitation of Christ* (1696).
[202] C. M. Haydon, *Anti-Catholicism in Eighteenth-Century England. A Political and Social
Study* (Manchester and New York, 1993), 164–203.
[203] Ch. Ch. MS Wake 6, fo. 44, 7 Jan. 1716.   [204] LPL MS 1134/2, fo. 140.
[205] LPL MS 1134/3, fo. 29.   [206] LPL MS Secker 3, fo. 334.
[207] LPL MS 1134/3, fo. 145.   [208] LPL MS 1134/2, fo. 23.
[209] KAO, U 386/F. See A. Williams, 'The Distribution of Catholic Chaplaincies in the
Early Eighteenth Century', *Recusant History*, 12 (1973–4), 16–25.

because of the numbers of Catholics there.[210] The incumbent of one of the Dover parishes in 1749 was wary of John Seaver, a Catholic who was to take oaths to the Church of England:

notwithstanding which I fear he will not prove the sincere person I hoped to find him: he hath appointed Sunday next for his Public renunciation. He is going to Canterbury for a few days and I have wrote to a very discreet and worthy clergy-man there to have an eye on his behaviour. Particularly whether he resorts to St. Stephen's [Hackington] amongst the Papists.

The suspicion was proved correct since Seaver did not make his renunci-ation.[211] In 1774 John Duncombe, preaching at the opening of the new church of St Andrew's, Canterbury, stressed that fact that popery had never been taught there.[212]

In 1758 Archbishop Secker reckoned that there were 160 Catholics in the diocese.[213] In 1780 there were reputedly 198 Catholics in the diocese, 30 of them at Boughton Blean, 24 at Little Chart, and 32 at Lynsted, including Simon Wilmot, a French dancing master and his family at Cranbrook.[214] The French Revolution brought exiled Catholic clergy and aristocracy to England: the Baron de Montesquieu and his family, for example, settled at Patrixbourne.[215] For many such refugees, Kent was the pathway to a new life and they came to Dover, Canterbury, and Lenham. In 1793 Dr Thomas Cooke, from the university of Paris and formerly chaplain to Louis XIV, became chaplain to the Hales family.[216] Some sympathetic members of the dean and chapter showed genuine concern about their fate, and were par-ticularly shocked by the grisly death of the Princess de Lambelle, who had visited the cathedral in the 1780s.[217] Emigré clergy were employed to teach French to the children of the dean and chapter. The emigrés often felt homesick when they saw Canterbury Cathedral. The sight of the cathedral reminded Canon Louet poignantly of his own church, which he had left behind.[218] Some members of the diocesan clergy met emigré priests

[210] Ch. Ch. MS Wake 6, fo. 44, Green to Wake, 7 Jan. 1716.

[211] LPL MS Secker 7, fos. 45 and 47, copy of letter from the incumbent of Dover to Herring, 15 Aug. 1749. Cf. a draft form in Wake's hand for admitting converts from the Church of Rome to the Established Church: LPL CM 19, fo. 19.

[212] J. Duncombe, *A Sermon Preached at the Consecration of St Andrew's Canterbury* (1774), 18.

[213] LPL MS Secker 3, fo. 334.   [214] LPL, VB 1/11, fo. 269; VG 3/1/a, fo. 497.

[215] LPL, VG 3/2/d, fo. 148.

[216] C. Buckingham, 'Some Notes on the Early Catholic Missions in Canterbury', *Kent Recusant History*, 6 (1982), 16–25.

[217] See *Poems of George Monk Berkeley*, p. dxiii.

[218] J. McManners, *French Ecclesiastical Society* (Manchester, 1960), 293.

socially. William Jones revealed that two neighbouring clergy had been to dine—one a papist, adding:

we don't quarrel with Papishes, but I must own, my own opinion of them is not so favourable to them as in times past; because I cannot find that their late troubles have lessened their pride or mended any of their doctrines, so have not answered what I suppose to have been the purpose of Divine Providence towards them.[219]

The number of exiles in Dover was particularly high. In 1793 it was reported that fifty-seven clergy were in Dover and that they ministered to the refugees there.[220] The presence of the military was one of the reasons why the Government, through the Aliens Act, tried to dissuade the French from staying in the town, for the exiles, though royalist, were still seen as a potential threat to the Anglican regime. In 1806 the behaviour of the Catholics suggested that they were now more anxious to make converts. It was noted at St Mary's, Dover that 'we have a popish priest, who goes by the name of Robertson, he is very zealous in endeavouring to make proselytes, but meets with very little success'.[221] Robertson was the alias of the Abbé Fleury who, in 1807, was moved on by the Dover magistrates. In the diocese of Rochester, which lay to the west of the diocese of Canterbury, the visitation articles issued by Bishop Horsley in 1796 enquired nervously about the behaviour of the exiled clergy, 'have you observed they hold much conversation with the common people?'[222] The Catholic Relief Act allowed the building of Catholic chapels, such as the one at Margate in 1802. By 1803 there were 600 Catholics in Kent, increasing to 3,301 by 1824.[223] The rise in numbers made the fear of popery seem more real, as the increased suspicion of Catholics in the early nineteenth century testifies. Indeed, during the early nineteenth century the diocesan clergy were amongst the most vociferous opponents of schemes for Catholic Emancipation.[224] Nevertheless, in the face of a perceived growth of Unitarianism in the period after 1780, a less squeamish attitude towards Catholicism, which was at least orthodox on the issue of Revelation, developed amongst some sections of the diocesan clergy. In 1802 Nehemiah Nisbett wrote against the vogue for applying the epithet 'the man of Sin' to the Church of Rome:

---

[219] Magdalen College, Oxford MS 471, fo. 57, Jones to Mrs Horne, 5 Dec. 1797.
[220] A. Bellenger, 'Seen but not Heard: French Exiled Clergy, 1789-1815', *Kent Recusant History*, 6 (1982), 152.
[221] LPL, VG 3/2/b, fo. 20.
[222] Quoted in Nichols, *Illustrations of Literary History*, vi. 673.
[223] LPL, MS Moore 2, fo. 186, William Chapman to Moore, 7 Nov. 1802; C. Buckingham, *Catholic Dover* (Canterbury, 1968), 32.
[224] See the petitions in the Journal of the House of Lords, IV (1821), 171, 222, 258, 348-9.

the application of St Paul's man of sin to the Church of Rome . . . appears to me to be radically defective, upon this ground, that however corrupt that Church may be supposed to be, she cannot, with any propriety, be said to have apostasized from the Christian faith; for the divine mission of our Lord is as much an article of her creed as it is ours; and the very corruptions of the Church of Rome are supported by an appeal to the authority of Scripture.[225]

The attitude towards Catholics provided a continuing counterpoint to the attitude towards Huguenots. In 1697 Celia Fiennes observed on her tour of Canterbury that

under the Cathedral is a large Church. This is given to the French Protestants in the town for the worshipping of God. It holds a vast number of people . . . it's so well arched, they cannot hear them in the Cathedral when they are singing—at least no ways to disturb them.[226]

Several Huguenots in the Canterbury area took Anglican orders in the eighteenth century as part of the gradual assimilation process whereby the 'strangers' became integrated into English cultural life.[227] John Jortin, for example, the ecclesiastical historian, and the son of a Huguenot exile, was the incumbent of Eastwell from 1737 to 1742. The Dutch and French congregations at Sandwich disappeared during the course of the century, but they maintained their separate identity at Canterbury. In the 1730s the blue-stocking Elizabeth Carter, the daughter of the curate of Deal, was sent to board at the house of Mr Le Sueur, the French minister at Canterbury, in order to learn French.[228] In the 1790s Hasted noted that the Huguenots looked after their own poor, and had their own services in the cathedral undercroft.[229] Rather as English nonconformists in this period attended both parish church and meeting house, so the French community maintained an amphibious relationship with the Church of England. A family of French refugees at Swalecliffe sometimes communicated with the French congregation in Canterbury, and sometimes in the parish church.[230]

Wake's 'fatherly concern' for them was part of his desire to forward ecumenical relations between the Church of England and other religious

---

[225] Nehemiah Nisbett, *An Attempt to Display the Original Evidences of Christianity* (1802), Preface, p. ix.

[226] *The Journeys of Celia Fiennes*, ed. C. Morris (1947), 121–2.

[227] R. D. Gwynn, *Huguenot Heritage: The History and Contribution of the Huguenots in Britain* (1985), 132.

[228] *Memoirs of the Life of Mrs Elizabeth Carter*, ed. M. Pennington (1807), 7.

[229] Hasted, *History of Kent*, xi. 132.

[230] Ch. Ch. MS Wake Visitation Returns B, fo. 964.

groups.[231] Indeed, the awareness that the Church should help support
oppressed Protestant communities throughout Europe indicates that the
Anglican Church could see its role in international terms and was one way
in which the diocesan clergy, and through them their parishioners, participated in events far away from Kent. Archbishop Herring contributed to a
charity which had been established to support Protestants in the Vaudois
who had suffered through renewed militant Catholicism in Germany from
the 1720s. He stressed 'our common Christianity' against Rome, and
prayed for 'the confusion of that bad system of religion, which is not only
the surest corruption of the Gospel, but the greatest disgrace to human
nature'.[232] In 1751 he urged the clergy of the diocese to be assiduous in
collecting money for the work of the Society for the Propagation of the
Gospel: 'it is with real concern, I assure you, that such assistance is now
become absolutely necessary to support and carry on this most charitable,
pious and extensive design, not less affecting the Honour and Property
than the Religion of this Protestant nation'.[233] The charity, to ministers
and schoolmasters in the Vaudois and Piedmont, was maintained throughout the century. Both Herring and Secker contributed to a fund for the relief of Hungarian Protestants.[234]

Clergy in the diocese participated in the long tradition of subscription
for other religious groups in distress. In the 1780s they gave to assist the
harrassed American clergy.[235] During the 1790s the 'charitable' aspect of
the Church was again invoked as clergy established a fund for the relief of
exiled Catholic clergy from France. In 1793 Archbishop Moore exhorted
the clergy of his diocese to 'cause a public collection of charity to be made
for the relief of the French clergy',[236] a fund reminiscent of that established
a century earlier for the relief of the Huguenots. The dean and chapter gave

---

[231] Ch. Ch. MS Wake 7, fo. 160, Thomas Green to Wake, 2 Sept. 1716. This is one of the
central arguments of Sykes' *Wake*. More generally see W. R. Ward, *The Protestant Evangelical
Awakening* (Cambridge, 1992), 51, 311, 343.

[232] Quoted in LPL MS Cornwallis 3, fo. 82, 28 May 1752.

[233] *Archbishop Herring's Letter to the Clergy of his Diocese, 12 February 1751* (1751). This
caused interest in the diocese: see Sayer Rudd, *God's Promise: A Great Incentive to Christian
Liberality. A Sermon Preached at Walmer in Kent, on Sunday, 12 July 1752 on the Occasion of the
General Collection of the Charity made within the Provinces of Canterbury and York by his
Majesty's special appointment in favour of the Incorporated Society for the Propagation of the
Gospel in Foreign Parts* (1752). For an analysis of the views of various archbishops to the
Moravians see C. J. Podmore, 'The Bishops and the Brethren: Anglican Attitudes to the
Moravians in the Mid-Eighteenth Century', *JEH*, 42 (1990), 622–46.

[234] LPL MS Secker 7, fos. 208–40: charities to French Protestants, 1754–67.

[235] CCAL, Chapter Act Book, 1775–1796, fo. 167.

[236] LPL MS Moore 8, fo. 128, 24 Apr. 1793.

£50 and the diocese raised £300.[237] Popular hostility towards Catholicism, however, ensured that the fund did not win the support of the laity; the clergy's generosity to the French emigré priests distanced them from their parishioners.[238]

THE CHURCH AND METHODISM

Attitudes to Methodism in the diocese show how suspicion of the divisive qualities of nonconformity could go hand in hand with sympathy. In some ways the emergence of Methodism highlights in an exaggerated form the problem which the Church had in defining and dealing with Protestant dissent more generally. The Kentish mission had begun as early as 1738 when Wesley, returning from America, landed at Deal and 'at once resumed his work . . . by reading prayers and preaching at the Inn'.[239] In 1740 John Lewis wrote to George Whitefield, assailing him for his youthful presumption and linking him to the famous enthusiast in the time of Richard I, the demagogue William Longbeard, whose behaviour had led to social disorder.[240] An effective summary of the main concerns about the early Methodists can be found in John Kirkby's *The Impostor Detected: or the Counterfeit Saint turn'd inside out* (1750), written 'for the use of the city of Canterbury where that mystery of iniquity has lately begun to work', after Wesley himself had preached in the Butter Market. Kirkby accused the Methodists of 'pretended light', and argued that Methodists were united with Deists in making Christianity look contemptible.[241]

The visitation returns of 1758 show that the development of Methodism in the diocese was slow (Map 4). Wesley had visited Canterbury in 1750, 1756, and 1758 when he preached to soldiers.[242] Nevertheless, the southeast of England was not a centre for evangelical opinions generally; the only two Evangelical Anglican clergy in the diocese were James Andrews and Henry Piers. Andrews had been educated at Exeter College, Oxford where he had met with evangelical views. He had been presented to a living in the Gloucester diocese and Bishop Warburton had made him promise that

---

[237] PRO, T 98/8, fo. 53; ibid., T 93/24: quoted in Bellenger, 'Seen But Not Heard', 153.
[238] A. Bellenger, 'The Emigré Clergy and the English Church, 1789–1815', *JEH*, 34 (1983), 399.
[239] L. Tyerman, *The Life and Times of the Rev. John Wesley, M.A., Founder of the Methodists*, 3 vols. (1890), i. 173.
[240] Bodl. MS Rawl. c. 412, fo. 318: 'A Letter to Mr Whitefield', 18 Feb. 1740.
[241] John Kirkby, *The Impostor Detected: or the Counterfeit Saint turn'd inside out* (1750).
[242] Tyerman, *Wesley*, ii. 69, 230, 309.

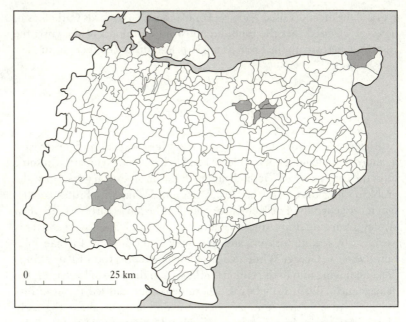

MAP 4. The Distribution of Methodist Meeting Houses in 1758

he would never again preach outside his parish. In 1765 Andrews was presented to Marden, in the Canterbury diocese. Warburton wrote to Archbishop Secker complaining of his behaviour at Stinchcombe, where, 'amongst his other freaks . . . it was his wont to have, on a Sunday, a female catechist, who when she had performed her part to the assembly, gave place to Mr. Andrews, who very orthodoxly dismissed all with his blessing'.[243] Andrews was in contact with Wesley and encouraged him during his visits to Kent. Yet it is also clear that Andrews was on friendly terms with High Churchmen in the diocese, such as George Berkeley, an indication of the links between Evangelicalism and High-Churchmanship.[244] Henry Piers, who had been converted by Charles Wesley in 1738, was collated to Upchurch in 1742 by Archbishop Potter and in to Bexley, in the peculiar deanery of Shoreham. Potter, High Churchman though he was, seems to have given support to several Evangelicals, as did other archbishops.

The Methodists found initial difficulties in the Weald, precisely the stronghold of Old Dissent. The distribution of Old Dissent and Methodism

[243] LPL MS Secker 3, fo. 232, Warburton to Secker, 5 Mar. 1767.
[244] BL Add. MS 39311, fo. 181, Andrews to Berkeley, 28 July 1766.

in the diocese modifies Currie's thesis that the former was strong where the Church of England was strong, and the latter was strong where the Church was weak.[245] It has been suggested that Methodism fared well among the lower orders since its Arminianism was more attractive than the arid Calvinism of the older sects.[246] This might explain its slow start in the Weald, for the most predominant form of dissent there was that of the General Baptists, whose Arminianism may have made the teachings of the Methodists appear redundant. In 1758 it was reported that in Smarden there were 45 Anabaptist families; 29 were 'General Anabaptists', 16 were 'Particular', and although, as the incumbent of Cranbrook noted, 'some itinerant Methodists lately began preaching in neighbouring villages towards the borders of Sussex', he added that 'they meet with little success'.[247] It was observed at Sandhurst that 'a Methodist did preach, or tried to, but met with no encouragement'.[248] In the few parishes in the area that held Methodists, such as Rolvenden, they were reported to be attending the parish church regularly.

Methodists developed a stronger hold in the coastal region to the north of the diocese, and in towns in the east. They made particular headway in Sheerness, appealing to the shipwrights and carpenters who were employed in the dockyard. John Murthwaite, the curate of Minster in Sheppey, suggested that proximity to London was one reason for Methodist success; Whitefield and Jones were able to keep in close contact.[249] He also attempted an analysis of why the Methodists had taken root in his parish:

Of late years they have greatly increased, but seem at present to be at a stand, and that spirit which they pretend to feel in the very act is not so turbulent and restless as formerly, allowing everyone to acquiesce in his own private testimony, tho' it be only in ye effect—a converted heart—a heart inclined by love, or filial fear of offending, to do those things which God commands. By what means it is that they have increased so much of late years I cannot easily account for, but believe it was owing at first to that thirst of novelty or spirit of opposition, which almost generally reigns, but especially in some particular peoples and places, who being banded together and united in interest, proceed afterwards as much from temporal as spiritual views.[250]

---

[245] R. Currie, 'A Micro-Theory of Methodist Growth', *Proceedings of the Wesley Historical Society*, 36 (1967), 65–73.

[246] M. R. Watts, *The Dissenters*, i. *From the Reformation to the French Revolution* (Oxford 1978), 438.

[247] LPL MS 1134/4, fo. 61; MS 1134/1, fo. 274.   [248] LPL MS 1134/4, fo. 9.

[249] LPL MS 1134/3, fo. 97.   [250] Ibid.

The garrison had long been noted as a problem area for the incumbent of the parish and early in the century the government had established a separate chapel for the use of the dockyard employees who were 'like one great family in the service of the government'.[251]

Methodist infiltration in 1758 was also apparent in Canterbury itself. The meeting was led by Edward Perronet, the son of the Evangelical vicar of Shoreham, Vincent Perronet, who had been styled the archbishop of the Methodists. Perronet was a descendant of a Swiss Reformed family which had established itself in Kent during the seventeenth century. Edward Perronet attracted listeners from all over the city and it is a measure of the charity that the Church of England could show to such groups that he leased the house where they met from the archbishop; it was in the Old Palace, next to the cathedral. (He died in 1791, and was buried in the Precincts.)[252]

The attitude of the archbishops towards the growth of Methodism indicates the difficulties in presenting the relationship between the Church and New Dissent as one of unrelieved hostility. Both Potter and Secker, who was bishop of Oxford when Wesley began his ministry in that city, showed little disapproval of the activities of the early Methodist leaders, and, as archbishop, Secker was anxious not to appear critical of their growth in his diocese. In 1761 he cautioned the curate of Minster in Sheppey to 'acknowledge whatever is good in any of the Methodists; acknowledge their intention to be good . . . even when they do wrong; say nothing to the disadvantage of any of them . . . beware of ridiculing any expression of theirs'.[253]

As one reared among the dissenters, Secker realized that the Anglican clergy might learn much from the Methodists.[254] He was aware that Methodism might lead to divisions within the Church but thought that the best way to curb its growth was for clergy to emulate its best features. In his charge of 1762 Secker told the clergy of his diocese that 'a chief reason why we have so little hold on our people is that we do not converse with them'. He pointed out that continental Protestants, Catholics, and 'both the Old Dissenters from our Church and those who are now forming new separations, gain and preserve a surprising influence amongst their followers by personal religious intercourse'.[255] He recognized that there was much

---

[251] Ch. Ch., MS Wake 22, fo. 203, Wren to Wake, 8 Mar. 1720.
[252] LPL MS 1134/1, fo. 191; Tyerman, *Wesley*, ii. 230.
[253] F. Baker, *John Wesley and the Church of England* (1970), 159; LPL MS Secker 3, fo. 247, Secker to Price, 26 May 1761.
[254] Baker, *John Wesley*.   [255] Secker, *Charges*, 285.

truth in the Methodists' criticisms; in his attempts to improve the pastoral performance of his clergy it could be argued that the archbishop had ends in view similar to those of the early Methodist leaders. In a proposed article of 1759 Secker exhorted clergy to preach 'diligently the doctrine of justification by faith in Christ; warning against the abuses of that doctrine and of separating themselves from the Church to follow unauthorized teachers'.[256] Secker was aware of the tendency for rationalistic sermons, yet he wondered whether the Methodists did not exaggerate the wrongs of the Anglican clergy. Mr Carrington, the Methodist preacher at Sheerness, had attacked both the behaviour and the preaching of the local clergy and Secker declared that

He has either heard worse sermons than other persons, or he hath a very bad memory, or he is an unfaithful Reporter, when he speaks as if the Gospel and satisfaction of Christ were scarce ever preached in our Churches, but only a dry morality. With respect to the former, I hope many can contradict him, and as to the latter, he should recollect; that our Saviour preached much of what he calls dry morality, and that the 10 Commandments are the moral law. Insisting on these is a necessary part of the duty of preaching Christ.[257]

To some extent Methodism lacked the political or social stigma of Old Dissent and the popular demonology associated with popery, and Secker realized that one reason why the Methodists did well was because leaders like Wesley could portray it as being a movement within the Church. He understood the aversion of many Methodists to separatism, and told the vicar of St John's, Thanet that if the Methodists in his parish had a place where they met, they ought to be licensed as dissenters, 'yet possibly some of them may be unwilling to call themselves Dissenters, and to be esteemed such by other persons. And in that case, it may be worth while to try what effect the fear of law will have upon them'.[258] He noted that Methodists had been suppressed at Rolvenden by 'Mr Moneypenny enforcing the Conventicle Act against them'. This refers to one of the *causes célèbres* of 1760 which has been seen as a turning point in the history of Methodism, making Wesley realize that he might be forced to secede from the Church. The case reached national attention, being reported in the newspapers, but the verdict was reversed on appeal to the King's Bench.[259]

[256] LPL MS Secker 7, fo. 99ᵛ, Secker to bishops of his province, 1759 (draft).
[257] LPL MS Secker 3, fos. 248–9, Secker to John Price, 28 June 1763. Whitefield had remarked that the inhabitants of Deal had need of his assistance as their minister did not preach to them the doctrine of Christ. Nicholas Carter retaliated in *A Sermon Preached at Deal: before the Mayor and Corporation, August 9th 1752* (1752).
[258] LPL MS Secker 3, fo. 242, Secker to Harrison, 11 Oct. 1765.
[259] Ibid., VG 2/5, s.v. 'Rolvenden'; Langford, *Polite and Commercial People*, 294.

John Walsh has hinted that hatred of Methodists in the parishes sometimes sprang from popular intolerance: it was not the clergy who always
stirred up the mob, but often the mob forced the clergy to declare themselves against the 'intruders'.[260] In 1767, for example, the freelance
preacher Nicholas Manners went to Wingham, where he came across a
Methodist minister. What followed is reminiscent of those acts of ritual
purification by which religious communities safeguarded themselves from
outsiders, so vividly described by Natalie Zemon Davis for the sixteenth
century:

I stood by the side of his house, and very soon about 500 people assembled; and all,
except a very few, seemed willing to hear. But that few interrupted the rest; for they
threw apples, eggs, turnips, etc. and when that did not prevent my preaching they
brought a drum, with which they made so much noise . . . threw dirt and water upon
me, tore my wig off, threw stones at me . . . and chased me out of town.[261]

By the visitation of 1786, incumbents reported that Methodist congregations had grown, but that most of their members still attended the parish
church. At St Alphege's it was noted that 'many . . . go to Cathedral in the
morning, to the Presbyterian meeting in the afternoon, and to the Methodist meeting at night'.[262] Clearly we should be wary of imposing a strict
denominational straitjacket on religious affiliations in this period. In any
case the spread of Methodism need not necessarily be seen as a condemnation of the Church. It has been suggested that the attraction of Methodism in part developed from the pastoral work carried out between 1660 and
1750 which made people more responsive to the revivalist message.[263]

The Methodist congregation at Sheerness had spread to the neighbouring parish of Queenborough.[264] At Birchington, another coastal parish, it
was observed that there were many recent Methodists, who were 'chiefly
women'.[265] But the picture was not one of unrelieved expansion. At Orlestone the Methodists had decreased and the incumbent of St Mary's, Dover
was pleased to note that they had declined, 'for want of fixed teachers'.[266]
Anglican clergy liked to contrast the stability and continuity of their own
ministry with the instability of Methodist leadership with its itinerant
preaching force. Fluctuations in the membership of the Methodist congregations could be affected by the behaviour of the Anglican minister in the

[260] J. D. Walsh, 'Methodism and the Mob in the Eighteenth Century', *SCH*, 8 (1972), 221.
[261] [Nicholas Manners], *Some Particulars of the Life and Experience of Nicholas Manners*
(York, 1785), 37–8. On 'pollution' see N. Z. Davis, 'The Sacred and the Body Social in
Sixteenth Century Lyon', *Past and Present*, 40 (1981), 40–70.
[262] LPL, VG 3/1/a, fo. 241.
[263] G. H. Jenkins, *Literature, Religion and Society in Wales, 1660–1730* (Cardiff, 1978), 309.
[264] LPL, VG 3/1/d, fo. 137.   [265] Ibid., fo. 433.   [266] LPL, VG 3/1/b, fo. 489.

parish, and by parishioners' attitudes towards him. At Eastchurch the curate was John Robertson from 1777 to 1785. In 1786 the vicar observed that a Methodist meeting had sprung up in Robertson's time; 'but it disappeared along with him, and I make no doubt that it was his general bad character which gave them any encouragement to attempt an establishment'.[267] Complaints had reached Archbishop Moore of Robertson's

crimes very unbecoming to the clerical function; many of your parishioners have been estranged from their church, from the persuasion that they could not hear anything good from a man of such bad principles, and those few who shall continue to go there, receive no benefit from his ministrations.

Moore revoked Robertson's licence on grounds of immorality.[268]

Incumbents in the diocese noted that the real growth in the Methodist congregations occurred during the 1790s (Map 5). By then, the Methodists were seen as rivals to the Established Church; it was remarked that they now met in the times of Anglican services, so that it was more difficult for them to attend both church and meeting house, and Wesley himself had come to ordain ministers. In Canterbury in 1806 it was reported that the 'numbers of Methodists had grown in every parish'.[269] The gradual alienation from the ministrations of the Anglican clergy was not, of course, universal. At St James', Dover the rector observed that the Methodists had no meeting house, 'and such of them as belong to Mr. Wesley's Society are not only punctual in their attendance at church, and at the sacrament, but in the course of twenty-three years I have often been called to visit them in sickness'. At St Clement's, Sandwich the Methodists 'come to church and conduct themselves very decently'.[270] This polarization amongst Methodists, between 'Church Methodists' and those who were now establishing themselves more firmly in a separatist posture, was, in part, a product of reaction to the French Revolution. In 1794 Charles Moore, the rector of Boughton Blean, noted a change in the Church's relationship with its rivals in the diocese. Whereas most eighteenth-century dissent had, he claimed, not tried to intrude on the Church, there were now more dangers. He particularly attacked itinerant preachers who 'dwell too much on the dark and gloomy side of things', and delivered a warning against instantaneous conversion, exalting faith above good works, and unsettled preachers.[271] It was easier in

---

[267] LPL, VG 3/1/c, fo. 46.
[268] LPL, VG 1/11, fo. 414: Licence revoked, 22 Dec. 1785.
[269] LPL, VG 3/2/a, fo. 30.   [270] LPL, VG 3/1/b, fo. 81; ibid., VG 3/2/d, fo. 10.
[271] Charles Moore, 'Against Love of Novelty in Religious Matters. Preached in Canterbury Cathedral, 26 May 1794' in his *Sermons*, iii., 340–62; J. Walsh, 'Methodism at the End of the Eighteenth Century', in R. E. Davies and E. G. Rupp (eds.), *A History of the Methodist Church in Great Britain*, 3 vols. (1965), i. 284, 303.

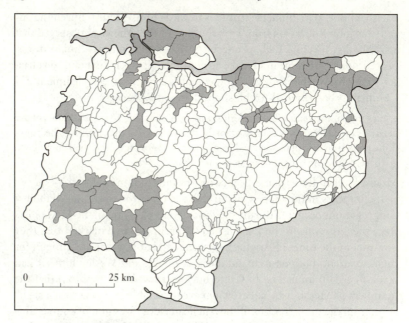

MAP 5. The Distribution of Methodist Meeting Houses in 1806

the 1790s for the authorities to label dissenters of any kind as potential revolutionaries, and this either brought nonconformists back within the Church, or increased their hostility towards the Establishment. At Biddenden, in 1806, the incumbent reported that 'whole families bred up as dissenters, hav[e] lately regularly attended the church'. But in towns such as Maidstone and Tenterden there was a marked growth not only amongst Methodists, but also in the orthodox congregations of Old Dissent.[272] Between 1789 and 1805 eighty-nine applications for new Baptist or Independent meeting houses were made in the diocese.[273] In some cases Methodism drew from dissent. The vicar of St Peter's, Sandwich observed that the Methodists had two meeting houses; one was established in 1794, the other had formerly belonged to the Presbyterians.[274]

The growth of Methodist meeting houses between 1786 and 1806 indicates a different temper in relations between them and the Church. The vicar of Lenham wrote to the archbishop in 1806,

---

[272] LPL, VG 3/2/c, fo. 53.
[273] LPL, VG 3/2/d, fo. 17. For the applications see CCAL, H/A, fos. 1–358.
[274] LPL, VG 3/2/c, fo. 18.

I am of the opinion that most of them would have returned to the bosom of the church, if the meeting house was not built; which attends, as it were, a rallying point for seducers from other churches in the neighbourhood to countervene my parishioners and keep up the seccession . . . If the legislative could be induced to repeal 10 Anne c2 and to confine every dissenting preacher to the chapel for which he is licensed, I am convinced such a regulation would give some little check to the progress of Methodism. Novelty and itinerancy are grand buttresses by which it is supported. These should be taken away, and the shepherds of fanaticism confined to one fold; their flocks would soon be surfeited with the dry husks and wastry garbage with which they are fed and return to that food which is nutritious and imperishable . . . I believe nothing more is required from the candidates for secession, but taking two oaths, subscribing against Popery and paying down a solitary half crown; surely something more should be required of these blue-aproned men before they issue forth to disturb the peace and harmony of parishes, and to disseminate their unrighteousness and disorganising principles in cottages and conventicles.

His suggestions are very similar to those proposed by the clergy of Lincolnshire in 1800 and the regulations in Sidmouth's Bill of 1811, which sought to curb dissenting itinerancy.[275]

Incumbents also complained that Methodism was spread by newcomers to their parishes. A meeting house was recorded at Sittingbourne in 1806, 'to which subscription the man who has lately taken the Rose Inn was a large subscriber'.[276] By this date there were a few congregations which belonged to Lady Huntingdon's connection, and it was reported that Rowland Hill, the friend of Hannah More and a prominent evangelical, had a meeting at Faversham. Amongst the non-Anglican denominations which increased at the end of the eighteenth century were the Jews, who had a synagogue at St Dunstan's, Canterbury, whose congregations, as the clergy noted in 1806, had grown during the war with France.[277] In the towns at least some of the blame for the development and growth of these groups must be placed on the lack of church accommodation. In 1793 Viscount Torrington observed that at Maidstone the parish church was 'low and roomy, but surely not half capacious enough for the Place: so that let the living be ever so valuable, still there is no resceptacle for churchmen; so the religious must fly into other persuasions.'[278]

Developments during the 1790s, particularly the increase in the number and in the organizational structure of meeting houses, hint at a breakdown

[275] *Report from the Clergy of a District in the Diocese of Lincoln* (1800); Clark, *English Society*, 365.
[276] LPL., VG 3/2/d, fo. 41.   [277] Hasted, *History of Kent*, xi. 102.
[278] *The Torrington Diaries*, ed. C. Brun Andrews, 4 Vols. (1934), iv. 153.

in that broad consensus between Anglican clergy and nonconformists which had existed for nearly a century. There were increasing complaints about the potential dangers which the Toleration Act gave to the Church. In 1806 Henry Lord, the rector of Barfreston, moaned of the Baptist congregations in his parish:

> I have been very earnest from a sense of duty in prevailing against their doctrines, and exhorting them to Church communion. The Toleration Act, I humbly conceive, is now too indulgent, because too much abused, and the injury the Church receives is daily but too apparent.[279]

None the less, visitation returns indicate that for much of the eighteenth century clergy in the Canterbury diocese seem generally to have treated dissent with respect. The vicar of St Lawrence, Thanet reported to Archbishop Moore in 1786, with some pride: 'I must do all my parishioners, both the Church of England, and like-wise the Dissenters, the justice to say that they attend the public worship of God on the Lord's day, at the Church and at the meeting house, with great punctuality, regularity and decency.'[280] What was of more concern to clergy was the growing sector of the population who did not attend any form of religious worship. How they attempted to deal with this, and how they tried to strengthen the Anglican presence in the parish, through pastoral care and parochial education, will be the subject of the next chapter.

[279] LPL, VG 3/2/a, fo. 30.   [280] LPL, VG 3/1/d, fo. 465.

6

The Church and the Parish

The previous chapter examined the clergy's attitude towards their rivals of Protestant dissent and Catholicism; this chapter looks at a third area of concern: the pastoral care of the laity. A large part of the case against the Church in the eighteenth century has been based on the alleged pastoral failure of its clergy in comparison to previous Puritan and later Evangelical and Tractarian groups. This adverse judgement has been strongly affected by the sources used by historians to evaluate the clergy's pastoral function, most notably the criterion of the number of services supplied, the evidence of which has suggested that clergy were rather under-deployed.[1] However, closer examination, especially of what might be called their back-up pastoral strategies and initiatives, reveals much in common between the clergy of the Church of England and their rivals.

The pastoral weakness of eighteenth-century clergy has been made much of by social as well as religious historians. E. P. Thompson has observed that 'the "magical" command of the Church and of its rituals over the populace . . . was becoming very weak', and R. W. Malcolmson has remarked that 'few clergymen, it seems, devoted much time to pastoral labours'.[2] Such criticisms raise the difficult problem of how the historian can properly measure the quality of pastoral work or, even more fundamentally, the relationship between the pastoral function of the clergy and the beliefs and behaviour of parishioners. A concentration on some of the more quantifiable aspects of Church life such as church attendance or the provision of services can all too readily lead the historian to be pessimistic. But are such indices reliable representations of faith, spiritual energy, or commitment to the Church as an institution?

Whilst several historians have recognized the pastoral endeavours displayed in the years immediately following the Restoration, it is still commonly supposed that the post-Restoration energy and enthusiasm gave way to complacency and inertia after 1689 or 1714, only to be reasserted during

[1] A. D. Gilbert, *Religion and Society in Industrial England. Church, Chapel and Social Change, 1740–1914* (1976), 27–9.

[2] Thompson, 'Patrician Society, Plebeian Culture', 390 and R. W. Malcolmson, *Life and Labour in England, 1700–1800* (1981), 85.

the Evangelical and Tractarian revivals.[3] This is in some ways a misleading view. The Toleration Act of 1689 made the pastoral responsibilities of the Anglican clergy appear even more central to the well-being of the Established Church, for in the absence of the exclusive support of the State, pastoral pressure was seen as the most effective method of making any headway against the presence of dissenters. As G. V. Bennett has noted, the Toleration Act 'partially disestablished' the Church of England, thereby forcing it to compete with other religious groups for allegiance.[4] Clergy could no longer rely on the combined efforts of the spiritual and secular courts to impose Anglicanism in the parishes, and it was only by the personal efforts of individual clergy, using their powers of persuasion rather than the weapons of legal coercion, that the Church was likely to make any impression against what appeared to be a growing band of people indifferent to the call of religion.[5]

It is time to take the pastoral endeavours of eighteenth-century clergy more seriously. Historians have rediscovered the centrality of the ideological dimension in eighteenth-century politics; they now need to recognize the ideological commitment, the vigour, and the urgency which informed Anglican work in the parishes.[6] We should not underestimate the extent to which clergy saw themselves as continuing, and in some cases fulfilling, the Reformation ideals of spreading Anglicanism and Christianity to the 'dark corners of the land'. Even Kent, supposedly in the forefront of the sixteenth-century Reformation, was still considered a *pays de mission* in the eighteenth century; despite all the efforts of the 'godly pastors' so admired by Patrick Collinson, the south-east of England continued to harbour

---

[3] For the Restoration period see Spurr, *Restoration Church of England*; R. A. Beddard, 'The Restoration Church', in J. R. Jones (ed.), *The Restored Monarchy* (1979), 155–75; D. Spaeth, 'Common Prayer?: Popular Observance of the Anglican Liturgy in Restoration Wiltshire', in S. J. Wright (ed.), *Parish, Church and People: Local Studies in Lay Religion, 1350–1750* (1988), 125–51. For the decline of this endeavour at the end of the seventeenth century see A. Whiteman, 'The Re-establishment of the Church of England, 1660–1663', *TRHS*, 5 (1955), 131. Some insight into the range of pastoral activity in the eighteenth century can be found in W. K. Lowther Clarke, *Eighteenth-Century Piety* (1944), 1–30.

[4] G. V. Bennett, 'Conflict in the Church', in G. Holmes (ed.), *Britain after the Glorious Revolution* (1969), 155–75.

[5] Gilbert Burnet, *A Discourse of the Pastoral Care* (1692), 176–214. This was commissioned by Tillotson: Birch, *Tillotson*, 264–8.

[6] Even Norman Sykes undersold the clergy on this point: *Gibson*, 228 and id., *From Sheldon to Secker*, 192, 223. For the political world see H. T. Dickinson, *Liberty and Property. Political Ideology in Eighteenth Century Britain* (1977); J. Brewer, *Party, Ideology and Popular Politics at the Accession of George III* (Cambridge, 1976); and Colley, *Defiance of Oligarchy*. J. C. D. Clark, *English Society* has taken religious ideology seriously, although he neglects the parochial dimension.

large pockets of religious ignorance.[7] In 1716, for example, Ralph Blomer, a prebendary of Canterbury Cathedral told his fellow clergy that 'we have, in truth (I am sorry to observe it) a sufficient share of this Duty of Preaching Christ to the Gentiles, without looking beyond the Bounds of our own Country. We have among ourselves a certain Leaven of Paganism, that is working upon the very vitals of Christianity'.[8]

EDUCATING THE PARISH

In clerical propaganda, the understanding of the faith demanded of parishioners was a distinctive feature of the Church, supposedly marking it off from the blind superstition of popery and the mindless enthusiasm of nonconformists. Parishioners had to be educated in their religious beliefs if they were to be saved from the seduction of rival creeds. In the mid-eighteenth century Archbishop Secker urged his clergy to remember that Christianity was a religion not 'of the clergy merely, but the common concern of all men'.[9] It was this assumption, so the propaganda ran, which separated the Church of England from the priestly oppression of Roman Catholicism, in which the laity were denied any true understanding of the faith. As John Cooke, a six-preacher of Canterbury Cathedral and the rector of St George's, Canterbury, told the lower house of Convocation in 1704: 'the barbarous policy of the Church of Rome may be discovered: to shut off the Scriptures from the people, to keep them, as if mad and distracted, in darkness, knowing they must necessarily rave against their keepers, the priests, whenever they come into the light.'[10] By contrast, the pastoral enterprise of Anglican clergy involved using a range of educational strategies and devices which, although initiated in earlier periods, were developed and extended during the eighteenth century.

The principal method by which Canterbury clergy tried to establish a simple and rudimentary knowledge of their religion and its obligations was through catechizing. This consisted of a series of questions and answers designed to disseminate basic tenets of the faith, and it had been central to

---

[7] On Kent in the Reformation see the magisterial study by Clark, *English Provincial Society*. Also, Collinson, 'Cranbrook and the Fletchers'.

[8] Ralph Blomer, *A Sermon Preach'd in the Cathedral and Metropolitical Church of Canterbury, at the Inthronement of His Grace, William Lord Archbishop of the Province, On Friday June 15th, 1716* (1716), 10.

[9] Secker, *Charges*, 22.

[10] John Cooke, *Thirty Nine Sermons on Several Occasions*, 2 vols. (1739), ii. 497. C. J. Sommerville, 'The Distinction between Indoctrination and Education in England, 1549–1719', *Journal of the History of Ideas*, 44 (1983), 387–406.

the pastoral endeavours of the Reformation period.[11] Archbishops after 1660 continued to urge their clergy to persist with this practice. Wake, for example, observed in 1724 that 'it is with a very sensible concern that I hear so many complaints of the gross ignorance of the common people in the things of God, and of the too general neglect of catechising, which seems to have been the chief occasion of it'.[12] It has been suggested that eighteenth-century clergy gradually let the habit die out, so that by the end of the period it was dropped altogether.[13] This is clearly not true of the Canterbury diocese, where visitation returns show that in 1716 82 per cent of parishes had catechizing, and in 1806 the majority of parishes catechized the young.[14] In some parishes there was not deterioration but improvement during the century. At High Halden, for instance, the curate reported in 1806 that although catechism used to take place only in Lent, it was now done throughout the summer, 'as Archbishop Secker recommended in his charge'.[15] This mirrors evidence from elsewhere.[16] It is true that, from the end of the seventeenth century, records indicate that most parish clergy in the Canterbury diocese limited catechizing to specific periods in the year, most commonly Lent, but how far this represents a decline from the practice of the early seventeenth century is difficult to judge. Moreover, visitation returns suggest that clergy were willing to catechize, but found only a seasonal response. The incumbent of Upper Hadres informed Wake in 1716 that he catechized 'every Sunday from Easter to Harvest, a season when I find children in the country can most conveniently come to church'.[17]

Both Wake and Secker wrote commentaries on the Catechism which were used by the parish clergy.[18] However, one incumbent told Wake in

---

[11] I. M. Green, '"For Children in Yeeres and Children in Understanding": The Emergence of the English Catechism under Elizabeth and the Early Stuarts', *JEH*, 37 (1986), 397–425. See his *The Christian's ABC. Catechisms and Catechizing in England, c.1530–1740* (Oxford, 1996).

[12] Sykes, *Wake*, i. 182.

[13] Overton and Relton, *English Church from the Accession of George I*, 294.

[14] Ch. Ch. MS Wake Visitation Returns A; LPL, VG 3/2/ a-d.   [15] Ibid., b, fo. 97.

[16] McClatchey, *Oxfordshire Clergy*, 144; Warne, *Church and Society in Eighteenth-Century Devon*, 49.

[17] Ch. Ch. MS Wake Visitation Returns A, fo. 25. Complaints about the neglect of catechizing were a commonplace in the early seventeenth century: Fincham, *Prelate as Pastor*, 257; Davies, *Caroline Captivity*, 137–44. Derek Hirst has shown that the problem was shared by Puritans: 'The Failure of Godly Rule in the English Republic', *Past and Present*, 132 (1991), 33–66.

[18] William Wake, *The Principles of the Christian Religion Explained; in a brief commentary upon the Church-Catechism* (1694); Thomas Secker, *Lectures on the Catechism of the Church of England with a Discourse on Confirmation*, 2 vols. (1769). Secker's *Lectures* had reached 15 editions by 1824, and had spawned various abridged versions: see Robert Lee, *An Analysis of Archbishop Secker's Lectures on the Church Catechism, arranged in a Course of Sermons* (1831).

1728, 'I have tried your Grace's explanation, but few attain to more than the late Dr Isham's Short Exposition', a comment which suggests the existence of a hierarchy of comprehension in the parish, and an awareness of the need to target particular groups. Other expositions used by the Canterbury clergy were those by Bishop Beveridge, Bishop Mann, Bishop Williams, Edward Synge, and Thomas Marshall.[19] In 1717 Daniel Somerscales, the vicar of Doddington, reported that in his parish he started with the Prayer Book catechism, then progressed to Dr Isham's 'and when any of the children can say that by heart he has a Bible and Common Prayer Book given him, and when he can answer all the questions at the end of each section in Bp. Beveridge's exposition 2s is given him'. In 1786 the incumbent of Hernehill gave books to those children who behaved best.[20] This is suggestive of the ways in which clergy might encourage the learning of religious truths. By far the most popular exposition in the diocese was *The Church Catechism Explained, by way of Question and Answer and Confirmed by Scriptural Proofs*, written by John Lewis. It was warmly welcomed by Thomas Bray who had it printed under the auspices of the Society for Propagating Christian Knowledge (SPCK) in 1700. Lewis's catechism was admired not only in the diocese but also throughout the rest of England. By 1714 it had run through seven English editions and by 1820 had reached fifty-eight editions; in 1738 it was the most frequently used catechism in the diocese of Oxford, as it was in Bristol in the 1760s. In 1713 it was translated into Welsh.[21] Lewis compiled it specifically for the poor and uneducated, after reading thirty other expositions, and after consulting neighbouring clergy, an indication of the attempt by some Canterbury clergy to get to grips with the problems of disseminating religious knowledge by pooling their pastoral experience.[22] Lewis pointed out how essential it was that parishioners should understand the tenets of the faith. Repeating the catechism was not an exercise in memory, but of comprehension; 'where the Grounds and Principles of our Holy Religion have never been well laid,

---

[19] Ch. Ch. MS Wake Visitation Returns D, fo. 271. William Beveridge, *The Church Catechism Explained* (1705); Isaac Williams, *A Familiar Exposition of the Church Catechism* (4th edn., 1776); Edward Synge, *An Abstract of the Church Catechism* (1744); Thomas Marshall, *The Catechism set forth in the Book of Common Prayer, briefly explained by Short Notes* (Oxford, 1679).

[20] SPCK, CR/1/7/5109, 16 Jan. 1717; LPL, VG 3/1/c, fo. 89.

[21] *Articles of Enquiry addressed to Clergy of the Diocese of Oxford at the Primary Visitation of Dr Thomas Secker, 1738*, ed. H. A. Lloyd Jukes (Banbury, 1957), 14 n. 5; 'Bishop Secker's Diocese Book' ed. E. Ralph, in P. McGrath (ed.), *A Bristol Miscellany*, Bristol Record Society, 37 (1985), 28–9; Jenkins, *Religion and Society in Wales*, 81.

[22] John Lewis, *The Church Catechism Explained, by way of Question and Answer and Confirmed by Scriptural Proofs* (1700), Preface, iii.

preaching rarely proves effectual; nor can it otherwise be expected, than that our Flocks should be rendered an easy prey to every seducer'.[23] Without such basic intelligence, other parts of the clerical function were redundant:

the preaching of the Sermons without Catechizing is like building without laying the Foundations; without this way of Instruction, the mind is rendered like a Ship without Ballast and can keep no steady course, but rolls and is tossed to and fro with every Wind of Doctrine and is in continual danger of oversetting.[24]

He set out the questions to be answered with texts from Scripture, so that pupils could learn the Bible too.

Like other commentators, Lewis emphasized the duty of parents and masters to send their dependants to be catechized; if they were remiss in fulfilling such duties they would have to answer 'to the great Judge of the Quick and the Dead'.[25] Of course the precise role that the laity were allowed to play in religious life was a matter of controversy throughout the period; the threat of schism and nonconformity ensured that Anglican clergy kept it under strict bounds. Nevertheless, the laity had the obligation to educate their children in basic religious beliefs, and some clergy reported that children were catechized at home. Canon Charles Smyth has termed Evangelicalism as the 'religion of the home', but it is clear that there was nothing original in such an encouragement of family religious life, so long as it remained preparatory and complementary to that supplied by the Church and did not become a substitute for regular attendance at public worship.[26] Indeed, it was warmly encouraged by mainstream Anglican clergy, who took pains to ensure that each family in the parish was supplied with a catechism for family use. At Folkestone in 1716 the incumbent acknowledged that the parish was too large for him to catechize all children, and that he depended on parents teaching children at home.[27] John Johnson, the High-Church vicar of Cranbrook, observed in 1716 that 'many people are . . . exceeding backwards in sending their youth to be catechized, yet I find they commonly teach them catechism in their houses'.[28]

Clergy realized that it was not only children who required instruction in the basic doctrines of the Church. Other groups which had to be targeted were servants and the youth of the parish. In some cases the generality of the parish needed teaching. The incumbent of Throwleigh informed

---

[23] Ibid., p. vii.   [24] Ibid.   [25] Ibid.
[26] C. H. Smyth, *Simeon and Church Order. A Study of the Origins of the Evangelical Revival in Cambridge in the Eighteenth Century* (Cambridge, 1940), 1–43.
[27] Ch. Ch. MS Wake Visitation Returns A, fo. 141.   [28] Ibid., fo. 103.

Secker in 1758 that besides catechizing children on Sunday afternoons he also catechized 'in the form of a sermon to bring people, for they are backward'.[29] Others claimed that they did not need to catechize publicly since, as one incumbent in the diocese explained, 'my constant preaching may be called catechising, for I never meddle with politics, nor controversy'.[30] The vicar of Wingham told Wake in 1716 that 'sometimes for the entertainment of the elder part of the congregation I have read to them Bp. Beveridge's large explication'.[31] George Stanhope produced an edition of Robert Parsons' *Directory*: 'My general intention of reducing the Christian Directory into a narrower compass is that it may be more suitable to the memory and leisure of vulgar readers.' Henry Brailsford, a minor canon at the cathedral, published in 1689 'for the parishioners of St. Mildred's, Canterbury' an abridgement of Bishop Pearson's exposition of the Creed, which consisted largely of a rewriting of his sermons.[32] By such means the parochial clergy attempted to diffuse the great works of Anglican scholarship to their parishioners. How far they succeeded in the accurate representation of complex doctrine is a question not easily answered.

Trends in sermon writing and delivery in the period can be linked to these pastoral problems. The often-noted move in the post-Restoration period to the plain style which came to be the hallmark of eighteenth-century sermons can be explained in part by the perceived need to get the Christian message across in a clear manner. And the constant need to repeat essential religious truths provides a partial explanation of the clerical habit of preaching sermons more than once.[33] The difficulties involved in the dissemination of basic truths led some clergy to appreciate manuals written by those usually seen as Evangelical clergy, and as such sometimes deemed hostile to the Establishment. In the 1760s the High-Church George Berkeley admired Thomas Haweis's sermons and found Henry Venn's *Complete Duty of Man* an 'excellent book' which was a great help to him in his parish at Bray: 'I bless God, many persons here seem disposed to receive his word with gladness, but it is shocking (for want of any information on ye subject . . .) how few of the many I have talked to here believed Jesus to be God.'[34]

---

[29] LPL MS 1134/4, fo. 306.   [30] Ch. Ch. MS Wake Visitation Returns A, fo. 27.

[31] Ibid., fo. 53.

[32] George Stanhope, *Parsons. His Christian Directory* (1699). Stanhope translated J. H. Ostervald's Catechism into English in 1702 and Rapin's *Salvation. Every Man's Great Concern* in 1728; Humphrey Brailsford, *The Poor Man's Help* (1689), dedication.

[33] C. H. Smyth, *The Art of Preaching. A Practical Survey of Preaching in the Church of England, 747–1939* (1940), 90–166.

[34] Henry Venn, *The Complete Duty of Man; Or, A System of Doctrinal and Practical Christianity* (1763); BL Add. MS 39311, fo. 252, Berkeley to Mrs Berkeley, 24 Nov. 1769.

It was largely only an elite within the parish, whose size and social com-position varied according to circumstances, which attained the kind of re-ligious commitment desired by the Church hierarchy, and complaints of the extent of irreligion in the period stemmed in part from the gulf between the standards set by the Church and the religious elite, and the actual at-tainment of many of the parishioners. Some visitation returns give the impression that a full understanding of the Protestant religion was out of the reach of the 'uneducated' and the 'uncivilized'. Other clergy sensed the threat of an increasing secularization to their didactic programme. The incumbent of Ivychurch grumbled in 1720 of 'this degenerate age' and in 1784 Archdeacon Backhouse moaned to a congregation at Deal that 'a just and awful sense of the Divine influence has diminished, is diminishing and ought to be increased'.[35] William Marsh, rector of Bicknor, complained to Moore in 1786 of 'the want seemingly of that inward and sincere regard for religion in the greatest part of the people, which the nature of it requires'.[36] However, such laments concerning the immorality and ungodliness of parishioners may have resulted not so much from a real decline in popular religious standards, as from a more exalted concept of what was pastorally tolerable and from a sense of nostalgia for an assumed age of faith when all understood and abided by the doctrines of the Church. The impression of gloom and failure is also a product of the kinds of source material available to the historian. In their correspondence and reports clergy inevitably con-centrated on their difficulties, making it likely that the modern student will miss what has been called the 'unspectacular orthodoxy' of many parish-ioners.[37]

The growth of religious ignorance and indifference is often seen as a con-sequence of a 'gentrification' of the clerical outlook, and evidence of an ever-widening gap between elite and popular culture, as a result of which the clergy were increasingly associated with the elite.[38] But such a view ig-nores the fact that the clergy often felt the need to instruct and reprove the

---

35 William Backhouse, *God the Author of Peace and Lover of Concord. A Sermon preached at the Parish Church of Deal, on Thursday, 29 July 1784. Being the Day Appointed and Commended by the King to be kept as a General Thanksgiving to Almighty God for the Peace* (Canterbury, 1784), 11.

36 LPL, VG 3/1/d, fo. 9.

37 M. Ingram, 'Religion, Communities and Moral Discipline in Late Sixteenth and Early Seventeenth-Century England: Case Studies', in K. von Greyerz (ed.), *Religion and Society in Early Modern Europe, 1500–1800* (1984), 181; Spaeth, 'Common Prayer', 125. For a subtle analysis of the social relations between clergy and parishioners see I. M. Green, '"Reformed Pastors" and *Bon Curés*: The Changing Role of the Parish Clergy in Early Modern Europe', *SCH*, 26 (1989), esp. 279–86.

38 Burke, *Popular Culture*, 207–43.

leading members of the laity in their parishes too. Some clergy saw as their crucial task the reform of the gentry. In an age so dependent on hierarchical assumptions it was seen as highly necessary for parish notables to live up to the religious codes desired by the Church and set a good example. Charles Moore, the incumbent of Boughton Blean, aimed his publications at the most fashionable in society. In a tract of 1790 he attacked one of the most important tenets of the aristocratic code—duelling—as an affront to Christian principles, since it was a form of suicide.[39] Urged on by the Church hierarchy, clergy often found that they had to place pressure on gentry to repair chancels and felt confident enough to prosecute them in the ecclesiastical courts for failure to do so, at least until the mid-eighteenth century.[40] In 1805 Thomas Dampier argued that the decline in religious practice was not because of the negligence of the clergy, lack of basic education, or the vogue for irreligious philosophy, but because of the spread of frivolity, idleness, and absenteeism amongst the gentry. He urged the necessity of having gentry resident on their estates to be an example to the rest of the parish.[41] Another area of conflict between clergy and gentry was the custom of gentry having their children baptized at home. This went against the ordinances of the Church which stated that baptism, save in cases of sickness, should be public and in church. Clerical efforts in this direction could cause unpopularity. As John Johnson complained in 1715, 'My only crime is ecclesiastical pride. I would not baptize his child at home while he was in perfect health; nor church his wife, till the child was baptized'.[42]

In their attempts to regularize the religious beliefs and behaviour of their parishioners, Anglican clergy shared ideals similar to those of the 'godly' of the early seventeenth century: both were trying to transform the attitudes and practices of the majority of the parish.[43] Post-Restoration Anglicanism inherited more from so-called Puritanism than the traditional interpretation of a two culture polarity allows. The Anglican hierarchy did not want Anglicanism to provide a cosy and lax alternative to the rigorous standards of the Puritans; in their own way they were just as concerned to spur on the

---

[39] Charles Moore, *A Full Inquiry into the Subject of Suicide. To which are added (As Being Closely Connected With the Subject) Two Treatises on Duelling and Gaming*, 2 vols. (1790). See D. T. Andrew, 'The Code of Honour and its Critics: The Opposition to Duelling in England, 1700–1850', *Social History*, 5 (1980), 417–430.

[40] For example, CCAL, Z/4/15, fos. 17 (1721), 153 (1741).

[41] Thomas Dampier, *A Sermon Preached Before the Lords Spiritual and Temporal, in the Abbey Church, Westminster, on Wednesday 20th February 1805* (1805), 13–15.

[42] Bodl. MS Ballard 15, fo. 115, Johnson to Charlett, 11 May 1715. Private baptism had increased during the 1640s and 50s: Sykes, *Sheldon to Secker*, 25.

[43] P. Collinson, *English Puritanism* (1983).

spiritually sluggish.[44] Recent scholarship has suggested that our traditional understanding of 'Puritanism' as a coherent oppositional creed is
defective. 'Puritan' doctrines such as sabbatarianism were not peculiar and
divisive beliefs, but rather part of the normal teaching of the English
Church.[45] Puritanism may have been politically defeated in 1660, but the
'Puritan' mentality made headway in the eighteenth century not at the expense of orthodox Anglican religion, but as an element within it. It is this
ethical rigorism, as well as any alleged clerical 'abuses', which explains
much contemporary anti-clericalism, and much of the disaffection shown
towards the Church. In trying to impose their demanding standards on
their flocks, the parish clergy might well offend, like their Puritan predecessors, traditional customs and modes of behaviour. Archbishop Wake
received news in 1725 of William Squire whose strict ideals led to battles
with his parishioners:

His predecessor, Mr Green . . . was as bad a preacher as well could be. His tongue
was too big for his mouth so that what he said was perfectly unintelligible. Besides,
he'd often fall asleep in the desk and nod in the pulpit. But for all this he was
beloved, for he had the sociable quality of drinking and playing all fours with the
graziers and Butchers all hours of the day and night.

It was concluded that 'what has made him so much disliked . . . is . . . the
people are generally too loose and dissolute to bear so grave, serious and
strict a monitor'.[46] Denominational histories have perhaps exaggerated the
differences between religious groups; from the standpoint of the parish,
such distinctions often look inconsiderable. Eighteenth-century Anglicanism, as much as Puritanism, Methodism, Evangelicalism, or Tractarianism, represented an attempt to mould religious sensibilities.

   One of the clearest testimonies to the Church's desire to reach the poor
and uneducated can be found in its involvement with the voluntary religious organizations which emerged at the end of the seventeenth century.
These bodies, headed by the SPCK, aimed to bring about religious and
social reformation through a concerted campaign at the parish level. It has
been customary for historians to link the support given by clergy to such
tasks with the 'moral revolution' of 1688 and the High-Church revival

   [44] For a contrast between Puritanism and Anglicanism see C. Hill, 'Occasional Conformity', in R. B. Knox (ed.), *Reformation, Conformity and Dissent: Essays in Honour of Geoffrey
Nuttall* (Epworth, 1977), 199-220. If Hill's account of the Restoration is correct, that the
populace preferred the Church of England because they thought it was lax, then they were to
be disappointed.

   [45] Collinson, *English Puritanism*; K. L. Parker, *The English Sabbath: A Study of Doctrine
and Discipline from the Reformation to the Civil War* (Cambridge, 1988).

   [46] Ch. Ch. MS Wake 10, fo. 191, Lewis to Wake, 31 May 1725.

during Anne's reign, but it is clear that the SPCK, the societies for Reformation of Manners, the religious societies, and, above all, the charity schools, which were the most tangible and long-lasting result of this endeavour, were supported by all shades of Churchmanship.[47] And it was not until after 1714 that much of the success of these organizations was achieved. If there was a religious revival in Anne's reign, the driving force behind it continued well into the period of the Whig ascendancy.[48]

It has been suggested that the different types of voluntary organization had separate aims and intentions and appealed to different sections of the clerical community; the SPCK being favoured by the more High-Church and Tory clergy, and the societies for Reformation of Manners claiming the adherence of the Whig party and Low-Church clergy.[49] But it is dangerous to adopt such a schematic approach. The blueprint for much of this enterprise can be found in the work of Josiah Woodward, the incumbent of Poplar who from 1703 was the perpetual curate of Maidstone. Woodward's *Account of the Rise and Progress of the Religious Societies* was highly influential and extolled the ability of such associations to revitalize the Church.[50] Although they were deemed to have been the breeding ground for High-Church views, it is clear that not all High Churchmen praised them wholeheartedly. George Stanhope, the dean of Canterbury and a prominent High-Churchman, warned such societies against any tendency to separatism, likening them to the religious conventicles that had played such a central role in the turmoil of the Civil War. He was concerned lest they might again become the agents of social and religious unrest by 'invading' the priestly office, and reminded them of the importance of a steadfast obedience to the regulations of the Church: 'there is no inconsistency between wishing all the Lord's people were prophets, and dreading the consequences of their thinking themselves prophets when they are not so.'[51] Stanhope was displaying a typical fear of religious fragmentation. To the work of the societies for Reformation of Manners he gave more praise.

---

[47] T. Isaacs, 'The Anglican Hierarchy and the Reformation of Manners, 1688–1738', *JEH*, 33 (1982), 391–411.

[48] E. Duffy, 'Primitive Christianity Revived: Religious Renewal in Augustan England', *SCH*, 14 (1977), 287–300.

[49] D. W. R. Bahlman, *The Moral Revolution of 1688* (New Haven, Conn., 1957), 67–70, 78, 86. More recently, S. Burtt, *Virtue Transformed. Political Argument in England, 1688–1740* (Cambridge, 1992), 22–3.

[50] Josiah Woodward, *An Account of the Rise and Progress of the Religious Societies in the City of London* (1698).

[51] George Stanhope, *The Duty of Rebuking, A Sermon preach'd at Bow Church* (1703), 23. For Anglican suspicion of the religious societies see J. D. Walsh, 'Religious Societies: Methodist and Evangelical, 1738–1800', *SCH*, 23 (1986), 282–3.

Their vision of a community imbued with religious principles appealed to his High-Church outlook and he told the Kent gentry and magistrates at the Assize of 1701 that 'the work of correcting vice and the Reformation of Manners is truly great and glorious'.[52] Whilst he had seen the dangers of a lay usurpation of the clerical role in the religious societies, he congratulated the Reformation societies for furthering the work of the Church:

> were the world what it ought to be, the vices you are labouring to reduce, should be effectually restrained by authority and corrections of another kind. The censures of the Church, which to a truly Christian spirit, would be a greater terror, than any punishment the sword or civil justice can affect. But since the degenerancy of mankind, the unhappy divisions among, and the unjustifiable separation from us . . . it is necessary to flee for succour to the Temporal magistrates.[53]

The ends that these societies had in mind anticipated some of the social aims of the Methodists: the regulation of behaviour, an end to swearing, and the reassertion of Sunday as a day devoted to worship mirrored the aims of creating a Christian Commonwealth.[54] Their intentions cannot be separated from those of the other agencies of religious revival; certainly in the Canterbury diocese clergy who supported one of these organizations often found themselves involved with the work of the others. By 1700 the SPCK had taken on much of the responsibility for the whole network, having diocesan clergy such as William Assheton, John Deffray, John Johnson, and Theophilius Dorrington as corresponding members. A copy of a letter to Humphrey Wanley describes a visit to towns and parishes in the area by John Skeate and Thomas Morrison, in their efforts to encourage the work of both the religious and Reformation societies. At Dover they found the incumbent John Macqueen 'a pious good man who, we were assured, would encourage any thing for promoting Reformation . . .'. They visited the religious society at Canterbury which consisted of thirty men and was in 'very good order'.[55] 'Afterward', the report continued,

> we took two or three officers to the publick houses and found twelve with company in them whereof one was a constable and the next day convicted them before the mayor, where were Mr. Alderman Gibbes, and Dr Taylor, a J.P. for the county, both churchwardens, who were very well pleased with what we had done . . . The whole city was alarmed with our proceedings and the same night we met with several of the constables who were mightily encouraged by what we had done . . . and promised to take some of the members belonging to the society out every Lord's Day and to

---

[52] Stanhope, *Duty of Rebuking*, 16.   [53] Ibid., 18.

[54] T. C. Curtis and W. A. Speck, 'The Societies for Reformation of Manners: A Case Study in the Theory and Practice of Moral Reform', *Literature and History*, 3 (1976), 45–64.

[55] SPCK MS Wanley, fo. 158.

divide themselves over the whole city . . . As to swearing, fruit being exposed to sale, and barbers' shaving on the Lord's Day, tis almost suppressed; we not hearing an oath all the while we were there, though we were in several public houses, and asking a barber if he could come to shave on the Lord's Day, told us he durst not do it being strictly forbid by the mayor.[56]

They also visited the Reformation society at Canterbury which had forty members, leaving them books and pamphlets.

Archbishop Tenison supported such societies as a way to reform the religious sensibilities of the nation. In a letter to Archdeacon Battely which was sent to all clergy in the diocese he confided:

My writing to you, at this time, is occasioned by a sensible growth of vice and Prophaness in the nation, which, to the great Affliction of all good men, appears not only in the corrupt practices of particular persons, but also in the endeavours that are used to subvert the general Principles of our Holy Religion . . . the preventing whereof belongs more immediately to us, who are the ministers of Christ, and, as such, are obliged to the utmost care and watchfulness in opposing these instruments of Satan. I doubt not, but many of the parochial clergy are sufficiently sensible both of their own duty and the danger we are in . . . but in some parts that are more remote, all of them may not so well understand either the arts or the industry of these enemies of Religion.[57]

He urged the clergy to set a good example and wished that

the clergy of every neighbourhood would agree upon frequent meetings, to consult for the good of Religion in general and to advise with one another about any difficulties that may happen in their particular areas . . . And these meetings may still be made a greater advantage to the clergy in carrying on the Reformation of men's lives and manners, by inviting the church-wardens of their several parishes with them . . . And we may very reasonably expect the happy effects of such a concurrence from the visible success of that noble zeal wherewith so many about the great cities in my neighbourhood, do promote true piety, and a Reformation of Manners.

John Lewis, however, in a letter to the SPCK pointed out some of the clergy's objections to such a scheme:

He can find but 2 clergymen within 10 miles round him whom he can confide in as favourers of the Design, that the clergy exposed it as a reviving of Presbyterian classes encouraging Fanaticism contrary to the 25 Henry cap 19, a breach of the 12th canon, an usurpation of the Rights of Convocation and an inlet to division and separation, that some reflected on the Archbishop's letter as unintelligible with regard to this matter, and are adverse to the Gentry's joining with them . . .[58]

[56] Ibid.
[57] Ch. Ch. MS Wake 6, fo. 335, Tenison to Battely, 4 Apr. 1699 (printed 1700), p. 1.
[58] SPCK, Minutes and Correspondence, 1698–1704, 281, Lewis to Mr Chamberlayne, 28 Feb. 1700.

Despite the initial support given to the societies for Reformation of Manners, they do not seem to have lasted very long in the diocese. There was some hostility to the role of the informers and even Stanhope had advised members to proceed with caution, and not to act on 'slight surmises'. The religious societies proved to be more tenacious, although they received criticism from both Low and High Churchmen. In 1716 Wake was concerned by the accusations of Jacobite infiltration.[59] The best-documented religious society in the diocese was the one established at New Romney by John Deffray, modelled on the instructions given by Josiah Woodward, keeping a strict conformity to the Church, and helping to educate children. Deffray claimed that both Tillotson and Tenison had supported the scheme but there had been some local opposition: 'when I promote a strict conformity to the Church, I am a papist with some. If I arm the younger sort with a clear sense of religion, against popery and vice, I am no better than a Presby[terian] . . .'.[60] He explained in 1701 that

when I first came to my parish, about ten years ago, I found to my great grief, the people very ignorant and irreligious; the place of divine worship indecently kept; the public services neither understood, nor attended; the ministrations of the lord's supper supported only by the piety of three or four communicants, and the divine ordinance of singing psalms almost laid aside. Now, whilst I considered by what means I might redress this general neglect of religion, I was of opinion that the setting up of such a society, as I had known in the city of London, would be very proper, but I feared it would be impracticable in the country; so that at first I began to teach three or four youths the skill of singing psalms orderly, and according to rules, which greatly attended, through the grace of God, to awaken their affections towards religion, and to give 'em a relish of it.[61]

One feature was the programme of visiting lecturers, whereby clergy from other parishes in the diocese came to address the society. After the lecture, members were free to discuss points raised. Amongst topics so debated were the position of St Peter and 'what does it behove us to know concerning the middle state of the soul after death?' Special attention was given to the young who were regularly catechized and examined. Members also attended Divine Service which contained a great deal of psalm-singing, hymns, and anthems. The importance of music in Deffray's attempts to spread religious piety and to win over the poor was such that the society had its own hymn book printed. Deffray was quick to point out that he chose the

[59] Ibid., CR 1/7/4889, Wake to Mr Chamberlayne, 5 Sept. 1716.
[60] Ch. Ch. MS Wake 7, fo. 100, Deffray to Wake, 26 Jan. 1716. For the society see *Old Romney Religious Society. Minutes of Meeting* (1701).
[61] Quoted in Woodward, *Account* (3rd edn., 1701), 41.

hymns himself: he did not want to be accused of giving too much power to the lay members of the society. He also made a collection of psalms and doxologies,

designed to promote the faith and adoration of the Ever Blessed Trinity, one of which he appoints to every psalm, it appearing to him of excellent use to make those sacred hymns as fit for the piety of the Christian Church as they were formerly for the Jewish Church.[62]

This indicates how one clergyman attempted to deal with the vogue for anti-Trinitarian beliefs, which were now thought to be spreading. Deffray claimed that the maintenance of the distinctive features of Anglican worship was the special aim of the society and in 1724 he asked Wake 'for more defences of the Athanasian creed'. He noted with approval the success of the Archbishop of Tuam's *Method*; 'it hath kept moving from hand to hand, and it hath a turn even among both gentry and clergy of our parts', and he wondered 'whether this excellent piece will put an end to Arianism . . .'.[63]

Deffray's use of music to attract the lower orders met with some success. He proudly informed the SPCK that 'to the joy of all pious souls, our shepherds, plough men, and other labourers at their work, perfume the air with the melodious singing of psalms, to the great Creator Redeemer, and Sanctifier of men'.[64] So impressive was the influence of Deffray's Society on the neighbourhood that Balthazar Regis, incumbent of Adisham, reported to the SPCK: 'I never saw the spirit of Religion in all my life in any place work to such a degree as here.'[65] The power of music in worship to attract parishioners was recognized by other members of the diocesan clergy. In 1704 Theophilus Dorrington published *A Discourse on Singing*, John Lewis noted the need for a collection of psalms—'the common people seeming to be most affected with that part of the service'—and Charles Bean asked 'whether by any means the common people may be prevailed upon to part with their drunken and obscene catches, in exchange for Divine hymns and authors, that they may have their affections in heaven while their hands are at the plough?'[66] Dean Horne observed in the 1780s that

---

[62] Ch. Ch. MS Wake 22, fo. 211, Deffray to Wake, 29 Mar. 1724; SPCK, CR 1/8/5438, John Deffray, 18 Nov. 1717. The hymn book: *The Christian's Daily Manual of Prayers and Praises* (1703).

[63] Edward Synge, *A Plain and Easy Method, whereby a Man of a Moderate Capacity may arrive at Full Satisfaction in all things that Concern his Everlasting Salvation* (1715); Ch. Ch. MS Wake 24, fo. 290, Deffray to Wake, 4 Nov. 1724.

[64] SPCK, CR 1/15/10374.

[65] Ch. Ch. MS Wake 15, fo. 45, Regis to Wake, 25 Mar. 1717.

[66] Ch. Ch., CR 1/15/10407.

at present, in many country churches, [church music] is either dismal or ridiculous, and our people are frequently induced to fall off to other religious assemblies, by the superior melody to be heard in them. There is hope, however, of some reformation in this part of divine worship, as many worthy clergymen have turned their thoughts this way.[67]

William Jones in 1787 saw the singing of music in church as one way of fostering religious unity within the parish, and he composed an anthem for Sunday schools.[68] Other clergy, however, were concerned that the existence of church bands tended to privilege certain sections of the congregation. The incumbent of Hollingbourne complained in 1758 of the

> very bad custom which prevails in this parish, as it does in very many country villages, for a particular set of people to assemble themselves in one part of the church on a Sunday . . . to sing psalms, which are many of them set to such tunes as the rest of the congregation cannot join in, and so much levity and indecency in them, as to savour more of ballad singing.[69]

Religious societies were sometimes accused of fostering Jacobite and extreme High-Church principles, but Deffray could be quite critical of 'high-flying' leaders in the diocese. One of the lecturers in 1710 was Thomas Brett, the later non-juror. Deffray told him that the society had read Brett's work on *Church Government*: 'I have often endeavoured to inculcate this weighty assertion that the Church of England only, of all parties within this realm, hath its government agreeable to that of the Apostles . . .'. But he raised the question whether the High-Church party was not being more disruptive than it allowed, and he was particularly anxious about their attacks on the Church hierarchy: 'as I love Episcopacy, I would not see the powers of the Metropolitan crushed.' He likened the partisan behaviour of Brett and the lower house of Convocation to 'bringing a Commonwealth in the Church'.[70]

[67] George Horne, 'Parish Churches', in *Olla Podrida* (27 Oct. 1787), 198.

[68] William Jones, 'The Nature and Excellence of Music. Preached at the Opening of a New Organ at Nayland, 29 July 1787', *Works*, vi. 110–37.

[69] LPL MS 1134/2, fo. 212. It may be that such worries reflected the clergy's concern that they had lost control of the service: see V. Gammon, 'Babylonian Perfomances: The Rise and Suppression of Popular Church Music, 1660–1870', in E. Yeo and S. Yeo (eds.), *Popular Culture and Class Conflict, 1590–1914* (Brighton, 1981), 62–84. In this light it is worth noting that the majority of those involved in the 1838 rising on behalf of Sir William Courtenay in the parish of Hernehill were members of the church band: B. Reay, 'The Last Rising of the Agricultural Labourers: The Battle in Bossenden Wood, 1838', *History Workshop Journal*, 26 (1988), 86, 95. In 1741 the rector of Chartham had tried to stop such singing, but the ecclesiastical courts supported the parishioners: E. W. Kemp, *An Introduction to the Canon Law of the Church of England* (1957), 71–3.

[70] Bodl. MS Eng. Th. c. 24, fo. 365, Deffray to Brett, 14 Mar. 1710.

Although the activities of Deffray's religious society appear to be unique in the diocese, and no evidence suggests that it survived beyond the 1730s, one of its concerns was more long-lasting, and was shared by many other parishes in the diocese: this was the establishment of a charity school. The role of eighteenth-century charity schools as an attempt to inculcate religious knowledge and in teaching parishioners to read, as part of a clerical campaign to ensure a better understanding of the Anglican position, has not yet been fully appreciated. It has even been questioned whether there was a charity school 'movement' at all; evidence from Leicestershire has suggested that they were little more than continuations of a process which had roots in the early seventeenth century.[71] Certainly, the aims behind the establishment of such schools echoed Reformation concerns to strengthen allegiance to the Church and to religious principles, yet the continuing lack of adequate educational provision for the poor shows how incomplete this aspect of the Reformation had been, even in a diocese which was supposed to have been in the vanguard of the new faith.[72] It is not easy to establish precise figures for educational resources in the diocese at the Restoration, but it would appear that only some twenty-five parishes had a regular form of parochial education. Predictably, these included some of the major towns in the diocese: Canterbury, Ashford, Dover, Sandwich, and Deal; also a clump of parishes in the fairly densely populated Weald: Maidstone, Tenterden, Cranbrook, Benenden, Biddenden, and Staplehurst. Another group was concentrated in the north-east: Margate, Birchington, Ash, and Wickhambreux.[73] But there were large areas of the diocese completely without such schools. By the end of the eighteenth century there had been a dramatic transformation, for by now nearly half of all parishes provided some kind of education for their children. Moreover, these new schools were situated in the areas of high population growth such as the parishes which bordered the north Kent coast, and there were now schools in Romney Marsh, which in 1660 had been neglected. The new schools were almost solely designed for the education of the poor and went further than the creations of the earlier religious reformers in that many of them were

---

[71] The standard work is still M. G. Jones, *The Charity School Movement. A Study of Eighteenth-Century Puritanism in Action* (Cambridge, 1938). J. Simon, 'Was there a Charity School Movement? The Leicestershire Evidence', in Brian Simon (ed.), *Education in Leicestershire, 1540–1940* (Leicester, 1968), 55–100; R. W. Unwin, *Charity Schools and the Defence of Anglicanism: James Talbot, Rector of Spofforth, 1700–1708*, Borthwick Papers, 65 (1984).

[72] Clark, *English Provincial Society*, 200–1, 215–16.

[73] R. Hume, 'Educational Provision for the Kentish Poor, 1660–1811: Fluctuations and Trends', *Southern History*, 4 (1982), 122–44.

open to girls as well as boys. The older schools, headed by the King's School in Canterbury, taught a largely classical syllabus and attracted the sons of neighbouring gentry, prosperous tradesmen, and clergy. Several of the grammar schools in the diocese also taught the classics and they suffered some kind of decline because this kind of education was not universally popular. In contrast, the new charity schools aimed to serve the needs of a less-well-educated cultural and social milieu, and tended to flourish in the more rural parishes. The role of the clergy in all this needs to be stressed; not only were they often instrumental in finding the finance for the schools, either by generous benefaction, as was the case with Richard Foster, who established a school at Crundale,[74] or more usually by raising subscriptions, but they were also often the teachers or guardians of the schools.

The schools were urged on parishes in the diocese by the SPCK, which saw its task as co-ordinating the movement and supplying clergy with advice and books. But it would be wrong to give the SPCK the credit for actually instigating the erection of a school in any particular parish; this was usually done by the local incumbent who had the task of encouraging the laity to give funds to supply tuition and books for the children, and, in many cases, clothing as well. The influence of clergy was often crucial: it was during Josiah Woodward's incumbency that four charity schools were established by subscription at Maidstone, each teaching thirty children.[75] In some parishes the schools became the objects of party hostility in the early eighteenth century. In Whig propaganda they were nurseries of Jacobitism. These accusations could cause difficulties for clergy who were trying to encourage subscriptions. In 1720 Robert Payne, the rector of Saltwood, told Wake that 'the only difficulty I meet with in its support arises from party rivalry'.[76] Schools in the diocese may have been particularly prone to such accusations because of the notorious affair of 1718—well publicized by Daniel Defoe—of the children smuggled out of London by the High-Church vicar of nearby Chislehurst in the Rochester diocese.[77] In Linda Colley's portrayal of 'Tory Anglicanism' support for charity schools is used as a sign of Tory political affiliation.[78] But the Whigs were just as aware of the need for such schools in educating the poor. Early on in his primacy Wake told Arthur Charlett, the master of University College, Oxford, that 'I do flatter myself that in time our Church will reap a singular benefit from

---

[74] CCAL, U3/116/25/1.   [75] SPCK, CR 1/3/3081.

[76] SPCK, CR 1/7/5163.

[77] On the political affiliation of the schools see C. Rose, '"Seminarys of Faction and Rebellion": Jacobites, Whigs and the London Charity Schools, 1716–1724', *HJ*, 34 (1991), 831–55.

[78] Colley, *Defiance of Oligarchy*, 110, 117.

these seminaries'.[79] There was plenty of support at Queenborough, where government influence was strong since the royal dockyards were situated there, for the school which was established and maintained by the Whig MPs who represented the borough.[80]

The charity school at Lydd was described in 1724 as being

under your Grace's protection, maintained by the vicar, curate, a religious society and £4 p.a. out of the offertory. The vicar gives £10 and the society £8 more. Better than 30 children are taught to read and write and cast accounts; who are brought to Church on all proper days, are cat[echized] every Sunday night, after 5 a bell tolling for that purpose; and some often undergo a public examination of every lecture approved by your Grace.[81]

At St Alphege's, Canterbury, a school was maintained by the subscriptions of clergy and gentry.[82] But ministers who lived in the poorer parishes found that the laity were not able to help. Wake was informed in 1722 that 'though Sittingbourne does not abound with people of substance I shall strive to begin there as I did here [Faversham] in promoting a charity school. And may providence succeed, as in this place, where . . . we have met with foreign and domestic support'.[83] The incumbent of Thurnham told Wake that 'a little to supply the want of one I pay for the schooling of some poor children and generally apply the sacrament money for that purpose'.[84] And even those parishes which had been lucky enough to receive an endowment for a school through a benefaction sometimes complained that it was difficult to obtain the money. Although Lady Joanna Thornhill had left the residue of her estate to support a school at Wye, William Nevar, the rector, grumbled to Wake in 1716 that nine years later the parish had still not acquired the benefaction.[85] The archbishop intervened to ensure that the money was paid. As late as 1817 it was noted that the £1,000 left by Baldwin Duppa in his will in 1720 had not been paid because it allegedly fell foul of the Mortmain Act.[86] Schools which were supported by subscriptions were not necessarily any more securely based. In 1725 it was complained that at Ashford 'the charity school is unhappily sunk by the total withdrawing of subscriptions which supported it'.[87] By contrast, the incumbent of

[79] Bodl. MS Ballard 3, fo. 59, Wake to Charlett, 6 Apr. 1716.
[80] Ch. Ch. MS Wake Visitation Returns A, fo. 343.
[81] Ch. Ch. MS Wake Visitation Returns C, fo. 237.
[82] Ch. Ch. MS Wake Visitation Returns B, fo. 126.
[83] Ch. Ch. MS Wake 9, fo. 172, Richard Tylden to Wake, 14 Mar. 1722.
[84] Ch. Ch. MS Wake Visitation Returns D, fo. 457.
[85] Ch. Ch. MS Wake 7, fo. 377, Nevar to Wake, 10 Oct. 1716.
[86] Parliamentary Papers, 1817, IX, *Report of the Commission for the Charities in England and Wales for the Education of the Poor*, 118.
[87] SPCK, CR 1/13/8482, John Tournay, 23 Sept. 1725.

Minster in Sheppey told Wake:

About three years since, I prevailed upon my neighbours to contribute for the in-
structing the children of all the poorer sort, I at first kept 3 or 4 to school at my own
charity, and then desired their assistance for augmenting the charity; they complied
and I hope it will be perpetual; having reason to expect a fixed salary from a charitable person of my acquaintance.[88]

It has been argued that the specifically religious role of the charity schools,
the education of parishioners in Christian principles, had virtually died out
by the 1730s.[89] Certainly a hindrance to the campaign was the Mortmain
Act of 1736 which forbade deathbed benefactions. Nevertheless, the use of
the schools continued to be advocated by clergy. William Marsh believed
that they were the best remedy for the ingrained religious ignorance of his
and other rural parishioners. He recommended to Secker in 1758 that:

as many pious and wealthy people are disposed to bequeath charitable legacies at
their death they could not do a better thing than to leave £10 or £12 p.a. in small
country parishes, for some to teach poor people's children to read, and say
cat[echism], for want of which, ignorance is entailed on this sort of folk, for many
generations. For parents not being able to read themselves, and having no school to
send their children to, or if they had not in a capacity many of them to pay for it, they
must almost necessarily be brought up without learning to read, these marry and
have families, which labour under the same disadvantage.[90]

The cause of parochial education received new impetus during the last two
decades of the eighteenth century with the foundation of the Sunday school
movement. Recent scholarship has tended to attribute this movement to
the Evangelical Revival,[91] but it is clear that its support came from across
the clerical spectrum. In the diocese the creation of such schools received a
great deal of support from George Horne, the dean of Canterbury, and
leader of the High-Church Hutchinsonians, and from the vice-dean,
George Berkeley. One of Berkeley's sermons was sold 'for the benefit of
charity schools', and Horne's sermons seem to have been successful in persuading the professional classes to give to this charitable cause.[92] In a sermon preached in 1785, *Sunday Schools Recommended*, which was dedicated
to George Hearne, the pioneer of religious education in the diocese and

---

[88] Ch. Ch. MS Wake Visitation Returns C, fo. 399.

[89] Jones, *Charity Schools*, 129.   [90] LPL MS 1134/1, f. 33.

[91] T. Laqueur, *Religion and Respectability: Sunday Schools and Working Class Culture,
1780–1850* (New Haven, Conn., 1976), 21–36.

[92] George Berkeley, *A Caution Against Socinianism given in a Discourse preached at the
Cathedral and Metropolitan Church of Christ, Canterbury; on Good Friday, 1787. And Published
for the Benefit of the Charity Schools in the Parish of St. Clement Danes* (Canterbury and
London, 1787).

rector of St Alphege's, Horne outlined the benefits of Sunday school education. He quoted Jonas Hanway, the well-known philanthropist, on the innocence of children, who were ready to be moulded by religious opinions, claiming that this work 'implores, above all the patronage and assistance of the clergy under whose direction and superintendence, it should, if possible be carried out'. He hoped that the success of the Sunday schools would make the next age less corrupt and more religious.[93]

The diocese was not in an area of the country noted for its Evangelical clergy, yet many parishes had instituted a Sunday school by the time of Archbishop Manners Sutton's primary visitation of 1806, usually through subscription or from the donation of a wealthy landowner. At Godmersham Jane Austen's cousin was the principal supporter of the school.[94] In speaking of an Evangelical Revival as the sole leaven to the dough of the eighteenth-century Church, historians have misjudged the strength of ordinary Anglican Churchmanship and its ability to initiate pastoral developments. Sunday schools need not be seen as very different from the charity schools; both institutions had common aims and received similar backing. In many cases the Sunday schools developed in parishes alongside the existing charity schools, or replaced them, being more suited to the emerging industrial and 'modern' working hours. Charles Moore, incumbent of Boughton Blean, set out the ends of the schools:

The points aimed at . . . are to furnish opportunities of instruction to the children of the poor, without interfering with any weekly industry . . . to inure them to early habits of regularity in their attendance at church and to teach them how to spend those leisure hours of Sunday to their own improvement, advantage and happiness, which are now almost universally consumed in idleness, profanation and riot.[95]

This was a common proposition made by defenders of both charity and Sunday schools, replying to criticism that such institutions might overeducate their pupils, making them idle and self-opinionated. The counter-argument was that such schools had a crucial role to play in maintaining social order: children would be educated to know their place, and the schools would inculcate humility and obedience. Moore believed that

the labour and industry of the lower class, [are] no hindrance to piety and religion . . . of whom it is very observeable, that the more diligent and industrious they are

---

93 George Horne, *Sunday Schools Recommended in a Sermon preached at the parish Church of St Alphege, Canterbury, on Sunday December the eighteenth, MDCCLXXV, with an Appendix on the Method of Forming and Conducting them* (Oxford and London, 1786), 15, 20; id., *A Charge Intended to have been Delivered to the Clergy of Norwich at the Primary Visitation of George, Lord Bishop of the Diocese* (Norwich, 1791), 21.

94 LPL, VG 3/2/b, fo. 78.   95 LPL, VG 3/1/c, f. 17.

in their several trades and occupations on the working days, the more consistent they are at their public devotion on Sundays.[96]

George Hearne, the rector of St Alphege's, Canterbury, was clearly dedicated to the cause and described part of his day's work:

I examine the most forward and explain to them the Catechism and the use of the Common prayer book. I exercize them in repeating after me the Lord's Prayer, and the Creeds and all the responses . . . We have gone through, likewise, Fox, on *Public Worship*, and his *Introduction*, and Crossman's Introduction, the *Church Catechism Broke into short questions*, and Mann's *Catechism*. The books in common use are *The Child's First Book*, Fisher or Dixon's Spelling Book, the Catechisms before mentioned, particularly Mann's, the *Divine Songs* of the pious and excellent Dr. Isaac Watts, and every child is furnished with a common prayer Book and Testament to carry to church.[97]

The list is interesting not only because it reveals something of the range of educational materials available to the late-eighteenth-century cleric in his attempt to spread the word, but also because it is indicative of the pastoral method of such clergy, disseminating religious principles through endless repetition, and relying on the printed word. Sunday schools were supported by the archbishop and by the cathedral at the end of the period. Archbishop Moore in 1790 gave certain fines which had been received for the renewal of leases at Eastbridge as a legacy for a school there and in 1811 Archbishop Manners Sutton demised the lease of Chislet manor for use of a school.[98] In 1811 a diocesan school for the education of the poor on Bell's plan was established,[99] and in 1823 the dean and chapter gave Sir Edward Knatchbull permission to build a National school.[100]

CHURCH SERVICES

Visitation returns are a prime source for the range and frequency of services held in the diocese, and have been used by historians as a guide to what

---

[96] Moore, *Sermons*, iii. 305.

[97] George Hearne, 'appendix', in Horne, *Sunday Schools*, 21. The works mentioned by Hearne are: Francis Fox, *The Duty of Public Worship Proved: to which are added directions for a devout behaviour there* (1713); id., *An Introduction to Spelling and Reading* (7th edn., 1754); Henry Crossman, *An Introduction to the Knowledge of the Christian Religion* (Colchester, 1742); *The Church Catechism Broke into Short Questions. To Which is Added an Explanation of Some Words, for the Easier Understanding Of It* (1730); Isaac Mann, *A Familiar Exposition of the Church-Catechism in Five Parts, to which are added prayers for the use of children and servants* (5th edn., 1771).

[98] Parliamentary Papers, 1817, IX, *Report of the Committee for the Charities in England and Wales for the Education of the Poor*, 89.

[99] Ibid., 93.   [100] CCAL, Dean's Book, 1793–1824, fos. 186, 288.

clergy were actually doing in the parishes, as well as shedding light on the broader question of the role of the Church in the community. A problem in interpreting the figures, statistics, and comments which survive for church attendance is the feeling of nostalgia held by many clergy (and some modern historians) for a golden age in which all allegedly came to church regularly. It was the clergy's wistful belief in the historical existence of this lost world which gave them the impression that they were living in a period of religious sloth and decline. But pastoral results which looked disappointing to them may well have been a real achievement. It was easy for clergy to take the regulations for attendance in the 1604 canons as actually descriptive of a bygone age of universal churchgoing, when in fact they were prescriptive, and by no means always obeyed.

For the Restoration period the records are scarce, yet is clear that the resumption of Anglican practice was often a difficult and laborious task. Despite the efforts of both Sheldon and Sancroft to ensure that parishes had a regular number of services it is difficult to discover how far they were successful in their aim. What is clear, if the period between 1660 and 1828 is taken as a whole, is that there was not the steady decline in the performance of Sunday duty during the eighteenth century which has been claimed by A. J. Russell.[101] Throughout this period the Church hierarchy continued to see 'whole service', both morning and afternoon prayer, as the ideal for each parish. In urban parishes this was usually put into practice. Exceptions to this were those Canterbury city parishes which were united after an Act of Parliament in 1681, in which incumbents treated their joint parishes as a single unit, giving morning service in one church and evening service in the other. But in the other towns in the diocese: Dover, Folkestone, Maidstone, Sandwich, Cranbrook, Ashford, Tenterden, and in many of the larger parishes, such as St Lawrence, Thanet, St Peter's, Thanet, Sittingbourne, and New Romney, incumbents reported that they performed both parts of the service.

The situation in the smaller rural parishes was different. In these incumbents often acknowledged that they only performed one service on a Sunday. This was especially true in winter. The incumbent of Warden explained in 1720 that although service was performed twice in summer, in winter, because there were few inhabitants and these lived a long way from the church, 'if I preach'd twice then I might preach to the walls'.[102] It was said of Fairfield that 'there is no coming to ye church some months in winter when the weather is very wet, by reason of floods, and much water lying

---

[101] Russell, *Clerical Profession*, 54–5.
[102] Ch. Ch. MS Wake Visitation Returns B, fo. 828.

round about'.[103] This did not mean, however, that parishioners were necessarily deprived of the chance to attend church twice. Many of the small parishes, which often had less than thirty houses, were held in plurality, one clergyman looking after two neighbouring parishes, or, in other cases, an incumbent of one parish acting as curate to a contiguous parish. This was particularly common in Romney Marsh. Some parishes there had very small numbers of inhabitants: in 1758 St Mary's in the Marsh had only seven houses, Leveland had eight, Barfreston was said to be 'uncommonly small' with eight houses, Birchington had four, Ripple had fifteen, Burmarsh had ten and Badlesmere had sixteen houses. Most of the inhabitants of these parishes were described as 'graziers' or 'lookers', being employed to look after sheep. The demands of farming routine clearly interfered with attendance, corroborating the theories of Currie, Gilbert, and Horsely that attendance did not so much reflect Church policy as external societal pressures.[104] Clergy claimed that even in the Marsh it was quite possible for inhabitants to attend a neighbouring parish church, since in spread-out parishes they often lived nearer a neighbouring church than their own. Even in cases where parishes were not held in plurality, there seems to have been no bar to inhabitants attending their own church one part of the day and a neighbouring church the other. This was particularly the case if their own incumbent did not preach at both services.

Edward Sedgwick, the curate of St Mary's in the Marsh, echoed the reports of many clergymen in this period when he told Secker of the 'unwillingness of people to attend unless there is a sermon, choosing rather to go to a neighbouring church where there is a sermon preached, than to stay at home and hear prayers only'.[105] The vogue for 'sermon-gadding', which has been seen as a feature of the early Anglican church, perhaps continued through the eighteenth century. At Ivychurch services were reduced from two to one as inhabitants refused to attend services where there was no sermon.[106] In this case the clergy of neighbouring parishes worked on a kind of unofficial rota, ensuring that they preached at different times, thereby enabling parishioners to hear two sermons. The vicar of Ospringe admitted that the 'church is generally full where there is a sermon, but scandalously

---

[103] Ch. Ch. MS Wake Visitation Returns A, fo. 197.

[104] Ibid., /1, fos, 37, 41, 87, 163, 3/ fos. 77, 233. R. Currie, A. Gilbert, and L. Horsely, *Churches and Churchgoers. Patterns of Church Growth in the British Isles since 1700* (Oxford, 1977), 98, 105.

[105] LPL MS 1134/3, fo. 77. Jane Austen took especial interest in sermons at Godmersham: *Jane Austen's Letters to her Sister Cassandra and Others*, ed. R. W. Chapman (2nd edn., 1952), 339: letter of 25 Sept. 1813.

[106] Davies, *Caroline Captivity*, 149–50; LPL MS 1134/2, fo. 244.

thin when there is none. The houses stand at a distance from ye church and ye people will resort to neighbouring churches, as they say, for the sake of hearing a sermon. This humour prevails much hereabouts.'[107] There is some indication that incumbents felt that the Protestant concentration on preaching had, perhaps, worked only too well. Wake was told in 1724 by the rector of Kingston, 'my parish, consisting of mean inferior people, our best endeavours are not sufficient to make them sensible how much prayers is their duty: it is my firm belief that if it was not for the sake of hearing a sermon, they would keep from the church altogether.'[108] Likewise, David Pratt, the rector of Harrietsham, reported that 'when we had prayers without a sermon, we had always exceeding few, and upon the least alteration of fine weather, scarcely any at all, so much that those expressions in the liturgy, that imply an assembly or congregation could not be represented with any sense of propriety.'[109]

Russell has argued that the professionalization of the clergy in the nineteenth century meant that clergy became more aware of their duty to offer services, notwithstanding the size of the congregation.[110] But it is clear that Secker urged similar objectives to his clergy. He told one incumbent that although 'several of the parishioners live at a distance, 11 are near it, and from these more than 2 or 3 may surely be gathered together, × 2 a Sunday in God's name'.[111] There is some indication that the pressure which Secker put on the clergy of his diocese ensured that in certain rural parishes the frequency of services increased. A diligent diocesan like Secker was able to chart variations in the number of services offered in any parish through a comparison of replies to his visitation enquiries with the returns submitted to previous archbishops. This kind of information enabled the archbishop to assess the diligence of his clergy. He wrote to Edward Filmer, the rector of Crundale, 'in the beginning of your incumbency, according to my predecessor's book, service was × 2. Now it is only 1'. He urged Filmer to resume full duty.[112]

The variation between town and country parishes within the diocese with regard to Sunday duty was mirrored in the regularity with which weekday services were performed. Incumbents of the more populous urban parishes offered some form of service in the week, whilst clergy in rural parishes complained of the futility of performing mid-week services when

---

[107] LPL MS 1134/3, fo. 171.   [108] Ch. Ch. MS Wake Visitation Returns C, fo. 31.

[109] Ch. Ch. MS Wake 9, fo. 113, Pratt to Wake, 25 Aug. 1721.

[110] Russell, *Clerical Profession*, 71.

[111] LPL MS Secker 3, fo. 235, Secker to Mr Leigh, 6 Dec. 1765.

[112] Ibid., fo. 149, Secker to Filmer, 8 Oct. 1758. Full duty was resumed, at least in summer: ibid., VG 3/1/a, f. 97.

there was no likelihood of a congregation. Even in towns the number of weekday services would vary according to the energies of the individual incumbent. Samuel Weller, the perpetual curate of Maidstone from 1712 to 1753, was clearly a model parish priest. In 1741 his services at All Saints included daily morning prayer, with evening prayer also on Saturday, holy days and eves, and daily in Lent. A sermon was also delivered on Good Friday.[113] Such a level of services offered was exceptional, yet most town parishes had services on Wednesdays and Fridays, especially during Lent. The problems facing the rural incumbents in this respect were greater. The rector of Aldington in 1758 maintained that he would have performed services on all holy days if there was any prospect of attendance 'among people so employed in country business for their bread'.[114] The vicar of Sellinge noted in 1806 that, 'few churches are better attended than this on Sundays, but with sorrow, I must beg leave to observe some farmers who will not refrain from working their men and cattle on Good Friday and on Fasts and Thanksgivings in opposition to every remonstrance'.[115] It was not so much that clergy were not prepared to offer the services as a general unwillingness of members of the laity to attend.

One reason which clergy regularly gave for the non-attendance of their parishioners was the presence of an alehouse. The role of the alehouse in the century before 1660 as a focus for an 'alternative society' within the parish has been well documented, but it has been suggested by Peter Clark that after the Restoration the alehouse became 'gentrified' and respectable, and was no longer seen as a threat to the Church.[116] Whether or not Clark's schema exaggerates the subversive nature of the alehouse in the early seventeenth century, it certainly underestimates the alarm with which it could be viewed by eighteenth-century clergy. Their concern with the competing attractions of the alehouse is another indication of the way in which 'Puritan' aims were absorbed into mainstream Anglicanism in the period after the Restoration. In 1663 the compiler of the Sheldon Catalogue was alarmed by the number of 'loose persons' and 'drinkers' at Eastwell.[117] Alehouses continued to be seen as forces for disorder, presenting a rival social centre to that of the church and encouraging drinking during times of divine service. John Johnson observed in 1708 that

---

[113] J. Russell, *History of Maidstone* (1843), 43.
[114] LPL MS 1134/a, fo. 13.   [115] Ibid., VG 3/2/d, f. 26.
[116] P. Clark, *The English Alehouse: A Social History* (1983), esp. pp. 145–250; see also K. Wrightson, 'Alehouses, Order and Reformation in Rural England, 1590–1660', in Yeo and Yeo, *Culture and Class Conflict*, 1–27.
[117] LPL MS 1126, fo. 36.

Habitual intemperance and sensuality do by degrees harden the heart and deaden all sense of religion in the minds of men, and when this is once done, all the most sacred obligations they are under to God and their superiors are soon forgotten. Houses of debauchery and drunken clubs are the great seminaries of atheism and irreligion, and consequently one great occasion of all the mischief that can light upon the kingdom.[118]

In 1750 John Bowtell felt that drunkenness was detrimental to the Anglican creed because it compromised the strength of understanding requisite for true faith.[119] The incumbent of the united parishes of Sibertswold and Coldred explained to Archbishop Moore in 1786 that 'there is a visible difference in the morals and behaviour of this parish (Sibertswold) and those of Coldred, which is united with this, which I can no other way account for, as they have long been united, save this has a public house'.[120] The rector of St Andrew's, Canterbury complained that 'there are some who commonly absent themselves from all public worship: these are reported to be principally persons employed in and about the inns and their neglect of public worship is understood to proceed in some measure from their employment'.[121] Patrick Colquhoun, a magistrate in Kent, commented in 1794 that 'an ill-governed public house is one of the greatest nuisances which can exist in civil society, for it spreads its poison far and wide'.[122] It is no wonder that the rector of Boughton Malherbe proudly boasted that 'my parishioners are careful to keep their bodies in temperance, soberness and chastity'.[123]

Absenteeism and disaffection were not merely promoted by alehouses. Those parishes in the diocese which were situated on the north and east Kent coast were likely to be affected by the activities of smugglers. So grieved the rector of Langley:

if not professedly, a disregard for religion unhappily prevails and which is chiefly to be attributed to the iniquitous practice of smuggling, in which contraband trade too many in this country are engaged in on the Sunday especially; to the subversion of all morality, decency and order, and in vain do the clergy labour to stem the torrent.[124]

---

[118] John Johnson, *Reasons Why Vice Ought to be Punished but Is Not, in a Sermon Preached at Maidstone in Kent, at the Assizes held there before Mr Justice Tracy, 17 March 1708* (1708), 13–14; KAO, U/20/5/1, Churchwarden's Accounts, 1663–1741: details of fines levied on Allez Symmons on 13 March 1705 for 'allowing tippling in his house on Sundays in service times'.

[119] John Bowtell, *A Sermon Preach'd at Staplehurst* (Canterbury, 1750), 13.

[120] LPL, VG 3/1/c, fo. 353.   [121] Ibid., /a, fo. 265.

[122] Patrick Colquhoun, *Observations and Facts relative to Licensed Ale-Houses* (1794), 19. For a wider context see J. Innes, 'Politics and Morals. The Reformation of Manners in Later Eighteenth Century England', in Hellmuth, *Transformation of Political Culture*, 57–118.

[123] Ch. Ch. MS Wake Visitation Returns B, fo. 230.   [124] LPL, VG 3/1/d, fo. 297.

Such comments have added significance in the light of a recent suggestion that south coast smuggling was often closely associated with Jacobitism, and thus represented another kind of potential threat to the position of the Church.[125] The powerlessness of the Church against such lawlessness was often deplored, especially when, as was often the case, leading members of the parish were involved. Thomas Patten, the incumbent of Whitstable from 1712 to 1764, was reputed to be a member of the notorious 'Seasalter Company' which participated in smuggling during most of the century.[126] The rector of Aldington declared the prevalence of smuggling was so great that the 'wisdom and power of Church and State' could not stop it.[127]

Clerical attacks on the influence of the alehouse and the Sunday smuggling trade were elements within a Protestant sabbatarianism which the Church tried to impose on the parishes. Part of the SPCK's programme was to send out tracts and pamphlets condemning the evils of drink and the dangers involved in disregarding Sunday worship. The practice of a holy life was seen as the best solution to these temptations. In 1751 John Bowtell maintained that legislation would not achieve this, the only real answer was true Christian zeal: 'not that which burns outrageously and betrays men with impudent and unaccountable actions . . . but that which is a just and becoming Assurance, and a true spirit of Piety, conducted with Prudence and Courage, labours to stop the current of Lewdness, Prophaneness and Atheism.'[128] But in the attempt to make Sunday into a day devoted to religion, ministers recognized that they might have to contend with different—and sometimes competing—understandings of the role and purpose of Sundays. In a statement reminiscent of the battles between 'godly' pastors of the early seventeenth century and their recalcitrant parishioners, the vicar of Ripple complained in 1758 that 'there are too many who seem to consider the Lord's Day merely as a day of rest, if not of festivity, but they are chiefly plough servants—stupid and ignorant'.[129] Some clergy indicated that part of the problem they faced in trying to enforce a more disciplined Sunday worship was the behaviour of the churchwardens. The vicar of Sheldwich, John Willis, brought Moses Eastes, a churchwarden, before the ecclesiastical courts for allowing the drinking of beer, ale, and brandy in the parish church, 'as in a common alehouse, in a most profane unseemly and disorderly manner'.[130] Benjamin Waterhouse,

[125] P. Monod, 'Dangerous Merchandise: Smugglers, Jacobitism and Commercial Culture in South-East England, 1690-1760', *JBS*, 30 (1991), 150–82.

[126] W. Harvey, *The Seasalter Company—a Smuggling Fraternity* (Whitstable, 1983), 6.

[127] LPL, VG 3/1/b, fo. 281.

[128] John Bowtell, *A Sermon Preach'd at Patrixbourne and Bridge* (Canterbury, 1751), 13.

[129] LPL, MS 1134/3, fo. 233.   [130] CCAL, X. 11. 20. fo. 30.

the rector of Hollingbourne, told Secker in 1758 that many irregularities occurred in his parish

through the neglect of Churchwardens. The Lord's Day is prophaned by trades-men opening their shops and selling such victuals as the people might and ought to be supplied with on other days, and not flesh meat only, but such eatables as are in no danger of spoiling . . . by their shaving . . . by alehouses being frequented by many . . . and I fear in very many other country villages also; the sad consequences of which wicked and licentious behaviour, I have represented in as full a manner as I possibly could, both from the pulpit and in private . . . but to little purpose . . . A charge to churchwardens in general would be attended with most happy con-sequences.[131]

William Marsh, vicar of Bapchild, complained that churchwardens in small country parishes were frequently illiterate and ignorant of their duties, 'and with all so deeply engaged in their worldly affairs, that they give themselves no concern about it. And if a minister was to exert himself, by enforcing the execution of these laws, he would be in danger of inflaming the whole parish'.[132]

Clergy had difficulty in classifying some of the non-attenders. The in-cumbent of St Dunstan's, Canterbury took a hard line: 'some few deserve rather the name atheists, deists, rather than dissenters for they neither go to church nor to the meeting houses, but profane the Lord's Day, by staying at home in their own houses, and have no family worship, which I have often reproved.'[133] It seems clear that some clergy were increasingly more con-cerned about this section of the parish than about dissenters, especially since dissent lost its radical overtones for most Anglican clergy during the eighteenth century. The rector of Norton reported in 1720 that 'none pro-fess to be dissenters, but some as bad or worse, who seldom come to church, neither do they go anywhere else, so it is hard to guess what religion they are of, or any, or none'.[134] Against these members of the parish, clergy had little recourse but to their own pastoral abilities. The curate of Whitstable ob-served that there were too many absentees in his parish, 'and will be so everywhere as long as the Toleration Act be abused'.[135]

There is no reason to suppose that this was a new problem for the clergy. Peter Clark has estimated that a fifth of the population of sixteenth-century Kent stayed away from church on a regular basis,[136] and eighteenth-century clergy seem to have had no worse a record in attracting their parishioners

[131] LPL MS 1134/2, fo. 122, Waterhouse to Secker, 17 June 1758.
[132] LPL MS 1134/1, fo. 33.   [133] Ch. Ch. MS Wake Visitation Returns C, fo. 73.
[134] Ch. Ch. MS Wake Visitation Returns B, fo. 614.   [135] LPL, MS 1134/4, fo. 212.
[136] Clark, *English Provincial Society*, 150.

to Sunday worship. Indeed several ministers claimed to attract the whole community to Sunday service.[137] Certainly the presence of non-attenders would vary according to the circumstances of the individual parish, and the abilities of the individual incumbent. It was easier for the clergy in the smaller rural parishes to obtain full attendance than in the towns. John Denne, the perpetual curate of Maidstone, replied to Secker in 1758:

Your Grace's diligent observation and long experience will naturally point out the reason why the inhabitants of large and populous parishes are more in danger of being corrupted than those small districts. They believe themselves here more at liberty because they are not, nor can possibly be, so well known. I can say with great truth that the higher ranks of people are religiously disposed . . . and I apprehend that the corruption of the lower orders is owing to that spirit of licentiousness, which reigns particularly in this place at all Parliamentary elections. The magistrates have it in their power to prevent much of this corruption by taking a proper care in licensing alehouses.[138]

Yet even in the larger and more populous parishes of the diocese it was possible for some incumbents to whittle down the number of non-attenders. The vicar of Folkestone reported in 1758 that the 'meanest are absent . . . bred up in ignorance and brutality . . . [but] lessened by two thirds since I came by my diligence in visiting the sick and poor and relieving their wants'.[139]

CELEBRATIONS OF THE EUCHARIST

The clearest division between town and country parishes in this period can be seen in the frequency with which the Eucharist was celebrated. Norman Sykes's view that, outside London and the major provincial cities, celebrations rarely rose above four times a year, ignores the fact that many smaller towns were able to achieve a rather higher rate (see Table 4).[140] Traditional interpretations of the relative infrequency of celebrations in the eighteenth century, at least when compared to the post-Tractarian situation, have emphasized the small part which the Eucharist played in Anglican worship in the Age of Reason: a feature of latitudinarian Churchmanship which was to change in the nineteenth century.[141] It is becoming increasingly clear, however, that conventional understanding of 'latitudinarianism' needs modification. As F. C. Mather has demonstrated, moderate High-Church

---

[137] For example, LPL MS 1134/4, fos. 161 (Smarden), 165 (Snargate), 231 (Thanington).
[138] LPL MS 1134/3, fo. 65.   [139] LPL MS 1134/2, fo. 100.
[140] Sykes, *Church and State*, 250–1, 253.   [141] Russell, *Clerical Profession*, 100–3.

TABLE 4. *Services in the Diocese of Canterbury (Percentage of Those Known)*

	Catechism		Divine service			Celebrations of Eucharist			
	All year	Lent	1 time	2 times	less than 4 times	4 times	5–8 times	9–12 times	More than 12 times
1716	29.1	52.9	45.2	30.3	20.8	41.7	16.0	3.4	6.9
1758	17.8	63.9	55.6	43.4	4.3	72.0	9.5	6.9	6.5
1806	5.6	47.0	53.0	35.0	2.6	67.0	4.3	6.5	6.9

Figures compiled from: 1716: Ch. Ch. MS Wake Visitation Returns A; 1758: LPL MS 1134/1–4; 1806: LPL MS VG 3/2/a–d.

views remained an essential part of eighteenth-century Anglicanism and the Eucharist retained a prominent position in the religion of Church of England clergy. It may very well have been that the infrequency of the Eucharist only served to highlight its importance.[142]

As far as attracting parishioners to take communion was concerned, there is little doubt that the Restoration clergy saw the effects of the Interregnum as disastrous. The 'Sheldon Catalogue' of 1663 and the returns to the Compton Census of 1676 gave some impression of the difficulties involved. Time and again clergy reported that although most of their parishioners attended the usual Sunday services, they were very reluctant to attend communion. At Wickhambreux in 1663 'not a quarter of them come to Communion, though most go to Church'.[143] The vicar of St Lawrence, Thanet wrote in 1676, 'though the most part of ye 1200 come constantly to the Church to prayers and sermon, yet few of them will be induced to receive the Communion by any arguments or perswasions'.[144] Many clergy compared this with a mythical pre-Civil War past when all parishioners received communion. At Cranbrook and Alkham, for instance, the incumbents claimed that numbers of communicants were not as great as they used to be.[145] Some recent historians would support the Restoration clergy's picture of a decline in the number of communicants, arguing that the Church under Laud in the 1630s had achieved a far better result.[146]

---

[142] F. C. Mather, 'Georgian Churchmanship Reconsidered: Some Variations in Anglican Public Worship, 1714–1830', *JEH*, XLX (1985), 282.

[143] LPL MS 1126, fo. 13.　　[144] CCAL, H/Z, fo. 195.　　[145] Ibid., fos. 15, 55.

[146] C. Haigh, 'The Church of England, the Catholics and the People', in id. (ed.), *The Reign of Elizabeth I* (1985), 169–220. J. Boulton, 'The Limits of Formal Religion: The Administration of Holy Communion in late Elizabethan and Early Stuart London', *London Journal*, 10 (1984), 136–49 discusses the use of attendance rotas and communion tokens to achieve this.

Although it seems likely that the Laudian regime was successful in bringing a larger number of parishioners to communion it does not mean that
this was approved by all. The argument that Laudian Churchmanship went
hand in hand with a form of popular parish Anglicanism will only hold if it
is made clear which aspects of Anglican worship were liked.[147] Certainly,
much Anglican worship had been highly esteemed: the sermons and services performed every Sunday had become, by the 1640s, so much a part of
the religious life of the nation that, in many areas of the country, they continued in some form or other throughout the 1640s and 50s, leading to the
riot on behalf of Anglican Christmas services in Canterbury in 1647.[148] In
any case, the evidence is problematic. John Lewis's survey of the diocese,
written in the 1730s, noted the high number of 'communicants' in 1640, but
it is more likely that this records the numbers of possible communicants or
people over sixteen, not the actual receivers.[149]

The Restoration clergy found the resumption of the sacrament one of
their hardest tasks. Even at the cathedral it was not until 1683 that the
Eucharist was given a regular weekly celebration, in response to pressure
from Sancroft who wanted this to be the norm in every cathedral in the land
as part of a campaign against the growth of dissent and immorality.[150] Dean
Tillotson, who was responsible for putting these demands into practice, informed the archbishop:

As to the Rubrick concerning communion in Cathedral Churches every Sunday, I
moved it last week to the Chapter, and we resolved to begin it next month, which was
as soon as we could engage a convenient number of our communicants, and I am
very glad your Grace designs it throughout ye province, because it is plainly required, and will I doubt not be of good example, and of great efficiency to promote
piety.[151]

Tillotson is often portrayed as the archetypal latitudinarian, unimpressed
by the outward forms of devotion, yet his latitudinarianism could embrace
a commitment to regular communion. In 1683 he published his popular
*Persuasive to Frequent Communion in the Holy Sacrament of the Lord's
Supper* in which he accounted for the reluctance to take communion by the

---

[147] A. Hughes, *The Causes of the English Civil War* (1991), 178 argues for the deep commitment to episcopacy and the Book of Common Prayer. See the discussion in Davies, *Caroline
Captivity*, 243–5.
[148] Everitt, *Community of Kent*, 230–40.   [149] LPL MS 1125.
[150] Bodl. MS Tanner 123, fo. 80, Thorp to Sancroft, 17 Oct. 1683.
[151] Bodl. MS Tanner 34, fo. 176, Tillotson to Sancroft, 11 Oct. 1683. Similar efforts were
made in other cathedrals to obtain a weekly sacrament. For Archbishop Dolben's efforts at
York in 1685 see *VCH, Yorkshire, The City of York*, 351.

Reformation stress on the dangers of receiving it unworthily, which had encouraged people not to receive it at all. He concluded:

I doubt not but it hath been a thing of very bad consequence to discourage men so much from the sacrament, as the way hath been of late years: and that many men who were under some kind of check before, since they have been driven away from the sacrament, have quite let loose the Reins, and prostituted themselves to all manner of impiety and vice. We exclaim against the Church of Rome with great impatience, and with a very just indignation, for robbing the people of half this Blessed Sacrament, and taking from them the cup of Blessing, the cup of Salvation: and yet we can patiently endure for some months, nay years, to exclude ourselves wholly from it.[152]

While dean of Canterbury, Tillotson received some savage criticism for his policies of moderation towards dissenters and for his supposed betrayal of Anglican orthodoxy, allegedly revealed in his famous observation to Prebendary William Beveridge, 'Doctor, doctor, charity is better than rubrics'.[153] In 1683 the writer of a pamphlet, *Some Select Queries humbly Offered to the Consideration of the Dean of Canterbury*, attacked Tillotson as a betrayer of Church of England principles and expressly blamed him for 'defacing the Altar piece of his own Cathedral, for fear of offending tender consciences'.[154] The dean mentioned the incident in a letter to the High Churchman Robert Nelson, whose best-selling *Festivals and Fasts* (1704) was a manual for Anglican worship. 'We only took down the sun over the screen behind the communion table which was done with so little noise that several days passed before it was taken notice of to be remov'd; and nothing done besides, not so much as the Table stirr'd out of its place.'[155] By the early eighteenth century it was also common for the sacrament to be celebrated once a month in the towns in the diocese, with an extra celebration at the major festivals. This was the case for most of the Canterbury parishes: Ashford, Cranbrook, Deal, Faversham, Folkestone, Maidstone, Sandwich, and Tenterden, conforming to Sancroft's Injunctions of 1688 which required the sacrament to be celebrated once every month in greater towns.[156]

[152] John Tillotson, *A Persuasive to Frequent Communion in the Holy Sacrament of the Lord's Supper* (1683), 69.

[153] Birch, *Tillotson*, 131.

[154] *Some Select Queries Humbly offered to the Consideration of the D—n of C—t—b—y* (1683).

[155] BL Add. MS 4236, fo. 223, Tillotson to Nelson, 19 Oct. 1680.

[156] Ch. Ch. MS Wake Visitation Returns A, fos. 59, 67, 80 (Canterbury parishes), 88 (Ashford), 103 (Cranbrook), 141 (Folkestone), 289 (Deal), 307 (Sandwich), 395 (Maidstone), 129 (Tenterden).

It was one of the aims of the Church in this period to make the communion service better understood and better attended. The vicar of Dymchurch admitted in 1676 that 'we have too many who neglect to come to ye
Communion'.[157] These were as much the object of clerical attention in the
diocese during Sancroft's Anglican revival as were the dissenters. Giles
Hinton told Sancroft in 1685:

> this year I presented four people for not coming to Holy Communion. They are men
> not formidable, otherwise than that they are old, and in this point most pernicious
> examples. I cannot follow them now as I would, but hope that in yr Grace's courts,
> effectual course may be taken that they be no longer hinderers of that Reformation
> that is begun among the younger sort.[158]

Much of the SPCK's activity was directed to this end. The packets of
pamphlets and tracts which were issued, via the corresponding members,
to various clergy in the diocese, were mainly concerned with explaining the
importance and necessity of attending the communion, especially to the
poor. Samuel Weller thanked the Society for printing tracts that could be
easily understood, 'as he is a great enemy to all voluminous writers upon
ye sacrament, so he was very much pleased to find such short and plain
treatises . . .'.[159]

The distribution of such pamphlets did not necessarily bring about any
perceptible change in the religious habits of parishioners. 'It is a great uneasiness to me in the discharge of my duties', the incumbent of Halstow
confessed to Wake, 'that after the greatest pains I can take, both in preaching and private admonition, my parishioners still neglect sending their
children to catechism and themselves to sacrament.'[160] Thomas William-
son, rector of St Dunstan's, Canterbury, resigned himself to the fact that, 'I
being a very old man . . . I take all the pains I can to win the souls to Christ
. . . I am heartily sorry that all my pains will not prevail with some to take
their Saviour in the sacrament.'[161] Many clergy, especially in the rural
parishes, claimed that they were willing to celebrate the sacrament more
often than four times a year, but that there was no possibility of getting any
communicants. Some found that several of the poorer parishioners refused
to attend the sacrament because they thought it not for them. John Johnson
was concerned by the 'false and superstitious notions which were one
reason for the backwardness of the people' which meant that there were
'still a great number of men well advanced in years who have never received

---

[157] CCAL, H/Z, fo. 61.
[158] Bodl. MS Tanner 124, fo. 48, Hinton to Sancroft, 29 Aug. 1685.
[159] SPCK, CR 1/14/4391214.   [160] Ch. Ch. MS Wake Visitation Returns A, fo. 326.
[161] Ibid., fo. 63.

the Sacrament'.[162] The reluctance of various sections of the parish to communicate was noticed by Secker: 'Some imagine that the sacrament belongs only to persons of advanced years, or great leisure, or high attainment in religion and it is a very dangerous thing for common people to venture on.'[163] In 1758 William Marsh, the vicar of Bapchild, bemoaned the fact that the lower orders stayed away from communion:

(I) beg leave to mention to your Grace, the great ignorance of the lower sort of people, and servants, in religious matters, not only indeed in this, but in all other parishes in this country, in which I have ever been concerned. There is hardly one in three, that I have ever met with, that knows who Jesus Christ is, and the need and design of his coming into the world, and servants, almost in general, are so ignorant of the Christian Religion as to think the HC calculated only for their masters and mistresses; it being very rare to see any of that sort at HC . . .

He administered the sacrament four times a year, 'and about ⅓ of the parish, householders generally receive it, and 10 or 12 other persons, but not many servants'.[164] The vicar of Sheldwich in 1720 picked out 'young, single persons' as those most reluctant to take communion.[165]

The clergy themselves were, perhaps, in part responsible for this situation. It was their insistence on the importance of the sacrament and their injunctions that parishioners should take it seriously which led sections of the parish to feel that they were unworthy to receive. George Berkeley, for many years vice-dean at the cathedral, warned his parishioners of the need to come to sacrament fully prepared: 'as (in respect of our natural food) it will as infallibly destroy any one of you to abstain from all food as to eat poison, so (in this case) it will be equally fatal to you, never to receive the Holy Communion as to come to it unprepared.'[166]

Other clergy stressed the momentous nature of the Eucharist. In 1682 the vicar of St Clement's, Sandwich wanted to move the communion table to the east end, because of the way in which the sacrament was 'prophanized', and the vicar of Elmstead in 1728 wished that the communion table was railed off, for the more decent administration of the rite.[167] John Johnson told Wake of the need to reassert communion as a badge of Church membership:

---

[162] Johnson, *Vade Mecum*, 195.   [163] Secker, *Charges*, 60.
[164] LPL MS 1134/1, fo. 34.   [165] Ch. Ch. MS Wake Visitation Returns B, fo. 638.
[166] Berkeley, *Sermons*, 89–90.
[167] The example of St Clement's, Sandwich is quoted in Woodruff, 'The Records of the Courts of the Archdeaconry and Consistory Court of Canterbury', 123; Ch. Ch. MS Wake Visitation Returns D, fo. 177.

I rejoice to understand that your Grace is disposed to revive Discipline; I take it for granted, that you mean true Primitive Discipline, without respect of persons, which in truth is the destruction of it. Now the first step towards this most Glorious end, I humbly conceive to be this, that the absolute necessity of communion with the Church to all that live within the pale of it, be universally pressed on the consciences of men. For if communion be not absolutely necessary to salvation, then excommunication can be no real punishment, nor can there be sufficient reason for men to undergo just penances for the regaining the communion, when they are deprived of it. Formal penance, and a capias are indeed a sort of punishment, but civil rather than spiritual, and they have but a very weak tendency to real Reformation, which I take to be the chief end of true discipline.[168]

Part of the way in which 'primitive discipline' could be demonstrated was by refusing the sacrament to those whom the clergy felt were unworthy. The Prayer Book recommended that parishioners wanting to take communion should send their names to the minister so that some kind of check could be made. This was not often practised in the diocese. As the rector of Frittenden explained to Wake, 'I must confess that I am so well pre-acquainted with my communicants that I trust I do conscientiously administer to such as have Christian disposition, and have prepared themselves to come to communicate with me without danger of receiving notorious sinners'.[169] Johnson himself acknowledged that he had never publicly expelled anyone from communion, but had 'privately admonished one or two to abstain, and they have accordingly absented themselves, and have again returned to Communion, after they had removed the scandals which were the occasion of my admonition'.[170]

Johnson aroused some controversy within the diocese for his *Unbloody Sacrifice* (1713), a work which stressed the 'proper' nature of the sacrifice at the Eucharist. Another incumbent, Thomas Wise, retaliated, arguing that Johnson's ideas represented the 'boldest step to Popery since the Reformation'.[171] Johnson's views were more fully taken up by later non-jurors, and although many Anglicans attacked what they considered to be the

[168] Ch. Ch. MS Wake Visitation Returns A, fo. 103. See his description of the erection of the altar in Bodl. MS Ballard 15, fo. 93, 14 Jan. 1710.

[169] Ch. Ch. MS Wake Visitation Returns A, fo. 109.   [170] Ibid., fo. 103.

[171] Johnson's work had been written partly against Thomas Wise's *The Christian Eucharist Rightly Stated* (1711). Wise responded in *The Christian Eucharist No Proper Sacrifice* (1714), 7, 9. Lewis wrote against Johnson: *The Bread and Wine in the Holy Eucharist Not A Proper, Material, Propitiatory Sacrifice* (1714) and id., *A Vindication of the Right Reverend the Lord Bishop of Norwich from the Undeserved Reflections of the Revd. Mr John Johnson* (1714). Thomas Brett supported Johnson in his *The Christian Altar and Sacrifice. A Sermon shewing that the Lord's Table is the Proper Altar, and the Sacrament of the Eucharist a Proper Sacrifice* (1713).

popish elements in his work, his stress on the centrality of the Eucharist to Anglican worship was generally shared.[172]

A constant question asked by archbishops of their diocesan clergy concerned the frequency of celebration and the numbers of communicants. Secker was particularly insistent on this point, and put pressure on incumbents to celebrate more frequently in the hopes of attracting more communicants.[173] Several rural parishes increased the number of times that the sacrament was offered, and it is also necessary to remember that when clergy reported that they celebrated the sacrament only four times this could mean that there were two Sundays at each of the major festivals which gave parishioners more chance to communicate.[174] The rector of Sandhurst maintained in 1786:

I now administer the sacrament once every six weeks; it used to be only 4 times a year; but being concerned to find very many deaf ears to my repeated calls, and hoping that something might happen to awaken them from their lethargy, and a present alarm of conscience might incite in them a desire of receiving Holy Sacrament, I thought it might answer a good end . . .[175]

He was able to add that the number of communicants had risen from thirty-two to forty-nine during the four years of his incumbency. The small rural parish of Bicknor, which had a quarterly celebration in 1758, had a monthly celebration in 1806.[176]

All clergy found the laity more reluctant to communicate than to attend divine worship and the often-quoted figures for attendance at communion in 1676 obtained by Francis Nicholson, the perpetual curate of Goodnestone-by-Wingham, were the product of a particular social situation and should not be seen as representative.[177] His list of 281 parishioners was headed by the Hales family and it is significant that both Nicholson and Sir Edward Hales declared themselves to be Roman Catholic when James II became king in 1685.[178] Nicholson had been a pupil of Obadiah Walker, the notorious master of University College, Oxford. His pastoral diligence succeeded in winning over to the Church a number of dissenters within the parish, but, as Peter Laslett has pointed out, the presence of a powerful and dominant family like the Haleses must have placed a

[172] *Reminiscences of the Reverend George Gilbert (1796–1874)*, ed. F. J. Shirley, ([Canterbury], 1938), 32.

[173] See his comments in LPL, VG 2/5, s.v. Hinxhill, Halstow, Hartlip, Milstead, Murston, Warden.

[174] This is similar to the 'staggering' at Cranbrook in the late sixteenth century: Collinson, 'Cranbrook and the Fletchers', 174.

[175] LPL, VG 3/1/a, fo. 585.   [176] Ibid., MS 1134/1, fo. 73; ibid., VG 3/2/a, fo. 51.

[177] CCAL, H/Z, fo. 82.   [178] Wood, *Athenae Oxonienses*, iv. 449.

great deal of social pressure on parishioners to attend the Established Church.[179] The Haleses were the leading landowners in the area, owning most of the land in the parish. In this respect Goodnestone conformed to the model of a village parish in which the combination of priest and squirearchy maintained the dominance of the Church of England. But such villages were more a feature of the Midlands than the South-East in the eighteenth century and few Kent parishes were true villages in this sense, many of them being closer, in origin, to small market towns. Nicholson reported that 128 parishioners communicated at the Easter communion in 1676, seven more had a sufficient reason for not attending, such as sickness, 'melancholy', or being away in London. He listed several who did not have any sufficient reason, two of whom had promised to communicate at the next celebration. Nicholson added that he had excluded William Wanstal from communicating because of his 'notorious drunkenness'. Apart from two Independents, the rest of the parish were too young to communicate, or 'else have not sufficient Christian knowledge to be communicants'. Nicholson's impressive achievement must be placed alongside parishes such as Smarden where less than 3 per cent of the parish were communicants.[180]

WORSHIP IN THE CATHEDRAL

Setting a standard for religious practice and providing the central focus for Anglican worship in the city and locality were seen as two of the major functions of the cathedral in this period. In the early years of the Restoration Archbishop Sheldon argued that 'our Cathedrals are the standard and Rule to all parochial churches of the solemnity and decent manner of reading the liturgy and administering the Holy Sacrament' and that if these were not well done it would be to the 'offense of some of our friends, the advantage of sectaries, and [the Church's] own just reproach'.[181] The weekly sacrament at the cathedral attracted a congregation from all over the city, providing a centrepiece for lay piety. Edward Hasted noted that 'on Sundays, when the altar is dressed up for the sacrament, it is covered with costly and splendid plate'.[182]

It is clear that the standards of cathedral worship were higher and the continuation of High-Church liturgical practices more thorough than the

[179] Laslett, *World We have Lost*, 91–2.   [180] CCAL, H/Z, fo. 174.
[181] Bodl. MS Tanner 282, fo. 65, Sheldon to Seth Ward, 4 June 1670.
[182] Hasted, *History of Kent*, xi. 372.

Church's later detractors claimed. At Canterbury a series of conscientious deans ensured that cathedral services were regularly performed. Tillotson, Stanhope, Friend, Moore, and Horne were all concerned with this aspect of their office, and Canterbury also gained a reputation for its good preachers. There was something of a debate in the period concerning the proper place for cathedral preaching. In the early seventeenth century sermons had usually been delivered in the Chapter House, which was known in consequence as the Sermon House. This was not liked by Laud, who thought the separation of preaching from liturgical worship a Puritan practice. He attempted to stop it and aroused some hostility. At the Restoration Meric Casaubon reiterated the potential danger of this separation of sermon and service which might encourage the 'prattlings of enthusiasts'. 'I conceive it to be one main reason that so few are acquainted, and by consequence, not more in love, with the service', he wrote.[183] And so, after the Restoration, the Sermon House was abandoned. Some Low-Church clergy in the diocese wanted the practice to be resurrected. John Lewis suggested to Archbishop Wake in 1716 that preaching in the cathedral would improve if this was done:

the Quire is very ill contrived for any considerable auditory, and that Venerable Body have thought fit for a long time to disuse the Sermon House commonly so called tho' a most commodious place for divine worship, and where on Sundays, morning prayer and preaching might be used without prejudice to the Cathedral service.[184]

Preachers' books indicate how far Anglican liturgical tradition was maintained at Canterbury. The cathedral was decorated for the major Church festivals, rosemary and bay being used at Christmas, with incense in the organ loft.[185] Sermons were regularly preached on the anniversaries of the great days within the history of the Church and nation: 30 January, the anniversary of Charles I's execution, when the pulpit was decked in mourning; 29 May, marking the accession of Charles II; and 5 November, the failure of the Gunpowder Plot and the arrival of William of Orange. During the Restoration period, probably while Turner was dean, a portrait of Charles I as martyr was placed in the choir.[186] These festivals were kept up throughout the eighteenth century: they became absorbed within the

---

[183] Meric Casaubon, *The Question to whom it Belonged Anciently to Preach* (1663), 2.

[184] Ch. Ch. MS Wake Visitation Returns A, fo. 434.

[185] CCAL, Preachers' Books, 1712–1766; 1767–1822; 1822–7; ibid, Treasurer's Book, 1669–70, fo. 37. This was a traditional form of decoration at Christmas. Pepys observed these as unusual decorations at the first Christmas after 1660: *Diary of Samuel Pepys*, i. 321, 23 Dec. 1660.

[186] Legg and Hope, *Inventories*, 281.

tradition of Whig High Anglicanism, providing a framework for Anglican piety, and helping to give a sense of tradition and permanence to the cathedral's activities. These anniversaries could be used to make political points: in 1723 Isaac Terry used the anniversary of Charles I's martyrdom to warn of the dangers of mixing with seditious persons, and to portray Charles as 'an illustrious example to his subjects of genuine piety.'[187]

The dignity and splendour of Canterbury services was noted by various commentators from John Evelyn in 1665, Celia Fiennes in 1697, to Viscount Torrington in the 1790s. George Berkeley was highly impressed by the service performed at Archbishop Cornwallis's primary visitation in 1770.

An honest scriptural sermon from Dr Tanner, expressly teaching the eternal power and Godhead of Jesus. The very finest anthem I ever heard; nothing like it did I ever hear even in the King's Chapel. At the entrance of the choristers into the choir, when the Archbishop was yet at the Western door, the organ joined the voices of all choristers, singing men and minor canons, thro' their melodious lanes the Canons, Dean, Archbishop and Bishop of Peterborough passed along . . .[188]

Dean Horne in particular was a stickler for seeing that such liturgical and musical standards were maintained. He wrote to Berkeley in 1788:

the anti-Laudian spirit on the subject of caps, hoods and surplices, I find is not yet extinct; But the spirit has exerted itself in a more serious way at Lambeth for our metropolitan, I hear, has lost all his plate: some fanatics or socinians have broken through the wall.[189]

What is striking about the liturgical concerns of the Canterbury chapter in the eighteenth century is the presence of prebendaries, who, far from typifying what historians have rather derogatively labelled 'the age of latitudinarianism', actively practised High-Church ideals. They are a testimony to the fact that there was an unbroken tradition of High-Church devotion and spirituality stretching from the Caroline divines of the early seventeenth century to the Oxford Movement.[190] It may be that eighteenth-century pre-Oxford Movement Churchmen were able to follow such ideals with

---

[187] Isaac Terry, *The Religious and Loyal Subject's Duty Consider'd, with regard to the present Government and the Revolution. A Sermon Preached in the Cathedral Church of Canterbury, on Wednesday, January 30, 1723. Being the Anniversary Fast of the Martyrdom of King Charles I* (1723).

[188] BL Add. MS 39311, fo. 272, Berkeley to Mrs Berkeley, 9 July 1770.

[189] BL Add. MS 39312, fo. 79, Horne to Berkeley, 13 Oct. 1788. The standard view of the 'dullness' of eighteenth-century worship is represented by H. Davies, *Worship and Theology*, iii. (Oxford, 1961), 38–75.

[190] On this point more generally see Nockles, 'Continuity and Change in Anglican High Churchmanship', *passim*.

less hostility than their successors. Prebendary Gilbert, for instance, re-membered hearing Archbishop Manners Sutton preaching a sermon in the cathedral in 1806 at his primary visitation on the subject of confession and its history, which by the mid-nineteenth century, he felt, would have seemed 'very popish'.[191]

The concern to tighten up the standards of liturgical practice may, how-ever, have had the effect of alienating some members of the public from cathedral life and worship. Various injunctions were made by the dean and chapter to regularize the behaviour not only of the choristers and minor canons but also of the public, who, at least in the first half of the period, seem to have treated the nave as a public meeting-place. This mirrors evi-dence from other cathedrals: in Durham in 1681 the chapter were irritated by children frolicking in the cloisters and playing cards on the altar.[192] At Canterbury there were complaints of the unruly behaviour and noise of the 'rabble' and of women walking about in 'pattens' during services. In 1712 the dean and chapter instructed its officers to 'prevent all rudeness and noyse by walking and talking in the Body and Isles of the Church in time of divine service and women bringing children with them unless they keep them quiet, and not suffer any Burden to be carry'd through the Church or make it a common thoroughfare'.[193] This did not mean, however, that the cathedral services, especially on Sundays, became divorced from the life of the city, only attended by a select group. The dean and chapter tried to en-courage attendance by making the times of services more convenient. In 1722, for instance, evening prayer was moved to three o'clock except in the summer.[194] In 1786 the rector of St Alphege's made a comment which illustrates the place of the cathedral within Canterbury life: 'Many persons in this town go to the Cathedral in the morning, to the Presbyterian meet-ing in the afternoon and to a Methodist meeting at night.'[195] This function of the cathedral at Canterbury, providing a model for services throughout the city and diocese, was advanced by members of the chapter against criti-cism in the 1820s and 30s: they argued that without the guidance and in-spiration of cathedral worship, parish worship would soon die out.[196]

---

[191] Gilbert, *Reminiscences*, 10.
[192] Quoted by K. V. Thomas, 'Children in Early Modern England', in G. Avery and J. Briggs (eds.), *Children and Their Books: A Collection of Essays to Celebrate the Work of Iona and Peter Opie* (Oxford, 1989), 68.
[193] CCAL, Chapter Act Book, 1711–26, fo. 14.
[194] Ibid., fo. 116.   [195] LPL, VG 3/1/a, fo. 241.
[196] George Pellew, *A Letter to the Right Honourable Sir Robert Peel. Bt. M.A. on the Means of 'Rendering Cathedral Churches More Conducive to the Efficiency of the Established Church'* (1837), 6-8, 32-7.

This survey of services offered in the diocese during the long eighteenth century has suggested the variety of practice which existed. The most significant difference seems to have been between rural and urban parishes; towns in the diocese were more likely to have a higher number of communion services as well as maintaining traditions of weekly services. It is thus misleading to suggest that the stronghold of Anglicanism in this period was the rural parish, while towns were more attractive to nonconformity.[197] Both nonconformity and Anglicanism prospered in an urban context and clergy indeed seem to have preferred to live in a town, even when they were beneficed to a nearby rural parish. The image of a rural idyll was not always shared by clergy in this century and they pleaded the unhealthiness of some rural areas and the need to send their children to good schools (as well as the company and stimulus to be derived from living near other clergy) as reasons why they preferred the town to the country. Secker pointed out to one incumbent that 'I greatly disapprove the custom which is growing very common place amongst clergymen that they quit their parishes, for a more sociable life in market towns'.[198] If Anglicanism was able to achieve notable success in rural parishes where squire and incumbent worked together on behalf of the Church, it could achieve comparable results elsewhere.

MONITORING THE PARISH: THE VISITATION PROCESS

The principal method by which archbishops monitored their diocesan clergy and advised them on pastoral matters was through the enquiries delivered before the visitation, the correspondence which was then produced, and the meetings with the clergy during the visitation tour. Through the collection of information concerning the state of the parishes, the numbers of services offered, the numbers of attenders, relations with dissenters, and the upkeep of the church fabric, they hoped to keep a firm eye on the pastoral outlook and activities of their clergy. The visitation itself gave archbishops the opportunity to address the clergy, drawing particular attention to current pastoral concerns. In some cases they were also an occasion for pronouncing on theological imperatives. In 1728, for instance, Wake took the opportunity to confront the vogue for anti-Trinitarian theology. He maintained that although such heterodox doctrines had been ably defeated by works of learned scholarship, the real work was to be done at the parish

---

[197] Gilbert, *Religion and Society*, 109–10.
[198] LPL MS Secker 3, fo. 225, Secker to Weller, 19 Apr. 1763.

level, in convincing parishioners of the centrality of the Trinity.[199] These archiepiscopal charges were frequently printed and later circulated to the clergy of the diocese and elsewhere.

The visitation procedure and especially the reliance of archbishops on their clergy to give them an accurate picture of their diocese, was a product of this period. Although the system had medieval origins, queries in the six-teenth and seventeenth centuries were more often directed to the church-wardens, and it is an indication of the increasing homogeneity of the clerical profession during the eighteenth century that archbishops now saw the clergy as the best source of information. Despite the vast differences in the wealth of the hierarchy and the parish clergy, a growing common interest, explained by an increasingly similar clerical background and education, bound members of the profession together. This is reflected in the lines of communication used in the visitation procedure.

Wake has been given credit for developing this system whilst he was bishop in Lincoln.[200] He told the Canterbury clergy in 1716 that it was his 'constant practice' as bishop of that large diocese to send queries to the clergy and 'being now by God's providence called to a new diocese, with the circumstances where of I am utterly unacquainted, I have the more need to desire the like assistance from you'. He urged them to 'deal very freely, and plainly with me in your answers'.[201] Succeeding archbishops followed this method and the excellent series of visitation queries and returns which exist for the period between 1716 and 1806 give vivid insights into the prob-lems of the Church as they appeared to clerical eyes.[202]

It took several decades after the Restoration for the regular course of vis-itations to emerge in the Canterbury diocese. Research into the Restoration Church has stressed the slowness with which the diocesan machinery re-turned to full working order and it is clear that the archbishop's diocese was no exception to this general rule.[203] Although there had been an archi-diaconal visitation in 1662, it was not until the spring of 1663 that Juxon held his primary visitation; the old and infirm archbishop delegating the re-sponsibility to the bishop of Hereford and the vicar-general, Sir Richard Chaworth.[204] The information obtained by the hierarchy at this visitation

---

[199] Ch. Ch. MS Wake Visitation Queries, 1728, 1.   [200] Sykes, *Wake*, i. 174–6.

[201] Ch. Ch. MS Wake Visitation Queries, 1716.

[202] Juxon's metropolitical visitation: LPL, VG 4/23, 24; Sancroft's visitation of 1682: LPL, VG/4 25; Tenison's visitation of 1695: LPL, MS 954, fo. 61. Returns 1716, 1720, 1724, 1728 (Ch. Ch. MSS Wake 284–7; A, B, C, D); 1758 (LPL MS 1134/1–4), 1786 (LPL, VG 3/1/a–d); 1806 (LPL, VG 3/2/a–d). See also *Articles of Visitation and Enquiry to be answered into at the Visitation of Thomas Archbishop of Canterbury, 1706* (1706).

[203] Whiteman, 'Re-establishment', 111.   [204] CCAL, Z/4/7, fo. 198.

was probably tabulated in the Sheldon survey of 1663. Not surprisingly, the material reflects the concern of the Church in these early years; the quality of the parish clergy and their loyalty to the Establishment, the financial value of the parishes, the state of the churches, the presence of dissenters, and the proportion of the parish 'conformable' to the services of the church. The archbishop asked similar questions at the visitation of the cathedral which usually happened during the first days of the diocesan visitation. In 1663 fifteen queries were addressed to the dean and chapter: by the end of the seventeenth century these were standardized to twelve.[205]

Despite the impressive efforts of Sheldon and Sancroft in many areas of Church life, their record as far as holding regular visitations was concerned fell behind that of their eighteenth-century successors. In part this can be explained by their pressing duties in London: significantly both these archbishops had good correspondents in the diocese who could keep them informed of the state of the parishes. Sheldon did not hold a diocesan visitation, but there are draft articles of 1667.[206] Sancroft instigated a visitation of the diocese in 1682 and 1688, though he did not visit in person, on account of ill-health and imprisonment during the trial of the seven bishops. In 1682 the bishop of Norwich represented Sancoft, in 1688 the bishop of Sodor and Man. Some indication of the irregularity and seeming novelty of the system at that time was noted by George Thorp to Sancroft: 'I have been asked since I came hither what was the design of this visitation to which I had an easy reply: the same that is, or should be, of all others . . . to do what good you could . . . concerning the state of your diocese . . . It was further said . . . it was a new thing to them . . .'.[207] Some of the inefficiencies of the system were pointed out to Sancroft by William Lloyd: 'I cannot see how your Grace can be well informed of the state of your diocese, if the articles be delivered at the visitation.' Lloyd made some suggestions which would tighten up the system. By giving clergy time to respond to the enquiries, Lloyd added, archbishops would be able 'to apply the pastoral care where it was most needed'.[208]

Thomas Brett, who, as a later non-juror might be thought sympathetic to the Restoration archbishops, found in 1701 that the lack of a regular visitation procedure had created problems for pastoral effectiveness in the diocese:

---

[205] CCAL., Z/2/7, fo. 292.
[206] Sheldon's draft articles in Bodl. MS Tanner 125, fo. 33. Early seventeenth-century archbishops were not regular visitors either: Fincham, *Prelate as Pastor*, 57.
[207] Bodl. MS Tanner 33, fo. 202, Thorp to Sancroft, 13 Apr. 1682; LPL MS 954, fo. 61.
[208] Bodl. MS Tanner 125, fo. 69, Lloyd to Sancroft, 18 Mar. 1682.

And now may it not justly be thought a Blemish to our most excellent Reformation, that more care should be taken in the days of Popery for the edification of the Church by the due execution of all episcopal functions than we take of them now. Let me speak of the office of confirmation . . . Our Church esteems it at least a very useful ordinance, and which ought by no means to be neglected, and that there are thousands in the Kingdom who are at years of discretion, and yet never have had an opportunity of being confirmed. I do not speak this to reflect on any of my Lords the Bishops: I believe we never had more vigilant Pastors, and such as have been more careful and regular in the performance of this particular office. To speak with relation to that particular Diocese wherein I have had the happiness to be fixed from my childhood our former Archbishops have thought it sufficient once in seven years or thereabouts to send some other Bishop to visit and confirm for them; this was done by Archbishop Sancroft; others such as Archbishop Sheldon and Archbishop Tillotson have neither come themselves nor sent any other . . .[209]

Brett's High-Church allegiance did not stop him from being more favourable to Tenison, recognizing that the archbishop's Whig principles in no way militated against an interest in pastoral concerns. He noted that Tenison in 1695 had been the first archbishop to visit the diocese in person since the Restoration:

his present Grace of Canterbury, my very good Lord and Patron, has almost kept to the strict letter of the Canon, and visited us very frequently and performed the office of Confirmation with the greatest order and solemnity imaginable; not in a hurry or muddle as I have seen it done in some other places where hundreds have been confirmed by the Bishop that neither heard the exhortation made, nor gave any answer to the question put to them, and probably knew nothing of the matter. But his Grace, my present Lord Archbishop, caused the chancel-doors to be shut, and admitted the people parish by parish.[210]

Nevertheless there were still drawbacks:

It is a misfortune that his Grace's time only permits him to confirm at 4 or 5 principal Towns of his diocese; so that at least one half of the People could not be brought to receive ordinance. And if this be the case of a Diocese which is none of the largest, what shall we think of those that are four times as big . . . If my present Lord Archbishop, who had done more than any of his predecessors for these hundred years, has not been able to discharge this Duty as it ought to be done, surely it is reasonable to think that his see needs an assistant suffragan.[211]

From the start of the eighteenth century visitations were held in the diocese every four years. This pattern appears to have been broken only during the period between 1728 and 1737, when Wake was very ill. Former returns

---

[209] Brett, *Account of Church Government*, 243–4.
[210] Ibid., 244.   [211] Ibid., 245.

were particularly useful to an archbishop during the early months of his translation; they provided a way by which he could learn something about the diocese under his care. The archbishops did not treat the visitations as a mere formality; they saw them as a source of valuable intelligence and as a means of forging some kind of professional bond between the Church hierarchy and the parish clergy. Wake's plea for frankness from his clergy encouraged several of them, notably John Lewis and John Johnson, to point out deficiencies which could be remedied. Both were especially concerned with the problems of confirmation. Lewis complained that his parishioners on the Isle of Thanet had 'no opportunity of being confirmed anywhere nearer than Canterbury, which is 15 miles from this place which is too far to go and come in a day and poor people cannot be at the expense of lying a night from home'.[212] Records show that late-seventeenth-century archbishops or their delegates confirmed at only three or four centres: in 1682 at Canterbury, Ashford, Sittingbourne, and Maidstone, and in 1695 at Canterbury, Ashford, and Sittingbourne.[213] Lewis wanted more confirmation centres to make it easier for people to attend. He suggested Sittingbourne, Faversham, Canterbury, Minster, Sandwich, Elham, Ashford, New Romney, Dover, Tenterden, and Cranbrook. Johnson told Wake that

I am not indeed sensible that any of your Grace's predecessors did ever perform the office of confirmation here; but many now alive do well remember that Abp. Sancroft did send first Bp. Lloyd of Norwich and then Bp. Levinz of Man to confirm in this place, and Dr. Thorpe, who was the Abp.'s chaplain did attend Bp. Lloyd in his confirmation, has often told me that they had a very great number of persons here.

He felt that holding a confirmation service at Cranbrook was one way of combating dissent in the area.[214] The incumbent of Hawkhurst reminded Wake in 1716 that there had been 'no Archbishop or Bishop in these parts to confirm for the last sixteen years'.[215] Eighteenth-century archbishops realized the validity of these complaints and expanded their visitation tours accordingly. Lewis thanked Wake in 1720 for his kindness 'in consideration of our distance from Canterbury to appoint Minster to be one of the places of confirmation'.[216] By the mid-century it was customary for archbishops to confirm at ten or more centres in the diocese.

One concomitant of this improvement was that there was a rise in the numbers confirmed. Bishop Lloyd informed Sancroft in 1682 that only 200

---

[212] Ch. Ch. MS Wake Visitation Returns A, fo. 420.   [213] LPL MS 954, fo. 61.
[214] Ch. Ch. MS Wake 7, fo. 103, Johnson to Wake, 11 Feb. 1716.
[215] Ch. Ch. Visitation Returns A, fo. 113.
[216] Ch. Ch. MS Wake 8, fo. 239, Lewis to Wake, 12 May 1720.

people were confirmed at Ashford, at a time when there were only four places of confirmation: 'But I am sure that many more would have come if due notice had been given.'[217] In 1688 the bishop of Sodor and Man acting for Sancroft was reported to have confirmed at Canterbury for 3¾ hours 'at a rate of 300 an hour'.[218] Successive archbishops from Wake, Potter, Herring, Secker, Cornwallis to Moore tried to formalize the procedure. Tickets were issued beforehand to parish clergy who were instructed to give them out only to those who had satisfied them that they had a clear understanding of what the ceremony entailed. This was very necessary since, as Lewis noted, it could be a 'very disorderly ceremony'. He moaned to Wake that he had 'often had occasion to observe that our common people have by tradition too many of the principles of paganism and popery'. He observed that in the *Usum Sarum* godfathers were ordered to bring children to be confirmed at the age of seven and that at the Council of Trent this was changed to twelve. 'But this can never be the contention of our Church, who though it mentions no age in particular, demands that they be more than children and show clear understanding; not by rote as parrots and magpies talk and chatter, but to be sensible what a solemn law, promise and profession was made in their names.'[219] He raised the case of an old woman in the Isle of Thanet who thought that the purpose of confirmation was to give bishops the opportunity to 'prod the flock'.[220] Lewis's concern and efforts to improve this were noticed by Archbishop Potter who, when confirming at Minster, described it as 'the most orderly and regular which he had ever seen'.[221] By the mid-century archbishops confirmed between 7,000 and 10,000 people at each visitation, and in 1815 Manners Sutton confirmed a total of 15,268.[222] The vivid picture given by the wife of a new bishop who was assisting Archbishop Cornwallis in 1774 indicates the numbers involved: 'my bishop's hands are so greasy from the pomatum; he has confirmed about 200.'[223] Archbishops could find the ordeal taxing. Tenison complained of a pain in his hip and foot after the 1706 visitation and in 1758 the tour spurred on Secker's gout.[224]

The Church hierarchy tried to ensure that the physical structure of the parish churches was maintained as a result of the archidiaconal visitations.

[217] Bodl. MS Tanner 124 fo. 2, Lloyd to Sancroft, 4 May 1682.
[218] Bodl. MS Tanner 28, fo. 83.   [219] Ch. Ch. MS Wake 22, fo. 203, 16 May 1724.
[220] Ch. Ch. MS Wake 9, fo. 302, Lewis to Wake, 14 Mar. 1724.
[221] BL Add. MS 28651, fo. 6ᵛ.   [222] LPL, VB 1/ 14, 104.
[223] Quoted in D. M. Owen, *Records of the Established Church in England*, British Records Association (1970), 42.
[224] Bodl. MS Ballard 6, fo. 103, Gibson to Charlett, 20 June 1706; *Letters between Mrs Eliza Carter and Mrs Catherine Talbot*, ed. M. Pennington, 2 vols. (1808), ii. 275.

These occurred far more regularly than the archbishop's visitations, usually being held twice a year, in the Spring and Autumn. Whereas the archiepiscopal visitations brought the diocesan clergy together at various centres in the diocese, archdeacons, particularly at their initial visitation, were more likely to conduct a 'parochial visitation' and inspect each parish church and parsonage or vicarage in turn. This was by far the best way for the Church hierarchy to ascertain the state of church fabric; detailed lists were made of the shortcomings found in each building and the churchwardens and incumbents were responsible for seeing that repairs or defects were amended, presenting a certificate of completion to the archdeacon's court.

One of the aims of the Restoration hierarchy was to put right the defects, and in some cases the spoilation, which had occurred to parish churches during the Interregnum. This included both physical damage and loss of items essential for the resumption of Anglican services. The Sheldon survey recorded that as late as 1663 several parishes were wanting in this respect. A particular deficiency was the absence of a Book of Common Prayer. Juxon had written to the commissary general of the diocese in 1662 asking him to 'send word how many of the Books you shall have occasion to use within the diocese . . . that the services may be performed within the limited time'.[225] This referred to the duty of incumbents who were to conform to the Act of Uniformity in 1662, to use the liturgy of the Prayer Book. As archdeacon of Canterbury from 1668 to 1670 Sancroft showed keen interest in the upkeep of the diocesan churches, and as archbishop he continued this.[226] Another need in the Restoration period was to restore the Anglican baptism service. During the 1660s new fonts were built at Marden, Nonington, Ripple, St Mary's at Cliffe, and Walmer. In the years immediately following the Restoration cups and patens were also given for the sacrament. As late as the 1760s Archbishop Secker gave £8 to the chapel at Sheerness, for purchasing a proper set of plate and utensils for communion. Before that it had been borrowed from a nearby public house.[227]

The first extensive survey of the parish churches which has survived belongs to Archdeacon Green's parochial visitations between 1711 and 1715. These demonstrate the great variation in the upkeep of the churches. Several churches needed whitewashing, some rebuilding, and the east window

---

[225] LPL MS 116, fos. 9, 16, 17; CCAL, W/Z/1, Juxon to Bishops of the Province, 25 July 1662.

[226] For example, his comments in Bodl. MS Tanner 99.

[227] N. Pevsner, *The Buildings of England, North East Kent* (3rd edn., 1983), 93. For Secker's gift to Sheerness see Nichols, *Literary Anecdotes*, iii. 751.

of Holy Cross was 'much decayed', but others, such as Hackington, were described as 'handsome and in excellent order'. Green informed Tenison in 1715:

On Thursday next I intend to proceed on the remaining 15 parishes, having visited 55 the last fortnight. I shall then have finished the whole 214 parishes. I shall think my trouble and charge doubly recompensed by the good effects which I hope from it. Everybody is sensible of ye alteration it has produced in ye churches and houses, so great I believe I may without vanity say, yt as to ye former especially, there is no diocese in England will be to compare with yt of your Grace's for the cleaness and decency of them. It has raised an ambition in the parishes of striving which shall make their churches finest . . .[228]

Similar records survive for surveys in 1751, by Archdeacon Head, who mounted an exhaustive enquiry into church fabric. In 1753 the archdeacon again held a parochial visitation. He commented that 'in general, the Churches and Houses within the Archdeaconry are put into good and decent repair, as appears by the returns that are made to the orders I gave at my parochial visitation'.[229] Archdeacon Backhouse conducted a parochial visitation in 1772, and Archdeacon Lynch in 1792 and 1793. Archdeacon Houston Radcliffe followed a similar pattern in 1805 and 1813.[230]

Another pastoral tool which was developed in this period was the creation of parochial libraries.[231] These were to be maintained by incumbents and passed on intact to their successors. The libraries can be seen as part of the effort to improve the pastoral abilities of clergy in this century, equipping incumbents with the knowledge by which they could defend Anglican doctrines and giving them guidance in pastoral care. Although parochial libraries had been urged since the Reformation, it was not until the Parochial Libraries Act of 1709 that they were enabled and safeguarded by law. The Act specified strict rules: the libraries were intended for poor cures and poor incumbents, in the first instance to livings worth £30 or less. A supply of appropriate books would help and encourage clergy to catechize parishioners. The SPCK took a special interest in promoting them, giving to designated parishes books and a case, for a £5 premium. The next half century

---

[228] CCAL MS Z.3.34: Archdeacon Green's Visitation Book, 1711–1715; LPL MS 954, fo. 15, Green to Tenison, 21 Apr. 1715.

[229] LPL MS 1134; MS 1138, fo. 68.

[230] CCAL, Box Dioc. I, fos. 16, 25. The role of the archdeacon was similar in other dioceses: W. A. Pemberton, 'The Parochial Visitations of James Bickham, D.D., Archdeacon of Leicester in the Years 1773 to 1779', *Transactions of the Leicestershire Archaeological and Historical Society*, 59 (1984–5), 52–68; id., 'The Parochial Inspections of Andrew Burnaby, D.D., Archdeacon of Leicester, 1793–97', ibid., 63 (1989).

[231] Yates, 'Parochial Library of All Saints, Maidstone', 159–74.

saw the establishment of several such libraries in the diocese, through a mixture of donations from the SPCK and clerical bequests. Richard Foster, the rector of Crundale from 1698 to 1729, left a library for the benefice in his will. He declared that the revenues of the living were so small that 'they are not like to enable an incumbent decently to maintain himself and family and likewise purchase many useful books; I do therefore give and bequeath all my books . . . as a parochial library under the protection of the Statute of the 7th year of Queen Anne'.[232] The inventory reveals 195 folios, 161 quartos, and 464 octavos. Not surprisingly the library contained a large number of theological works, including editions of the Fathers in Greek and Latin, ecclesiastical history, and pamphlets concerning recent issues, especially the events of 1688–9. John Bowtell, the vicar of Patrixbourne, another poor living, bequeathed his library to his successors. Other parish libraries were founded at Detling, Doddington, Preston-by-Wingham, Thurnham, Maidstone, Faversham, and Elham. Most of these did not contain the range of works found in Foster's library; the books given by the SPCK were of a more practical nature, suitable for use in charity schools, and concerned with exhorting parishioners to attend communion and with the regulation of vices. At Maidstone, however, the incumbent Samuel Weller was successful in acquiring for the town a substantial portion of Thomas Bray's library. By 1740 a library for the use of religious societies and other well-disposed persons was established at Eastbridge Hospital in Canterbury.[233]

Archbishops, in their visitation enquiries, urged that the contents of these libraries should be well looked after, demanding that proper catalogues were kept up. Although only a handful of parishes within the diocese had a formal library, there are indications that other livings had some books, even if a much smaller number. Secker, for instance, commented on the books at Cranbrook.[234] And, of course, it was not necessary to have a formal library. A study of clerical wills from the diocese has revealed that most clergy had some religious or theological books in their possession, which might be lent out to interested parties.[235] The period also saw the growth of community libraries such as that at Margate which in 1790 had nearly 600 titles of sermons, a testimony to the popularity of religious and theological reading matter.[236] It was also possible for diocesan clergy to borrow books

---

[232] CCAL, Y/4/31: catalogue of Books.
[233] LPL MS Secker 3, fo. 150: 'A Catalogue of the Parochial Library of Detling, 10 November 1758'; fo. 153: 'Doddington'.
[234] LPL, VG 2/5, s.v. 'Cranbrook'.   [235] Ignjatijevic, 'Canterbury', 21.
[236] P. Kaufman, *Libraries and their Users: Essays in Library History* (1696), 173.

from the cathedral library. The cathedral was spending £600 p.a. on books by the early nineteenth century.[237] The close relationship which existed between Lambeth and Canterbury enabled the cathedral library to receive duplicate volumes from the archbishops' library, and some members of the dean and chapter encouraged parish clergy to borrow them. Archdeacon Lisle told Samuel Pegge, the antiquarian and vicar of Godmersham from 1731 to 1751, 'I have desired Mr Norris to send to you at any time such books of the library as you shall desire . . . and I think it very reasonable and proper that a collection of books should always be open for the assistance of any clergyman in the diocese, for the prosecution of his studies'.[238]

An enduring feature of the pastoral concern of the eighteenth-century clergy as revealed by the visitation process was that it was not the monopoly of any one brand of Churchmanship. During the early years of the eighteenth century, for instance, when religious parties were at their height, it is clear that the leaders of both the Whig and Tory clerical groupings shared a common interest in pastoral matters. Whatever the divisions between the laity, polarities between members of the clergy were not so clear-cut. Johnson recognized that the pastoral problems he faced in Cranbrook transcended politics. He told Wake,

I am sensible my enemies will impute all the hardships I am under to my disaffection (as they call it) to the present government, but it is true that my difficulties in serving the cure were well nigh as great in the reign of Her late Majesty; when my loyalty was not in the least questioned, as they are at present.[239]

The tragedy of party conflict in the Canterbury diocese was that it detracted from a uniform policy of pastoral reform. It is fashionable to suggest that clerical differences in this period were all embracing and to neglect the fact that their similarities were to prove just as important.[240] Both the Whig Lewis and the Tory Johnson submitted for Wake's consideration detailed proposals for reform. They both stressed the need for better pastoral oversight and for a uniform clerical policy on matters concerning relations with dissenters and with parishioners. Lewis complained to Wake:

The want of uniformity among the clergy occasions difficulties to a strict and regular clergyman. I have been often told of my neighbouring clergy their baptising in private houses according to the form of public baptism; of their marrying at Canterbury at any time, and I have been ensued as unnecessarily troublesome

[237] B. Botfield, *Notes on the Cathedral Libraries of England* (1849), 149.
[238] Bodl. MS Eng. d. 43, fo. 65, Lisle to Pegge, 18 Jan. 1738.
[239] Ch. Ch. MS Wake Visitation Returns A, fo. 104.
[240] Studies which concentrate on clerical differences along party lines include: G. Every, *The High Church Party, 1688–1718* (1956) and Speck, *Tory and Whig*.

because I would not do the same. The different ways of the clergy's praying before sermons, some using an exhortation to pray, others using a form of prayer is attended with ill consequences, to the very great prejudice of our ministry.[241]

Through visitation procedures, pastoral directives, and correspondence with individual clergy in their diocese, the archbishops attempted to procure a consistent pastoral front. No doubt this had always been part of archiepiscopal policy; it had clearly been dear to Laud's heart.[242] Nevertheless, the party divisions of the early eighteenth century made the need to find a common outlook and a common purpose even more pressing. Ralph Blomer, a Canterbury prebendary, wrote to Wake in 1716, 'May your Grace have the satisfaction of seeing us more and more united, and the honour of being the principal agent in so great and Christian a work!'[243] It was in large measure the pastoral concern of the eighteenth-century archbishops which united their clergy and served to soften clerical party rivalry. Linda Colley has suggested, in her attempt to demonstrate how far early eighteenth-century tensions were kept alive, that a vigorous promotion of pastoral issues was characteristic of the Tory opposition to the Whig regime. She is correct in seeing that the eighteenth-century clergy were by no means as pastorally uninvolved as traditional interpretations allow, but she is wrong to claim this as unique to the Tories.[244] The pastoral preoccupations of the post-Revolution and Hanoverian Church, headed by archbishops such as Tillotson, Tenison, Wake, Potter, Secker, Cornwallis, Moore, and Manners Sutton served to reconcile many clergy to the new regimes. The desire to improve the standard and frequency of parochial worship, the attempt to decrease the numbers of non-attenders at services, the importance placed on receiving the sacrament, the wish to extend parochial education, and the concern shown for the fabric of the churches were central aspects of Hanoverian Churchmanship. It would be greatly underestimating the task of the Church hierarchy to suggest that parish clergy fulfilled their obligations of the pastoral office without any prompting. Whilst some parish clergy were more aware of their pastoral concerns than were Church dignitaries, others had to be prodded into action. Part of the problem, as many clergy reiterated, was that ministers were often more popular amongst their parishioners if they did not appear to be too demanding. Moreover, parish clergy could resent what they felt to be undue interference by archbishops. Secker confided to one incumbent:

---

[241] Ch. Ch. MS Wake Visitation Returns A, fo. 427v. For Johnson: ibid., fos. 103–4.
[242] See H. R. Trevor-Roper, *Archbishop Laud, 1573–1645* (2nd edn., 1962), 145–210.
[243] Ch. Ch. MS Wake 6, fo. 176, Blomer to Wake, 20 Apr. 1716.
[244] Colley, *Defiance of Oligarchy*, 117, 154.

I hope all my clergy will come in a little time to understand that I desire to give only equitable directions and those to be equitably interpreted. Your admonition to me against the Temptation of Power is very kind. I have need to be admonished against all temptations, and shall be obliged to be admonished by those who are under my care for doing me that good office as they see occasionally hoping that they will permit me in my turn to do them the same. But if I know myself at all I am not desirous of exerting Power for the sake of exerting it, but only for the Discharge of the Trust committed to me.[245]

Criticism of the pastoral work of the Anglican clergy has usually been presented as coming from outside the Church. But it is clear that attempts to improve the pastoral role of the clergy came as strongly from within as it did from outsiders. Archbishop Howley, in 1832, paid tribute to the efforts of the previous half century to promote reforms within the Church which had improved its pastoral mission. In his eyes, the pastoral successes of the Anglican clergy in the diocese of Canterbury, from at least the 1780s, could be seen in the greater diffusion of scriptural knowledge and in the education of the poor. He was aware that 'the efficiency of the Church depends on the faithfulness and diligence of the parochial clergy', recognizing that 'in most cases, the state of the schools, the numbers prepared for confirmation, attending the services of the Church, and partaking of the Lord's supper, may be taken as a tolerable criterion of the ability and diligence of the pastor'.[246]

The Anglican pastoral system needed constant vigilance from archbishops and archdeacons. The information collected at visitations enabled conscientious archbishops to see where improvement was needed. As Secker remarked, 'custom is no reason for indulging what is wrong'.[247] Such pressure from the hierarchy to increase the pastoral commitments of their clergy continued that process of 'clerical professionalization' which has been analysed in the early seventeenth century and also has clear parallels with the aims of the Catholic hierarchy in eighteenth-century Europe.[248] The suggestion that in eighteenth-century France the long-term result of this pastoral enterprise was positive may well have been true of the diocese of Canterbury.[249] What is difficult to ascertain is the way in which parishioners responded to this educational endeavour. How far

[245] LPL MS Secker 3, fo. 202, Secker to Holdsworth, 9 Nov. 1758.
[246] Howley, *Charge*, 24–5.
[247] LPL MS Secker 3, fo. 253, Secker to Pomfret, 23 Oct. 1762.
[248] O'Day, *Profession*.
[249] R. Briggs, '*Ideés and Mentalités*: The Case of the Catholic Reform Movement in France', *History of European Ideas*, 7 (1986), 14. Also C. Langlois, *Le Diocèse de Vannes au xix siècle, 1800–1830* (Paris, 1974).

people's lives were changed by it; how far they were led to abandon old heterodoxies and superstitions, is hard to discover. Yet the essential truths of the Christian doctrine may have been better known by more parishioners at the end of the period than at the start. In the 1820s the majority of cottages in the parish of Hernehill contained a Bible, Prayer Book, or Anglican hymn book, whereas in the mid-seventeenth century it had been known for its illiterate and uneducated parishioners.[250] Christina Larner postulated a distinction between 'belief' and 'faith', whereby faith is a term used for an optional belief which needs education and instruction to sustain it.[251] It is possible to suggest that the pastoral strategies explored in this chapter represent the ways in which clergy and others were grappling towards an interpretation of faith which attempted to replace social and communal criteria for orthodoxy with individual and internal definitions founded on educated understanding.[252] Much has been written about the eighteenth century as a period of decline in faith.[253] It may be, however, that rather than supporting the case for de-christianization or secularization, the evidence presented here suggests that we are witnessing a change in the nature of faith, rather than an absolute decline. In the archbishops' efforts to exhort their clergy to fulfil their pastoral role and in clergy's struggles to educate their parishioners in a better understanding of Anglicanism, the Church of England was attempting to make the eighteenth century not into an age of reason, or of unreflecting belief, but into an age of faith.

---

[250] B. Reay, 'Last Rising of the Agricultural Labourers', 95.

[251] C. Larner, *Witchcraft and Religion. The Politics of Popular Belief* (Oxford, 1984), 21.

[252] Cf. C. J. Sommerville and J. Edwards, 'Debate: "Religious Faith, Doubt and Atheism"', *Past and Present*, 128 (1990), 152–61.

[253] For a classic statement on this theme see M. Vovelle, *Piété baroque et déchristianisation en Provence au xviiie siècle. les attitudes devant la mort d'aprés les clauses des testaments* (Paris, 1973) and id., *Religion et révolution: la déchristianisation de l'an ii* (Paris, 1976).

Conclusion

To return to the three major themes of this book as outlined in the introduction, what conclusions can be drawn about the nature of the Restoration
in the diocese of Canterbury; the aims behind, and the quality of, the pastoral care delivered by the clergy; and the issue of Church reform? First,
what is clear, is that these topics were intimately related. At the Restoration
a major pastoral task for the clergy was to further the reformation in the
parishes,[1] and the subject of reform in a number of areas of the Church's
life (such as recruitment to the profession; pastoral care; church finances;
and church courts) was discussed, and in some cases put into practice, at the
highest levels.[2] Moreover, for most of the period covered by this book
Church reform was framed under the topic of Church 'reformation', which
is suggestive of the interconnection between the themes of 'reformation'
and 'reform'.[3]

Second, the Restoration in the diocese of Canterbury was a complex
process which, although it was accomplished more smoothly and more
quickly in some areas of the Church's operation than in others, effectively
shaped the position of the Church for the next 170 years, establishing the
agenda both for how the Church saw itself as an institution, and for how the
Church related to the wider world. The Restoration, and the memory of
the Civil War which had necessitated a re-establishment of the Church in
the first place, set into train two developments which worked in tandem: the
tightening up, and even homogenizing of the clerical profession and
the Church as an institution; and at the same time the strengthening of the
Church's links with the wider world. For instance, this book has shown that
alongside the traditional concentration on the divisions within the clerical
estate, we need to recognize those factors which went some way to create a
Church which was essentially a homogeneous organization. Whilst differences within clerical wealth remained, other forces, such as a similar socio-
economic background, a common education, and an increasingly shared
political outlook, enabled the clergy to achieve a fair degree of unity. Moreover, through their use of patronage, archbishops were able to influence the

---

[1] See above, pp. 5, 233, 255, 264–6.   [2] See above, pp. 83, 87, 147–8, 200–1, 255, 264–6.
[3] See 'Bishop Edmund Gibson's Proposals for Church Reform', ed. S. Taylor, *From
Cranmer to Davidson. A Church of England Miscellany*, Church of England Record Society
(forthcoming).

nature of the clergy in their diocese, which, as we have seen, meant that the clergy in the diocese of Canterbury were arguably more under the control of the Church's hierarchy than in other regions. Alongside this development, however, this book has stressed that we need to pay attention to the ways in which the Church as an institution related to society at large. From the Restoration onwards, in most areas of the Church's operation, such as the treatment of nonconformists, the reacquisition of property, and the furthering of the clergy's pastoral role, a common theme emerged: the imperative of working with, rather than against, the laity, and this suggests that the received picture of the Church's contacts with society needs to be more nuanced. In the epilogue to his magisterial study of sixteenth- and early seventeenth-century Kent, Peter Clark claimed that after the Restoration the Church came steadily under gentry influence.[4] But in describing the Church in the diocese as gentry-dominated, historians have obscured the central tension in the clergy's relationship with society: the need to maintain a separate identity and to preserve Church rights without antagonizing the wider world. This was always a difficult balance to achieve, yet post-Restoration clergymen, learning from Laud's disastrous policy of alienating the laity, recognized that they could do little to further Anglicanism if they aroused lay hostility.[5] The Church needed lay support against the inroads of dissent and to preserve its influence in what was seen as an increasingly corrupt and irreligious age. It had to work within a framework in which the possibilities for manœuvre were limited by the attitudes and demands of those around it. As shown in the ways in which the clerical profession was perceived, in the administration of Church lands, in the economic relationship between the parish clergy and their flocks, and in attitudes towards dissent and parishioners, the relationship between the Church and society in Kent had distinct links to those policies pursued by pre-Laudian Churchmen as described by Professor Collinson.[6] It is time that the post-Restoration, pre-Victorian clergy were seen in the same light. Instead of the conventional picture of the century as one in which Church interests were increasingly subordinated to secular considerations, it might be argued that clergy during the long eighteenth century were surprisingly successful in eliciting support for the Church's pastoral programme. This was clearly shown in the backing given by the laity for the work of the Church in the parish, in providing funds for schools, and in keeping churches in repair.[7]

---

[4] Clark, *English Provincial Society*, 402–5.   [5] Pruett, *Parish Clergy*, 178.

[6] Collinson, *Religion of Protestants, passim*. See also Fincham, *Prelate as Pastor, passim*.

[7] W. M. Jacob has suggested that the involvement of the laity in Church life in the parishes

Third, this book suggests that we need to place the pastoral work of the clergy in the long eighteenth century in a rather different perspective from that usually favoured by historians. As such, its findings have implications for the study of other centuries and suggests that we need to develop a new historiographical framework, which modifies the conventional periodizations and characterizations of older ecclesiastical histories. On the one hand, the pastoral work of the clergy in the parishes shows that too much weight has been placed on the success of the Church in the sixteenth and early seventeenth centuries in furthering Anglicanism.[8] Much has been written concerning the successes of the Reformation in spreading religious literacy and in bringing Anglicanism to the hearts and minds of parishioners.[9] Yet it is becoming clear that this task had by no means been accomplished in the sixteenth century: a good case can be made for the claim that these objectives were better carried through in the eighteenth century, particularly in matters of religious education, catechizing, and even in some cases, the number of services offered by the clergy. On the other hand, veneration of the Evangelical and Oxford Movements has encouraged historians to lose sight of the degree to which some of their attitudes were anticipated by eighteenth-century clergy, such as the stress on developing new methods of religious instruction, and the maintenance of 'orthodox' doctrine.[10] Further, the evidence presented here fits in with Mark Smith's argument that the 'unreformed establishment' was more vital than we used to think; and that that vitality was reflected in its general pastoral effectiveness.[11] This book would also support Smith's contention that there was much continuity between the 'reformed' and 'unreformed' establishments: both were pastorally alive, and we should thus see the pastoral developments of the nineteenth century as emerging from eighteenth-century initiatives, rather than representing a new departure after 1830.[12]

Fourth, by 1828 the Church of England in the diocese of Canterbury had demonstrated its capacity not only to initiate new pastoral strategies but also to reform and revitalize itself. On his death in that year one admirer of Archbishop Manners Sutton praised 'the extraordinary services which the late archbishop has graciously permitted to render to the Church of

made the Church 'a people's Church': *Lay People and Religion in the Early Eighteenth Century* (Cambridge, 1996), 19.

[8] On this see G. Parker, 'Success and Failure during the First Century of the Reformation', *Past and Present*, 136 (1992), 43–82.

[9] *Inter alia*, A. G. Dickens, *The English Reformation* (1964).

[10] Haig, *Victorian Clergy*; Virgin, *Church in Age of Negligence*.

[11] Smith, *Religion in Industrial Society*, 273.   [12] Ibid., 191.

England during the most busy period of her history since the Reformation'.[13] It has indeed been observed that the years between 1810 and 1820
saw a 'remarkable movement' in three important branches of the Church's
work: religious education; foreign missions; and church building.[14] The
National Society for Educating the Poor in the Principles of the Established
Church was formed in 1811, under Manners Sutton's presidency, and had
founded 690 schools by 1833, with its first in the Canterbury diocese being
established in 1823.[15] On a wider canvas, it can be suggested that the
Society provided a model for the Church to act in a corporate capacity in
the absence of convocations, including as it did all the bishops as vice-
presidents, along with leading laymen. As far as church building was concerned, Manners Sutton was instrumental in obtaining a parliamentary
grant of £1 million in 1818 for building new churches and in founding the
Church Building Society (1817, incorporated 1818), which, as its first venture in the diocese, financed the new chapel in the parish of Folkestone
which was consecrated in 1822.[16]

If the Church in the diocese of Canterbury can be shown to have been
participating in reform before 1828, the methods by which it did so can be
related to those highlighted in other recent studies. The role played by the
Hutchinsonians and then the Hackney Phalanx in the cathedral and the
diocese, with the support of archbishops (in particular, Secker, Moore, and
Manners Sutton), confirms Peter Nockles' and Arthur Burns' view of a
vigorous pre-Oxford Movement High Churchmanship which not only kept
alive 'orthodox' doctrine and Churchmanship but was also keen to reform
the Church as an institution.[17] Moreover, the mechanisms whereby this
group established its influence within the diocese supports Clive Dewey's
insistence on the role of patronage as being the principal means by which
the 'unreformed Church' engaged with issues of reform.[18] However, it
might be suggested that both Nockles' and Dewey's analyses in particular
have focused on a too narrowly defined group of clergy: High Churchmanship was more widely diffused within mainstream Anglicanism than either
allows; as Nockles himself admits, there was much overlap between those
who would after 1830 be separated into High and Low Church camps.[19]
Further, Dewey's suggestion that in using the extensive patronage network

---

[13] Joshua Watson, quoted in Rowden, *Primates*, 434.

[14] Rowden, *Primates*, 397.   [15] See above, p. 254.

[16] See above, pp. 177. LPL, ICBS records show that between 1818 and 1828 21 churches in
the diocese received grants.

[17] Nockles, *Oxford Movement in Context*; Burns, 'The Diocesan Revival'.

[18] Dewey, *Passing of Barchester*, 6.

[19] Nockles, *Oxford Movement in Context*, 310. See also G. F. A. Best, 'Church Parties and

available to archbishops of Canterbury, Archbishop Manners Sutton took 'a conscious decision' to distribute patronage on 'new meritocratic lines', and that he was the 'real pioneer' behind Church reform,[20] exaggerates the novelty of his method, and ignores the efforts of his predecessors in reforming their diocese and in using patronage as a means of doing this, so that in many respects interest in church reform should be seen as a continuing tradition, and not something confined to a specific period.

Furthermore, some of the methods used by the ecclesiastical reformers of the 1830s and 40s, such as the use of statistics and the collecting and collating of information, were precisely the tools used by Church's leaders in the long eighteenth century to gain information about their clergy and to see where pastoral pressure needed to be applied. The surviving series of visitation returns can be seen as attempts by new primates to familiarize themselves with their diocese, as are the charts, tables, and the material supplied for the various Parliamentary enquiries of the pre-1828 period. David Eastwood has acknowledged the role of the clergy in collecting information needed by the expanding state in the years before 1830; less attention has been paid to the ways that clergy used these methods to reform their own institution.[21]

One of the leading authorities on the nineteenth-century Church, James Obelkevich, admitted some time ago that until we knew more about the eighteenth-century Church, there was the danger that we would exaggerate the novelty of the Victorian reforms.[22] It has indeed been argued that by 1828 all those elements which are usually seen as integral to the reforms of the 1830s and 40s, with one exception (the Ecclesiastical Commission), were in place: orthodox theology was preserved; the SPCK and SPG had been revitalized; the National Society had been founded (1811); and there was a network of people willing to take reform seriously.[23] Nevertheless, Peter Virgin has campaigned against an upbeat picture of the Church in this period, maintaining that this one exception was crucial: if the eighteenth-century Church was so alive, and willing to participate in reform, why was there no Ecclesiastical Commission before the 1830s?[24] This is, however, to view eighteenth-century developments from what has

Charities: The Experience of Three American Visitors to England, 1823/4', *EHR*, 78 (1963), 243–62.

20 Dewey, *Passing of Barchester*, 6, 139.

21 D. Eastwood, '"Amplifying the Province of the Legislature": The Flow of Information and the English State in the Early Nineteenth Century', *Historical Research*, 62 (1989), 276–94.

22 Obelkevich, *Religion and Rural Society*, 179.

23 Dewey, *Passing of Barchester*, 11.   24 Virgin, *Age of Negligence*, 27.

been called a 'reform perspective'; judging an organization from the position of future changes, and the dangers of that perspective need to be exposed.[25] J. H. Plumb once warned that the preoccupation of historians with what would subsequently be deemed to be antiquated machinery and abuses might blind them to improvements which had occurred: he called this 'the methodist view of history'.[26] Furthermore, Jeffrey Chamberlain has noted that although the Church as an organization may have needed reform this does not mean that those who operated it were inattentive or lax.[27] Yet, although the most sustained recent study of the end of old corruption has restated the case for the importance of the Evangelical Revival in shaping the reform of the political world,[28] it significantly has picked out the Church as the one institution which was immune to reform before 1828: it was the 'decade of reform' after 1830 which, in Philip Harling's opinion 'abruptly reversed the "long" eighteenth-century trend towards a wealthier and less responsible clergy'.[29] But, as we have seen, statements about the wealth of the clergy need careful handling. Undoubtedly clergy were wealthier in 1828 than they had been in 1660, but some of the wilder estimates about the Church's wealth (as Harling himself acknowledges) were highly exaggerated. To suggest that clergy were less responsible in 1828 than they had been in 1660 is problematic, and probably unmeasurable, and certainly plays down the pastoral work of the clergy. Another indication of the reforming capabilities of clergy before 1828 within the diocese, is that those who were to be instruments of the 'diocesan revival' after 1830 (Arthur Burns' new model archdeacons and rural deans) were all men who had been appointed before 1828. This again complicates our understanding of the periodization between the 'unreformed' and the 'reformed' Church.[30]

---

[25] J. Innes and J. Styles, 'The Crime Wave: Recent Writing and Criminal Justice in Eighteenth-Century England', *JBS*, 25 (1986), 383.

[26] J. H. Plumb, *In The Light of History* (1972), 37.　　　[27] Chamberlain, 'Sussex', 36.

[28] Harling, *Waning of Old Corruption*, 7–8, 66–7, 162.　　　[29] Ibid., 202.

[30] Burns, 'Diocesan revival'. Archdeacon James Croft had been rector of Saltwood from 1812 to 1819, and was archdeacon from 1825 until 1869. Rural deans appointed after 1837 included Julius Deedes (curate of Hastingleigh, rector of Wittersham, 1828 and vicar of Marden, 1847–79); George Rashleigh (curate of Meopham, 1807, curate of Harrietsham, 1828, vicar of Little Hardres, 1827–74); Francis Lockwood (curate of Sturry, 1826, rector of Mersham, 1827); John Poore (rector of Murston, 1814, rector of Bicknor, 1816); Morgan Walter Jones (vicar of Ospringe, 1815–48); Thomas Morris (rector of St James', Dover, 1818–54); Charles Handley (curate of Marden, 1812, vicar of Hernehill, 1816–65); Charles James Burton (curate of Marden, 1816, vicar of Lydd, 1821); Thomas Wood (vicar of Ashford, 1826); James Bellamy (vicar of Sellinge, 1822–74); John Hodgson (curate of Tunstall, 1818, perpetual curate of Owre, 1820–6, vicar of Sittingbourne, 1826–35, and vicar of St Peter's, Thanet, 1834–57); Wyndham Knatchbull (rector of Westbere, 1811–23, rector of Bircholt, 1821–36, rector of Aldington, 1823–68); and William Baylay (vicar of St John's, Thanet, 1810–28).

But it would be wrong to suggest that all areas of the Church's operation were running smoothly in the early nineteenth century. As various chapters of this book have shown, there were signs of renewed tension in the period after 1790, both within the Church as an organization, and between the Church and dissent and between the Church and lay society, which indicate that, in some areas at least, the models of consensus and flexibility which had developed since the Restoration were under strain. Tenants found that Church landlords were more aggressive about the management of their property, and in the bleaker economic climate from the 1790s there were fresh anxieties over the collection of tithes. Significantly too, it was precisely in this period that the policy of 'tactful affability' between the Church and various dissenting bodies can be seen to break down in a number of parishes. These developments can in large measure be related to the wider impact of the French Revolution within British society, and the consequent labelling of those who did not wholly conform to the Church as being schismatic, reminiscent of those who had so shattered the Church's position in the 1640s and 50s.[31] But admitting that there were some severe difficulties for the Church in the early nineteenth century does not mean that the reform programme was abandoned, and, further, we should acknowledge that these difficulties were period-specific, and should not, as has so often been the case, be seen as a condemnation of the Church of England during the long eighteenth century as a whole. Moreover, within the diocese of Canterbury at least, there was little sign even in 1828 of those party divisions within the clerical body which would so riddle the Church in the Victorian era.[32]

All in all, the history of the diocese of Canterbury within the period covered by this book can be placed alongside the growing body of evidence which suggests that the Church of England played a far more central and dynamic role within English religious, social, and political life than has sometimes been maintained. The comparison with other regions indicates that the Canterbury experience was by no means untypical.[33] In the period between the upheavals of the mid-seventeenth century and the early nineteenth century, the history of the Church in the Canterbury diocese is something of a success story. At the start, its role was by no means clear, but within the provinces it fashioned itself into an agent of religious and

---

[31] D. W. Lovegrove, *Established Church, Sectarian People. Itinerancy and the Transformation of English Dissent, 1780–1830* (Cambridge, 1989).

[32] Nockles, *Oxford Movement in Context*, 310–17.

[33] See the comments in S. Gilley, 'Christianity and the Enlightenment: An Historical Survey', *History of European Ideas*, 1 (1981), 103–21.

political stability. Perhaps its very success in meshing itself within local society accounts for the problems the Church had in adapting to social change; it was too well entrenched within the world around it for rapid alteration. Nevertheless, at Canterbury there is little evidence of that self-satisfied inertia which has been such a potent image of Church life in this period. The life of the diocese of Canterbury in the long eighteenth century does not reflect stagnation so much as comparatively successful conservatism. Despite the stress on continuities with the past, there were strong signs of modernity and change. All in all, the most significant feature of the life of the Church, as shown by this study, was its capacity to respond to developments rather than totally to ignore them. In its attitudes towards dissenters, and especially in its attempt to spread literacy and inculcate religious understanding in its parishioners, the Church was participating in activities usually associated with the Enlightenment. The desire for efficiency, improvement, and change was not just a prerogative of the Church's critics; rather this was a goal aimed for within the Church.[34]

On its own terms, the Church in Canterbury largely fulfilled its role of creating political and social stability and spreading Christian doctrine. When challenge to the old regime did occur in Canterbury as elsewhere in the 1830s and 40s, involving a reorganization of the diocese and the cathedral, which led to changes in the training of clergy, in the financial role of the Church, and in its position vis à vis the dissenting population, it was not nearly so violently anticlerical as the attacks on the Church in France in the 1790s. And even when change did come about, it was not necessarily so rapid or so complete as some have suggested. As Frances Knight has reminded us, many of the patterns which had been established during the long eighteenth century for the way in which the Church operated within society, such as its pastoral imperatives, the methods in which churches were financed, and the double allegiance to Anglicanism and dissent, continued at least until the 1850s.[35] The changes affecting the Church in the

---

[34] See, for example, F. Bussby, *Winchester Cathedral, 1079–1974* (Southampton, 1979); C. J. Stranks, *This Sumptuous Church. The Story of Durham Cathedral* (1973); A. Tindal Hart, 'The Age of Reason, 1660–1831', in W. R. Matthews and W. M. Atkins (eds.), *A History of St. Paul's Cathedral* (1957), 172–249; P. Mussett, 'The Reconstituted Chapter, 1660–1820', in N. Yates and P. A. Welsby (eds.), *Faith and Fabric. A History of Rochester Cathedral, 604–1994* (Woodbridge, 1996), 77–114; D. M. Owen, 'From the Restoration until 1822', in Aylmer and Cant, *History of York Minster*, 233–71; A. Whiteman, 'The Church of England, 1542–1837', in *VCH, Wiltshire*, iii. 44–71; and R. G. Wilson, 'The Cathedral in the Georgian Period, 1720–1840', in I. Atherton, E. Fernie, C. Harper-Bill, and Hassell Smith (eds.), *Norwich Cathedral; Church, City and Diocese, 1096–1996* (1996), 576–614. See also the unpublished theses relating to particular regions cited in the bibliography.

[35] Knight, *Nineteenth-Century Church*, 23.

period after 1828 did not necessitate the repudiation of the position of the Church within society as it had evolved in the long eighteenth century, but rather drew on eighteenth-century developments to fit it for the demands of a new and different age.

BIBLIOGRAPHY

I. MANUSCRIPT SOURCES

Bodleian Library, Oxford

Additional MS c. 308 (Gilbert Sheldon)
MSS Ballard 3, 6, 15 (Arthur Charlett)
MS Eng. Lett. b. 46 (John Lewis)
MS Eng. Lett. c. 43 (John Lewis)
MS Eng. Lett. d. 43 (Samuel Pegge)
MS Eng. Misc. b. 46 (John Lewis)
MSS Eng. Th. c. 24, 25, 30, 43, 38, 53 (Thomas Brett)
MS Gough Kent 19
MS Rawlinson 93
MS Rawlinson c. 155 (John Lewis)
MS Rawlinson c. 412 (John Lewis)
MS Rawlinson c. 441 (John Lewis)
MSS Rawl. Letters 7, 29, 59, 106 (William Sancroft)
MS Rawl. Poet 181
MS Sancroft 99 (Notes on Parishes, 1668)
MS Sancroft 119 (Abstract of Leases, 1661–71)
MSS Tanner 25, 26
MS Tanner 28
MS Tanner 31
MS Tanner 33 (William Sancroft)
MS Tanner 34
MSS Tanner 36, 36*
MS Tanner 38
MS Tanner 39
MS Tanner 44
MS Tanner 45
MS Tanner 48
MS Tanner 122 (Sancroft: benefice book, 1678)
MSS Tanner 123–6, 126* (Diocese of Canterbury)
MS Tanner 127 (Archbishopric)
MS Tanner 128 (Canterbury Cathedral)
MS Tanner 141 (Sheldon)
MS Tanner 240 (Nicholas Battely)
MS Tanner 280

MS Tanner 282
MS Tanner 300
MS Tanner 315
MS Tanner 333 (John Battely)
MS Dep. c. 233 (Edmund Gibson)

British Library

Additional MSS
   4236 (Birch Collection)
   5811 (Cole Collection)
   28651 (John Lewis)
   34106 (Thomas Brett)
   39311–12 (George Berkeley)
   Harleian MS 3790 (William Sancroft)
Harleian MS 7377 (Gilbert Sheldon and William Sancroft)
Althorp Papers (Charles Poyntz)

Cambridge University Library

MS Add. 8134 (George Horne)
MS Add. 6958 (William Pitt)

Canterbury Cathedral Archives and Library

Dean and Chapter Act Books: 1670–1710; 1710–26; 1727–41; 1741–60; 1761–75; 1775–94; 1794–1824; 1824–54
Deans' Books: 1691–1717; 1718–42; 1742–61; 1761–70; 1770–6; 1777–92; 1793–1822; 1822–54
Register Z: 1660–2
General Registers, 26–42: 1662–1828
Box Dioc. I
Unmarked Box
F/A, Induction boxes
MSS Fabric
Treasurers' Books, 1660–1828
Dr Benson's Book, 1757–1804
Dr Potter's Book, 1746–65
Bunce's Schedule, III (1805)
Preachers' Books: 1712–66; 1767–1822
Precentors' Books: 1753–65; 1766–9; 1780–9; 1802–3
Oblation Books: 1709–12; 1712–20; 1721–44
Sykes' Charity
Petitions
Canterbury Letters: To 1661; 1661–1790
Auditors' Letters

Register of Books Borrowed and Returned
MS 298 (Prebendary Welfitt's Diary)
MS H/A (Applications for Registration of Dissenting Meeting Houses)
MS H/Z (Original Returns to 1676 Compton Census)
MS U 47 (French Church Records)
MS W/Z (Diocese of Canterbury Records)
MS X (Archdeaconry of Canterbury, Court records)
MS Z (Archdeaconry of Canterbury, Court records)
MS Z. 3. 34 (Archdeacon Green's Visitation Book)
MS Z. 26 (Leases, 1660–1)
MS Z. 3. 19 (Archdeacon's Visitation, 1710)
MSS U3/1–200 (Parish Records deposited in CCAL)
MS U 40 (Licences, Nonconformist Meeting Houses)
MS Lit. E 16 (John Barwick)
Add. MS 19 (Notitia Diocesis Cantuar)
Add. MS 43 (Account Book of Simon D'Evereux)
Add. MS 80 (Thomas Monins)
Add. MS 91 (Ashford)
Add. MS 298 (Canon Welfitt's Diary)

Christ Church, Oxford

Wake MSS
Arch. Epist. W.
Wake Letters 6–10 (Canterbury Diocese, 1716–26)
Wake Letters 20–4 (Miscellaneous, 1715–26)
MSS 284–7 (Visitation Returns, Diocese of Canterbury, A–D: 1716–28)

Kent Record Office, Maidstone

MS Guildford
MSS U/ (Parish Records from Canterbury Diocese)
MSC/148 (Duke of Dorset)

Lambeth Palace Library

Archbishops' Registers (Juxon to Manners Sutton)
VB 1/1–15 (Act Books, 1663–1828)
G 4/23–4 (Juxon's Metropolitical Visitation)
VG 25 (Visitation, 1682)
MS 1134/1–4 (Visitation Returns, 1758)
VG 2/5 (Secker Speculum)
VG 2/7 (Returns, 1810–11)
VG 3/1/a–d (Visitation Returns, 1786)
VG 3/2/a–d (Visitation Returns, 1806)
Convocation Papers

MS 639 [Nonconformists]
MSS 923, 929, 941, 942 (Edmund Gibson)
MSS 950, 952–4, 958 (Thomas Tenison)
MS 1029 (Thomas Tenison)
MS 1024, 1037 (John Lewis)
MS 1120 (Queen Anne's Bounty)
MS 1121 ('Sons of Clergy')
MS 1125 (John Lewis)
MS 1126 (Sheldon Catalogue)
MS 1133 (Account of Archbishop Wake's MSS)
MS 1134 (Visitation of Diocese of Canterbury, 1751)
MS 1137 ('Account of ye Canterbury Diocese . . . 1685')
MS 1138 ('Account of the archdeaconry in ABp Herring's time')
MS 1153 (Poor Vicars in the dioceses of Canterbury and Ely)
MS 1163 (A. C. Ducarel)
MSS 1349–50 (Thomas Secker)
MS 1483 (Secker's Account Book)
MS 1742 (Edmund Gibson)
MS 1770 (William Wake: diary, 1705–26)
MSS 2180–3, 2219–21 (Thomas Brett)
MS 2598 (Autobiography of Archbishop Secker)
MS 2686 (Thomas Tenison)
MSS Potter
MSS Herring
MSS Secker
MSS Cornwallis
MSS Moore
MSS E[state] D[ocuments] 1808, 1916, 2029–30, 2036, 2042
MS T[emporalities] C 4
MS TC 9 (1805 'View of Estates')
MSS TG 24, 36 [Account Books]
MSS TR 9, 12, 14, 17, 18, 19, 20, 21, 30, 32, 34, 35 36, 37 [Estates]
MSS TS 2, 5, 6, 140 [Archbishops' Woods]
Cartae Miscellenae
'Unsorted fiats'
General Licences
Caution Books, 1758–85; 86–1828
Incorporated Church Building Society Records, 1818–28

Magdalen College, Oxford
MS 471 (George Horne)

Public Record Office

State Papers 36, 1729: State Papers Domestic, George II

SPCK, Archives, St Marylebone, London

MS Wanley
SPCK, Minutes and Correspondence, 1698–1704
SPCK, Abstract Letter Books, 1708–71: CR 1/1–25

Westminster Abbey Muniments

MS 25096 (Miscellaneous)

Dr Williams's Library, London

MS 34/4 (Evans MS)
MS 38/6 (Thompson MS)

2. PRIMARY PRINTED SOURCES

The place of publication is London unless otherwise stated.

2.1. CORRESPONDENCE, DIARIES, MEMOIRS, ETC.

Archer, Issac, and William Coe, *Two East Anglian Diaries, 1641–1729*, ed. Matthew Storey, Suffolk Records Society, 36 (1994).

Austen, Jane, *Jane Austen's Letters to her Sister Cassandra and Others*, ed. R. W. Chapman (2nd edn., 1952).

Barratt, D. M. (ed.), *Ecclesiastical Terriers of Warwickshire Parishes*, 2 vols. (Oxford, 1955–71).

Byng, John [Viscount Torrington], *The Torrington Diaries*, ed. C. Bruyn Andrews, 4 vols. (1934–8).

Calendar of State Papers, Domestic.

Carter, Elizabeth, *Memoirs of the Life of Mrs Elizabeth Carter, with a New Edition of her Poems*, ed. Montagu Pennington, 2 vols. (2nd edn., 1808).

—— *A Series of Letters between Mrs. Elizabeth Carter and Miss Catherine Talbot, from the Year 1741 to 1770*, ed. Montagu Pennington, 2 vols. (1808).

Cole, R. E. G., *Speculum Dioeceseos Lincolniensis sub Episcopus Gul: Wake et Edm: Gibson*, Lincoln Record Society, 4 (Lincoln, 1913).

Cook, Michael (ed.), *The Diocese of Exeter in 1821: Bishop Carey's Replies to Queries Before Visitation*, 2 vols. (Torquay, 1958–60).

Cowper, Spencer, *Letters of Spencer Cowper, Dean of Durham, 1746–74*, ed. E. Hughes, Surtees Society, 145 (1950).

Defoe, Daniel, *A Tour Thro' The Whole Island of Great Britain*, ed. G. D. H. Cole, 2 vols. (1968).

Dering, Edward, *The Diaries and Papers of Sir Edward Dering*, ed. M. F. Bond (1976).

—— *The Parliamentary Diary of Sir Edward Dering, 1670–73*, ed. B. D. Henning (New Haven, Conn., and London, 1940).

Doddridge, Philip, *Calendar of the Correspondence of Philip Doddridge, D.D. (1702–51)*, comp. G. F. Nuttall (1979).

English Historical Documents, 10, *1714–1783*, ed. D. B. Horn and M. Ransome (1957).

Evelyn, John, *The Diary of John Evelyn*, ed. E. S. de Beer., 6 vols. (Oxford, 1955).

Fiennes, Celia, *The Journeys of Celia Fiennes*, ed. Colin Morris (1947).

Gilbert, George, *Reminiscences of the Reverend George Gilbert, 1796–1874*, ed. F. J. Shirley ([Canterbury], 1938).

Guy, J. R., *The Diocese of Llandaff in 1763. The Primary Visitation of Bishop Ewer*, South Wales Record Society (1991).

Hearne, Thomas, *Reliquae Hearniae. The Remains of Thomas Hearne*, ed. John Buchanan-Brown (1966).

Herring, Thomas, *Archbishop Herring's Visitation Returns 1743*, ed. S. L. Ollard and P. C. Walker, Yorkshire Archaeological Society Record Series, 71, 72, 75, 77 (1928–32).

—— *Letters from the Late Most Reverend Dr Thomas Herring, Lord Archbishop of Canterbury, to William Duncombe, Esq; deceased, from the year 1728–1757*, ed. John Duncombe (1777).

Historical Manuscripts Commission, 6th Report.

—— *7th Report.*

—— *9th Report.*

—— *Manuscripts of the Earl of Egmont, Diary of Viscount Percival, afterwards First Earl of Egmont*, 3 vols.

—— *Report on the Finch Manuscripts.*

—— *Report on the Manuscripts of His Grace the Duke of Portland*, 5 vols.

Hovenden, Robert (ed.), *The Register Books of Christninges, Marriages, and Biurialls within the Precinct of the Cathedrall and Metropolitical Church of Christe of Canterburie* (1878).

Hull, Felix (ed.), *Dr John Warner's Visitations of the Diocese of Rochester, 1663 and 1670*, Kent Archaeological Society, 1 (1991), pts. 3, 4, 5.

Josselin, Ralph, *The Diary of Ralph Josselin, 1616–1683*, ed. Alan MacFarlane, British Academy, Records of Social and Economic History, NS, 3 (1976).

Larking, L. B., *Proceedings in Kent*, Camden Society Publications (1862).

Lodge, E. C., *The Account Book of a Kentish Estate, 1616–1704*, British Academy (1927).

Melling, Elizabeth (ed.), *Kent Sources*, v, *Some Kentish Houses* (1965).

Morgan, Paul (ed.), *Inspections of Churches in the Diocese of Worcester, 1674, 1676, 1684 and 1687*, Worcester Historical Society, 12 (1986).

Newman, John Henry, *Apologia Pro Vita Sua, Being a History of His Religious Opinions*, ed. Martin J. Svaglic (Oxford, 1967).

North, Roger, *The Autobiography of Roger North*, ed. Augustus Jessop (1890).
Nichols, John (ed.), *Illustrations of the Literary History of the Eighteenth Century*, 8 vols. (1817–58).
—— *Literary Anecdotes of the Eighteenth Century*, 9 vols. (1812–16).
Nicolson, William, *The London Diaries of William Nicolson, Bishop of Carlisle, 1702–1718*, ed. C. Jones and G. Holmes (Oxford, 1985).
Pepys, Samuel, *The Diary of Samuel Pepys*, ed. R. Latham and W. Matthews, 11 vols. (1970–83).
Percy, Thomas, *The Correspondence of Thomas Percy and Richard Farmer*, ed. Cleanth Brooks (Baton Rouge, La., 1946).
[Beilby Porteus], *Life of Bishop Beilby Porteus, by a Lay Member of Merton College* (1810).
Price, Joseph, *A Kentish Parson. Selections from the Private Papers of the Revd Joseph Price of Brabourne, 1767–1786*, ed. G. M. Ditchfield and B. Keith-Lucas (Canterbury, 1990).
Pyle, Edmund, *Memoirs of a Royal Chaplain, 1729–1763. The Correspondence of Edmund Pyle, D.D., Chaplain in Ordinary to George II, with Samuel Kerrich, D.D., Vicar of Dersingham, Rector of Wolferton and Rector of West Newton*, ed. A. Harsthorne (1905).
Ransome, Mary (ed.), *The State of the Bishopric of Worcester, 1782–1808*, Worcester Historical Society, NS, 6 (1969).
—— *Wiltshire's Returns to the Bishop's Visitation Queries, 1783*, Wiltshire Record Society, 27 (1972).
Secker, Thomas, *Articles of Enquiry Addressed to the Clergy of the Diocese of Oxford at the Primary Visitation of Dr Thomas Secker*, ed. H. A. Lloyd-Jukes, Oxfordshire Record Society, 38 (1957).
—— *The Autobiography of Thomas Secker Archbishop of Canterbury*, ed. J. S. Macauley and R. W. Greaves (Lawrence, Kan., 1988).
—— 'Bishop Secker's Diocese Book', ed. Elizabeth Ralph, in Patrick McGrath (ed.), *A Bristol Miscellany*, Bristol Record Society's Publications, 37 (1985), 23–69.
—— *The Correspondence of Bishop Secker*, ed. A. P. Jenkins, Oxford Record Society, 57 (1991).
—— *The Speculum of Archbishop Thomas Secker*, ed. J. Gregory, Church of England Record Society, 2 (1995).
Turner, Thomas, *The Diary of Thomas Turner, 1754–1765*, ed. David Vaisey (Oxford, 1984).
Walpole, Horace, *The Yale Edition of Horace Walpole's Correspondence*, ed. W. S. Lewis, 48 vols. (New Haven, Conn., 1937–83).
Ward, W. R. (ed.), *Parson and Parish in Eighteenth-Century Hampshire: Replies to Bishops' Visitations, Hampshire Records Series*, 13 (1995).
—— (ed.), *Parson and Parish in Eighteenth-Century Surrey. Replies to Bishops' Visitations*, Surrey Record Society, 34 (1994).

Whiteman, Anne (ed.), *The Compton Census of 1676: A Critical Edition*, British Academy Records of Social and Economic History, NS, 10 (1986).

Woodward, George, *A Parson in the Vale of the White Horse. George Woodward's Letters from East Hendred, 1753-61*, ed. Donald Gibson (Gloucester, 1983).

2.2. PAMPHLETS, SERMONS, AND OTHER CONTEMPORARY PUBLICATIONS

[Anon.], *An Account of the Rules of the Society for the Relief of the Widows and Orphans of Poor Clergymen, Canterbury, 20 August 1751* (1751).

[Anon.], *A Brief Account of the Many Prosecutions of the People Call'd Quakers in the Exchequer, Ecclesiastical and other Courts* (1731).

[Anon.], *The Christian's Daily Manual of Prayers and Praises* (1703).

[Anon.], *The Duty and Obligation of the Clergy to Observe Such Occasional Days of Fasting and Thanksgiving, as are Occasioned by Royal Authority . . . Consider'd in answer to Mr Johnson's Late Tract, intitiled, The Case of Occasional Days and Prayers. By a Clergyman of the Diocese of Canterbury* (1722).

[Anon.], *A Letter Written by a Country Clergyman to Archbishop Herring, in the Year MDCCLIV* (1771).

[Anon.], *The Life of Dean L——ch by a Yeoman of Kent. No Canterbury Tale. And shall they escape for such Wickedness?* (1748).

[Anon.], *Personal the Best Pledge of Public Reform. Addressed to Inferiors. In which their Duty to the Country is ascertained by the Care she takes of them. By a Clergyman in the Diocese of Canterbury* (1795).

[Anon.], *A Race for Canterbury: or Lambeth Ho! A Poem, Describing the Contention for the Metropolitical See* (1747).

Articles of Visitation and Enquiry concerning Matters Ecclesiastical; exhibited to the Churchwardens and Side-Men of every Parish within the Archdeaconry of Canterbury (Canterbury, 1720).

Assheton, William, *A Sermon Preached at the Anniversary Meeting of the Sons of Clergymen in St Paul's Cathedral, 5 December 1699* (1700).

Backhouse, William, *God the Author of Peace and Lover of Concord. A Sermon preached at the Parish Church of Deal, on Thursday, July 29, 1784* (Canterbury, 1784).

Bate, James, *Human Learning Highly Useful to the Cause of True Religion. A Sermon preached in Canterbury Cathedral, on Thursday, September 13, 1753, at the annual meeting of the Gentlemen educated at Canterbury School* (Canterbury, 1753).

Battely, John, *Antiquitates Rutupinae* (Oxford, 1711).

—— *A Sermon Preach'd before the Queen, in Christ's-Church, Canterbury, May vi 1694* (1694).

Battely, Nicholas, *The Antiquities of Canterbury in Two Parts. I. The Antiquities of Canterbury . . . published by William Somner . . . II. Cantuaria Sacra* (1703).

Bearcroft, Philip, *A Sermon Preached before the Incorporated Society for the*

Propagation of the Gospel in Foreign Parts; at their anniversary meeting in the parish church of St Mary-le-Bow, on Friday February 15 1744 (1744).

Bean, Charles, *The Obligations of the Clergy to Promote a Legal Subjection to His Majesty, and Mutual Charity among their Fellow Subjects. Considered in a Sermon Preach'd at Ashford in Kent on June 22, 1716* (1716).

Bennett, William, *The Case of the Minor Canons and Inferior Officers of the Cathedrals of the New Foundation, particularly with reference to Canterbury* (Canterbury, 1839).

Berkeley, George, *A Caution Against Socinianism given in a Discourse preached at the Cathedral and Metropolitical Church of Christ, Canterbury; on Good Friday, 1787* (Canterbury and London, 1787).

—— *The Danger of Violent Innovations in the State Exemplified from the Reigns of the Two First Stuarts, in a Sermon preached at the Cathedral and Metropolitical Church of Christ, Canterbury on Monday, Jan. 31, 1785* (Canterbury, 1785).

—— *Sermons*, ed. Eliza Berkeley (1799).

Berkeley, George-Monck, *Poems by the late George-Monck Berkeley*, ed. Eliza Berkeley (1797).

Beveridge, William, *Synodicon* (Oxford, 1672).

—— *The Theological Works of William Beveridge*, 12 vols. (Oxford, 1842–8).

Birch, T., *The Life of the Most Reverend Dr John Tillotson* (1752).

Blackburne, Francis, *The Confessional; or a Full and Free Inquiry into the Right, Utility, Edification, and Success of Establishing Systematical Confessions of Faith and Doctrine in Protestant Churches* (1766).

Blomer, Ralph, *A Discourse Concerning Conscience. With an Appendix Occasioned by the Death of the Reverend Dr Grandorge, Late Prebendary of Canterbury, and Chaplain to the Right Honourable the late Earl of Thanet. A Sermon Preach'd in the Cathedral-Church of Canterbury, February 1 1729/1730* (1730).

Blomer, Ralph, *A Sermon Preach'd in the Cathedral and Metropolitical Church of Canterbury, at the Inthronement of His Grace, William Lord Archbishop of the Province, On Friday June 15th, 1716* (1716).

Blomer, Thomas, *A Full View of Dr Bentley's Letter to the Lord Bishop of Ely. In a Discourse to a Friend* (1710).

Botfield, Beriah, *Notes on the Cathedral Libraries of England* (1849).

Bowers, Thomas, *The Value of Church and College Leases Considered and the Advantages of the Lessees made very Apparent* (2nd edn., 1722).

Bowtell, John, *A Sermon Preach'd at Patrixbourne and Bridge* (Canterbury, 1751).

—— *A Sermon Preach'd at Patrixbourne . . . to prove the dissenters are impos'd upon by their Teachers and Ought to Conform to the Church of England, as by Law established* (1711).

—— *A Sermon Preach'd at Staplehurst* (Canterbury, 1750).

Boys, John, *General View of the Agriculture of the County of Kent, with Observations on the Means of its Improvement* (1794).

Brett, Thomas, *Account of Church Government and Governors* (1701).

—— *The Christian Altar and Sacrifice. A Sermon shewing that the Lord's Table is the Proper Altar, and the Sacrament of the Eucharist a Proper Sacrifice* (1713).

—— *The Dangers of a Relapse. A Sermon Preach'd at the Royal Chapel at St James's Chapel on May 29 1713. Being the Day of Thanksgiving to Almighty God, for having put an end to the Great Rebellion* (1713).

—— *A Discourse Concerning the Necessity of Discerning the Lord's Body in the Holy Communion* (1720).

—— *Dr Brett's Vindication of Himself, From the Calumnies Thrown upon him in Some Late Newspapers, Wherein he is Falsly Charged with Turning Papist* (1715).

—— *The Extent of Christ's Commission to Baptise. A Sermon Shewing the Capacity of Infants to Receive, and the Utter Incapacity of Dissenting Teachers to Administer Infant Baptism* (1712).

—— *The Independency of the Church upon the State, As to its Pure Spiritual Powers: Proved from the Holy Scriptures* (1717).

—— *A Letter of Advice to Thomas Brett LL.D and a Seasonable Rebuke for Offences Given by Him to God and the King* (1715).

—— *A Letter to the Author of Lay Baptism Invalid* (1710).

—— *The Life of the Reverend Mr John Johnson* (1745).

B[ulteel], J[ean], *A Relation of the Troubles of the three forraign Churches in Kent. Caused by the Injunctions of William Laud, Archbishop of Canterbury. Anno Dom 1634* (1645).

Burnet, Gilbert, *A Discourse of the Pastoral Care* (1692).

—— *A History of My Own Time*, 6 vols. (1828).

—— *A Sermon Preached at the Funeral of the Most Reverend Father in God, John Tillotson, Archbishop of Canterbury* (1694).

Butler, Weeden, *Some Account of the Life and Writings of the Reverend Dr George Stanhope, Vicar of Lewisham and Deptford and Dean of Canterbury* (1797).

[C. A.], *The Farmers and the Clergy. Six Letters to the Farmers of England on Tithes and Church Property* (2nd edn., 1831).

Carter, Nicholas, *A Sermon Preached at Deal: before the Mayor and Corporation, August 9th 1752* (1752).

Casaubon, Meric, *A King and His Subjects Unhappily Fallen Out and Happily Reconciled. Being the Substance of a Sermon with very little Alteration fitted for the present time. Preached in the Sermon House, Canterbury Cathedral, 15 January 1643* (1660).

—— *Of the Necessity of the Reformation. In and Before Luther's Time* (1664).

Cobbett, William, *History of the Protestant Reformation* (1824).

—— *Rural Rides*, ed. G. Woodcock (1967).

[Chamberlayne, E.], *Angliae Notitia; or, the Present State of England*, 2 vols. (18th edn., 1692).

Colquhoun, Patrick, *Observations and Facts relative to Licensed Ale-Houses, in the City of London and its Environs . . . by a Magistrate acting for the Counties of Middlesex, Surrey, Kent and Essex* (1794).

Cooke, John, *Thirty Nine Sermons on Several Subjects*, 2 vols. (1739).

Cooke, Shadrach, *Legal Obedience the Duty of a Subject: considered in a Sermon at the Archdeacon of Canterbury's Visitation at Sittingbourne* (1718).

Cornwallis, Frederick, *A Sermon Preached before the Incorporated Society for the Propagation of the Gospel in Foreign Parts; at their Anniversary meeting in the parish church of St. Mary le Bow, on Friday February 20, 1756* (1756).

—— *A Sermon Preached before the Right Honourable the Lords Spiritual and Temporal in Parliament assembled in the Abbey-Church Westminster, on Wednesday January 30, 1751. Being the day to be observed as the day of the Martyrdom of King Charles I* (1751).

Cornwallis, James, *A Sermon Preached in the Cathedral and Metropolitical Church of Christ, Canterbury, On Friday, February 4, 1780. Being the Day Appointed to be Observed as a Day of General Fasting and Humiliation* (Canterbury, 1780).

[Croft, Herbert], *The Naked Truth* (1675).

Crossman, Henry, *An Introduction to the Knowledge of the Christian Religion* (Colchester, 1754).

Cull, Francis, *The Nature and Necessity of Preaching the Gospel: deliver'd in a Visitation Sermon, before the Revd. Dr Samuel Lisle Archdeacon of Canterbury, June 9 1731, at Wye, in Kent* (1732).

Culmer, R., *Cathedrall Newes from Canterbury; shewing The Canterburian Cathedrall to bee in an Abbey-like, corrupt, and rotten condition, which calls for a speedy Reformation, or Dissolution* (1644).

—— *The Ministers Hue and Cry* (1651).

Curteis, T. S., *A Sermon Preached at the Time of the Subscription for Voluntary Contributions, set on foot under sanction of Parliament* (1798).

Curteis, Thomas, *Advice to a Son at the University, designed for Holy Orders* (1725).

Dampier, Thomas, *A Sermon Preached Before the Lords Spiritual and Temporal, in the Abbey Church, Westminster, on Wednesday, 20th February 1805* (1805).

Davies, David, *The Case of Labourers in Husbandry* (1795).

Delafaye, Theodore, *Inoculation an Indefensible Practice. A sermon preached at the United Parish Churches of St Mildred's and All Saints, in the city of Canterbury, 3 June 1753* (1753).

Denne, John, *A Sermon Preached in the Parish-Church of Maidstone, in Kent; on Friday 2 November 1753, at the Anniversary election of a Mayor for that Corporation* (1754).

Disney, John, *Considerations on the Propriety and Expediency of the Clergy, acting in the Commission of the Peace* (1781).

—— *Memoirs of the Life and Writings of Arthur Ashley Sykes* (1785).

Dorrington, Theophilus, *A Discourse on Singing in the Worship of God* (1714).

—— *The Dissenting Ministry in Religion, Censur'd and Condemn'd from the Holy Scriptures* (1703).

—— *A Familiar Guide to the Right and Profitable Receiving of the Lord's Supper* (1700).

—— *Family Devotions for Sunday Evenings throughout the Year*, 4 vols. (1693–5).

—— *Family Instructions for the Church of England* (1705).

—— *Reformed Devotions in Meditations, Hymns and Petitions*, 4th edn. (1696).

—— *The True Foundation of Obedience and Submission to His Majesty King George. Stated and Confirm'd and the late Happy Revolution Vindicated* (1714).

—— *A Vindication of the Christian Church in the Baptizing of Infants* (1701).

Ducarel, A. C., *The History and Antiquities of the Archiepiscopal Palace of Lambeth* (1785).

—— *A Repertory of the Endowments of Vicarages in the Diocese of Canterbury* (1763).

Duncombe, John, *The Civil War between the Israelites and Benjamites Illustrated and Applied in a Sermon Preached in the Parish-Church of St. Andrew, in the City of Canterbury, on Friday, February 27, 1778* (Canterbury and London, 1778).

—— *An Elegy, Written in Canterbury Cathedral* (1778).

—— *The History and Antiquities of the Three Archiepiscopal Hospitals at and near Canterbury* (1785).

—— *The History and Antiquities of the two parishes of Reculver and Hearne* (1784).

—— *A Sermon Preached at the Consecration of the Parish-Church of St Andrew in the City of Canterbury, Monday 4 July 1774* (Canterbury, 1774).

Eachard, John, *The Grounds and Occasions of the Contempt of the Clergy* (1670).

Ecton, John, *A State of the Proceedings of the Corporation of the Governors of the Bounty of Queen Anne, for the Augmentation of the Maintenance of the Poor Clergy* (1719).

—— *Thesaurus Rerum Ecclesiasticarum* (1742).

Edwards, Thomas, *Gangraena* (1646).

Fox, Francis, *The Duty of Public Worship Proved: to which are added directions for a devout behaviour there* (1713).

Friend, William, *A Sermon Preached before the House of Commons, at St Margaret's Westminster, on Thursday, January 30, 1755. being appointed to be observed as the day of the Martyrdom of King Charles I* (1755).

Gibson, Edmund, *The Bishop of London's Three Pastoral Letters* (1732).

—— *Codex Juris Ecclesiastici Anglicani: or, the Statutes, Constitutions, Canons, Rubricks and Articles of the Church of England, Methodically Digested under their Proper Heads. With a Commentary, Historical and Judicial*, 2 vols. (1713).

Gostling, William, *A Walk In and About the City of Canterbury* (6th edn. Canterbury, 1825).

Greene, Thomas, *The Great Wickedness of Perjury, and of the Present Rebellion. A Sermon Preach'd at the Cathedral-Church of Canterbury, on Sunday, November 20, 1715* (1715).

—— *The Late Rebellion an Effect of the Madness of the People. A Sermon preached at the Cathedral-Church of Canterbury, on Thursday, June 7th* (1716).

Hall, George, *God Appearing Before the Tribe of Levi* (1655).

Hancock, John, *Arianism not the Primitive Christianity: or, the Antenicene Fathers vindicated from the Imputation of being Favourable to that Heresy, design'd as an Answer (in part) to Mr Whiston's Primitive Christianity Reviv'd* (2nd edn., 1719).

Hasted, Edward, *The History and Topographical Survey of the County of Kent*, 4 vols. (Canterbury, 1778–99); 12 vols. (2nd edn., Canterbury, 1797–1801).

[Hayter, Thomas], *An Examination of a Book, lately printed by the Quakers; intitled, A Brief Account . . . so far as the Clergy of the Diocese of Canterbury are concern'd in it* (1738).

Herring, Thomas, *Archbishop Herring's Letter to the Clergy of his Diocese, 12 February 1751* (1751).

—— *A Sermon Preach'd at the Cathedral Church of York, September the 22nd 1745; on Occasion of the Present Rebellion in Scotland* (York, 1745).

—— *A Sermon Preached before the Incorporated Society for the Propagation of the Gospel in Foreign Parts; at their anniversary meeting in the parish church of St Mary Le Bow, on Friday February 17, 1737–8* (1738).

—— *Seven Sermons on Public Occasions* (1763).

Heseltine, William, *A Tenant's Statement of the Conduct Recently Pursued towards him by the Dean and Chapter of Canterbury, on the Occasion of his Renewing his Lease* (2nd edn., 1839).

Heylyn, Peter, *Cyprianus Anglicanus* (1668).

Higden, William, *A View of the English Constitution* (1707).

Hinde, Samuel, *England's Prospective-Glasse: A Sermon at a Metropolitical Visitation held at the Cathedral Church of Christ in Canterbury, on the 29th of April 1663* (1663).

Hodgson, C., *An Account of the Augmentation of Small Livings by the Governors of the Bounty of Queen Anne's* (1826).

—— *Instructions for the use of Candidates for Holy Orders* (1817).

Hooker, Richard, *The Works of Richard Hooker*, ed. John Keble, *et al.* (7th edn., Oxford, 1883).

Horne, George, *The Antiquity, Use and Excellence of Church Music. A Sermon Preached at the Opening of A New Organ in the Cathedral Church of Christ, Canterbury, on Thursday, July 8, 1784* (Oxford, 1784).

—— *The Character of True Wisdom, and the Means of Attaining it. A Sermon preached in the Cathedral Church of Christ, Canterbury, before the Society of Gentlemen educated in the King's School, on Thursday, August 26 1784* (Oxford, 1784).

—— *Commentary on the Book of Psalms*, 2 vols. (Oxford, 1776).

—— *The Duty of Contending for the Faith. A Sermon preached at the Primary Visitation of the Most Reverend John, Lord Archbishop of Canterbury, in the Cathedral and Metropolitical Church, on Saturday, July 1st, 1786. To which is subjoined a Discourse on the Trinity in Unity* (Oxford, 1786).

—— *A Letter to the Right Hon. the Lord North, Chancellor of the University of Oxford, Concerning Subscription to the XXXIX Articles* (Oxford, 1834).

Horne, George, *A Sermon Preached Before the Sons of the Clergy in the Cathedral Church of St Paul, Thursday 6 May 1762* (1762).

—— *Sunday Schools Recommended in a Sermon preached at the parish church of St Alphege, Canterbury, on Sunday December the eighteenth, MDCCLXXXV with an Appendix on the Method of Forming and Conducting them* (Oxford and London, 1786).

—— *The Works of the Right Reverend George Horne*, 4 vols. (1818).

Howley, William, *A Charge Delivered at his Primary Visitation in August and September, 1832* (1832).

Hutton, Matthew, *A Sermon Preach'd Before the Honourable House of Commons, at St Margaret's Westminster, on Friday, Jan. 30, 1740–1. Being the day appointed to be observed as the day of the Martyrdom of King Charles I* (1741).

—— *A Sermon Preached before the House of Lords, in the Abbey-Church of Westminster, on Monday, Jan. 30, 1743–4. Being the day appointed to be observed as the day of the Martyrdom of King Charles I* (1744).

—— *A Sermon Preached before the Incorporated Society for the Propagation of the Gospel in Foreign Parts; at their anniversary meeting in the parish church of St. Mary-le-Bow, on Friday February 21, 1745* (1745).

Hyde, Edward, Earl of Clarendon, *The History of the Rebellion and Civil Wars in England*, 3 vols. (Oxford, 1819).

—— *The Life of Edward, Earl of Clarendon. Containing I. An Account of the Chancellor's Life . . . to the Restoration in 1660 II. Continuation of the History of England. Written by Himself* (Oxford, 1759).

An Hymn to be Sung by the Children of the Charity-Schools, belonging to the parish of Maidstone. On Sunday October the 16th, 1785, when a Sermon will be preached for the Support of the Schools by the Revd. T. Cherry (Maidstone, 1785).

Jackson, Jeremiah, *A Sermon Preached at Sittingbourne, on Wednesday, June 11, 1800, at the Visitation of the Lord Archbishop of Canterbury* (Canterbury and London, 1800).

Johnson, John, *The Case of Occasional Days and Prayers, containing a defence for not solemnising the Accession Day* (1716).

—— *The Case of Pluralities and Non Residence Rightly Stated* (1694).

—— *The Clergyman's Vade-Mecum; or, an Account of the Ancient and Present Church of England; the Duties and Rights of the Clergy, and of their Privileges and Hardships* (1706) [6th. edn., 1751].

—— *Collected Sermons* (1738).

—— *Reasons why Vice Ought to be Punished, but is not, in a Sermon Preached at Maidstone in Kent, at the Assizes held there before Mr Justice Tracy, 17 March 1708* (1708).

—— *A Sermon Preach'd at Canterbury School Feast. With a Preface, Shewing that the Alphabetical Letters were never used by any before Moses, and he first learned an Alphabet from God* (1727).

—— *The Unbloody Sacrifice and Altar Unvail'd and Supported*, 2 vols. (1714–24).

Jones, David, *Some Remarks upon Modern Education. A Sermon Preach'd in the Cath-edral-Church of Canterbury, on Thursday, September 5, 1728. At the Anniversary Meeting of the Gentlemen educated at the King's School There* (1729).

[Jones, William], *A Letter to John Bull from his Second Cousin Thomas Bull* (1793).

[——], *One Penny-worth of Truth from Thomas Bull to his Brother John* (Canterbury, 1793).

—— *Popular Commotions Consider'd as Signs of the Approaching End of the World. A Sermon preached in the Metropolitical Church of Canterbury, on Sunday Septem-ber 26, 1789* (1789).

—— *The Theological, Philosophical and Miscellaneous Works of the Rev. William Jones, M.A., Minister of Nayland, Suffolk. To which is prefixed a short account of his life and writings by William Stevens*, 12 vols. (1801).

Jortin, John, *Remarks on Ecclesiastical History*, 5 vols. (1751–73).

Kennett, White, *The Case of Impropriations and of the Augmentations of Vicarages and other Insufficient Cures* (1704).

Kirkby, John, *The Impostor Detected: or the Counterfeit Saint turn'd inside out* (1750).

Laud, William *The Works of William Laud*, ed. W. Scott and J. Bliss, 7 vols. (1847–60).

Laurence, Edward, *The Duty and Office of a Land Steward* (Dublin, 1731).

Lee, Robert, *An Analysis of Archbishop Secker's Lectures on the Church Catechism, arranged in a Course of Sermons* (1831).

Le Neve, John, *Lives and Characters of the Protestant Archbishops of Canterbury* (1720).

Lewis, John, *Agreement of the Lutheran Churches and the Church of England* (1715).

—— *The Bread and Wine in the Holy Eucharist Not A Proper, Material, Propitiatory Sacrifice* (1714).

—— *A Brief History of the Rise and Progress of Anabaptism in England. To which is prefixed some account of Dr Wicliff* (1738).

—— *The Case of Obeying Such Fasts and Festivals as are appointed by the King's Authority* (1716).

—— *The Church Catechism Explained, by way of Question and Answer and Confirmed by Scriptural Proofs* (1700).

—— *The Clergy of the Church of England Vindicated, in a Sermon preach'd in the Metropolitical Church of Christ, Canterbury, on Tuesday, May 16, 1710* (1710).

—— *The History and Antiquities as well Ecclesiastical as Civil of the Isle of Tenet in Kent* (2nd edn., 1736).

—— *The History and Antiquities of the Abbey and Church of Faversham* (1727).

—— *The History of the Life and Sufferings of the Reverend and Learned John Wicliffe. D. D.* (1720).

—— *The Life of Mayster Wyllyam Caxton* (1737).

—— *Presbyters Not Always an Authoritative Part of Provincial Synods. Being An Examination of a Part of Dr Brett's . . . Account of Church Government* (1710).

—— *A Sermon Preach'd at the Cathedral Church of Canterbury. On January the 30th,*

1718. Being the Day of the Martyrdom of the Blessed King Charles the First (1718).

Lewis, John, *A Specimen of the Gross Errors in the Second Volume of Mr Collier's Ecclesiastical History: being a Vindication of the Right Reverend and Learned Dr Gilbert Burnet, late Bishop of Sarum* (1724).

—— *Two Letters In Defence of the English Liturgy and Reformation. Being Remarks on Four Sermons, lately preach'd by Dr. Thomas Bisse* (1717).

——*A Vindication of the Right Reverend the Lord Bishop of Norwich from the Undeserved Reflections of the Revd. Mr John Johnson* (1714).

Lisle, Samuel, *A Sermon Preached before the House of Lords, in the Abbey-Church, Westminster, on Wednesday, April 14, being the Day Appointed by His Majesty's Royal Proclamation for a General Fast, on the Occasion of the Present War* (1744).

Lowth, Simon, *Catechetical Questions* (1673).

—— *Historical Collections Concerning Church Affairs . . . a Reply to Dr Hody* (1696).

—— *A Letter to Edward Stillingfleet* (1687).

—— *Of the Subject of Church Power* (1685).

Mann, Isaac, *A Familiar Exposition of the Church-Catechism in Five Parts, to which are added prayers for the use of children and servants* (5th edn., 1771).

[Manners, Nicholas], *Some Particulars of the Life and Experience of Nicholas Manners* (York, 1785).

Marsh, Richard, *The Advantage of Learnng in Religion. A Sermon Preach'd in the Cathedral-Church in Canterbury, September 1st, 1715. At the Anniversary Meeting of the Clergy and Gentlemen Educated at the King's School* (1715).

Marshall, Thomas, *The Catechism set forth in the Book of Common Prayer, briefly explained by Short Notes* (Oxford, 1679).

Masters, Richard, *History of the College of Corpus Christi..Cambridge* (1753).

Maurice, Henry, *A Letter Out of the Country* (1689).

Mills, Benjamin, *An Examination of the Remarks made by a Curate of the Diocese of Canterbury, on the Account of A Controversy between the author of The Trial of Mr Whitefield's Spirit, and Benjamin Mills* (1741).

Moore, Charles, *A Full Inquiry into the Subject of Suicide. To which are added (As Being Closely Connected With the Subject) Two Treatises on Duelling and Gaming*, 2 vols. (1790).

—— *The Sermons of Charles Moore*, 3 vols. (1818).

Du Moulin, Lewis, *A Short and True Acount of the Several Advances the Church of England Hath Made Towards Rome* (1680).

Du Moulin, Peter, *The Great Loyalty of the Papists* (1673).

[——], *A Letter to a Person of Quality, Concerning the Fines Received by the Church at its Restoration. By a Prebendary of the Church of Canterbury* (1668).

[——], *A Replie to a Person of Honour* (1695).

——*A Sermon Preached in the Metropolitical Church of Canterbury, October 17. MDCLXXII. At the Funeral of the very Reverend Thomas Turner, D.D. Dean of Canterbury* (1672).

Du Moulin, Peter, *A Vindication of the Sincerity of the Protestant Religion in the point of obedience to Sovereignes, opposed to the doctrine of rebellion, authorised and practised by the Pope and Jesuits* (1664).

Nares, Edward, *Sermons Composed for Country Congregations* (1803).

Nelson, Robert, *A Companion for the Festivals and Fasts of the Church of England* (1704).

Newton, William, *An Essay against Unnecessary Curiosity in Matters of Religion. Applied particularly to the Doctrine of the Blessed Trinity* (1720).

Nicholls, Charles, *The Hue and Cry after Priests* (1651).

Nisbett, Nehemiah, *An Attempt to display the Original Evidences of Christianity in their Genuine Simplicity* (1807).

—— *Britain's Victories from God. A Sermon Preached on Thursday, the 29th of November, before the Worshipful the Mayor and Jurats of the Town and Port of Sandwich* (Canterbury, 1798).

—— *Ezekiel's Warning Applied to the Threatened Invasion of Great Britain. A Sermon Delivered at Ash 8 March 1797* (Canterbury, 1797).

D'Oyly, G., *The Life of William Sancroft, Archbishop of Canterbury* 2 vols. (1821).

Old Romney Religious Society Minutes of Meeting (1701).

The Nonconformist's Memorial; Being An Account of the Lives, Sufferings and Printed Works of the Two Thousand Ministers Ejected from the Church of England . . . Originally Written by Edward Calamy, ed. Samuel Palmer, 3 vols. (2nd edn., 1803).

Parker, Samuel, *An Account of the Government of the Christian Church for the First Six Hundred Years* (1683).

—— *A Discourse of Ecclesiastical Politie, wherein the Authority of the Civil Magistrate over the Conscience of Subjects in Matters of Religion is Asserted* (1670).

—— *Religion and Loyalty: or, The Power of the Christian Church within itself. The Supremacy of Sovereign Powers over it. The Duty of Passive Obedience, or Non Resistance to all their Commands* (1684).

Parsons, Philip, *Six Letters to a Friend on the Establishment of Sunday Schools* (1786).

Paske, Thomas, *The Copy of a Letter Sent to an Honourable Lord* (1642).

Pegge, Samuel, *Light Shining in Darkness; or, the Effects of the Christian Institution, Antiently, Upon the Recusant Pagan, And at Present, Upon the Modern Infidel. Preached at Christ's Church, Canterbury, on St. John's Day, 1742* (1742).

—— *Popery, an Encourager of Vice and Immorality; a Sermon Preach'd at the Cathedral Church of Canterbury, on Occasion of the Present Unnatural Rebellion* (1745).

Pellew, George, *A Letter to the Right Honourable Sir Robert Peel. Bt. M.A. on the Means of 'Rendering Cathedral Churches More Conducive to the Efficiency of the Established Church'* (1837).

Pierce, Thomas, *A Collection of Sermons upon Several Occasions* (Oxford, 1671).

The Poll of the Electors for Members of Parliament to represent the City of Canterbury (Canterbury, 1796).

Potter, John, *The Archbishop of Canterbury's Letter to the Right Reverend Lord Bishops of His Province* (Stamford, 1737).

—— *The Theological Works of the Most Reverend Dr John Potter, Late Lord Archbishop of Canterbury*, 3 vols. (Oxford, 1753-4).

Priestley, Joseph, *Letters to Dr Horne, Dean of Canterbury* (Birmingham, 1787).

Pusey, E. B., *Remarks on the Prospective and Past Benefits of Cathedral Institutions, in the Promotion of Sound Religious Knowledge, Occasioned by Lord Henley's Plan for their Abolition* (1833).

Radcliffe, Houston, *A Sermon Preached in His Majesty's Chapel at the Consecration of William Lord Bishop of Chester, Sunday Jan. 20 1788* (1788).

Randolph, Thomas, *The Advantages of Publick Education. A Sermon preach'd in the Cathedral-Church at Canterbury, on Thursday, September 13, 1733* (Oxford, 1733).

Reading, John, *Anabaptism Routed: or a Survey of the Controverted Points concerning 1. Infant Baptism 2. Pretended Necessity of Dipping 3. The Dangerous Practise of Rebaptising* (1655).

—— *Christmas Revived; or, an Answer to objections made against the Observance of a Day in Memory of our Saviour Christ His Birth* (1660).

—— *The Ranter's Ranting, with the Apprehending Examinations and Confession of John Collins* (1650).

—— *A Sermon Lately Delivered in the Cathedral Church of Canterbury, Concerning Church-Musick* (1663).

—— *A Speech made before the King's Most Excellent Majesty Charles II, on the shore where he landed at Dover, by John Reading who presented his Majesty with a Bible, the Gift of the Inhabitants there, May 25th 1660*.

Regis, Balthasar, *The Mystery of Godliness Consider'd, and Oppos'd to the Mystery of Iniquity. In a Sermon preach'd at the Visitation in Canterbury, May Fifth, 1721* (1721).

Report from the Clergy of a District in the Diocese of Lincoln, Convened for the Purpose of Considering the State of Religion in the several Parishes of the said District, as Well as the Best Mode of Promoting the Belief and Practice of it . . . (1800).

The Return Made by the Governors of the Bounty of Queen Anne (1736).

Rudd, Sayer, *God's Promise: A Great Incentive to Christian Liberality. A Sermon Preached at Walmer in Kent, on Sunday, 12 July 1752 on the Occasion of the General Collection of the Charity made within the Provinces of Canterbury and York by his Majesty's special appointment in favour of the Incorporated Society for the Propagation of the Gospel in Foreign Parts* (1752).

Salmon, N., *The Lives of the English Bishops From the Restauration to the Revolution*, 2 vols. (1731-8).

Sancroft, William, *Sermons preached by the Most Reverend Father in God, William Sancroft, late Archbishop of Canterbury* (1703).

Sandys, Edwin, *The Importance of An Early Acquaintance with the Scriptures. A*

Sermon Preached on the Anniversary of the King's School, at the Cathedral, Canterbury, on August the 27th, 1812 (Canterbury, 1812).

Scott, William, *The Substance of the Speech of the Right Honourable Sir William Scott, delivered in the House of Commons, Wednesday April 7th 1802. Upon a motion for leave to bring in a Bill relative to the Non-Residence of the Clergy, and other affairs of the Church* (1802).

Secker, Thomas, *Eight Charges Delivered to the Clergy of the Dioceses of Oxford and Canterbury* (1769).

—— *Lectures on the Catechism of the Church of England with a Discourse on Confirmation*, 2 vols. (1769).

—— *The Works of Thomas Secker, LL.D late Lord Archbishop of Canterbury. To which is prefixed, A Review of his Grace's Life and character, by Beilby Porteus, D.D. late lord Bishop of London*, 8 vols. (1769).

Sheldon, Gilbert, *David's Day of Deliverance and Thanksgiving. A Sermon Preached before the King at Whitehall, 28 June 1660, being the Day of Solemn Thanksgiving for the Happy Return of His Majesty* (1660).

Sherlock, Thomas, *The Option; or, an Enquiry into the Grounds of the Claim made by the Archbishop of Canterbury* (1756).

Smith, James, *The Errors of the Church of Rome Detected* (Canterbury, 1777).

Some Select Queries Humbly offered to the Consideration of the D——of C——t——b——y (1683).

Stanhope, George, *The Christian's Pattern; or a Treatise on the Imitation of Christ* (1696).

—— *The Danger of Hard-Heartedness to the Poor. A Sermon preached at a meeting of the Gentlemen concerned in promoting the Charity Schools in London and Westminster 31 May 1705* (1705).

—— *The Duty of Juries. A Sermon preached at the Lent Assizes, holden at Maidstone in Kent . . . April the Ist, 1701* (1701).

—— *The Duty of Rebuking, A Sermon preach'd at Bow Church December 18 1702 before the Societies for the Reformation of Manners . . . to which is added a Post-Script to the Religious Societies* (1703).

—— *The Duty of Witnesses. A Sermon, preach'd at the Summer Assizes holden at Maidstone in Kent . . . August the 5th 1701* (1701).

—— *The Early Conversion of Islanders, a Wise Expedient for Propagating Christianity. A Sermon Preached before the Society for the Propagation of the Gospel in Foreign Parts* (1714).

—— *The Grounds and Principles of the Christian Religion by J. T. Oestervald. Translated by George Stanhope* (1704).

—— *A Paraphrase and Comment upon the Epistles and Gospels. Appointed to be used in the Church of England on all Sundays and Holy Days throughout the Year. Designed to Excite Devotion and Promote the Knowledge and Practice of Sincere Piety and Virtue*, 4 vols. (1705).

—— *Parsons. His Christian Directory* (1699).

—— *Salvation. Every Man's Great Concern (by R. Rapin). Done into English by George Stanhope* (1699).

—— *A Sermon Preached at the Annual Meeting of the Sons of the Clergy 7 December 1697* (1698).

—— *A Sermon Preach'd before the Archbishop . . . the Bishops and the Clergy of Canterbury. Done from the Latin* (1705).

—— *The Truth and Excellence of the Christian Religion. In Sixteen Sermons, preached at the lecture founded by the Hon. Robert Boyle* (1701-2).

Stillingfleet, Edward, *Origines Britannicae* (1685).

Sydall, Elias, *The Clergy Farther Vindicated. A Sermon Preach'd in the Cathedral-Church of Canterbury, at the Primary Visitation of William Ld Archbishop of Canterbury, on Saturday June 16th 1716* (1716).

—— *The Insupportable Yoke of Popery, and the Wickedness of Bringing it again upon these Kingdoms . . . In a Sermon Preach'd at the Cathedral-Church of Canterbury, on Saturday November 5 1715* (1715).

Sykes, Arthur Ashley, *An Answer to that part of Dr Brett's Sermon which relates to the Incapacity of persons not episcopally ordained to administer Christian Baptism* (1712).

Synge, Edward, *An Abstract of the Church Catechism* (1744).

—— *A Plain and Easy Method, whereby a Man of a Moderate Capacity may arrive at Full Satisfaction in all things that Concern his Everlasting Salvation* (1715).

Tenison, Edward, *The True Copies of Some Letters, Occasion'd by the Demand for Dilapidations in the Archiepiscopal See of Canterbury* (1716).

[Tenison, Thomas], *Articles of Visitation and Enquiry to be answered into at the Visitation of Thomas Archbishop of Canterbury, 1706* (1706).

[——], *Memoirs of the Life and times of the Most Reverend Father in God, Dr Thomas Tenison, late Archbishop of Canterbury* (1716).

—— *A Sermon Concerning the Folly of Atheism* (1691).

Terry, Isaac, *The Religious and Loyal Subject's Duty Consider'd, with regard to the present Government and the Revolution. A Sermon Preached in the Cathedral Church of Canterbury, on Wednesday, January 30, 1723. Being the Anniversary Fast of the Martyrdom of King Charles I* (1723).

Thorp, George, *The Fifth Note of the Church Examined* (1688).

Tillotson, John, *Life of Tillotson* (1717).

—— *A Persuasive to Frequent Communion in the Holy Sacrament of the Lord's Supper* (1683).

—— *Sermons*, 12 vols. (1757).

Todd, Henry John, *Catalogue of the Archiepiscopal Manuscripts in the Library at Lambeth Palace* (1812).

—— *Some Account of the Deans of Canterbury; from the New Foundation of that Church, by Henry the Eighth to the Present Time* (Canterbury and London, 1793).

Venn, Henry, *The Complete Duty of Man: Or, A System of Doctrinal and Practical Christianity* (1763).

[Vokins, Joan], *God's Mighty Power Magnified: as Manifested and Revealed in his Faithful Handmaid Joan Vokins* (1691).

Wade, John, *The Black Book: or Corruption Unmask'd!* (1820).

Wake, William, *The Principles of the Christian Religion Explained; in a brief commentary upon the Church-Catechism* (1694).

—— *The State of the Church and Clergy of England* (1703).

Warner, Ferdinando, *The Ecclesiastical History of England, to the Eighteenth Century*, 2 vols. (1756–7).

Wesley, John, *Works*, 14 vols. (1872).

Wharton, Henry, *A Treatise of the Celibacy of the Clergy, wherein its Rise and Progress are Historically Considered* (1688).

—— and George Stanhope, *A Defence of Pluralities, or, Holding two benefices with cure of souls, as now practised in the Church of England* (1692).

Whitfield, Francis, *The Utility and Importance of Human Learning, stated in a Sermon Preached in the Parish Church of Ashford in Kent. On Wednesday, August 14, 1782* (Canterbury and London, 1782).

Wilkins, David, *Concilia Magnae Britanniae et Hiberniae*, 4 vols. (1737).

—— *Leges Anglo-Saxonicae Ecclesiasticae et Civiles* (1721).

Williams, Isaac, *A Familiar Exposition of the Church Catechism* (4th edn., 1776).

Williams, John, *The Difference between the Church of England and the Church of Rome* (1687).

—— *A Vindication of the Sermons of Archbishop Tillotson Concerning the Divinity and Incarnation of our Blessed Saviour* (1695).

Willis, Browne, *Parochiale Anglicanum: or, the names of all the churches and chapels within the dioceses of Canterbury etc . . .* (1733).

Wise, Thomas, *The Christian Eucharist No Proper Sacrifice* (1714).

—— *The Christian Eucharist Rightly Stated* (1711).

—— *The Faithful Stewards: or, the Pastoral Duty Open'd: in a Visitation-Sermon Preach'd at St Margaret's Church in Canterbury, June the Ist. 1710* (1710).

—— *The Folly of Apostacy from God and from the King. A Sermon preach'd at the Cathedral Church of Canterbury, October 18, 1715* (1726).

—— *Fourteen Discourses on some of the Most Important Heads in Divinity and Morality; Deliver'd all of them (except the 13th) upon Saints or other Solemn Days, at the Cathedral and Metropolitical Church of Canterbury* (1717).

—— *Religion and Loyalty. A Sermon preach'd at the Parish Church of St Alphege in Canterbury, August the Ist, 1715* (1715).

—— *The Truth of the Christian Religion. Written originally in Italian for the Benefit of the Court of Savoy, by the Marquis of Pianezza* (1703).

Wood, Anthony, *Athenae Oxonienses*, ed. Philip Bliss, 4 vols. (1813–20).

Woodward, Josiah, *An Account of the Rise and Progress of the Religious Societies in the City of London* (1698).

2.3. PARLIAMENTARY SOURCES

An Act for Vesting Several Sums of Money, Given for Charitable Uses, in the Arch-bishop of Canterbury, the Bishop of Ely and the Dean of Canterbury; and to im-power them to place the same with the Governors of Queen Anne's Bounty (1727).
Journals of the House of Lords.
Parliamentary Papers, 1810, X, *Returns on the Residence of Beneficed Clergy.*
Parliamentary Papers, 1812, X, *Abstract of the Number and Classes of Non-Resident Incumbents, and of the Number of Resident Incumbents, According to the Diocesan Returns for the Year 1810.*
Parliamentary Papers, 1812, X, *Abstract of the Number of Resident and Licensed Curates, with the Amount of the Salaries of Curacies, According to the Diocesan Returns for the Year 1810.*
Parliamentary Papers, 1817, IX, *Report of the Commissioners for the Charities in England and Wales for the Education of the Poor.*
Parliamentary Papers, 1835, XXII, *Report of the Commissioners appointed by His Majesty to inquire into the Ecclesiastical Revenues of England and Wales.*
Parliamentary Papers, 1837, XLI, *Return of all the Remonstrances made to the Church Commissioners respecting the union of the Sees of St Asaph and Bangor and Further . . . Return Memorials . . . Relating to Cathedrals.*

2.4 PERIODICALS

Gentleman's Magazine.
Mercurius Publicus.
Olla Podrida.

3. SECONDARY SOURCES

3.1. REFERENCE WORKS

Butchaell, G. D., and T. U. Sadleir, *Alumni Dublinienses, 1505–1905*, 2 vols. (1924).
Dunkin, E. H. W., Claude Jenkins, and E. A. Fry, *Index to the Act Books of the Arch-bishops of Canterbury, 1663–1859*, Index Library, lv, lxiii, 2 vols. (1929–38).
Foster, J., *Alumni Oxonienses. The Members of the University of Oxford, 1500–1714; their Parentage, Birthplace, and Year of Birth, with a Record of their Degrees*, 4 vols. (Oxford, 1891–2).
—— *Alumni Oxonienses. The Members of the University of Oxford, 1715–1886: their Parentage, Birthplace, and Year of Birth, with a Record of their Degrees*, 4 vols. (Oxford, 1888).
Houston, Jane (ed.), *Index of Cases in the Records of the Court of Arches, 1660–1913*, British Record Society (1972).

Le Neve, John, *Fasti Ecclesiae Anglicanae, 1541–1857*, iii. *Canterbury, Rochester and Winchester Dioceses*, comp. J. M. Horn (1974).

Matthews, A. G., *Calamy Revised* (Oxford, 1934).

—— *Walker Revised* (Oxford, 1947).

Robinson, F. J. G., *et al.*, *Eighteenth Century British Books: An Author Union Catalogue*, 5 vols. (Folkestone and Newcastle upon Tyne, 1981).

Venn, J., and J. A. Venn, *Alumni Cantabrigienses. A Biographical List of All Known Students, Graduates and Holders of the University of Cambridge, from the Earliest Times to 1900, Part I. From the Earliest Time to 1751*, 4 vols. (Cambridge, 1922–7).

—— —— *Alumni Cantabrigienses. A Biographical List of All Known Students, Graduates and Holders of the University of Cambridge, from the Earliest Times to 1900, Part II. From 1752 to 1900*, 6 vols. (Cambridge, 1940–54).

Victoria County History of Kent.

Victoria County History of Yorkshire.

Wing, Donald, *Short Title Catalogue, 1641–1700*, 3 vols. (1945–51).

3.2. BOOKS

Abbey, C. J., *The English Church and its Bishops, 1700–1800*, 2 vols. (1887).

—— and J. H. Overton, *The English Church in the Eighteenth Century*, 2 vols. (1878).

Addleshaw, G. W. O., and F. Etchells, *The Architectural Setting of Anglican Worship. An Inquiry into the Arrangements for Public Worship in the Church of England from the Reformation to the Present Day* (1948).

Ashton, John, *Chap-books of the Eighteenth Century* (1882).

Aston, N., *The End of an Elite: The French Bishops and the Coming of the Revolution, 1786–1790* (Oxford, 1992).

Aylmer, G. E., and R. Cant (eds.), *A History of York Minster* (Oxford, 1977).

Bahlman, D. W. R., *The Moral Revolution of 1688* (New Haven, Conn., 1957).

Baker, Frank, *John Wesley and the Church of England* (1970).

Barnard, L. W., *John Potter. An Eighteenth-Century Archbishop* (Ilfracombe, 1989).

—— *Thomas Secker. An Eighteenth-Century Primate* (Lewes, 1998).

Barrie-Curien, V., *Clergé et pastorale en Angleterre au xviiième siècle: le diocèse de Londres* (Paris, 1992).

Bate, F., *The Declaration of Indulgence 1672: A Study in the Rise of Organised Dissent* (1908).

Bebb, E. R., *Nonconformity and Social and Economic Life, 1600–1800* (1935).

Bennett, G. V., *The Tory Crisis in Church and State, 1688–1730. The Career of Francis Atterbury, Bishop of Rochester* (Oxford, 1975).

—— *White Kennett, 1660–1728, Bishop of Peterborough* (1957).

Best, G. F. A., *Temporal Pillars. Queen Anne's Bounty, the Ecclesiastical Commissioners and the Church of England* (Cambridge, 1964).

Bewes, W. A., *Church Briefs, or Royal Warrants for Collections for Charitable Objects* (1896).

Bill, E. G. W., *Education at Christ Church, Oxford, 1660–1800* (Oxford, 1988).

Black, Jeremy (ed.), *Britain in the Age of Walpole* (1985).

Bosher, R. S., *The Making of the Restoration Settlement. The Influence of the Laudians, 1649–62* (1951).

Bossy, J., *Christianity in the West, 1400–1700* (Oxford, 1985).

—— *The English Catholic Community, 1570–1850* (1975).

Boulay, F. R. H. Du, *The Lordship of Canterbury* (1966).

Boyle, J., *In Quest of Hasted* (Chichester, 1984).

Bradley, Ian, *The Call to Seriousness. The Evangelical Impact on the Victorians* (1976).

Bradley, J. E., *Religion, Revolution and English Radicalism. Non-conformity in Eighteenth-Century Politics and Society* (Cambridge, 1990).

Brewer, J., *Party, Ideology and Popular Politics at the Accession of George III* (Cambridge, 1976).

Brooks, N., *The Early History of the Church of Canterbury. Christ Church from 597 to 1066* (Leicester, 1984).

Brose, O. J., *Church and Parliament: The Reshaping of the Church of England, 1828–1860* (Stanford, Calif., and London, 1960).

Browning, R., *Political and Constitutional Ideas of the Court Whigs* (Baton Rouge, La., 1982).

Buckingham, Christopher, *Catholic Dover* (Canterbury, 1968).

Bullock, F. W. B., *The History of Training for the Ministry of the Church of England, 1800–1874* (St Leonard's-on-Sea, 1955).

Burke, P., *Popular Culture in Early Modern Europe* (1978).

Burtt, S., *Virtue Transformed. Political Argument in England, 1688–1740* (Cambridge, 1992).

Bushaway, B., *By Rite. Custom, Ceremony and Community in England, 1700–1800* (1982).

Bussby, F., *Winchester Cathedral, 1079–1974* (Southampton, 1979).

Callahan, W. J., and D. Higgs (eds.), *Church and Society in Catholic Europe of the Eighteenth Century* (Cambridge, 1983).

Cameron, Euan, *The European Reformation* (Oxford, 1990).

Capp, B., *Astrology and the Popular Press: English Almanacs, 1500–1800* (1500–1800).

—— *Cromwell's Navy: The Fleet and the English Revolution, 1648–1660* (Oxford, 1990).

Carpenter, E. F., *Thomas Sherlock, 1678–1761* (1936).

—— *Thomas Tenison, Archbishop of Canterbury. His Life and Times* (1948).

Carpenter, S. C., *Eighteenth Century Church and People* (1959).

Chadwick, W. O., *The Victorian Church*, 2 vols. (1966–70).

Chalklin, C. W., *Seventeenth Century Kent: A Social and Economic History* (2nd edn., Rochester, 1975).

Chamberlain, Jeffrey S., *Accommodating High Churchmen. The Clergy of Sussex, 1700–45* (Urbana, Ill. and Chicago, 1997).

Champion, J. A. I., *The Pillars of Priestcraft Shaken. The Church of England and its Enemies, 1660–1730* (Cambridge, 1992).

Chatfield, Mark, *Churches the Victorians Forgot* (Trowbridge, 1979).

Christie, Ian R., *Stress and Stability in late Eighteenth Century Britain: Reflections on the British Avoidance of Revolution* (Oxford, 1984).

Churchill, I. J., *Canterbury Administration: The Administrative Machinery of the Diocese of Canterbury Illustrated from Original Records*, 2 vols. (1933).

Clark, J. C. D., *English Society, 1688–1832. Ideology, Social Structure and Political Practice during the Ancien Regime* (Cambridge, 1985).

Clark, Peter, *The English Alehouse: A Social History, 1200–1830* (1983).

—— *English Provincial Society from the Reformation to the Revolution: Religion, Politics and Society in Kent, 1500–1640* (Hassocks, 1977).

Clarke, Basil F. L., *The Building of the Eighteenth-Century Church* (1963).

Claydon, Tony, *William III and the Godly Revolution* (Cambridge, 1996).

Colchester, L. S. (ed.), *Wells Cathedral. A History* (Wells, 1987).

Coleby, A. M., *Central Government and the Localities: Hampshire, 1646–1689* (Cambridge, 1987).

Colley, Linda, *In Defiance of Oligarchy: The Tory Party 1714–1760* (Cambridge, 1982).

Collinson, P., *The Birthpangs of Protestant England. Religious and Cultural Change in the Sixteenth and Seventeenth Centuries* (1988).

—— *The Elizabethan Puritan Movement* (Berkeley, Calif., 1967).

—— *English Puritanism* (1983).

—— *Godly People. Essays on English Protestantism and Puritanism* (1983).

—— *The Religion of Protestants. The Church in English Society, 1559–1625* (Oxford, 1982).

—— Nigel Ramsay, and Margaret Sparks (eds.), *A History of Canterbury Cathedral* (Oxford, 1995).

Cowper, J. Meadows, *The Lives of the Deans of Canterbury, 1541 to 1900* (Canterbury, 1900).

Cox, N., *Bridging the Gap. A History of the Corporation of the Sons of the Clergy over 300 years. 1655–1978* (Oxford, 1978).

Cragg, G. R., *Puritanism in the Period of the Great Persecution, 1660–1688* (Cambridge, 1957).

Cross, C., *Church and People, 1450–1660* (1976).

Cross, F. W., *History of the Walloon and Huguenot Church at Canterbury* (Canterbury, 1898).

Currie, R., A. Gilbert, and L. Horsley, *Churches and Churchgoers. Patterns of Church Growth in the British Isles since 1700* (Oxford, 1977).

Curtis, L. P., *Chichester Towers* (New Haven, Conn., and London, 1965).

Daley, A. A., *History of the Isle of Sheppey* (1904).

Davidoff, L., and C. Hall, *Family Fortunes. Men and Women of the English Middle Class, 1780–1850* (1987).

Davies, H., *Worship and Theology in England*, iii. (Oxford, 1961).

Davies, Julian, *The Caroline Captivity of the Church. Charles I and the Remoulding of Anglicanism 1625–1641* (Oxford, 1992).

Davis, J. F., *Heresy and Reformation in the South East of England, 1520–1559* (1983).

Dearnley, Christopher, *English Church Music, 1650–1750* (1970).

Delumeau, Jean, *Le Catholicisme entre Luther et Voltaire* (Paris, 1971) [English tr., London, 1977].

Derry, W., *Dr Parr. A Portrait of the Whig Doctor Johnson* (Oxford, 1966).

Dewey, C., *The Passing of Barchester. A Real Life Version of Trollope* (Leicester, 1991).

Dickinson, H. T., *Liberty and Property. Political Ideology in Eighteenth Century Britain* (1977).

Douglas, D. C., *English Scholars, 1660–1730* (2nd edn., 1951).

Downey, J., *The Eighteenth Century Pulpit* (Oxford, 1969).

Eastwood, David, *Governing Rural England. Tradition and Transformation in Local Government, 1780–1840* (Oxford, 1994).

Edwards, D. L., *Christian England*, ii. *From the Reformation to the Eighteenth Century* (1983).

—— *A History of the King's School, Canterbury* (1957).

Elliott, P., *The Sociology of the Professions* (1972).

Elliott-Binns, L., *The Early Evangelicals* (1953).

Evans, E. J., *The Contentious Tithe. The Tithe Problem and English Agriculture, 1750–1850* (1976).

Everitt, A., *The Community of Kent and the Great Rebellion* (Leicester, 1966).

—— *Continuity and Colonisation: The Evolution of Kentish Settlement* (Leicester, 1986).

—— *The County Committee of Kent in the Civil War*, University of Leicester, Department of Local History, Occasional Papers, 9 (1957).

—— *Landscape and Community in England* (1985).

—— *The Pattern of Rural Dissent: The Nineteenth Century*, University of Leicester, Department of Local History, Occasional Papers, 4 (1972).

Every, G., *The High Church Party, 1688–1718* (1956).

Fincham, K., *Prelate as Pastor. The Episcopate of James I* (Oxford, 1990).

Firth, C., and R. Raith (eds.), *Acts and Ordinances of the Interregnum, 1642–1660*, 2 vols. (1911).

Fletcher, A., *Reform in the Provinces: The Government of Stuart England* (Princeton, NJ and London, 1986).

Gardiner, Dorothy, *A History of Lambeth Palace* (1953).

Gascoigne, J., *Cambridge in the Age of the Enlightenment: Science, Religion and Politics from the Restoration to the French Revolution* (Cambridge, 1989).

Gentles, I. J., and W. J. Sheils, *Confiscation and Restoration; The Archbishopric Estates and the Civil War*, Borthwick Papers, 59 (York, 1981).

Gibson, Margaret, *Lanfranc of Bec* (Oxford, 1978).

Gibson, W. A., *The Achievement of the Anglican Church, 1689–1800. The Confessional State in Eighteenth-Century England* (Lampeter, 1995).

—— *Church, State and Society, 1760–1850* (Basingstoke, 1994).

Gilbert, A. D., *Religion and Society in Industrial England. Church, Chapel and Social Change, 1740–1914* (1976).

Golden, R. M. (ed.), *Church, State and Society under the Bourbon Kings of France* (Kansas, 1982).

Graham, Elspeth, Hilary Hind, Elaine Hobby, and Helen Wilcox (eds.), *Her Own Life. Autobiographical Writings by Seventeenth-Century Englishwomen* (1989).

Grant Robertson, C., *All Souls: Oxford College Histories* (1899).

Greaves, R. W., *On the Religious Climate of Hanoverian England*, Inaugural Lecture, Bedford College (1963).

Green, I. M. *The Christian's ABC. Catechisms and Catechizing in England, c.1530–1740* (Oxford, 1996).

—— *The Re-establishment of the Church of England, 1660–1663* (Oxford, 1978).

Gwynn, R. D., *Huguenot Heritage: The History and Contribution of the Huguenots in Britain* (1985).

Haig, Alan, *The Victorian Clergy* (Beckenham, 1984).

Haigh, C., *Reformation and Resistance in Tudor Lancashire* (Cambridge, 1976).

Hall, F. M., R. S. Stevens, and J. Whyman, *The Kent and Canterbury Hospital, 1790–1987* (Ramsgate, 1987).

Harling, Philip, *The Waning of Old Corruption. The Politics of Economical Reform in Britain, 1779–1846* (Oxford, 1996).

Harris, T., P. Seaward, and M. Goldie (eds.), *The Politics of Religion in Restoration England* (Oxford, 1990).

Hart, A. Tindal., *The Life and Times of John Sharp, Archbishop of York* (1949).

Harvey, W., *The Seasalter Company—a Smuggling Fraternity* (Whitstable, 1983).

Heal, F., *Hospitality in Early Modern England* (Oxford, 1990).

—— *Of Prelates and Princes. A Study of the Economic and Social Position of the Tudor Episcopate* (Cambridge, 1980).

Heath, Peter, *The English Parish Clergy on the Eve of the Reformation* (1969).

Heeney, Brian, *A Different Kind of Gentleman. Parish Clergy as Professional Men in Early and Mid-Victorian England* (New Haven, Conn., 1976).

Henning, B. D. (ed.), *The House of Commons, 1715–1754*, 2 vols. (1984).

Higham, F., *Catholic and Reformed. A Study of the Anglican Church, 1559–1662* (1962).

Hill, C., *The Economic Problems of the Church from Archbishop Whitgift to the Long Parliament* (Oxford, 1956).

—— *Religion and Politics in Seventeenth-Century England* (Brighton, 1986).

—— *Society and Puritanism in Pre-Revolutionary England* (1966).

Hinde, Wendy, *Catholic Emancipation. A Shake to Men's Minds* (Oxford, 1992).

Hobbes, Mary (ed.), *Chichester Cathedral. An Historical Survey* (Chichester, 1994).

Hobsbawm, E. J. E. and G. F. E. Rudé, *Captain Swing* (1969).

Hoffman, P. T., *Church and Community in the Diocese of Lyon, 1500–1789* (New Haven, Conn., 1984).

Hole, Robert, *Pulpits, Politics and Public Order in England, 1760–1832* (Cambridge, 1990).

Holmes, G., *Augustan England. Professions, State and Society, 1680–1730* (1982).

—— *Politics, Religion and Society in England, 1679–1742* (1986).

Hook, W. F., *Lives of the Archbishops of Canterbury*, 11 vols. (1879).

Horn, Pamela, *The Rural World, 1780–1850* (1980).

Hufton, O., *Bayeux in the Late Eighteenth Century. A Social Study* (Oxford, 1967).

Hughes, Ann, *The Causes of the English Civil War* (1991).

Hunt, W. H., *The Puritan Moment: The Coming of Revolution in an English County* (Cambridge, Mass., 1983).

Hutton, Ronald, *The Restoration: A Political and Religious History of England and Wales, 1658–1667* (Oxford, 1985).

Hylsom-Smith, Kenneth, *The Churches in England from Elizabeth I to Elizabeth II*, ii. *1689–1833* (1997).

Jacob, M. C., *The Newtonians and the English Revolution* (Hassocks, 1976).

Jacob, W. M., *Lay People and Religion in the Early Eighteenth Century* (Cambridge, 1996).

Jenkins, G. H., *Literature, Religion and Society in Wales, 1660–1730* (Cardiff, 1978).

Jenkins, R. C., *Diocesan Histories: Canterbury* (1880).

Jones, M. G., *The Charity School Movement. A Study of Eighteenth-Century Puritanism in Action* (Cambridge, 1938).

Kauffman, Paul, *Libraries and their Users: Collected Papers in Library History* (1969).

Keane, John, *Tom Paine. A Political Life* (1995).

Keith-Lucas, B., *Parish Affairs. The Government of Kent under George III* (Maidstone, 1986).

Kemp, E. W., *An Introduction to the Canon Law of the Church of England* (1957).

Knight, F., *The Nineteenth-Century Church and English Society* (Cambridge, 1995).

Knowles, Dom David, *The Religious Orders of England*, 3 vols. (Cambridge, 1957).

Lacey, D. R., *Dissent and Parliamentary Politics in England, 1661–1689* (New Brunswick, NJ, 1969).

Landau, Norma, *The Justices of the Peace, 1679–1760* (Berkeley, Calif. and Los Angeles, Calif., 1984).

Langford, Paul, *A Polite and Commercial People, England 1727–1783* (Oxford, 1989).

—— *Public Life and the Propertied Englishman, 1689–1798* (Oxford, 1991).

Langlois, C., *Le Diocèse de Vannes au xix siècle, 1800–1830* (Paris, 1974).

Laqueur, T., *Religion and Respectability: Sunday Schools and Working Class Culture, 1780–1850* (New Haven, Conn., 1976).

Larner, C., *Witchcraft and Religion. The Politics of Popular Belief* (Oxford, 1984).

Laslett, Peter, *The World We Have Lost—Further Explored* (1983).

Lee-Warner, E., *The Life of John Warner* (1901).

Legg, J. Wickham, *English Church Life from the Restoration to the Tractarian Movement, Considered in Some of its Neglected or Forgotten Features* (1914).

—— and W. H. St J. Hope, *Inventories of Christchurch, Canterbury* (1902).

Lessenich, R. P., *Elements of Pulpit Oratory in Eighteenth Century England, 1660–1800* (Cologne and Vienna, 1972).

Lovegrove, D. W., *Established Church, Sectarian People. Itinerancy and the Transformation of English Dissent, 1780–1830* (Cambridge, 1989).

Lowther Clarke, W. K., *Eighteenth Century Piety* (1944).

McAdoo, H. R., *The Spirit of Anglicanism. A Survey of Anglican Theological Method in the Seventeenth Century* (1965).

Macaulay, Thomas Babbington, *The History of England From the Accession of James II*, 4 vols. (Everyman edn., 1906).

McCahill, M. W., *Order and Equipoise; The Peerage and the House of Lords, 1783–1806* (1978).

McClatchey, D., *Oxfordshire Clergy, 1777–1869. A Study of the Established Church and the Role of its Clergy in Local Society* (Oxford, 1960).

Machin., G. I. T., *The Catholic Question in English Politics 1820–1830* (Oxford, 1964).

McManners, J., *French Ecclesiastical Society under the Ancien Regime; A Study of Angers in the Eighteenth Century* (Manchester, 1960).

Malcolmson, R. W., *Life and Labour in England, 1700–1800* (1981).

Marshall, P. J., and Glyndwr Williams, *The Great Map of Mankind. British Perceptions of the World in the Age of the Enlightenment* (1982).

Marshall, W. M., *George Hooper, 1640–1727. Bishop of Bath and Wells* (Milbourne Port, 1976).

Mason, T. A., *Serving God and Mammon: William Juxon, 1582–1663* (Cranbury, NJ, 1985).

Mather, F. C., *High Church Prophet. Bishop Samuel Horsley (1733–1806) and the Caroline Tradition in the Later Georgian Church* (Oxford, 1992).

Mathieson, W. L., *English Church Reform, 1815–40* (1923).

Matthews, W. R., and W. M. Atkins, *A History of St Paul's Cathedral* (1957).

Monod, Paul Kleber, *Jacobitism and the English People, 1688–1788* (Cambridge, 1989).

Morgan, E. S., *The Puritan Family: Religion and Domestic Relations in Seventeenth-Century New England* (New Haven, Conn., 1944).

Morgan, J., *Godly Learning: Puritan Attitudes Towards Reason, Learning and Education, 1560–1640* (Cambridge, 1986).

Namier, L. B., *The Structure of Politics at the Accession of George III* (1929; 2nd edn., 1957).

—— and John Brooke (eds.), *The History of Parliament: The House of Commons, 1754–1790*, 3 vols. (1964).

Nokes, D., *Jonathan Swift: A Hypocrite Reversed* (Oxford, 1985).

Nockles, Peter B., *The Oxford Movement in Context. Anglican High-Churchmanship, 1760–1857* (Cambridge, 1994).

Norman, E. R., *Church and Society in England, 1770–1970: A Historical Study* (Oxford, 1976).

Obelkevich, James, *Religion and Rural Society: South Lindsey, 1825–1875* (1976).

O'Day, R., *The English Clergy: The Emergence and Consolidation of a Profession, 1558–1642* (Leicester, 1979).

—— and F. Heal, *Continuity and Change: Personnel and Administration of the Church in England, 1500–1642* (Leicester, 1976).

Owen, Dorothy M., *The Records of the Established Church in England Excluding Parochial Records*, British Records Association, Archives and the User, 1 (1970).

Overton, J. H., and F. C. Relton, *The English Church from the Accession of George I to the End of the Eighteenth Century, 1714–1800* (1906).

Pailin, David A., *Attitudes to Other Religions: Comparative Religion in Seventeenth and Eighteenth Century Britain* (Manchester, 1984).

Parker, K. L., *The English Sabbath: A Study of Doctrine and Discipline from the Reformation to the Civil War* (Cambridge, 1988).

Parker, R. A. C., *Coke of Norfolk: A Financial and Agricultural Study, 1707–1842* (Oxford, 1975).

Perry, G. G., *A History of the Church of England*, 3 vols. (1861–4).

Perry, T. W., *Public Opinion, Propaganda and Politics in Eighteenth-Century England. A Study of the Jew Bill of 1753* (Cambridge, Mass., 1962).

Peters, R., *Oculus Episcopi: Administration in the Archdeaconry of St Albans (1580–1625)* (Manchester, 1963).

Pevsner, N., *The Buildings of England, North East Kent* (3rd edn., 1984).

Plongeron, B., *La Vie quotidienne du clergé français au xviiième siècle* (Paris, 1974).

Phillips, J. A., *Electoral Behaviour in Unreformed England: Plumpers, Splitters and Straights* (Princeton, NJ, 1982).

Plumb, J. H., *In the Light of History* (1972).

Porter, Roy, *English Society in the Eighteenth Century* (Harmondsworth, 1982).

Pruett, John H., *The Parish Clergy Under the Later Stuarts: The Leicestershire Experience* (Urbana, Ill., 1978).

Ravitch, N., *Sword and Mitre. Government and Episcopate in France and England in the Age of Aristocracy* (The Hague, 1966).

Reader, W. J., *Professional Men: The Rise of the Professional Classes in Victorian England* (1966).

Reay, Barry, *The Last Rising of the Agricultural Labourers. Rural Life and Protest in Nineteenth-Century England* (Oxford, 1990).

Redwood, John, *Reason, Ridicule and Religion. The Age of Enlightenment in England, 1660–1750* (1976).

Reedy, G. R., *The Bible and Reason. Anglicans and Scripture in Late Seventeenth-Century England* (Philadelphia, 1975).

Rivers, I., *Reason, Grace, and Sentiment. A Study of the Language of Religion and Ethics in England, 1660–1780*, i. *Whichcote to Wesley* (Cambridge, 1991).

Roberts, D., *Paternalism in Early Victorian England* (1979).

Rowden, A. W., *The Primates of the Four Georges* (1916).

Rowse, A. L., *Reflections on the Puritan Revolution* (1986).

Rupp, E. G., *Religion in England, 1688–1791* (Oxford, 1986).

Russell, Anthony, *The Clerical Profession* (1980).

Russell, John, *History of Maidstone* (1843).

Sack, James J., *From Jacobite to Conservative. Reaction and Orthodoxy in Britain, 1760–1832* (Cambridge, 1993).

Savidge, A., *The Foundation and Early Years of Queen Anne's Bounty* (1955).

Sedgwick, Romney (ed.), *The History of Parliament: The House of Commons, 1715–54*, 2 vols. (1970).

Shaw, W. A., *A History of the English Church During the Civil Wars and Under the Commonwealth*, 2 vols. (1900).

Simon, W. G., *The Restoration Episcopate* (New York, 1965).

S[mith], G[eorge], *A Chronological History of Canterbury Cathedral* (Canterbury, 1883).

Smith, Mark, *Religion in Industrial Society. Oldham and Saddleworth, 1740–1865* (Oxford, 1994).

Smith, R. A. L., *Canterbury Cathedral Priory. A Study in Monastic Administration* (Cambridge, 1943).

Smith, R. J., *The Gothic Bequest. Medieval Institutions in British Thought, 1688–1863* (Cambridge, 1987).

Smyth, C. H., *The Art of Preaching. A Practical Survey of Preaching in the Church of England, 747–1939* (1940).

—— *Simeon and Church Order. A Study of the Origins of the Evangelical Revival in Cambridge in the Eighteenth Century* (Cambridge, 1940).

Soloway, R. A., *Prelates and People: Ecclesiastical Social Thought in England, 1783–1852* (1969).

Sommerville, C. J., *Popular Religion in Restoration England* (Gainesville, Fla., 1977).

Speck, W. A., *Society and Literature in England, 1700–1760* (Dublin, 1983).

—— *Stability and Strife. England 1714–1760* (1977).

—— *Tory and Whig, The Struggle in the Constituencies, 1701–1715* (1970).

Spiller, M. R. G., *Concerning Natural Philosophy. Meric Casaubon and the Royal Society* (The Hague, 1980).

Spufford, Margaret, *Contrasting Communities: English Villagers in the Sixteenth and Seventeenth Centuries* (Cambridge, 1974).

—— *Small Books and Pleasant Histories: Popular Fiction and its Readership in Seventeenth-Century England* (1981).

—— (ed.), *The World of Rural Dissenters, 1520–1755* (Cambridge, 1993).

Spurr, John, *The Restoration Church of England, 1646–1689* (New Haven, Conn., and London, 1991).

Staley, V., *The Life and Times of Gilbert Sheldon* (1913).

Stephen, L., *A History of English Thought in the Eighteenth Century*, 2 vols. (1876).

Stone, Lawrence, *The Family, Sex and Marriage in England, 1500–1800* (1977).

Storey, R. L., *The End of the House of Lancaster* (1966).

Stoughton, John, *Religion in England under Queen Anne and the Georges, 1702–1800*, 2 vols. (1878).

Stranks, C. J., *Anglican Devotion* (1951).

—— *This Sumptuous Church. The Story of Durham Cathedral* (1973).

Sutch, V. D., *Gilbert Sheldon. Architect of Anglican Survival (1640–1675)* (The Hague, 1973).

Sutherland, L. S., and L. G. Mitchell (eds.), *The History of Oxford*, v. *The Eighteenth Century* (Oxford, 1986).

Sutherland, L., *Politics and Finance in the Eighteenth Century*, ed. A. Newman (1984).

Sykes, N., *Church and State in England in the Eighteenth Century* (Cambridge, 1934).

—— *Edmund Gibson, Bishop of London. 1669–1748. A Study in Politics and Religion in the Eighteenth Century* (Oxford, 1926).

—— *From Sheldon to Secker. Aspects of English Church History, 1660–1768* (Cambridge, 1959).

—— *William Wake, Archbishop of Canterbury, 1657–1737*, 2 vols. (Cambridge, 1957).

Tackett, T., *Priest and Parish in Eighteenth-Century France* (Princeton, NJ, 1977).

Taylor, S. J. C. (ed.), *From Cranmer to Davidson. A Church of England Miscellany* (Woodbridge, 1999).

Teale, W. H., *Lives of English Divines* (1846).

Temperley, Nicholas, *The Music of the English Parish Church* (Cambridge, 1979).

Thirsk, J. (ed.), *The Agrarian History of England and Wales*, iv and v (Cambridge, 1967, 1984–5).

Thomas, K. V., *Man and the Natural World* (Harmondsworth, 1983).

—— *Religion and the Decline of Magic* (1971).

Thompson, E. P., *The Making of the English Working Class* (Harmondsworth, 1963).

Thompson, J. A. F., *The Later Lollards* (Oxford, 1977).

Thompson, K. A., *Bureacracy and Church Reform: The Organizational Response of the Church of England to Social Change, 1800–1965* (Oxford, 1970).

Timpson, T., *Church History of Kent. From the Earliest Period to the Year MDCC-CLVIII* (1859).

Todd, Margo, *Christian Humanism and the Puritan Social Order* (Cambridge, 1987).

Tompson, R. S., *Classics or Charity? The Dilemma of the Eighteenth-Century Grammar Schools* (Manchester, 1971).

Towler, R., and P. Coxon, *The Fate of the Anglican Clergy* (1979).

Turner, G. Lyon, *Original Records of Nonconformity under Persecution and Indul-gence* (1911).

Twiss, Horace, *The Public and Private Life of Lord Chancellor Eldon*, 2 vols. (3rd edn., 1846).

Tyacke, N., *Anti-Calvinists. The Rise of English Arminianism, c. 1590–1640* (Oxford, 1987).

Tyerman, L., *The Life and Times of the Rev. John Wesley, M.A., Founder of the Methodists*, 3 vols. (1890).

Underdown, D., *Revel, Riot and Rebellion: Popular Politics and Culture in England, 1603–1660* (Oxford, 1985).

Unwin, R. W., *Charity Schools and the Defence of Anglicanism: James Talbot, Rector of Spofforth, 1700–1708*, Borthwick Papers, 65 (1984).

Vann, Richard T., *The Social Development of English Quakerism, 1655–1755* (Cambridge, Mass., 1969).

Varley, E. A., *The Last of the Prince Bishops. William Van Mildert and the High Church Movement of the early Nineteenth Century* (Cambridge, 1992).

Vopa, A. J. La, *Grace, Talent and Merit: Poor Students, Clerical Careers and the Clerical Profession in Eighteenth Century Germany* (Cambridge, 1988).

Vovelle, M., *Piété baroque et déchristianisation en Provence au xviie Siècle. les attitudes devant la mort d'après les clauses des testaments* (Paris, 1973).

—— *Religion et révolution: la déchristianisation de l'an ii* (Paris, 1976).

Virgin, P., *The Church in an Age of Negligence. Ecclesiastical Structure and Problems of Church Reform, 1700–1840* (Cambridge, 1989).

Ward, W. R., *Georgian Oxford. University Politics in the Eighteenth Century* (Oxford, 1958).

—— *The Protestant Evangelical Awakening* (Cambridge, 1992).

—— *Religion and Society in England, 1750–1850* (1972).

Warne, Arthur, *Church and Society in Eighteenth-Century Devon* (Newton Abbot, 1969).

Watt, Tessa, *Cheap Print and Popular Piety, 1550–1640* (Cambridge, 1991).

Watts, M. R., *The Dissenters*, i. *From the Reformation to the French Revolution* (Oxford, 1978).

—— *The Dissenters*, ii. *The Expansion of Evangelical Nonconformity* (Oxford, 1995).

Webb, Sidney, and Beatrice Webb, *English Local Government from the Revolution to the Municipal Corporations Act*, 9 vols. (1906–29).

Webster, A. B., *Joshua Watson. The Story of a Layman, 1771–1855* (1954).

Western, J. R., *Monarchy and Revolution: The English State in the Sixteen Eighties* (Blandford, 1972).

White, G. Cecil, *A Versatile Professor. Reminiscences of the Rev. Edward Nares, D.D.* (1903).

White, R. J., *Dr Bentley: A Study in Academic Scarlet* (1965).

Whiting, C. E., *Nathaniel Lord Crewe, Bishop of Durham (1674–1721) and his Diocese* (1940).

Whitmore, L. E., *Recusancy in Kent: Studies and Documents* (priv. pr., 1973).

Williams, E. N., *The Eighteenth-Century Constitution, 1688–1815* (2nd edn., Cambridge, 1970).

Wilson, B. R., *Religion in Secular Society* (1966).

Winstanley, D. A., *The University of Cambridge in the Eighteenth Century* (Cambridge, 1922).

Woodruff, C. E., and William Danks, *Memorials of the Cathedral Priory of Christ in Canterbury* (1912).

Wordsworth, C. W., *Scholae Academicae: Some Aspects of the Studies at the English Universities in the Eighteenth Century* (Cambridge, 1877).

—— *Social Life at the English Universities in the Eighteenth Century* (Cambridge, 1874).

Wrightson, K., and D. Levine, *Poverty and Piety in an English Village: Terling, 1525–1700* (New York, 1979).

Yates, N., *Buildings, Faith and Worship. The Liturgical Arrangement of Anglican Churches, 1600–1900* (Oxford, 1991).

—— *Kent and the Oxford Movement* (Gloucester, 1983).

—— Robert Hume, and Paul Hastings, *Religion and Society in Kent, 1640–1914* (Woodbridge, 1994).

—— and P. A. Welsby (eds.), *Faith and Fabric. A History of Rochester Cathedral, 604–1994* (Woodbridge, 1996).

3.3. ARTICLES

Addy, J., 'Bishop Porteus' Visitation of the Diocese of Chester, 1778', *Northern History*, 13 (1977), 175–98.

Andrew, D. T., 'The Code of Honour and its Critics: The Opposition to Duelling in England, 1700–1850', *Social History*, 5 (1980), 417–30.

—— 'On Reading Charity Sermons: Eighteenth-Century Anglican Solicitation and Exhortation', *JEH*, 43 (1992), 581–91.

Aston, Nigel, 'Horne and Heterodoxy: The Defence of Anglican Beliefs in the Late Enlightenment', *EHR*, 108 (1993), 895–919.

Barry, Jonathan, 'Bristol as a "Reformation city", c. 1640–1780', in Nicholas Tyacke (ed.), *England's Long Reformation, 1500–1800* (1998), 261–84.

—— 'The Politics of Religion in Restoration Bristol', in Tim Harris, Paul Seaward, and Mark Goldie (eds.), *The Politics of Religion in Restoration England* (Oxford, 1990), 163–190.

Baskerville, S. W., 'The Political Behaviour of the Cheshire Clergy, 1705–1752', *Northern History*, 23 (1987), 74–97.

Beddard, R. A., 'Bishop Cartwright's Death-Bed', *Bodleian Library Record*, 11 (1984), 220–30.

—— 'Cathedral Furnishings of the Restoration Period: A Salisbury Inventory of 1685', *Wiltshire Archaeological Magazine*, 66 (1971), 147–55.

Beddard, R. A., 'The Church of Salisbury and the Accession of James II', *Wiltshire Archaeological Magazine*, 67 (1972), 132–48.

—— 'Of the Duty of Subjects: A Proposed Fortieth Article of Religion', *Bodleian Library Record*, 10 (1981), 229–36.

—— 'The Privileges of Christchurch, Canterbury: Archbishop Sheldon's Enquiries of 1671', *AC*, 87 (1973), 81–100.

—— 'The Restoration Church', in J. R. Jones (ed.), *The Restored Monarchy 1660–88* (1979), 155–75.

—— 'Sheldon and Anglican Recovery', *HJ*, 19 (1976), 1005–17.

Bellenger, A., 'The Emigré Clergy and the English Church, 1789–1815', *JEH*, 34 (1982), 392–410.

—— 'Seen but not Heard: French Exiled Clergy, 1789–1815', *Kent Recusant History*, 6 (1983), 5–11.

Bennett, G. V., 'Conflict in the Church', in *Britain after the Glorious Revolution*, ed. Geoffrey Holmes (1969), 155–75.

—— 'The Convocation of 1710: An Anglican Attempt at Counter-Revolution', *SCH*, 7 (1971), 311–19.

—— 'King William III and the Episcopate', in id. and J. D. Walsh (eds.), *Essays in Modern English Church History in Memory of Norman Sykes* (1966), 104–31.

—— 'Patristic Tradition in Anglican Thought, 1660–1900', *Oecumenica* (Gutersloh, 1972), 20–43.

—— 'The Seven Bishops: A Reconsideration', *SCH*, 15 (1978), 267–87.

Best, G. F. A., 'Church Parties and Charities: The Experience of Three American Visitors to England, 1823/4', *EHR*, 78 (1963), 243–62.

—— 'The Protestant Constitution and its Supporters, 1800–1829', *TRHS*, 5th ser., 8 (1958), 107–27.

—— 'The Road to Hiram's Hospital', *Victorian Studies*, 5 (1961–2), 135–50.

Bettey, J., 'Bishop Secker's Diocesan Survey', *Dorset Natural History and Archaeological Society*, 95 (1973–4), 74–5.

Blackwood, B. G., 'Plebeian Catholics in Later Stuart Lancashire', *Northern History*, 25 (1991), 160–73.

Borsay, P., 'The English Urban Renaissance: The Development of Provincial Urban Culture, c. 1680–c.1760', *Social History*, 5 (1977), 581–603.

Boulton, J., 'The Limits of Formal Religion: The Administration of Holy Communion in Late Elizabethan and Early Stuart London', *London Journal*, 10 (1984), 136–49.

Bradley, J. E., 'The Anglican Pulpit, the Social Order and the Resurgence of Toryism During the American Revolution', *Albion*, 21 (1989), 361–88.

Brigden, Susan, 'Youth and the Reformation', *Past and Present*, 95 (1982), 37–67.

Briggs, R., '*Idées and Mentalités*: The Case of the Catholic Reform Movement in France', *History of European Ideas*, 7 (1986), 9–19.

Brooke, C. N. L., J. M. Horn, and N. L. Ramsay, 'A Canon's Residence in the Eighteenth Century: The Case of Thomas Gooch', *JEH*, 39 (1988), 546–7.

Buckingham, C., 'Some Notes on the Early Catholic Missions in Canterbury', *Kent Recusant History*, 6 (1982), 16–25.

Cameron, Euan, 'The "Godly Community" in the Theory and Practice of the European Reformation', *SCH*, 33 (1986), 131–53.

Cantor, G. N., 'Revelation and the Cyclical Cosmos of John Hutchinson', in L. J. Jordonova and R. Porter (eds.), *Images of the Earth* (Chalfont St Giles, 1979), 3–22.

Chalklin, C. W., 'The Compton Census of 1676: The Dioceses of Canterbury and Rochester', *A Seventeenth Century Miscellany*, Kent Records, 17 (1960), 153–74.

—— 'The Financing of Church Building in the Provincial Towns of Eighteenth-Century England', in Peter Clark (ed.), *The Transformation of English Provincial Towns 1600–1800* (1984), 284–310.

Chamberlain, Jeffrey S., 'The Limits of Moderation in a Latitudinarian Parson: or, High-Church Zeal in a Low Churchman Discover'd', in Roger D. Lund (ed.), *The Margins of Orthodoxy. Heterodox Writing and Orthodox Response, 1660–1750* (Cambridge, 1995), 195–215.

Clark, J. C. D., 'Eighteenth Century Social History', *HJ*, 30 (1984), 773–88.

—— 'England's Ancien Regime as a Confessional State', *Albion*, 21 (1989), 450–74.

Clark, Richard, 'Why was the Re-Establishment of the Church of England Possible? Derbyshire: A Provincial Perspective', *Midland History*, 8 (1983), 86–105.

Clay, C., '"The Greed of Whig Bishops"?: Church Landlords and their Lessees, 1600–1760', *Past and Present*, 87 (1980), 128–57.

Collinson, P., 'Shepherds, Sheepdogs and Hirelings: The Pastoral Ministry in Post-Reformation England', *SCH*, 26 (1989), 185–220.

Cox-Johnson, A., 'Lambeth Palace Library, 1610–1664', *Transactions of the Cambridge Bibliographical Society*, 2 (1955), 105–26.

Currie, R., 'A Micro-Theory of Methodist Growth', *Proceedings of the Wesley Historical Society*, 36 (1967), 65–73.

Curtis, T. C., and W. A. Speck, 'The Societies for Reformation of Manners: A Case Study in the Theory and Practice of Moral Reform', *Literature and History*, 3 (1976), 45–64.

Daeley, J. I., 'Pluralism in the Diocese of Canterbury, During the Administration of Archbishop Parker, 1559–75', *JEH*, 18 (1967), 33–49.

Davis, J. F., 'Lollard Survival and the Textile Industry in the South-East of England', *SCH*, 3 (1966), 191–201.

Davis, N. Z., 'The Sacred and the Body Social in Sixteenth Century Lyon', *Past and Present*, 40 (1981), 40–70.

Ditchfield, G. M., and Bryan Keith-Lucas, 'Reverend William Jones of Nayland (1726–1800): Some New Light on His Years in Kent', *Notes and Queries*, 238 (1993), 337–42.

Draper, Gillian, 'The First Hundred Years of Quakerism in Kent. Part I', *AC*, 112 (1993), 317–40.

Duffy, E., 'Correspondence Fraternelle': The SPCK, the SPG, and the Churches of Switzerland in the War of the Spanish Succession', in D. Baker (ed.), *Reform and Reformation: England and the Continent, c. 1500–c. 1750*, *SCH*, Subsida 2 (1979).

—— 'Primitive Christianity Revived: Religious Renewal in Augustan England', *SCH*, 14 (1977), 287–300.

Eastwood, D., '"Amplifying the Province of the Legislature": The Flow of Information and the English State in the Early Nineteenth Century, *Historical Research*, 62 (1989), 276–94.

Evans, E. J., 'The Anglican Clergy of Northern England', in Clyve Jones (ed.), *Britain in the First Age of Party, 1680–1750. Essays Presented to Geoffrey Holmes* (London and Ronceverte, 1987), 221–40.

—— 'Some Reasons for the Growth of English Rural Anti-Clericalism, c. 1750–c.1830', *Past and Present*, 66 (1975), 84–109.

Field, Clive D., 'A Godly People? Aspects of Religious Practice in the Diocese of Oxford, 1738–1936', *Southern History*, 14 (1992), 46–73.

Fletcher, A., 'The Enforcement of the Conventicle Acts, 1664–1679', *SCH*, 21 (1984), 234–46.

Gammon, V., 'Babylonian Performances: The Rise and Suppression of Popular Church Music, 1660–1870', in E. Yeo and S. Yeo (eds.), *Popular Culture and Class Conflict, 1590–1914* (Brighton, 1981), 62–84.

Gardiner, D., 'The Berkeleys of Canterbury', *AC*, 69 (1956), 117–24.

Gascoigne, J., 'Church and State Allied: The Failure of Parliamentary Reform of the Universities, 1688–1800', in A. L. Beier, D. Cannadine, and J. M. Rosenheim (eds.), *The First Modern Society. Essays in English History in Honour of Lawrence Stone* (Cambridge, 1989), 401–29.

—— 'Politics, Patronage and Newtonianism: The Cambridge Example', *HJ*, 27 (1984), 1–24.

Gentles, I., 'The Sale of Bishops' Lands in the English Revolution, 1646–1660', *EHR*, 95 (1980), 573–96.

Gilley, S., 'Christianity and the Enlightenment: An Historical Survey', *History of European Ideas*, 1 (1981), 103–21.

Goldie, M., 'John Locke and Anglican Royalism', *Political Studies*, 31 (1983), 61–85.

—— 'The Political Thought of the Anglican Revolution', in R. A. Beddard (ed.), *The Revolutions of 1688* (Oxford, 1991), 102–27.

—— 'The Theory of Religious Intolerance in Restoration England', in Ole Peter Grell, Jonathan I. Israel, and Nicholas Tyacke (eds.), *From Persecution to Toleration. The Glorious Revolution and Religion in England* (Oxford, 1991), 331–68.

Greaves, R. W., 'An Eighteenth Century High Churchman', *Theology*, 19 (1934), 272–86.

Greaves, R. L., 'The Role of Women in Early English Nonconformity', *Church History*, 52 (1983), 299–311.

Green, I. M., 'Career Prospects and Clerical Conformity in Early Stuart England', *Past and Present*, 90 (1981), 70–115.

—— 'The First Five Years of Queen Anne's Bounty', in Rosemary O'Day and Felicity Heal (eds.), *Princes and Paupers in the English Church, 1500–1800* (Leicester, 1981), 231–54.

—— '"For Children in Yeeres and Children in Understanding": The Emergence of the English Catechism under Elizabeth and the Early Stuarts', *JEH*, 37 (1986), 397–425.

—— 'The Persecution of "Scandalous" and "Malignant" Parish Clergy During the English Civil War', *EHR*, 104 (1979), 507–31.

—— '"Reformed Pastors" and *Bon Curés*: The Changing Role of the Parish Clergy in Early Modern Europe', *SCH*, 26 (1989), 249–86.

Gregory, J., 'Anglicanism and the Arts: Religion, Culture and Politics in the Eighteenth Century', in Jeremy Black and Jeremy Gregory (eds.), *Culture, Politics and Society in Britain, 1660–1800* (Manchester, 1991), 82–109.

—— 'Christianity and Culture: Religion, the Arts and the Sciences in England, 1660–1800', in Jeremy Black (ed.), *Culture and Society in Britain, 1660–1800* (Manchester, 1997), 102–23.

—— 'The Eighteenth-Century Reformation: The Pastoral Task of Anglican Clergy after 1689', in John Walsh, Colin Haydon, and Stephen Taylor (eds.), *The Church of England c. 1689–c. 1833. From Toleration to Tractarianism* (Cambridge, 1993), 67–85.

—— 'Gender and the Clerical Profession in England, 1660–1850', in Robert Swanson (ed.), *Gender and the Christian Religion*, *SCH*, 34 (1998), 235–71.

—— '*Homo-religiosus*: Masculinity and Religion in the Long Eighteenth Century', in Tim Hitchcock and Michele Cohen (eds.), *English Masculinities, 1660–1800* (1999), 85–110.

—— 'A Just and Sufficient Maintenance: Some Defences of the Clerical Establishment in the Eighteenth Century', in W. J. Sheils and Diana Woods (eds.), *The Church and Wealth*, *SCH*, 24 (1987), 321–32.

—— 'The Making of a Protestant Nation; "Success" and "Failure" in England's Long Reformation', in Nicholas Tyacke (ed.), *England's Long Reformation, 1500–1800* (1998), 307–33.

—— 'Persecution, Toleration, Competition and Indifference: The Church of England and its Rivals in the Long Eighteenth Century', in C. D'Haussy (ed.), *Quand religions et confessions se regardent* (Paris, 1998), 45–60

Gugerli, D., 'Protestant Pastors in Late Eighteenth-Century Zurich: Their Families and Society', *Journal of Interdisciplinary History*, 22 (1992), 369–385.

Guy, J. R., 'Perpetual Curacies in Eighteenth Century South Wales', *SCH*, 16 (1979), 327–33.

Gwyn, R. D., 'James II in the Light of his Treatment of Huguenot Refugees in England, 1685–1688', *EHR*, 92 (1977), 820–33.

Habbakuk, H. J., 'Landowners and the English Civil War', *Economic History Review*, 2nd ser., 18 (1985), 130–51.

Haigh, C., 'The Church of England, the Catholics and the People', in id. (ed.), *The Reign of Elizabeth I* (1985), 169–220.

Harling, Philip, 'Rethinking "Old Corruption"', *Past and Present*, 147 (1995), 127–58.

Harrat, S., 'Queen Anne's Bounty and the Augmentation of Livings in the Age of Reform', *Transactions of the Leicestershire Archaeological and Historical Society*, 61 (1987), 8–18.

Heal, F., 'The Archbishops of Canterbury and the Practice of Hospitality', *JEH*, 33 (1982), 544–63.

Hembry, P., 'Episcopal Palaces, 1533–1660', in E. W. Ives, R. J. Knecht, and J. J. Scarisbrick (eds.), *Wealth and Power in Tudor England. Essays Presented to S. T. Bindoff* (1978), 146–66.

Hill, C., 'Occasional Conformity', in R. B. Knox (ed.), *Reformation, Conformity and Dissent: Essays in Honour of Geoffrey Nuttall* (Epworth, 1977), 199–220.

Hirschberg, D. R., 'Episcopal Incomes and Expenses, 1660–c.1760', in Rosemary O'Day and Felicity Heal (eds.), *Princes and Paupers in the English Church 1500–1800* (Leicester, 1981), 211–30.

—— 'The Government and Church Patronage in England, 1660–1760', *JBS*, 20 (1980–1), 109–39.

Hirst, Derek, 'The Failure of Godly Rule in the English Republic', *Past and Present*, 132 (1991), 33–66.

Holiday, P. G., 'Land Sales and Repurchases in Yorkshire after the Civil Wars, 1650–1670', *Northern History*, 5 (1970), 67–92.

Holmes, G., 'Religion and Party in Late Stuart England', repr. id., *Politics, Religion and Society in England, 1679–1742* (London and Ronceverte, 1986), 181–216.

Holtby, R. T., 'Thomas Herring as Archbishop of York, 1743–1747', *Northern History*, 30 (1994), 105–21.

Hoskins, W. G., 'Harvest Fluctuations and English Economic History, 1620–1759', *Agricultural History Review*, 16 (1968), 15–131.

Hughes, A., 'Local History and the Origins of the Civil War', in R. Cust and A. Hughes (eds.), *Confict in Early Stuart England. Studies in Religion and Politics, 1603–1642* (1989), 224–52.

Hughes, E., 'The Professions in the Eighteenth Century', *Durham University Journal*, 44 (1952), 46–55.

Hume, Richard, 'Educational Provision for the Kentish Poor, 1660–1811: Fluctuations and Trends', *Southern History*, 4 (1982), 122–44.

Hurwich, J. J., 'Dissent and Catholicism in English Society: A Study of Warwickshire, 1660–1720', *JBS*, 16 (1976), 24–58.

—— '"A Fanatick Town": The Political Influence of Dissenters in Coventry 1600–1720', *Midland History*, 4 (1977), 15–47.

Ingram, M., 'Religion, Communities and Moral Discipline in Late Sixteenth and

Early Seventeenth-Century England: Case Studies', in K. von Greyerz (ed.), *Religion and Society in Early Modern Europe, 1500-1800* (1984), 177-93.

Innes, Joanna, 'Politics and Morals. The Reformation of Manners Movement in later Eighteenth Century England', in Eckhart Hellmuth (ed.), *The Transformation of Political Culture. England and Germany in the Late Eighteenth Century* (Oxford, 1990), 57-118.

―― and J. Styles, 'The Crime Wave: Recent Writing and Criminal Justice in Eighteenth-Century England', *JBS*, 25 (1986), 380-435.

Isaacs, T., 'The Anglican Hierarchy and the Reformation of Manners, 1688-1738', *JEH*, 33 (1982), 391-411.

Jacob, W. M., 'A Practice of a Very Hurtful Tendency', *SCH*, 16 (1979), 315-26.

James, F. G., 'Clerical Incomes in Eighteenth-Century England', *Historical Magazine of the Protestant Episcopal Church*, 18 (1949), 311-25.

James, M. R., 'The Political Importance of the Tithes Controversy in the English Revolution, 1646-1660', *History*, 26 (1941), 1-18.

Jones, M. V., 'The Divine Durant: A Seventeenth-Century Independent', *AC*, 83 (1968), 193-203.

Jordan, W. K., 'Social Institutions in Kent, 1480-1660. A Study of the Changing Pattern of Social Aspirations', *AC*, 75 (1961), 1-168.

Kain, R. J. P., 'The Tithe Commutation Surveys', *AC*, 89 (1974), 101-18.

Kaufman, Paul, 'Reading Vogues at English Cathedral Libraries of the Eighteenth Century', *Bulletin of the New York Public Library*, 67 (1963), 643-72.

Kuhn, A. J., 'Glory or Gravity: Hutchinson vs Newton', *Journal of the History of Ideas*, 22 (1961), 303-22.

―― 'Nature Spiritualised: Aspects of Anti-Newtonianism', *English Literary History*, 41 (1974), 400-12.

Landau, Norma, 'The Laws of Settlement and the Surveillance of Immigration in Eighteenth-Century Kent', *Continuity and Change*, 3 (1988), 391-420.

Langford, P., 'Convocation and the Tory Clergy, 1717-61', in E. Cruickshanks and J. Black (eds.), *The Jacobite Challenge* (Edinburgh, 1988), 107-22.

―― 'The English Clergy and the American Revolution', in Eckhart Hellmuth (ed.), *The Transformation of Political Culture. England and Germany in the Late Eighteenth Century* (Oxford, 1990), 275-307.

―― 'Old Whigs, Old Tories and the American Revolution', *Journal of Imperial and Commonwealth History*, 8 (1980), 106-30.

Laslett, P., 'The Gentry of Kent in 1640', *Cambridge Historical Journal*, 9 (1948), 148-64.

Lee, Colin, '"Fanatic Magistrates": Religious and Political Conflict in Three Kent Boroughs, 1680-1684', *HJ*, 35 (1991), 43-61.

Lucas, P., 'A Collective Biography of the Students and Barristers of Lincoln's Inn', *Journal of Modern History*, 46 (1974), 227-62.

McDowell, R. B., 'The Anglican Episcopate, 1780-1945', *Theology*, 50 (1947), 202-9.

Marshall, J., 'The Ecclesiology of the Latitude-Men, 1600–1689: Stillingfleet, Tillotson and "Hobbism"', *JEH*, 36 (1985), 407–27.

Marshall, William M., 'Episcopal Activity in the Hereford and Oxford Dioceses', *Midland History*, 8 (1983), 106–20.

Mate, M., 'Property Investment by Canterbury Cathedral Priory, 1250–1400', *JBS*, 23 (1983–4), 1–21.

Mather, F. C., 'Church, Parliament and Penal Law: Some Anglo-Scottish Interactions in the Eighteenth Century', *EHR*, 92 (1977), 540–77.

—— 'Georgian Churchmanship Reconsidered: Some Variations in Anglican Public Worship, 1714–1830', *JEH*, 36 (1985), 255–83.

Maynard, W. R., 'Pluralism and Non-Residence in the Archdeaconry of Durham, 1774–1856': The Bishop and Chapter as Patrons', *Northern History*, 26 (1990), 103–30.

—— 'The Response of the Church of England to Economic and Demographic Change: The Archdeaconry of Durham, 1800–1851', *JEH*, 42 (1991), 437–62.

Mayo, C. H., 'The Social Status of the Clergy in the Seventeenth and Eighteenth Centuries', *EHR*, 37 (1922), 258–66.

Mingay, G. E., 'The Agricultural Depression, 1730–1750', *EHR*, 8 (1956), 323–38.

Mitchison, R., 'Pluralities and the Poorer Benefices in Eighteenth-Century England', *HJ*, 5 (1962), 188–90.

Monod, P., 'Dangerous Merchandise: Smugglers, Jacobitism and Commercial Culture in South-East England, 1690–1760', *JBS*, 30 (1991), 150–82.

Morrill, J. S., 'The Attack on the Church of England in the Long Parliament, 1640–42', in D. Beales and G. Best (eds.), *History, Society and the Churches* (Cambridge, 1985), 105–24.

—— 'The Church in England, 1642–9', in J. S. Morrill (ed.), *Reactions to the English Civil War* (1982), 89–114.

—— 'The Religious Context of the English Civil War', *TRHS*, 5th ser., 34 (1984), 155–78.

Necheles, R. F., 'The Curés in the Estates General of 1789', *Journal of Modern History*, 46 (1974), 89–114.

Norrey, P. J., 'The Restoration Regime in Action: The Relationship between Central and Local Government in Dorset, Somerset and Wiltshire', *HJ*, 31 (1988), 789–812.

Nuttall, G. F., 'Dissenting Churches in Kent before 1700', *JEH*, 54 (1963), 175–89.

Oakley, A., 'The Hill Family of Canterbury, St Paul, Mapmakers', in Margaret Sparks (ed.), *The Parish of St Martin and St Paul, Canterbury* (Canterbury, 1980), 68–70.

O'Day, R., 'The Anatomy of a Profession: The Clergy of the Church of England', in W. Prest (ed.), *The Professions in Early Modern England* (1987), 25–63.

O'Higgins, J., 'Archbishop Tillotson and the Religion of Nature', *Journal of Theological Studies*, 24 (1973), 123–42.

Parker, G., 'Success and Failure during the First Century of the Reformation', *Past and Present*, 136 (1992), 43–82.

Pemberton, W. A., 'The Parochial Inspections of Andrew Burnaby, D.D., Archdeacon of Leicester, 1793–97', *Transactions of the Leicestershire Archaeological and Historical Society*, 63 (1989), 34–56.

—— 'The Parochial Visitations of James Bickham, D.D., Archdeacon of Leicester in the Years 1773 to 1779', *Transactions of the Leicestershire Archaeological and Historical Society*, 59 (1984–5), 52–72.

Phillips, John A., 'The Social Calculus: Deference and Defiance in Later Georgian England', *Albion*, 21 (1989), 426–49.

Podmore, C. J., 'The Bishops and the Brethren: Anglican Attitudes to the Moravians in the Mid-Eighteenth Century', *JEH*, 42 (1990), 622–46.

Pruett, J. H., 'Career Patterns among the Clergy of Lincoln Cathedral, 1660–1750', *Church History*, 44 (1975), 204–16.

Quinn, J. F., 'Yorkshiremen Go to the Polls: County Contests in the Early Eighteenth Century', *Northern History*, 21 (1985), 137–74.

Ramsbottom, John. D., 'Presbyterians and Partial Conformity in the Restoration Church of England', *JEH*, 43 (1992), 249–70.

Reay, B., 'The Last Rising of the Agricultural Labourers: The Battle in Bossenden Wood, 1838', *History Workshop Journal*, 26 (1988), 79–101.

—— 'The Quakers, 1659 and the Restoration of the Monarchy', *History*, 63 (1978), 193–213.

Richards, T., 'The Religious Census of 1676. An Inquiry into its Historical Value', *Supplement to the Transactions of the Honourable Society of Cymmrodorion* (1927), 1–17.

Richey, R., 'The Origins of British Radicalism: The Changing Rationale for Dissent', *Eighteenth Century Studies*, 7 (1973–4), 179–92.

Roberts, M. J. D., 'Private Patronage and the Church of England, 1800–1900', *JEH*, 32 (1981), 199–223.

Robertson, J. C., 'The Condition of Canterbury Cathedral at the Restoration in A.D. 1660', *AC*, 10 (1876), 93–8.

Rose, C., '"Seminarys of Faction and Rebellion": Jacobites, Whigs and the London Charity Schools, 1716–1724', *HJ*, 34 (1991), 831–55.

Rubinstein, W. D., 'The End of "Old Corruption" in Britain, 1780–1860', *Past and Present*, 101 (1982), 55–86.

Schochet, Gordon J., 'The Act of Toleration and the Failure of Comprehension: Persecution, Nonconformity, and Religious Indifference', in Dale Hoak and Mordechai Feingold (eds.), *The World of William and Mary. Anglo-Dutch Perspectives on the Revolution of 1688–89* (Stanford, Calif., 1996), 165–87.

Scott, Jonathan, 'Radicalism and Restoration: The Shape of the Stuart Experience', *HJ*, 31 (1988), 453–68.

Seaward, Paul, 'Gilbert Sheldon, the London Vestries, and the Defence of the

Church', in Tim Harris, Paul Seaward, and Mark Goldie (eds.), *Politics of Religion in Restoration England* (Oxford, 1990), 49–74.

Sharp, B., 'Popular Political Opinion in England, 1660–1685', *History of European Ideas*, 10 (1989), 13–29.

Sharp, R., 'New Perspectives on the High Church Tradition: Historical Background, 1730–80', in Geoffrey Rowell (ed.), *Tradition Renewed. The Oxford Movement Conference Papers* (1986), 4–23.

Shirley, J., 'John Lewis of Margate', *AC*, 64 (1951), 39–56.

Simon, J., 'Was there a Charity School Movement? The Leicestershire Evidence', in Brian Simon (ed.), *Education in Leicestershire 1540–1940* (Leicester, 1968), 55–100.

Slatter, M. Doreen, 'The Records of the Courts of Arches', *JEH*, 4 (1953), 139–61.

Smith, Ruth, 'Intellectual Contexts of Handel's English Oratorios', in C. Hogwood and R. Luckett (eds.), *Music in Eighteenth-Century England. Essays in Memory of Charles Cudworth* (Cambridge, 1983), 119–34.

Sommerville, C. J., 'The Distinction between Indoctrination and Education in England, 1549–1719', *Journal of the History of Ideas*, 44 (1983), 387–406.

—— and J. Edwards, 'Debate: "Religious Faith, Doubt and Atheism"', *Past and Present*, 128 (1990), 152–61.

Spaeth, D. A., 'Common Prayer?: Popular Observance of the Anglican Liturgy in Restoration Wiltshire', in S. J. Wright (ed.), *Parish, Church and People: Local Studies in Lay Religion, 1350–1750* (1988), 125–51.

Speck, W. A., '"Whigs and Tories Dim their Glories": English Political Parties under the First Two Georges', in John Cannon (ed.), *The Whig Ascendancy. Colloquies on Hanoverian England* (1981), 61–75.

—— 'William—and Mary', in Lois G. Schwoerer (ed.), *The Revolution of 1688/9: Changing Perspectives* (Cambridge, 1991), 131–46.

Spurr, J., 'The Church of England, Comprehension and the Toleration Act of 1689', *EHR*, 104 (1989), 927–46.

—— '"Latitudinarianism" and the Restoration Church', *HJ*, 31 (1988), 61–82.

—— 'Schism and the Restoration Church', *JEH*, 41 (1990), 408–24.

Stone, L., 'The Size and Composition of the Oxford Student Body', in id. (ed.), *The University in Society*, 2 vols. (1974), 3–110.

Sykes, N., 'Bishop Butler and the Primacy. Did He Decline the See of Canterbury in 1747?', *Theology*, 33 (1958), 132–7.

—— 'The Election and Inthronization of William Wake as Archbishop of Canterbury', *JEH*, 1 (1950), 96–101.

Tatham, G. B., 'The Sale of Episcopal Lands during the Civil Wars and the Commonwealth', *EHR*, 22 (1908), 91–108.

Tatton-Brown, T., 'The Parish Church of St. Laurence, Godmersham: A History', *AC*, 106 (1989), 45–82.

Taylor, S., 'Archbishop Potter and the Dissenters', *Yale University Library Gazette*, 67 (1993), 118–26.

—— 'Church and Society after the Glorious Revolution', *HJ*, 31 (1988), 973–87.

—— '"Dr Codex" and the Whig "Pope": Edmund Gibson, Bishop of Lincoln and London, 1716–1748', in R. W. Davis (ed.), *Lords of Parliament. Studies, 1714–1917* (Stanford, 1995), 9–28.

—— '"The Fac Totum in Ecclesiastic Affairs"? The Duke of Newcastle and the Crown's Ecclesiastical Patronage', *Albion*, 24 (1992), 409–33.

—— 'Sir Robert Walpole, the Church of England and the Quakers Tithe Bill of 1736', *HJ*, 28 (1985), 51–77.

Thirsk, J., 'The Sales of Royalist Land during the Interregnum', *Economic History Review*, 2nd ser., 5 (1952/3), 188–207.

Thomas, K. V., 'Children in Early Modern England', in G. Avery and J. Briggs (eds.), *Children and Their Books: A Collection of Essays to Celebrate the Work of Iona and Peter Opie* (Oxford, 1989), 45–78.

—— 'Women and the Civil War Sects', *Past and Present*, 13 (1958), 42–57.

Thomas, R., 'The Seven Bishops and their Petition, 18 May 1688', *JEH*, 12 (1961), 56–70.

Thompson, E. P., 'The Moral Economy of the English Crowd in the Eighteenth Century', *Past and Present*, 50 (1971), 76–136.

—— 'Patrician Society, Plebeian Culture', *Journal of Social History*, 8 (1974), 382–405.

Torre, Angelo, 'Politics Cloaked in Worship: State, Church and Local Power in Piedmont, 1570–1770', *Past and Present*, 134 (1992), 42–92.

Underdown, David, 'Cornelius Burges and the Corporation of Wells. A Case Concerning Bishops' Lands', *EHR*, 78 (1963), 18–42.

Valenze, Deborah M., 'Prophecy and Popular Literature in Eighteenth-Century England', *JEH*, 29 (1978), 75–92.

Venn, J. A., 'Matriculations at Oxford and Cambridge, 1544–1906', *Oxford and Cambridge Review* (1908), 48–66.

Walsh, J. D., 'Methodism and the Mob in the Eighteenth Century', *SCH*, 8 (1972), 213–27.

—— 'The Origins of the Evangelical Revival', in G. V. Bennett and J. D. Walsh (eds.), *Essays in Modern English Church History* (1966), 132–62.

—— 'Religious Societies: Methodist and Evangelical, 1738–1800', *SCH*, 23 (1986), 279–302.

Ward, W. R., 'The Tithe Question in England in the Early Nineteenth Century', *JEH*, 16 (1965), 67–81.

Whiteman, A., 'The Church of England, 1542–1837', in *VCH, Wiltshire*, iii (1956), 28–56.

—— 'The Re-establishment of the Church of England, 1660–1663', *TRHS*, 5 (1955), 111–32.

—— 'Two Letter Books of Archbishops Sheldon and Sancroft', *Bodleian Library Record*, 4 (1953), 24–45.

Whitley, W. T., 'Militant Baptists, 1660–1672', *Transactions of the Baptist Historical Society*, 1 (1909), 148–55.

Wilde, C. B., 'Hutchinsonianism, Natural Philosophy and Religious Controversy in Eighteenth-Century Britain, *History of Science*, 18 (1980), 1–24.

—— 'Matter and Spirit as Natural Symbols in Eighteenth-Century British Natural Philosophy', *British Journal of the History of Science*, 15 (1982), 99–131.

Williams, A., 'The Distribution of Catholic Chaplaincies in the Early Eighteenth Century', *Recusant History*, 12 (1973–4), 16–25.

Williams, B., 'The Duke of Newcastle and the Election of 1734', *EHR*, 12 (1897), 448–88.

Winnifrith, Sir J., 'Land Ownership in Appledore, 1500–1900', *AC*, 97 (1981), 1–6.

Woodruff, C. E., 'Letters Relating to the Condition of the Church in Kent, during the Primacy of Archbishop Sancroft (1678–90)', *AC*, 21 (1895), 172–97.

—— 'The Parliamentary Survey of the Precincts of Canterbury Cathedral in the Time of the Commonwealth', *AC*, 49 (1938), 195–222.

—— 'The Records of the Courts of the Archdeaconry and Consistory Court of Canterbury', *AC*, 41 (1929), 89–104.

—— 'A Seventeenth-Century Survey of the Estates of the Dean and Chapter of Canterbury in East Kent', *AC*, 38 (1926), 29–44.

—— 'Some Seventeenth Century Letters and Petitions from the Muniments of the Dean and Chapter of Canterbury', *AC*, 42 (1930), 93–139.

—— 'A Survey of the Sussex Estates of the Dean and Chapter of Canterbury, Taken in 1671', *Sussex Archaeological Collections*, 53 (1910), 192–7.

Wrightson, K., 'Alehouses, Order and Reformation in Rural England, 1590–1660', in Eileen Yeo and Stephen Yeo (eds.), *Popular Culture and Class Conflict* (Hassocks, 1981), 1–27.

Wykes, David L., 'Friends, Parliament and the Toleration Act', *JEH*, 45 (1994), 42–63.

—— 'They "assemble in greater numbers and [with] more dareing then formerly": The Bishop of Gloucester and Nonconformity in the late 1660s', *Southern History*, 17 (1995), 24–39.

Yates, N., 'The Parochial Library of All Saints, Maidstone, and other Kentish Parochial Libraries', *AC*, 99 (1983), 159–74.

Zell, M., 'The Personnel of the Clergy in Kent in the Reformation Period', *EHR*, 89 (1974), 513–33.

3.4. THESES

Acheson, R. J., 'The Development of Religious Separatism in the Diocese of Canterbury, 1590–1660', University of Kent Ph.D. thesis, 1983.

Addy, J., 'Two Eighteenth-Century Bishops of Chester, William Markham and Beilby Porteus', University of Leeds Ph.D. thesis, 1972.

Albers, Jan, 'Seeds of Contention: Society, Politics and the Church of England in Lancashire, 1689-1790', Yale University Ph.D. thesis, 1988.

Barratt, D. M., 'The Condition of the Parish Clergy between the Reformation and 1660, with Special Reference to the Dioceses of Oxford, Worcester and Gloucester', University of Oxford D.Phil. thesis, 1949.

Bezodis, P. A., 'The English Parish Clergy and their Place in Society, 1600-1800', Fellowship dissertation, Trinity College, Cambridge, 1949.

Burns, R. Arthur, 'The Diocesan Revival in the Church of England, c. 1825-1865', University of Oxford D.Phil thesis, 1990.

Chamberlain, Jeffrey S., '"The Changes and Chances of this Mortal Life": The Vicissitudes of High Churchmanship and Politics among the Clergy of Sussex, 1700-1745', University of Chicago Ph.D. thesis, 1992.

Clark, R., 'Anglicanism, Recusancy and Dissent in Derbyshire, 1603-1730', University of Oxford D.Phil. thesis, 1979.

Collins, M. H. P., 'The Making of a Nonjuror. The Theological and Ecclesiastical Opinions of Dr Thomas Brett, 1700-1715; A Study in Withdrawal from the Anglican Establishment', University of Oxford B.Phil. thesis, 1977.

Davie, N. A. J., 'Custom and Conflict in a Wealden Village; Pluckley, 1500-1700', University of Oxford D.Phil thesis, 1987.

Davies, C. Euan, 'The Enforcement of Religious Uniformity in England, 1668-1700, with Special Reference to the Dioceses of Chichester and Worcester', University of Oxford D.Phil. thesis, 1982.

Davies, T. A., 'The Quakers in Essex, 1655-1725', University of Oxford D.Phil thesis, 1986.

Etherington, J. M., 'The Life of Archbishop Juxon, 1582-1663', University of Oxford B.Litt. thesis, 1954.

Findon, J. C., 'The Nonjurors and the Church of England, 1689-1716', University of Oxford D.Phil. thesis, 1979.

Ford, R. F., 'Minor Canons at Canterbury Cathedral: The Gostlings and their Colleagues', University of California D.Phil. thesis, 1984.

Haydon, C. M., 'Anti-Catholicism in Eighteenth-Century England', University of Oxford D.Phil. thesis, 1985.

Heaton, D. A., 'A Study of the Structure of Corporate Estate Management of the Lands of the Dean and Chapter of Canterbury, 1640-1760', University of Kent MA thesis, 1971.

Holland, Susan Mary, 'Archbishop George Abbot: A Study in Ecclesiastical Statesmanship', University of London Ph.D. thesis, 1991.

Humphries, P. L., 'Kentish Politics and Public Opinion, 1768-1832', University of Oxford D.Phil. thesis, 1981.

Ignjatijevic, G. L., 'The Parish Clergy in the Diocese of Canterbury and Archdeaconry of Bedford in the Reign of Charles I and under the Commonwealth', University of Sheffield Ph.D. thesis, 1986.

Jacob, W. M., 'Clergy and Society in Norfolk, 1707–1806', University of Exeter Ph.D. thesis, 1982.

McKay, J., 'John Tillotson (1630–1694): A Study of his Life and of his Contribution to the Development of English Prose', University of Oxford D.Phil. thesis, 1951.

Marshall, W. M., 'The Administration of the Dioceses of Hereford and Oxford, 1660–1760', University of Bristol Ph.D. thesis, 1978.

Murray, Nancy L. V., 'The Influence of the French Revolution on the Church of England and its Rivals, 1789–1802', University of Oxford D.Phil. thesis, 1975.

Newman, A. N., 'Elections in Kent and its Parliamentary Representation, 1715–1754', University of Oxford D.Phil. thesis, 1957.

Nockles, P. B., 'Continuity and Change in Anglican High Churchmanship, 1792–1850', University of Oxford D.Phil. thesis, 1982.

Potter, Jean Margaret, 'The Ecclesiastical Courts in the Diocese of Canterbury', 1603–1665', University of London M.Phil. thesis, 1973.

Rycroft, Philip, 'Church, Chapel and Community in Craven, 1764–1851', University of Oxford, D.Phil thesis, 1988.

Salter, J. L., 'Warwickshire Clergy, 1660–1714', University of Birmingham Ph.D. thesis, 2 vols., 1975.

Seaward, P., 'Court and Parliament: The Making of Government Policy, 1661–1665', University of Oxford D.Phil. thesis, 1986.

Shuler, J. C., 'The Pastoral and Ecclesiastical Administration of the Diocese of Durham, 1721–71; With Particular Reference to the Archdeaconry of Northumberland', University of Durham Ph.D. thesis, 1975.

Smith, M. G., 'A Study of the Administration of the Diocese of Exeter during the Episcopate of Sir Jonathan Trelawney, Bart, 1689–1707', University of Oxford B.D. thesis [1964].

Snape, M. F., '"Our Happy Reformation": Anglicanism and Society in a Northern Parish, 1689–1789', University of Birmingham Ph.D thesis, 1994.

Spaeth, Donald A., 'Parsons and Parishioners: Lay-Clerical Conflict and Popular Piety in Wiltshire Villages, 1660–1740', Brown University Ph.D. thesis, 1985.

Taylor, S. J. C., 'Church and State in England in the Mid-Eighteenth Century: The Newcastle Years, 1742–1762', University of Cambridge Ph.D. thesis, 1987.

White, Barbara, 'Assize Sermons, 1600–1720', Newcastle Polytechnic (CNAA) Ph.D. thesis, 1980.

Whiteman, E. A. O., 'The Episcopate of Dr Seth Ward, Bishop of Exeter (1662 to 1667) and Salisbury (1667–88/89) with Special Reference to the Ecclesiastical Problems of his Time', University of Oxford, D.Phil. thesis, 1951.

Whitfield, P. W., 'Change and Continuity in the Rural Church: Norfolk, 1760–1840', University of St Andrews Ph.D. thesis, 1977.

Young, B., '"Orthodoxy Assail'd": An Historical Examination of Some Metaphysical and Theological Debates in England from Locke to Burke', University of Oxford D.Phil thesis, 1990.

INDEX

Tenison, Archbishop Thomas 26, 27, 28,
    32, 33, 34, 35, 36, 50, 92, 98, 137, 160,
    209, 216, 245, 246, 277
Tenterden 72, 150, 186, 249, 278
  church services 255, 265
  nonconformists 196, 208, 217, 230
terriers 156
Terry, Isaac 272
Test Acts 65
testimonials 84
Teynham family 206, 218
Thanet, *see* Isle of Thanet
Thanet, Earl of 174
Thomas, Keith 187
Thompson Census 214
Thompson, E. P. 233
Thornhill, Lady Joanna 251
Thornycroft family 218
Thoroughgood, Nicholas 193 n. 76
Thorp, George 32, 62–3, 79, 86, 112, 132,
    198, 199, 201–2, 206, 276
Throwley 170, 238–9
Thurnham 251, 282
Tillotson, Archbishop John 27, 28, 29–30,
    31, 34, 47, 49, 60–1, 62–3, 82, 98, 132,
    138, 140, 211, 246, 264–5
Timpson, Thomas 181
tithes 16, 115, 120, 146, 147–60, 167, 293
Todd, Henry 60
Toleration Act (1689) 182, 207, 210, 214,
    232, 234, 261
Tories 66, 90, 91, 95–6, 97, 119, 174, 216,
    243, 250
  and Anglicanism 97–8, 250, 283, 284
Torrington, Viscount 231, 272
Tractarians 1, 18, 82, 233–4, 242
  see also Oxford Movement
Trollope, Anthony 69
Tunstall 292 n. 30
Tunstall, James 33
Turner, Eliza 127
Turner, Thomas 42, 61, 111, 112, 135, 139
Turney, Mr 97
12*d* Act (1559) 201

Ulcomb 147
Ullock, Henry 93
Underdown, David 185
Uniformity, Act of (1662) 188, 280
union of parishes 160, 163, 255
Unitarians 57, 59, 65, 220
universities 54–5, 67–8, 75, 77–80
University College, London 67–8

Upper Hardres 236
urban development 129–30
urban properties 123–4
  in Canterbury 126–30

valuation of lands 116
Vann, Richard 213
Vaudois 222
Venn, Henry 239
Venours, Marquis of 204
Ventriss, Thomas 184, 193
vicarages 149, 150, 161, 162
Virgin, Peter 74, 291
visitation system 18–19, 26, 87, 274–81,
    285
Vokins, Joan 198–9

Wade, John 105, 144
Wake, Archbishop William 2, 25, 26, 27, 28,
    29, 30, 31, 35, 36, 41, 51, 62, 74, 88, 96,
    99, 114, 117, 138, 236, 246, 250–1, 275,
    277, 278
  and anti-Trinitarian theology 274–5
  chaplains 32
  and foreign protestants 221–2
  political affiliation 97, 98
Waldershare 97
Walker, Obadiah 269
Walloons 17, 73, 202
Walmer 280
Walsh, John 228
Walton, Brian 47
Wanley, Humphrey 244
Wanstal, W. 270
war with France 131, 141–2, 143
Warburton, Bishop 223–4
Warden 255
Warner, John 134, 188
Warwickshire 149–50
Waterhouse, Benjamin 260–1
Watson, Bishop 144
Weald, the 148, 149, 185–6, 193, 196
Welfitt, Canon 63, 137
Weller, Samuel 214, 258, 266, 282
Wesley, Charles 60
Wesley, John 60, 100–1, 223, 227
West Langdon 150, 214
Westbere 186, 292 n. 30
Wharton, Henry 32, 171
Whigs 52, 66, 90–1, 95, 96, 97–8, 150, 170,
    174, 215, 243, 250
  and Anglicanism 52, 97–8, 250, 272, 283
Whitefield, George 223, 225